The Science of
SWIMMING

PRENTICE-HALL INTERNATIONAL, INC., *London*
PRENTICE-HALL OF AUSTRALIA, PTY. LTD., *Sydney*
PRENTICE-HALL OF CANADA, LTD., *Toronto*
PRENTICE-HALL OF INDIA PRIVATE LTD., *New Delhi*
PRENTICE-HALL OF JAPAN, INC., *Tokyo*

The Science
of SWIMMING

JAMES E. COUNSILMAN, PH.D.

Swimming Coach and
Professor of Physical Education

Indiana University
Bloomington, Indiana

PRENTICE-HALL, INC. / *Englewood Cliffs, N.J.*

Library of Congress Catalog Card No.: 68-10089

This book is dedicated to my coach,
the late Ernst Vornbrock;
to my wife, Marjorie;
and to all the boys
who have trained with me.

Preface

The following quotation is taken from the inscription in the foyer of the Science Building of the Seattle World's Fair of 1962:

> To learn about the world around him, a scientist must ask, observe, suppose, experiment, and analyze:
>
> In asking—the right question must be posed
>
> In observing—the significant must be distinguished from the unimportant
>
> In supposing—a workable answer (or hypothesis) may be predicted, but a scientist must be ready to abandon it
>
> In experimenting—the right instrument must be chosen or borrowed from the tool kit of some other branch of science.
>
> In analyzing—the scientist must, with his mind and his imagination, draw conclusions from the data his research has revealed.

The coach must ask himself: "Am I a scientist?

"Am I asking questions of other coaches, the athletes, and other experts?"

"Am I constantly observing objectively, evaluating, and reevaluating, or have I reached the point where I look, but am not aware of what I see?

"Am I supposing or trying to find a workable answer for the problems which confront me. Once I arrive at a conclusion, am I then inflexible or do I always keep an open mind?

"Am I experimenting? If possible, do I use tools from other areas of science such as motion pictures, physiological tests, and psychological tests. Do I also use tests within my area; tests of strength, flexibility, agility? In experimenting, do I, within reasonable limits, try new ideas, that is, isometric contractions, and so on?

"In analyzing, am I arriving at logical conclusions or are my conclusions colored by prejudice, inadequate thinking, poor background, and lack of imagination?"

The average coach does not always have the tools to do research or the time to investigate thoroughly all the related areas that interest him. He is often too busy teaching, coaching, and taking care of the details involved in his job to devote much time to the available literature. There are, however, questions that arise in the course of his experience that stimulate his curiosity. Since curiosity is the beginning of all true learning, the coach can use his curiosity as a means of self-motivation in his search for knowledge. The human pursuit of knowledge seems to follow a three-phase pattern: the first phase is curiosity which comes when the person's interest is aroused and he begins to look at things, it is to be hoped, with some degree of objectivity; the second phase is that of confusion which comes about when the person is unable to analyze the situation immediately and sees no possible answer to the question or sees the possibility of several answers; the third phase is that of the search for the answer or the quest for knowledge. This is the never-ending phase, the one that will always keep man busy.

The true scientist is curious. He is able to recognize the problem he is confused about, and often his confusion is what keeps him in search of the truth. In athletics, the intelligent coach and athlete are constantly searching for new approaches and improved methods. These are the people who advance our sport. Other people, less inspired and creative, adopt their techniques.

How far the sport of swimming has advanced in the past one hundred years can only be answered during the next hundred years. Eventually, we will know how a swimmer should train and how he should perform his stroke mechanics. We will never know all the answers to all the questions, for as we learn answers, our knowledge and insight to recognize other problems and questions expands. This search for knowledge will continue and perhaps unlock the knowledge that will make a forty second 100-meter freestyle possible.

This book is written to introduce the coach and athlete to the first two phases of learning, and perhaps to a bit of the third phase—to stimulate curiosity, to confuse, and to aid somewhat in the search for knowledge.

The sequence drawings of the strokes that are used in this book, in every case, were taken from underwater movies of world record holders. Minor changes have been made where obvious deviations from good stroke mechanics were observed. The head-on drawings in all the sequences were made from pictures taken about three feet below the surface of the water in order that the kick, as well as the arm stroke could be observed simultaneously.

I want to express my appreciation to all of the athletes whose pictures appear in this book and to the coaches and athletes who contributed so much, particularly to Chapter XIV, "The Training Schedules of Some Champions." The primary reason our sport has developed so rapidly is that, in the sport of swimming, coaches and athletes willingly share their ideas and knowledge. The only real *secret* to success is hard, intelligent work and that *secret* is available to everyone.

I have been criticized for the Hurt-Pain-Agony concept of training for swimmers. I feel, however, that no success should come easily. If it did, it would not be highly valued. The harder we strive for a goal, the more significant that goal becomes when it is finally achieved. This is not to say that the concept has evolved merely to provide a difficult goal; it remains the most effective stress/adaptation method we know about at this time.

Not every swimmer or every coach can be a winner. With intelligent, hard work, each can achieve the best that is within him or within his team, and this is the standard he will be measured by, both by other persons and himself.

My self-image is more important to me
Than what my neighbor's opinion might be.

JAMES E. COUNSILMAN

Bloomington, Indiana

Contents

X

Dry Land Exercises, 276

XI

Age-Group Swimming, 312

XII

Organization of Practice, 327

XIII

Some Additional Principles of Training, 347

XIV

The Training Schedules of Some Champions, 378

Index, 447

The Science of
SWIMMING

I

Mechanical Principles Involved in Swimming

Knowledge of the mechanics involved in swimming strokes must be based on certain mechanical principles which apply directly to swimming. Most incorrect ideas concerning stroke mechanics result either from misunderstanding and improper application of these principles, or from complete disregard or lack of knowledge of them.

Incomplete understanding of these principles generally results in such misconceptions as the idea that the swimmer should pull with a straight arm in the crawl, butterfly, and backstroke. Complete disregard of principles is indicated in this statement made by one coach: "There is nothing to stroke mechanics. Every time I work on my swimmers' strokes, they go slower. If I leave them alone, they go faster." This statement points up the important principle that poor coaching is worse than no coaching. A swimmer will often develop a better stroke if he is left alone than if he is taught improperly.

A coach or swimmer who wants only to know the "how" of the various strokes and not the "why" lacks intellectual curiosity and, at best, can hope to do only a mediocre job of teaching or acquiring proper stroke mechanics. A swimmer must use not only his body, but also his intellect; this is what makes swimming such a challenging and enjoyable activity. Much of this book will be devoted to describing how the various strokes are swum, but an equal amount will be devoted to the "why."

Not only should the swimmer and coach know what to do and why to do it in a certain way, they should also know what not to do and why certain mechanical defects should be avoided. Throughout the chapters on stroke mechanics, these factors will be discussed.

A discussion follows of some of the mechanical principles which apply to the swimming strokes. A knowledge of these principles will enable the reader to understand more readily the next four chapters.

RESISTANCE AND PROPULSION

At any given time a swimmer's forward speed is the result of two forces. One force is tending to hold him back. This is *resistance* (or drag), caused by the water he has to push out of his way or pull along with him. The force which pushes him forward is called *propulsion*, and is created by his arms and legs.

A swimmer, in order to swim faster, must do one of the following: (1) decrease resistance, (2) increase propulsion, or (3) use a combination of these two. In studying stroke mechanics, one must attempt to devise the proper techniques to accomplish this. Probably the greatest improvements in stroke mechanics in recent years have been in the reduction of resistance. For example, breaststroke swimmers swim in a much flatter position now than in years past; they also create less resistance by using a narrower kick.

The study of conditioning is largely concerned with the type of training

FIG. I–1.   Resistance and Propulsion

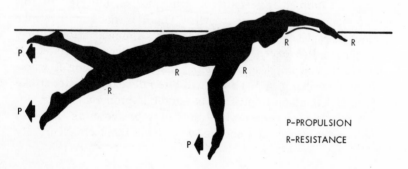

P–PROPULSION
R–RESISTANCE

that will best enable the swimmer, physiologically, to maintain the highest possible level of propulsion and the least amount of resistance throughout the race. As a swimmer fatigues during a race, he becomes less capable of creating force, and his body position becomes less streamlined. The whole study of competitive swimming resolves itself into solving these problems. Keep this in mind as we examine the "why" of the strokes.

Resistance

The study of fluid mechanics is complex, and involves many concepts which require knowledge of calculus to be understood. For this discussion, however, only simple terms will be used.

There are three types of water resistance: (1) frontal or head-on resistance, (2) skin friction, and (3) tail suction or eddy resistance.

1. Frontal resistance is the resistance to forward progress that is created by the water immediately in front of the swimmer or any part of his body. It is depicted in Figure I–2 by arrows. This type of resistance is very important when considering stroke mechanics.

2. Skin friction, caused by the resistance of the water immediately next to the body, is represented in Figure I–2 by dotted lines. While this type of resistance is important in airplanes, boats, and highspeed objects, it is of less consequence in swimming. Recently, a number of swimmers have speculated that shaving the hair on the legs, arms, and body would decrease skin resistance appreciably and, thereby, increase the swimmer's speed by virtue of the lessened resistance. There is no valid evidence, however, to substantiate this theory. The common practice has been to shave only the hair of the arms and legs. It is possible, although it has never been proven satisfactorily, that shaving the hair from the arms and legs may increase the swimmer's sensitivity to the "feel" or pressure of the water and, consequently, improve his coordination. It is more

FIG. I–2. Three Types of Water Resistance

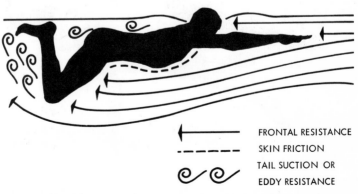

	FRONTAL RESISTANCE
	SKIN FRICTION
	TAIL SUCTION OR EDDY RESISTANCE

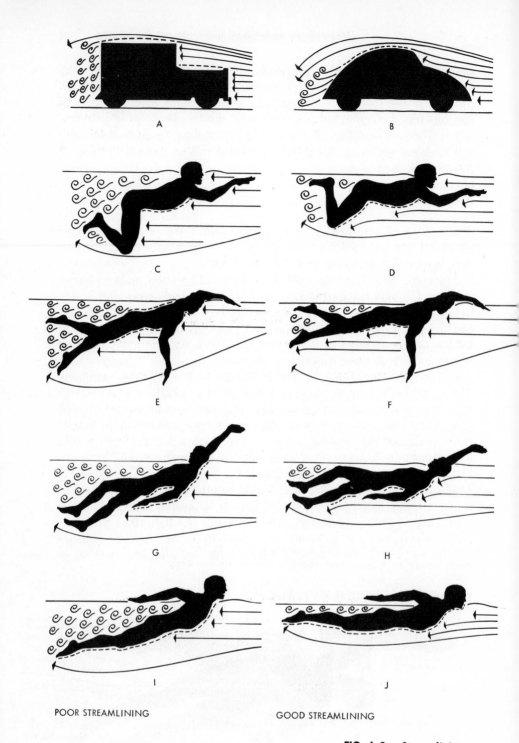

POOR STREAMLINING   GOOD STREAMLINING

FIG. 1—3.   Streamlining

likely, however, that any improvement in performance that appears to result from shaving is either a normal improvement resulting from training or from the psychological effect the shaving might induce in the swimmer.

3. The third type of resistance is called tail suction or eddy resistance, and is caused by the water that is not able to fill in behind the poorly streamlined parts of the body, so that the body must pull along a certain number of water molecules. Tail suction is represented in Figure I–2 by the curled lines. Tail suction or eddy resistance is an important type of resistance to consider in designing boats, cars, and airplanes. Designers have spent as much time streamlining the backs of these vehicles as they have their fronts.

Designers can change the shape of a vehicle, but there is little that can be done, other than through diet and body building, to change the swimmer's body shape. However, the body position in the water can be changed in order to streamline it more effectively and thus create less resistance, particularly frontal resistance, and tail suction or eddy resistance.

Figure I–3 shows how the body can be placed in such a position as to create greater or lesser amounts of resistance. A swimmer's body can also create greater resistance through poor streamlining on the lateral plane. For instance, if the hips and legs wiggle back and forth, the frontal and eddy resistances are again increased and the swimmer slows down.

Propulsion

Propulsion is the force that drives the swimmer forward, and is created by the swimmer's arms and sometimes by his legs. Actually, it is caused

FIG. I–4. Movement of the Swimmer's Body in the Lateral Plane Increases Frontal and Eddy Resistance of the Body

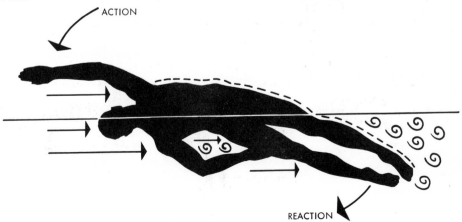

by the resistance the hands and feet create as they push the water backwards.

A principle that will be considered frequently in the mechanics of all strokes is Newton's *Third Law of Motion,* or the action-reaction law. Sir Isaac Newton formulated this law over 250 years ago, and it states that every action has an equal and opposite reaction. For example, when a runner is running forward, he pushes the ground backward and downward with his back leg; the reaction is to push him forward and upward with the same amount of force.

The same principle applies in swimming. If a swimmer, as in Figure I–5, pushes backward with a force of 25 pounds with his hands and five pounds with his feet, the resultant force of 30 pounds is used to push him forward.

You will notice that in Figure I–5 a question mark has been placed

FIG. I–5.   Application of Newton's Third Law of Motion

150 LBS. REACTION

150 LBS. ACTION

A

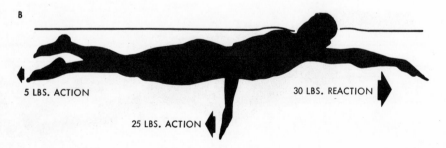

B

5 LBS. ACTION

30 LBS. REACTION

25 LBS. ACTION

after the "5 pounds" of force contributed by the kick. This brings up the question of the function of the kick in the crawl and back-crawl strokes. Everyone knows that a person swims faster when he uses his kick as well as his arms. Is this because the kick (1) increases propulsion, (2) decreases resistance, or (3) does both of these? Research by the writer indicates that at fast speeds the kick contributes nothing to the propulsion created by the arms. This question will be discussed in more detail in Chapter II.

Newton determined that every action has an equal and opposite reaction. In other words, the reaction is in precisely the opposite direction, or at 180 degrees to it. If a swimmer pushes the water directly downward, the resultant reaction pushes him directly upward.

If the swimmer tries to *climb up* on top of the water, he will have little success. Some swimmers do ride slightly higher out of the water than others, but this is probably due to the fact that they are more buoyant than other swimmers and, perhaps, are traveling at a faster speed. When they try to ride higher in the water, most swimmers raise their heads. Although this puts the front part of the body up higher, it has the additional effect of submerging the lower part, as shown in the poorly streamlined positions of Figure I–3. This results in an arm pull and kick which are less effective in propelling the person forward. The swimmer must then use a relatively greater proportion of his propulsive force to overcome the increased resistance. Some of the force of the arm pull must also be used to compensate for lifting the head higher out of the water.

As a swimmer increases his speed, the water resistance underneath him increases without a corresponding increase in the water resistance on top of him. His body acts very much like an airfoil, and he rises slightly higher in the water. This principle becomes apparent when water skiers are observed. As the boat pulls the skier at an increasingly faster rate of speed, the skier will rise in the water until he is literally skimming over it. At the low speeds at which humans swim, we must be

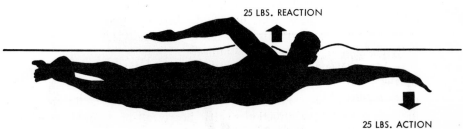

25 LBS. REACTION

25 LBS. ACTION

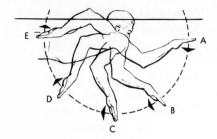

1. THE DROPPED-ELBOW PULL

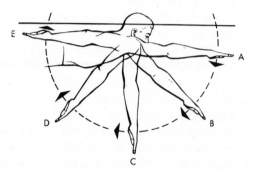

2. THE STRAIGHT ARM PULL

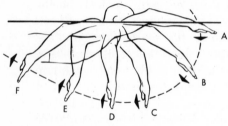

3. THE CORRECT PULL

FIG. I–7.   Pulls Affect Propulsion

resigned to always swimming in the water, not on top of it or skimming over it.

Many people believe that a swimmer should try to ride high in the water so as to create less resistance. This is much like trying to lift oneself by one's bootstraps. A swimmer can, however, ride too low by pushing water upward with his hands, thereby forcing himself downward. He can also carry his head too low in the water, causing a lower body position and increased resistance.

In Figure I–6, for example, the diagram illustrates how force applied by the hand tends to push the swimmer upward (this force is acting against gravity). It would be much better if this force could be applied more in a backward direction so that nearly all of it could be used to push the swimmer forward.

PULL. There are three types of pull, with variations, which can be used in the crawl or butterfly strokes and which contribute varying amounts (according to their effectiveness) to the propulsion of the total stroke. They are: (1) the dropped elbow arm pull, (2) the straight arm pull, and (3) the proper arm pull.

1. The dropped elbow arm pull is the poorest type of pull and provides the swimmer with very little forward propulsion, since very little water is pushed backward. It is the type of stroke usually used by beginners. It is often advisable to emphasize to beginners that the elbows should not bend; as the beginning swimmer learns not to drop his elbow he can be changed to the proper arm pull.

2. The straight arm pull is better than the dropped elbow arm pull so far as effectiveness is concerned, but at points A and B (see Figure I–7) the force applied downward is too great, and at points D and E the force applied upward is too great. This tends to push the swimmer upward at points A and B and downward when the hand is at D and E.

3. The best pull is that which will minimize the upward and downward components of the straight arm pull and provide a greater push backward; it is represented in Figure I–7 as the proper pull. It begins almost as a straight arm pull except that the elbow is higher. The elbow bends during the pull and then nearly straightens as the pull finishes. The arm stroke will be discussed in detail in the next chapter. It is a fairly complex movement and cannot be described adequately in a few sentences.

HAND POSITION. The question always arises: how should the hand be held during the arm pull in order to create the greatest amount of propulsion? This was studied by the writer a number of years ago, and plaster casts were made of the same hand in various positions (Figure I–8). These casts were then tested in a wind tunnel to see how much resistance each hand position would create. In this manner the relative amount of propulsion created by each position could be measured.

Originally, five hand positions were studied: (A) hand flat, fingers and thumb together, (B) hand flat, fingers together but thumb out at the side, (C) hand flat, fingers held apart, (D) hand cupped, fingers held together, and (E) hand flat, wrist and fingers extended slightly.

The resistance created by the various hand positions was in the descending order in which they are listed above, with the greatest amount first. There was practically no difference in the amount of resistance created by the first three positions. In positions (D) and (E), however, it was observed that both frontal and eddy resistance were decreased significantly. This study indicated that the swimmer should not cup his hands or extend his wrist, since he will thus lose some propulsion, primarily through loss of frontal and eddy resistance.

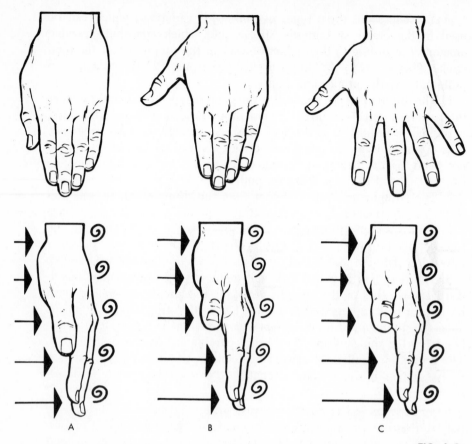

FIG. I–8.

Why should a swimmer not swim with his fingers spread apart? It can and has been done, as in the case of Fred Schmidt, former world record holder in the 100-meter butterfly. However, more muscular energy will be expended by the wrist and finger flexor muscles when the fingers are held in a spread position than when they are held together. Fatigue will result more easily and this will necessarily affect swimming speed, particularly over a longer race. To test this, spread your fingers widely apart for a few minutes and you will feel the additional strain. It is also likely that energy will be used needlessly if the swimmer forces his fingers together too tightly.

As a sidelight to this study, the writer decided to find whether frontal or eddy resistance contributes more to hand resistance. The flat hand with the fingers together was supplied with a half round surface in front

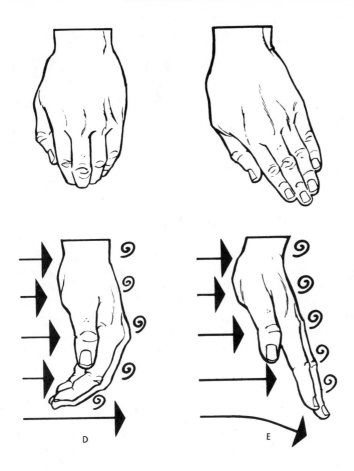

to streamline the frontal plane [Figure I–9, Position (A)]. In the second position, the posterior section of the hand was supplied with a half round surface [Figure I–9, Position (B)]. The first position (A) created the most resistance. This would seem to indicate that eddy resistance is more important than frontal resistance and that, at least theoretically, more propulsion is derived from the back of the hand than from the front of it.

A swimmer can try these various hand positions as he swims. Usually he will be able to feel the difference. Another method of testing this theory, although it is not recommended by driver education instructors, is to hold the hand out of a car window while the car is in motion, and to feel the varying amounts of resistance created by the hand in the various positions.

Research in the area of fluid mechanics indicates that it may be possi-

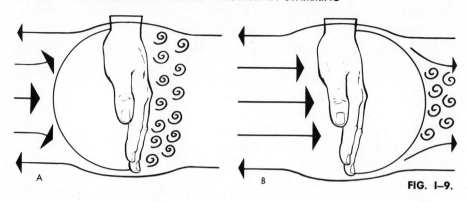

A   B   **FIG. I–9.**

ble that a hand with the fingers spread slightly may produce a bit more pull than a closed-finger hand. Concerning minor deviations in finger position, it is important to remember the following principle, which is applicable to all phases of stroke mechanics: *do not subordinate fundamental principles to minor details.* Priority should be given to the basic principles. In hand positioning for the pull it is fundamental that the hand be flat, not cupped. The fact that the thumb may be held out at the side, away from the fingers, as in Figure I–10, is a minor detail. The

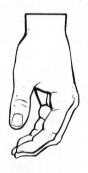

FIG. I–10.

cupping of the hand does reduce the pull considerably, and the thumb being separated from the hand does not appreciably affect propulsion. First, straighten the hand; then correct the thumb position, if you wish.

The practice of subordinating minor details to fundamental principles holds true for all phases of stroke mechanics. Many so-called perfectionists make very poor teachers and coaches because they are unable to discern that which is important from that which is of minor significance. This often occurs when a swimmer tries to imitate a champion or when a coach tries to convey his impressions of that champion's stroke to a swimmer. He may only observe an imperfection or idiosyncrasy in the champion's stroke and go right by the fundamentals the champion is using. Remember that even the best of swimmers has stroke defects. That he does well in spite of these defects is doubtless due to one of two factors: (1) his tremendous ability, strength, or conditioning overcomes these defects, or (2) the defects are so minor that they are of little significance in his performance. Even so, in the latter case they are not worth consciously imitating.

EVENNESS OF THE APPLICATION OF PROPULSION

This principle might also be termed "the continuity of movement" principle. An even application of propulsion is more efficient in propelling the body forward than is a fluctuating application of force. This is why the crawl stroke is faster than the butterfly stroke or breaststroke.

Some people predict that the butterfly stroke will someday surpass the crawl stroke in speed. This is not likely, although when both arms are pulling during the butterfly stroke, there is more total propulsive force than there is at any time during the crawl stroke. When the arms are recovering in the butterfly stroke, they can contribute no propulsion, so the swimmer's speed decelerates.

The mechanics of a stroke should be designed to permit the body to travel at as even a forward speed as possible. In other words, stop-and-go swimming should be avoided. If a swimmer permits himself to accelerate and decelerate in a stop-and-go manner, much of the force he could be using to overcome water resistance will be lost in overcoming inertia. The price of acceleration is costly, as can be realized when one tries to push an automobile that is stopped (Figure I–11). Once the inertia of the car is overcome and it is rolling forward, less force is needed to keep it moving than was used to overcome the inertia. The same is true of swimming. As much as possible of the force created by the arms and legs should be used to overcome the drag created by the water and should not be used to pay the price of acceleration.

In the crawl and backstroke this can be accomplished by beginning to pull one arm before, or immediately as, the other arm finishes the pull, providing a smooth, constant application of forward propulsion from the arms. In the butterfly stroke the arm pull begins almost as soon as

FIG. I—11. The Cost of Overcoming Inertia

the arms enter the water; any prolonged glide of the arms up front will permit the body to decelerate.

In the breaststroke there should be a slight glide after the arms are extended forward, since this manner provides the best use of the momentum developed by the kick. This momentum causes the body to plane or level off and create less resistance. If the swimmer waits too long in this glide position, his forward momentum will decrease too much, his feet will drop, and he will once again have to pay the excessive price of acceleration.

ACTION-REACTION LAW APPLIED TO RECOVERY

Some coaches have said that they are not concerned with what happens out of water since the propulsive phase of the stroke occurs underwater. The mechanics of the recovery of the arms, which in three of the four competitive strokes is out of water, does have an effect upon the efficiency and speed of the swimmer. An improper recovery can break the rhythm of the swimmer's stroke and cause him to pull improperly; that is, he may pull too fast or too slow or even shorten his pull, or possibly introduce too long a glide into his arm stroke.

One of the obvious ways a poor recovery can harm the swimmer's stroke is by increasing his frontal and eddy resistance. Let us return to Newton's action-reaction law. If the recovery is made in a wide sweeping manner (as in Figure I–12) in a counter-clockwise direction, the reaction is a movement of the hips or feet in the opposite or clockwise direction.

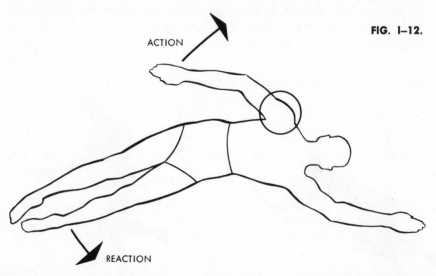

ACTION

FIG. I–12.

REACTION

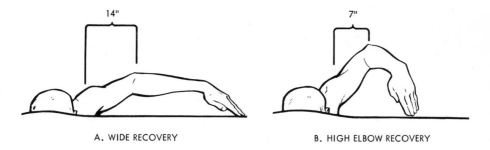

A. WIDE RECOVERY   B. HIGH ELBOW RECOVERY

FIG. I–13.   Shortening the Radius of Rotation

The muscle that recovers the arm also attaches to the body at the shoulder. A muscle does its work by shortening. When it does shorten, it exerts an equal force at each end. This lateral movement caused by a wide recovery can be illustrated by having the swimmer lie in the water and support his feet with a tube or kick board. Using a wide recovery (in either the backstroke or crawl) will result in a readily observable movement of the feet in the opposite direction (as illustrated in Figure I–12).

In the backstroke the arms can be recovered directly overhead, almost completely eliminating the lateral reaction of the body. In the crawl stroke the lateral reaction of the body can be minimized by decreasing the radius of rotation of the recovering arm, that is, by lifting the elbow up and bringing the hand in, as shown in illustration (B), Figure I–13. In the butterfly stroke the distorting effect of one recovering arm is canceled by the same effect of the other arm. Thus lateral body movement is not generally a concern in this stroke.

TRANSFER OF MOMENTUM PRINCIPLE

It is quite easy to transfer the momentum of one part of the body to another part or to the rest of the body. This principle is used in many movements we perform in and out of the water. The momentum developed by the arms during the wind-up before the swimmer makes a racing dive is transferred to his entire body and helps him get greater distance in his dive (see Figure I–14).

This principle also applies to the recovery of the arms in the crawl, butterfly, and backstrokes. In the backstroke recovery the arms develop momentum in a circular motion (Figure I–15). Immediately before the recovering arm goes into the water, it has developed momentum in a

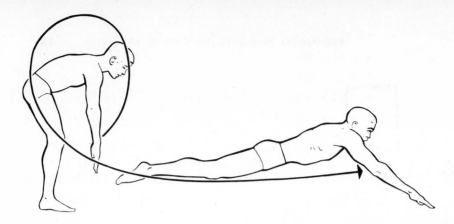

FIG. I–14. Transfer of Momentum: Racing Dive

downward direction (point A). If the arm is checked or slowed in its motion immediately before it enters the water (point B), this momentum of the arm is transferred to the body and it forces the upper body and head downward (illustration 1). A person can hardly see a backstroke race without noting at least one swimmer whose head bobs up and down as a result of this stroke defect. To avoid this bobbing motion the backstroker needs merely to let the arm continue into the water with the momentum it developed during the recovery. The water resistance will tend to dissipate most of this momentum (illustration 2).

Slowing the speed of the recovering arm or arms in the crawl or butterfly strokes immediately before the arms enter the water also has detrimental effects. This will be discussed in subsequent chapters.

THE THEORETICAL SQUARE LAW

The resistance a body creates in water (or any fluid or gas) varies approximately with the square of its velocity. To illustrate this fact, let us use an airplane going 100 mph and say that it creates 1000 pounds of resistance. When the airplane doubles its speed to 200 mph, it does not

FIG. I–15. Transfer of Momentum: Backstroke Arm Recovery

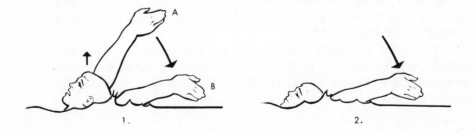

SPEED: 100 M.P.H.   200 M.P.H.   300 M.P.H.
RESISTANCE: 1000 LBS.   4000 LBS.   9000 LBS.

FIG. I–16.   An Application of the Theoretical Square Law

simply double its resistance; rather, the resistance increases by four times, or to 4000 pounds. If the plane increases its speed to 300 mph, it now increases its resistance by nine times (Figure I–16). This law also applies to the swimmer's speed and resistance in water. A direct and practical application of this law to the swimming strokes is found in the speed with which the recovering arm enters the water.

If a person throws his arm in the water twice as fast as before, he creates four times as much resistance to forward progress. A rushed recovery, therefore, not only breaks rhythm but also, by increasing the resistance to forward progress, tends to put the brakes on the swimmer and slow him down. What should determine the speed of recovery? The swimmer cannot take too long to place his hand in the water slowly in order to create little resistance. The speed of the recovering arm should correspond to a large degree with that of the pulling arm. Usually it will be a bit faster, but not appreciably so. It is difficult to recover quickly with one arm and, at the same time, pull steadily with the other. A close parallel in the speed of the pull and the speed of the recovery is an important factor in rhythm.

When a swimmer doubles the speed of his arms going through the water, he creates four times as much propulsion, if he uses the same stroke mechanics. It is a physiological law that the energy expenditure of a muscle approximately cubes with the speed of the muscle's contraction. In other words, when the speed of the pulling arm is doubled, the energy expenditure is increased eight times. Thus, while a faster arm pull does increase propulsion, it also disproportionately increases energy expenditure and oxygen consumption. This explains why swimmers who spin their arms while swimming frequently tire quickly. It also shows why the middle and long races should be paced.

BUOYANCY

As experience shows, a lightly loaded boat is easier to pull or push through the water than a heavily loaded one of the same size and shape.

It displaces less water, consequently floats higher and creates less resistance, as well as having less inertia to overcome.

A light buoyant swimmer floats higher and creates less resistance than a heavier, less buoyant swimmer of the same size. Swimmers vary in body build, bone size, muscular development, weight distribution, relative amounts of adipose fat tissue, lung capacity, and so on. All of these factors affect the individual's buoyancy and floating position. A large-boned boy with a heavy frame floats lower in the water than does a lighter swimmer, but probably has more muscle to move him through the water.

A few years ago our team had two world record holders who were examples of the extremes in buoyancy. Tom Stock, world record holder in the backstroke, was so buoyant that he could float on his back in a horizontal position, while Chet Jastremski, world record holder in the breaststroke, could not float in any position.

II

The Crawl Stroke

The previous chapter, dealing with fluid mechanics, contains many principles which apply directly to swimming the crawl stroke. These principles and the others in this chapter are included in order to bring about a better understanding of exactly what the swimmer should do, why he should do it and, in many cases, what he is already doing. I do not expect that a swimmer, after reading this chapter, will go into the water and think of all the details mentioned herein at one time. Many of the desired stroke mechanics occur naturally with some swimmers, others have to be acquired through a thorough understanding of them plus good coaching.

Good stroke mechanics frequently occur in gifted persons who may not be aware of what they are doing. Lacking an understanding of stroke mechanics, a person may try to eliminate something in his stroke, such as a lateral thrust of the feet, which is desirable. Many misconceptions concerning the proper method of swimming the crawl stroke result from not knowing why a certain movement is made.

BODY POSITION

The big improvement in the stroke mechanics of the crawl stroke in recent years can be attributed primarily to the decreased resistance swimmers create rather than to increased forward propulsion. The once undreamed-of, sub-seventeen minute 1500-meter swim is becoming commonplace, not because our swimmers are so much bigger and more powerful than before, but because they are better conditioned and, even more important, are swimming through the water with much less resistance.

Horizontal Body Alignment

Body position in the crawl stroke should be as streamlined and flat as possible, while still permitting the feet to be deep enough in the water for effective action. Any additional drag caused by poor body position decreases the swimmer's speed. The popular belief that the swimmer should force himself to ride high in the water and thereby create less resistance has led to a great many problems. The most widely accepted, but nevertheless improper, method of achieving this position has been to raise the head high and lift the shoulders high in the water by arching the back. This *hydroplaning* position may elevate the head and shoulders, but it also causes the back to arch and the hips and legs to drop excessively in the water, thereby increasing resistance or drag. Those who advocate this style say that the swimmer should kick harder to keep his legs and hips up. It is important to emphasize that the swimmer's energy should be devoted toward driving himself forward through the water, not toward lifting him on top of it. To lift oneself up out of the water, one must work against gravity.

To measure the difference in drag (negative resistance) when the head was held in two positions (position A, in which the water line broke at the hairline level, and position B, in which the water line broke at the eyebrow level), a swimmer was towed by the apparatus illustrated in Figure II–6. The tension created on the towing line was recorded and measured. The drag measurements in Figure II–1 are an average of three trials at each position, and show clearly that, at all speeds measured (between 1.1 feet per second and 7.03 feet per second), position A created less resistance than did position B. As the swimmer was dragged at the higher speeds, there was less difference. Unfortunately, the drag created by the body when the head was held in an intermediate position was not measured. This research suggests that when the head is held in position A, which most coaches feel is somewhat high, there is a significant increase in the drag.

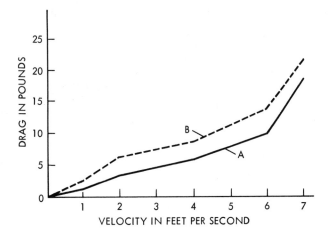

Position A. Drag created by subject with head held in normal position, with water line at hairline level.

Position B. Drag created by subject with head held in a high position, with water line at eyebrow level.

FIG. II–1.   Drag Measurements with Head in Two Positions

A common idea, illustrated by the following typical statement, reveals another error in analysis: "The swimmer should press the water downward with his hands in order that he may ride high in the water." This style of trying to climb over the water has been advocated for all strokes at one time or another. In the case of the crawl, it has been stated that one should emphasize the press of the water downward during the first part of the arm stroke so the swimmer can achieve this high body position. If this reasoning were valid, the swimmer, after finishing the first part of his pull, would have nothing to support him and would drop until the other arm entered the water and started to press downward. This would result in a constant up and down motion of the body and increase the total resistance offered by the swimmer, in addition to being very costly in energy expenditure. It is true that some swimmers swim in a higher position than others; this higher position in the water apparently does decrease the drag or resistance of such swimmers. In the previous chapter I stated that I believed this high position to be the result of two factors: buoyancy and speed. A light-boned person of slight build will naturally float in a slightly higher position than will a large-boned, heavily muscled person. The difference in their buoyancy is apparent from the positions in which they float. A large-boned boy would be foolish to try to ride in the high position held by a light-boned boy. He will naturally ride in a lower position and create more drag, but, due to the nature of his physique, will have more muscle power with which

1. LIFTING AND LOWERING HEAD TO BREATH

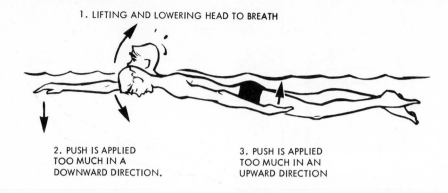

2. PUSH IS APPLIED
TOO MUCH IN A
DOWNWARD DIRECTION.

3. PUSH IS APPLIED
TOO MUCH IN AN
UPWARD DIRECTION

FIG. II–2. Three Stroke Defects that Cause Excessive Up and Down Movement of Body

The horizontal alignment of the body in the vertical plane is most frequently disturbed by the following three stroke defects:

1. When the head is lifted out of the water to breathe, the rest of the body is forced downward. When the head is lowered, the rest of the body rises slightly.

2. When the force of the first part of the pull is directed too directly downward, it results in a climbing motion during the first part of the pull.

3. If the elbow is straight at the end of the pull, it causes the force of the armstroke to be directed upward, resulting in a force that pulls the body down into the water.

to pull his body through the water. A buoyant swimmer, however, does have a definite advantage, particularly in the long events, since he can keep his legs high in a streamlined position without kicking too hard. The second factor which makes a swimmer ride higher is the speed at which he swims. A boat with an aquafoil does not ride higher in the water by pushing directly downward; it rises upon the foils in the same manner as does a water skier. As the boat goes faster, the pressure underneath the foils increases and the horizontal level of the boat rises in the water.

The comparison of a boat on aquafoils to a swimmer is not a true parallel, in that the former case involves speeds great enough to cause an elevation of the center of gravity of the boat by several feet, while the speed of the swimmer is only a fraction of the speed of the boat, and the amount of elevation is measured in inches or fractions of inches. Even at top speeds the swimmer swims primarily through the water

1. ROTATE THE HEAD ON ITS AXIS INSTEAD
OF LIFTING AND LOWERING IT (NOTICE THE MOUTH
IS IN THE CONCAVITY IN BACK OF THE BOW WAVE).

3. INSTEAD OF PUSHING UPWARD
THE FORCE SHOULD BE APPLIED
IN A MORE BACKWARD DIRECTION
(NOTICE ELBOW BEND).

2. INSTEAD OF PUSHING DOWNWARD,
THE FORCE SHOULD BE APPLIED
IN A MORE BACKWARD DIRECTION
(NOTICE ELBOW HIGH POSITION).

FIG. II–3. Methods of Correcting the Stroke Defects Shown in Figure II–2

and not on top of it. Fish and dolphins reportedly attain speeds of 30 mph and more while swimming through the water; the top speed a human can achieve is around 4 mph. The answer to faster swimming, therefore, is not in trying to lift oneself higher in the water, but in streamlining more effectively and applying force more efficiently.

It becomes obvious that the swimmer should avoid excessive up and down movements of the body. (See Figure II–2.)

To correct the three defects illustrated in Figure II–2 the swimmer should: (1) rotate the head on its axis (not lift and lower it) and breathe to the side closer to the bottom of the bow wave, (2) press the hands in a more backward direction rather than directly downward, and (3) bend the elbow and continue to try to push the water in a more backward rather than upward direction. Figure II–3 illustrates the stroke with these corrections made.

Lateral Body Alignment

Good lateral body alignment appears to be as important as horizontal alignment in achieving maximum efficiency and speed. Since any side to side movement of any part of the body causes increased resistance, excessive movements in this plane should be avoided. A swimmer whose head, shoulders, hips, and feet weave excessively back and forth sideways is placing himself at a great disadvantage. A good way to describe this fault to the swimmer is to tell him he is dragging along half of the water in his lane, whereas a more efficient swimmer moves less than a quarter of the water in his lane. The less water a swimmer has to push out of his way or drag along with him, the better. It is helpful to the coach to view a swimmer frequently from directly in back and at a height of ten to twenty feet—or even higher—for at this point the lateral movement becomes most apparent. Movies taken at this point will show the swimmer how much he really does *wiggle*.

It is important to realize that, although a swimmer may swim in an almost straight line, his movements to accomplish this are all circular or rotary or variations and combinations of this type of movement. When a swimmer is in the water he is suspended in a fluid, and any circular movement of his arm, either in the recovery or the pull of his arm or in the movements of his leg, will tend to have a reaction which will distort his body alignment in the opposite direction.

When a person stands on the ground and swings his arm upward to the side in a sweeping movement, the feet are pushed in the opposite direction. This is an illustration of Newton's third law of motion (action-reaction) discussed in Chapter I. The floor upon which the person stands theoretically is pushed sidewards by the feet. Actually the floor absorbs the reactions of the arm movement. If the person jumps into the air and, while suspended in the air, swings his arm sidewards in the same manner, his feet will move in the opposite direction to that of the arms.

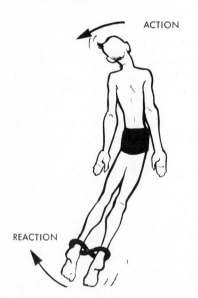

FIG. II–4.   **Sideward Flexion of Neck Causing Lateral Deviation of Body Alignment**

ACTION

REACTION

Another way of demonstrating this fact is to have the swimmer place his feet in an inner tube and lie face down in the water, both hands at his sides. He should then recover one arm only in a wide circular motion and observe that his feet will swing to the opposite side. This motion of the feet can be minimized by changing the arm recovery from a wide sweeping motion to one with a high elbow and the hand close under the elbow (Figure I–13).

Lateral alignment of the body can also be destroyed by pulling the arm too far across either side of a line running vertically and directly under the center of gravity of the body. It would appear that the best way to pull his arm through the water would be on a line directly under the swimmer's body. As will be shown, good swimmers do not do this, but pull in a curved pattern near, across, and around this middle line.

The lateral or sidewards flexion of the head off the longitudinal axis of rotation, an action frequently committed by the swimmer when he breathes, not only throws the head out of alignment, but also affects the rest of the body. Figure II–4 shows how this action can have its reaction in the rest of the body.

Another faulty stroke technique which causes excessive lateral movement, particularly of the shoulders, is checking or slowing the speed of the recovering arm by muscular effort before the hand and arm enter the water. When this occurs, much of the momentum of the recovering arm is transferred to the upper body and causes lateral movement.

It can be seen from the foregoing discussion that many factors are operating to destroy the swimmer's body alignment or streamlining, and that the coach and swimmer must constantly be alert to keep this type of movement of the body at a minimum. As stated before, this movement becomes most apparent when viewed as the swimmer swims directly away or toward the observer.

If it is possible to combine one force that distorts the body alignment in one direction simultaneously with another force that destroys alignment in the opposite direction, they may cancel one another and the body will remain in relatively straight alignment. An example of this technique is illustrated in Figure II–8, in which the reaction to the recovering of the arm in a clockwise direction throws the feet out of alignment in the opposite (or counter-clockwise) direction, while the kick of the foot in a sideward direction keeps the hips and feet in.

THE FLUTTER KICK

The Role of the Kick—Propulsive or Stabilizing

The arm stroke in the crawl is the main source of propulsion and, in the case of most swimmers, the only source of propulsion. The kick serves primarily as a stabilizer and means of keeping the feet high in a streamlined position. As mentioned before, the lateral thrust of the kick serves to cancel out the effect of the recovering arm in disturbing body alignment.

A comparison may be made between the crawl stroke and an automobile with a separate front and rear wheel drive (Figure II–5). The front wheels are turning at a rate of 30 mph while the rear wheels are turning at a speed of only 20 mph. What will be the total speed of the car? Will the rear wheels contribute anything to the speed of the car?

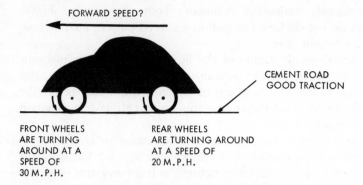

FORWARD SPEED?

CEMENT ROAD
GOOD TRACTION

FRONT WHEELS
ARE TURNING
AROUND AT A
SPEED OF
30 M.P.H.

REAR WHEELS
ARE TURNING AROUND
AT A SPEED OF
20 M.P.H.

Questions: 1. What will be the speed of the car?
            2. Does the power applied to the rear wheels contribute to the forward speed of the car?

Answers: 1. Somewhere between 20 and 30 mph, probably about 25 mph.
            2. No. The rear wheels serve as a drag rather than a propulsive force.

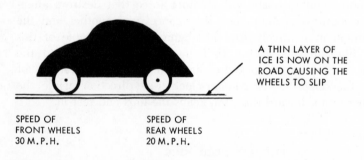

A THIN LAYER OF
ICE IS NOW ON THE
ROAD CAUSING THE
WHEELS TO SLIP

SPEED OF
FRONT WHEELS
30 M.P.H.

SPEED OF
REAR WHEELS
20 M.P.H.

Question: Do the rear wheels now contribute to the forward speed of the car?
           Yes. The rear wheels are turning faster than the road is going under them.

FIG. II–5. **Demonstration of How a Lesser Force Can Contribute to a Greater Force**

This illustration is parallel to the extent that the swimmer can pull himself through the water faster than he can kick himself through the water. In the case of the car, the rear wheels add nothing to the speed of the car, but serve rather as a drag. The total speed of the car, therefore, would be less than 30 mph. This comparison is not completely accurate since the swimmer's arms and legs do not have a similar amount or kind of traction with the water that the tires have with the road; thus, they slip. It would be accurate if the car were on an icy road and the forward speed were only 15 mph, while the speed of the front and rear wheels remained 30 and 20 mph respectively. In this case, the rear wheels would be turning faster than the road was going under them and would then contribute to the total speed of the car.

The question of whether the swimmer gets any propulsion from his kick depends on whether the feet can push the water backward faster than the arms are pulling the body through the water. If, in order to achieve this speed, the swimmer had to kick as hard as possible, would he not be better off to use this energy to pull himself through the water with his arms, using only enough energy in kicking to maintain body alignment?

To test whether a swimmer receives any propulsion from the kick, I used the apparatus pictured in Figure II–6, in which the subjects were towed toward the device at various speeds in a glide position, without kicking and again while kicking. The tension on the towing rope was measured to see if it was greater, the same, or less when kicking than when just being towed in a glide position. Generally at the lower speeds of under five feet per second, when the swimmer kicked at maximum effort, the tension on the rope decreased. However, when the swimmer was pulled at speeds greater than five feet per second, he not only did not contribute anything to the speed at which he was being towed, but,

FIG. II–6. Equipment Used to Measure the Effectiveness of the Flutter Kick at Various Speeds

The operator (A) turns the on-off switch (B) to the motor (C). The motor drives the shaft (D) at various speeds depending on the pulley arrangements. The towing rope (E) wraps around the shaft and pulls the swimmer (F) toward the platform (G). The resistance caused by the swimmer exerts a force on the towing rope to pull the platform toward the swimmer. The platform is fixed to the side of the pool by the strain gauge beams (H). The force on the towing rope is measured by the strain gauge beams and recorded on an electronic recorder (I).

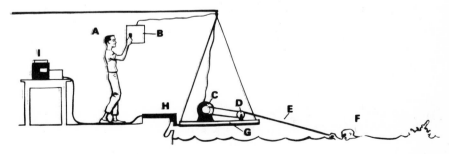

in some instances, actually created an increased drag as a result of his kicking. There were individual differences; some swimmers' kicks became ineffective at four feet per second.

The trouble with this experiment, as with most experiments, is that the data can be interpreted in different ways. No crawl swimmer swimming a distance event (the 1500-meters event, for example) at a ràte of four or five feet per second would be expected to kick as hard as possible for the full distance. The trend is in exactly the opposite direction. The longer the race, the less emphasis placed on the kick by the swimmer. He decreases his emphasis for two reasons: (1) he is going at a slower speed and his body is riding in a slightly lower position in the water, consequently he does not have to kick as hard as he does when he sprints, and (2) the swimmer's heart can supply only so much blood to active muscles. If the swimmer kicks exceedingly hard, too much blood is channelled to the leg muscles and there is less blood available to the muscles which pull the arms through the water, with the result that they fatigue more easily. I have long advocated a reduced emphasis of the kick, particularly in distance swimming. In recent years world records have been set in the distance events by swimmers with reduced kicks, some of whom kicked as few as two beats per arm cycle.

As the crawl swimmer sprints, he rides slightly higher in water. If he does not increase the tempo and effort of his kick, the front part of his body will rise and his legs will drop further into the water. For this

FIG. II–7. Energy Cost of Swimming with Legs Only, Arms Only, and Whole Stroke

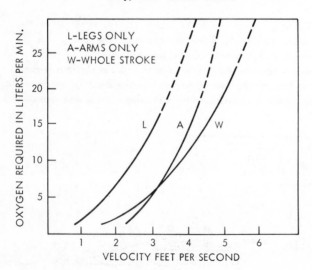

reason, some swimmers who use a two beat kick (two beat per arm cycle) in the distance events will switch to a six beat kick when sprinting.

Adrian, Singh, and Karpovich determined the energy cost of the leg kick, arm stroke, and whole stroke of the crawl stroke on twelve subjects of both sexes. They summarized on the basis of their data:

> The energy cost of the leg kick is greater than that of the arm stroke and whole stroke. The energy cost of the arm stroke is less than that of the whole stroke at the low velocities, but becomes greater than the whole stroke as the velocity increases.
>
> Formulas for the prediction of oxygen requirement for the leg kick and arm stroke were determined for the group and for the best swimmer. A similar formula for the whole stroke from data of the best swimmer was also determined.
>
> Evidence was obtained to substantiate the belief that the leg kick should be kept at minimum velocity when competing in the 1500-meter crawl.
>
> In general, the efficiency of the leg kick is less than 1 per cent, whereas the arm stroke average efficiency is 2.24 per cent. The efficiency of the whole stroke was slightly higher than that cited in other studies, ranging from 1.71 to 3.99 per cent.[1]

The data in the Adrian, Singh, and Karpovich experiment indicates that as the swimmer swam faster and approached top speed, the kick became an increasingly important factor. This has also long been my opinion; as early as 1949 I advocated a reevaluation of the function of the kick in the crawl stroke. In an article entitled "Theory of the Flutter Kick,"[2] I suggested that the flutter kick was a stabilizing rather than propulsive force. The article raised a flurry of protest from proponents of the *heavy kick*. Disagreement continues today, but, in my opinion, the argument was settled by the success of swimmers using a reduced kick. Whether they use a two or six beat kick, our great swimmers of the present are not using the big, heavy kick that was previously advocated.

A swimmer can kick too much, but he can also kick too little. The degree of effort needed in the kick must be experimented with and, in the final analysis, the swimmer should adopt the method that allows him to swim the fastest. This, of course, will vary, within limits, with different swimmers and with the distances they are swimming. Great natural swimmers make the adjustment unconsciously; others must be taught to develop the proper pattern.

[1] Marlene Adrian, Mohan Singh, and Peter Karpovich, unpublished research project, and personal correspondence with Peter Karpovich, Springfield College, Springfield, Mass., October 1965.
[2] James E. Counsilman, "Theory of the Flutter Kick," *Beach and Pool*, XXIV, No. 6 (June 1949), 12.

From the fact that the kick is used as a stabilizer and neutralizer, and does not act as a propulsive force in the crawl stroke, it does not follow that less emphasis should be placed on conditioning the legs in workout. The movements of the legs are very important and, at times, quite vigorous. If they are not conditioned properly, they will fatigue and become less effective in their stabilizing role, thereby allowing hips and legs to drop too low and to move about laterally, creating unwanted resistance. If the kick is mechanically poor and does not move the swimmer effectively while he is on the kick board, it will perform its job less efficiently and may even create additional drag when he is swimming.

I believe that a person should have an efficient kick and that the legs should be conditioned. I also recommend that the swimmer kick while swimming; however, I do not believe that the primary function of the kick is propulsion.

The Timing of the Kick

If the function of the kick is primarily that of a stabilizer or neutralizer and streamliner, then coordination of the kick with the arms is very important. If the hips are permitted to roll with the shoulders, the feet will be in a good position to thrust sidewards at the proper time, as mentioned previously.

This lateral thrust is apparent in underwater movies of good crawl swimmers. With practice a person can train himself to observe this movement from out of the water. At the beginning of the arm recovery, as the arm is swung forward in an arc by the deltoid muscle, there is a movement of the legs in the opposite direction. The swimmer must, therefore, kick outward in the opposite direction to the arm recovery in order to neutralize the effect of the recovery.

Another important point regarding the timing of the arms and the legs is concerned with the end of the pull. As the arm finishes its pull, it is pushing backward and upward. This action will cause the hips to be pulled further underwater if the downbeat of the kick does not correspond with this upward movement of the arm. I have studied underwater movies of many great crawl swimmers and, in every case, this particular timing has been evident regardless of whether they were using a two or six beat kick.

There are several kick patterns used with the crawl stroke. The role of the two beat kick in cancelling the distorting effect upon hips and legs of the act of recovering the arm will be discussed first.

THE TWO BEAT CROSS-OVER KICK IN THE CRAWL STROKE. This variation of the crawl stroke has been used by many great swimmers, most of whom are not aware of what they are doing. I have never seen a swimming meet in which some of the swimmers were not using this kick.

In 1960 I published an article [3] which began by stating:

> The difficulty in writing an article of this sort is that many people will not read it carefully and will misinterpret the writer in a number of ways he can anticipate. First, that it is his intention to coach all swimmers to use the horizontal or cross-over kick, ... Second, that many swimmers who are better adapted to the conventional type of kick may try to change their kicks, with detrimental effects.

As predicted, I was misinterpreted and misquoted. Many people believe that I advocate this style for all crawl swimmers. The facts are that my teams have had as low as 10 per cent and as high as 30 per cent using this type of kick. Figure II–8 and the accompanying description depict and describe this type of crawl stroke.

If the swimmer is using this type of kick and is swimming well, he should be allowed to continue to use it. Some swimmers, as has been mentioned earlier, use it when swimming distance events and use the six beat kick "when sprinting."

The two beat cross-over kick is used most often by swimmers with a wide, flat recovery. These people may use this type of recovery because they lack sufficient shoulder flexibility to recover with high elbows. Usually, they have large shoulder blades, which restrict arm and shoulder movement. The wide, flat arm recovery causes a greater lateral movement of the hips which can be more effectively cancelled out by a horizontal and lateral thrust of the leg than by a diagonal and upward thrust used in the six beat kick. Such swimmers should use shoulder stretching exercises to improve shoulder flexibility in order to be able to recover with a higher elbow and with the hands in closer to the body, thereby reducing the amount of lateral movement.

It is virtually impossible to imitate the two beat cross-over kick on the flutter board. The swimmer using this kind of kick, however, should condition his legs by kicking in the same way as other crawl swimmers; that is, by kicking the conventional flutter kick on the board and also by kicking some breaststroke kick each day in order to strengthen the abductor and adductor muscles of the legs.

THE STRAIGHT TWO BEAT KICK IN THE CRAWL STROKE.   When a two beat kick is used by crawl swimmers who also use a high elbow recovery, it is not necessary that a large lateral thrust of the legs, as illustrated in Figure II–8, be used. In such cases, the leg action is similar to that of

---

[3] James E. Counsilman, "The Cross-over Kick in the Crawl," *Junior Swimmer*, I, No. 11 (November 1960), 6-7.

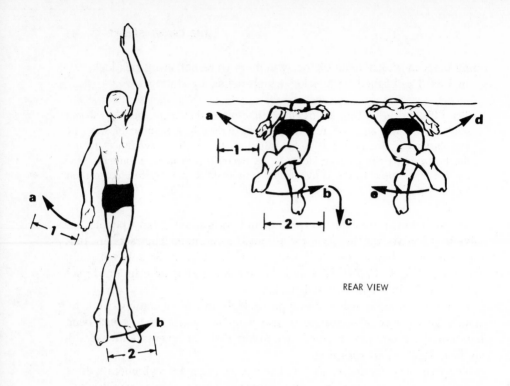

FIG. II–8. The Two Beat Cross-over Kick in the Crawl Stroke

In this series of illustrations, the manner in which the cross-over kick is timed with the crawl arm stroke is shown. In illustrations 1 and 2 the left arm has finished its pull and is ready to begin its recovery (in a clockwise direction). At this same moment the right leg is crossed over the top of the left leg and is ready to thrust horizontally in a counterclockwise direction. These two distorting forces cancel each other, as shown previously in Figure I–5.

The kick covers the distance (b) during the time the arm covers the distance (a). This timing is similar in all cross-over kicks. After the horizontal thrust of the kick, the foot travels downward (c) and the other foot crosses on top of it, as shown in illustration 3. As the right arm ends its pull and is ready to begin its recovery (d), the left leg has crossed over the right and is ready to thrust sideward (e).

the two beat cross-over kick except that the legs do not cross over, one above the other. This type of swimmer usually has relatively buoyant legs and does not require a lot of kicking action to keep his legs in a high, horizontal position. The leg kick and arm pull action is timed in such a way that the downward thrust of the leg coincides with the upward thrust of the arm on the same side as it finishes its pull. In this manner the tendency of the arm to pull that side of the body downward is cancelled to a large extent by the tendency of the downward thrust of the leg kick to raise that side of the body. This particular timing of the downward thrust of the kick with the upward push of the arms is also noticeable in all three types of crawl stroke described in this chapter, when they are swum properly.

Swimmers using this type of stroke generally fall into this type of timing without any conscious effort.

Since the two beat crawl swimmer kicks so few times per arm cycle, it sometimes appears that movement of the legs has stopped. Underwater movies of both two beat cross-over and straight two beat crawl swimmers show that in some swimmers the legs continue to move all of the time, but so slightly that they seem to be relaxed and merely drifting with the water currents; in others, the legs appear at times to stop completely and to be held more rigidly, serving as rudders to keep the body in straight alignment.

Both Patty Caretto and Steve Krause, in 1965, used a straight two beat kick crawl stroke when they set their world records in the 1500 meter freestyle events. The swimmer pictured in Figure II–18 is using this stroke.

THE SIX BEAT KICK IN THE CRAWL STROKE.   Most swimmers develop a six beat kick crawl stroke. There are slight variations of the kick and the manner in which the diagonal thrust of the feet is made. Some six beat kick crawl swimmers use a hesitation and drag of their feet on every third kick at the point at which each foot is at the bottom of the kicking cycle. This *drag* kick serves as a rudder in keeping straight body alignment. Certainly this drag effect of the feet creates an increase in resistance, but may more than compensate for this by its advantageous effect on general body alignment. In the sequence drawings of the crawl stroke presented at the end of this chapter (Figure II–25), the swimmer is using a normal six beat kick as used by most crawl swimmers.

THE MECHANICS OF THE FLUTTER KICK.   A swimmer kicks differently while kicking on the board than he does when he is swimming. The swimmer's body rolls when he swims, and remains relatively flat while he is kicking on the board. It seems to be impossible to simulate this rolling motion.

I have worked on the general assumption that the more effective the kick is in propelling the individual kicking on the flutter board, everything else being equal, the more effective will be its role as a streamlining and stabilizing force.

Too often the swimmer, particularly the beginning competitive swimmer (perhaps because he has been instructed to do so), kicks too hard and too high in the water. He tends to bend his knees too much and move his upper legs too little. While kicking on the board, the swimmer should try to keep the rocking motion of the shoulders to a minimum.

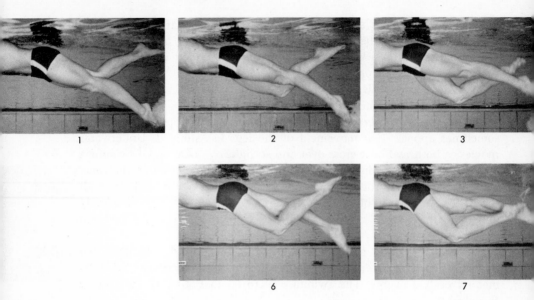

FIG. II–9.   **The Mechanics of the Flutter Kick**

This series of photographs shows the mechanics of the flutter kick as it should be done when the swimmer is practicing drills on the kick board.

1. The feet are at their maximum spread (approximately 18 inches). The left leg is at the bottom of its downbeat and the right leg is at the peak of the upbeat.

2. The left leg, with no bend in the knee, starts upward. Swimmers should constantly be reminded of kicking upward with a straight leg, because if the leg were to be bent at the knee on the upbeat, it would create a negative force that would hold the swimmer back. The right leg starts the downbeat by driving downward with the upper leg and a simultaneous bending at the knee; this leaves the foot in almost the same position as in 1.

3. The left leg continues upward, still with no flexion at the knee. The right leg starts downward vigorously with the upper leg being forced downward. The knee starts to extend and, as the right foot passes by the left leg, the instep is in a line parallel with the ankle of the right foot.

4. The left leg, nearing the top of its upbeat, starts to flex slightly as the right leg nears completion of the downbeat. The right knee is actually at the deepest point it will go and from this point on it will start upward, even though the right foot will continue downward.

5. The upper part of the left leg starts downward and the left foot continues upward. The right leg is at the bottom of the downbeat with the knee completely extended.

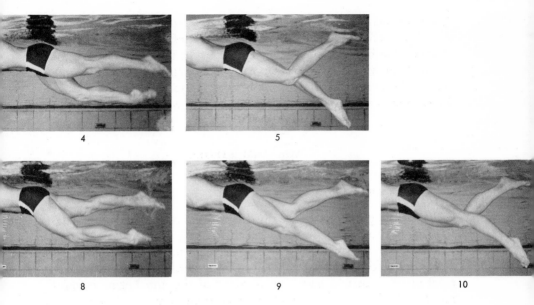

4   5

8   9   10

6. The left leg with the knee at its maximum bend is **ready** to begin its downbeat. The straight left leg knee has started its upbeat.

7. The left leg is now well into the propulsive phase of its kick. The right leg continues its recovery with a straight leg.

8. The propulsive phase of the left leg is now almost fully completed. The right leg shows a slight flexion at the knee.

9. The left knee nears complete extension as the flexion in the right knee increases.

10. The feet are again at their maximum spread and the kick cycle is about to begin again.

The feet should not come high out of the water, but should churn up the water as they kick upward and come close to the surface. The feet should separate on the vertical plane between ten to sixteen inches.

It is sometimes helpful during kicking drills to substitute larger, heavier boards for regular weight kicking boards; this practice has the twofold purpose of overloading the kicking muscles and overlearning the proper mechanics of a more subdued kick. Figure II–9 pictures the mechanics of a good flutter kick when used in a kicking drill on the kick board. This kick is too large for use when combined with the arms.

Many swimmers kick more efficiently with their toes pointed inward than with their feet pointed straight back. No conscious effort, however, should be made to *toe in*. The natural torsion of the femur or the angle at which the bone of the upper leg is set into the hip joint determines the angle at which the upper leg and, consequently, the foot should be held. If the swimmer merely *plantar flexes* or stretches his foot backward, the amount of *toeing in* that is desirable for him will be attained naturally.

THE ARM STROKE

The Recovery

The crawl arm stroke can be divided into the pull and recovery phases. It is an oversimplification for a coach to state, "I don't care what the swimmers do out of water, it's what they do under water that counts." As we have seen, a wide sweeping recovery can cause excessive movement of the hips and legs. The recovery of the arm begins before the pull has finished. The elbow of the recovering arm is out of the water while the hand is still under water pushing backward and outward. As the arm is halfway through the pull, it should cross the mid-line of the body. During the last part of the pull the arm should push backward, outward, and upward toward the side in order that the swimmer might *round out* into his recovery. This rounding-out motion conserves the momentum developed during the last part of the pull. The swimmer does this for the same reason that a baseball player who hits a double does not run in a straight line to first and then take a sharp 90° left turn to run to second. The baseball player does not want to dissipate the momentum of his run to first base by making a sharp change in direction, so he *rounds out* his run.

The elbow should leave the water first and start to swing upward and forward with the hand trailing behind it. The effect that the wide, flat arm swing has upon body alignment has already been discussed.

A common style of recovering the arm stroke has been to leave the elbow almost stationary after it lifts and rotate the upper arm (Figure II–10) in order that the hand might swing forward and pass in front of

FIG. II–10. An Incorrect Recovery of the Arm in the Crawl Stroke

the elbow before the elbow passes the shoulder. The hand is usually then driven deeply into the water. This type of arm recovery was popularized by the Australian swimmers. Although it was not adopted by Murray Rose, it was used by other outstanding Australians. It is my

FIG. II—11. Variation in Shoulder Flexibility of Two Champion Swimmers

The boy on the left has below-average shoulder flexibility, while the boy on the right has better than average shoulder flexibility.

feeling that this arm recovery causes the arm to lose the momentum acquired during the last part of the pull and to increase the amount of work that the muscles which recover the arms must do.

If all swimmers had equal flexibility in the shoulders, everyone's recovery might be similar. Since flexibility in the shoulder joints varies from one person to the next, different types of recovery must be used. The boy on the left in Figure II—11 has very limited shoulder flexibility. In order to recover his arm and clear it over the water without dragging it in the water, he must use a little more roll of his body and a flatter and wider sweep of his arms during the recovery than would a more flexible swimmer. This, of course, results in a greater reaction or lateral thrust of his legs. To keep his legs in alignment, this type of swimmer frequently has to adopt a two beat cross-over kick. Such a swimmer can increase his shoulder flexibility through stretching exercises; his increased flexibility will enable him to lift his elbows higher and bring his hands in closer to his body during the recovery.

The arm recovery in most cases should be a controlled relaxed movement. There should not be undue tension in the arm or shoulder, yet the arm should be controlled sufficiently to prevent centrifugal force from pulling the hand outward and prevent the arm from flopping loosely in an uncontrolled manner.

Electromyographic studies [4] of swimmers show that, as the first part

[4] Michio Ikai, Kihachi Ishii, and Mitsumasa Miyashita, "An Electromyographic Study of Swimming," Laboratory for Physiologic Research in Physical Education, School of Education, University of Tokyo, Japan, *Research Journal of Physical Education,* 7, No. 4 (April 1964), 47-54.

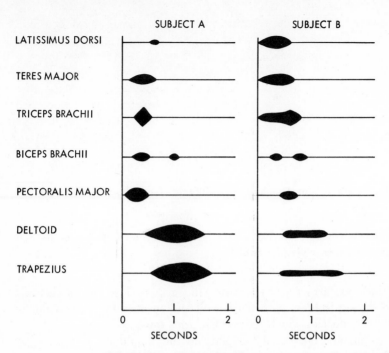

FIG. II–12. **Electromyographic Records of Two Swimmers Swimming the Crawl Stroke**

Subject A—Member of the University Swimming Club (University of Tokyo), but not classified as a top swimmer.

Subject B—One of the top competitive crawl swimmers in Japan.

The two figures above are diagrams of the muscular pattern activities rearranged from the original record of the electromyograms. The amplitude of these figures indicates the degree of contraction of the muscles as measured by electromyographic equipment. The horizontal line (abscissa) shows the beginning, the duration, and the end of the contraction of each muscle in seconds.

The difference in the muscle contraction pattern of these two swimmers is obvious. The poorer swimmer (Subject A) uses more muscular effort to recover his arms, as evidenced by the large contractions of the arm recovery muscles, the deltoid and trapezius. The better swimmer uses three of the arm depressor muscles to a greater extent than does the poorer swimmer, thereby giving the better swimmer a stronger and more forceful pull. The latissimus dorsi of the better swimmer contracts early in the arm pull and the pectoralis major enters into arm depression action when the latissimus contraction is half completed. The sequence of contraction of these two muscles is reversed in the poorer swimmer. In both swimmers, at the completion of the arm pull, at approximately .6 of a second, there is an overlapping of the contraction of the arm depressor and the arm recovery muscles.

of the recovery is made, the recovery muscles (primarily the deltoid and trapezius) contract vigorously to provide the momentum to recover over the water. After this initial contraction phase, the recovery muscles decrease their amount of contraction and the momentum developed during this early phase seems almost great enough to carry the arm through the rest of the recovery, in what is referred to as modified ballistic movement. There should be sufficient contraction to prevent the arm from flopping loosely, but there should be no sustained, vigorous contraction of these muscles, which would have the effect of tiring them and using energy better used to pull the swimmer through the water. I believe that recovery of the arms should be primarily a controlled ballistic movement with enough controlled tension exerted by the muscles to make the arms do what the swimmer wants them to do. The swimmer who complains of being *tight in the shoulders* has probably exerted too much tension and tired the deltoid and trapezius muscles to the point of extreme fatigue. Conscious relaxation (which must necessarily be only partial if the swimmer is to continue to move) must be practiced during the second half of the recovery if the swimmer is to overcome the tightness.

The Japanese study learned further that top swimmers use their recovery muscles less vigorously and for a shorter period than do poorer swimmers (Figure II–12). Good swimmers also used three of their arm depressor muscles (latissimus dorsi, teres major, and triceps brachii) longer and more vigorously than did the poorer swimmers.

In the case of the swimmer who must use a wide, flat recovery, the movement can be even more ballistic, that is, more of a throwing motion, permitting the centrifugal force of the initial part of the recovery to carry the arm forward.

During the first part of the recovery the hand should be carried with the palm facing almost backward and slightly upward, and with the wrist in a relaxed position. As the hand swings forward past the shoulder, it should be in line with the elbow. At this point the hand should start to lead the elbow and, even though the wrist does not flex or extend, the palm of the hand should start to face the water. Gravity will accelerate the movement of the arm slightly at this point. The swimmer should be careful not to accelerate the speed of his arm movement during its recovery due to muscular effort. If the arm recovery is rushed, the rhythm of the stroke is destroyed and the swimmer tends either to rush the pulling arm and drop the elbow or delay the beginning of the pull until the recovering arm enters the water, consequently developing an excessive glide in the stroke. It is almost impossible to recover one arm fast and to pull steadily at the proper speed with the other. A rushed recovery also creates more resistance and holds the swimmer back. The resistance to forward progress which the recovering arm creates as it enters the

FIG. II–13.   Don Schollander

Don Schollander, winner of four Gold Medals in the 1964 Olympic Games and World Record holder in the 200-meter and 400-meter freestyle, is pictured in this series of out of water shots. Schollander uses a high elbow recovery with a normal reach entry into the water. Don carries his head slightly higher than most crawl swimmers.

water varies approximately with the square of the speed at which it is placed in the water. Thus, when a person doubles the speed with which the recovery arm enters the water, the resistance to forward progress is increased by four times.

Figure II–13 shows a sequence of pictures of Don Schollander's arm recovery with the high elbow and normal reach entry into the water.

The Arm Pull

THE ENTRY OF THE HAND INTO THE WATER.   The elbow should be slightly bent when the hand enters the water, and the hand should enter the water before the rest of the arm. The palm of the hand should be facing diagonally downward as it enters the water. This type of entry is called the *normal reach entry*.

The *early entry arm recovery* was once felt to hold the advantage over the *normal reach entry*. In this recovery the hand enters the water almost immediately in front of the head, purportedly assuring the swimmer of a deep catch with the elbow up. The difficulty comes when underwater movies reveal that swimmers respond by digging their hands in too

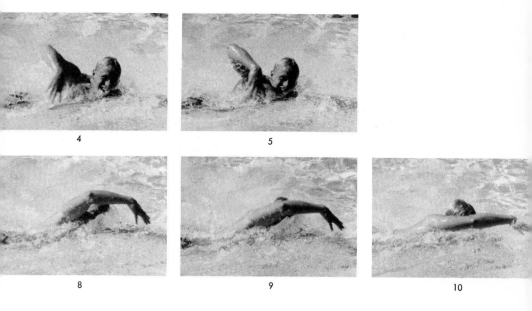

deeply and pushing them forward and upward, frequently dropping the elbow. The normal recovery as described above and as illustrated in the sequence on the crawl stroke is recommended over either digging deeper or overreaching.

This latter technique has been the object of emphasis by many coaches and swimmers who advise stretching or reaching out with the hand as it

FIG. II–14.   Elevation of the Shoulder

In illustration A the subject has the shoulder held in the position recommended during the arm pull. In illustration B the subject has reached upward and has elevated his shoulder and shoulder blade. This position should be avoided in all swimming strokes.

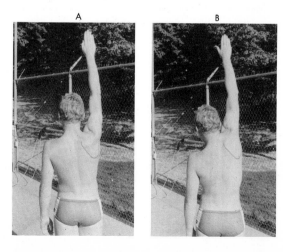

enters the water. It is true that the elbow should be almost completely extended as soon as the hand enters the water, but there should be no elevation of the shoulder by rotating and moving the shoulder blade and collar bone upward (Figure II–14). This unnecessary movement will disturb the swimmer's lateral body alignment and weaken his pull. To illustrate this to a swimmer, have him do a supine straight arm pullover with a weight he can just lift. He will find that the same weight is harder or impossible to lift from this position. This principle applies to all swimming strokes. Another effective method of putting across this idea to a swimmer is to tell him that elevation of the shoulders (it is easier for him to understand and feel this movement when you refer to elevation and rotation of the shoulder blades) is forbidden except on racing dives and push-offs. The easiest way for a swimmer to fall into using this mechanical defect is for his coach to repeatedly use the term *reach*. Once the swimmer's elbow is completely extended, the only way the swimmer can reach or stretch his hand further forward in front of his body is through elevation of the shoulders. The term *reach* is banned during stroke mechanic sessions in our pool.

EVENNESS OF APPLICATION OF PROPULSIVE FORCE. Once the arm is in the water it must not glide too long, but should begin its pull almost immediately. The term *almost* is relative and must be explained in the light of this situation. Some swimmers leave one hand extended in the glide position too long and permit the other hand to complete its pull and recover before the first hand begins to pull. This type of stroke has been called the *glide* or *catch-up* stroke and was popularized after the 1932 Olympic Games when some observers concluded it was this element in the strokes of the Japanese swimmers that accounted for their success.

In this stroke one arm is held in front in the gliding position while the other arm pulls and recovers and *catches up* with the resting arm (Figure II–15). The resting arm then takes over and pulls and recovers while the first arm rests. The logic of this theory was that one arm would always be resting and the swimmer would not tire so easily. This stroke was and still is often taught by having the swimmer hold onto a kick board with one hand while the other hand completes its pull and recovery; it, in turn, goes to work after the other hand grasps the board. Faulty stroke mechanics such as this are unfortunately taught to many beginning swimmers today. The fault lies in the fact that this type of stroke permits the propulsive force applied to the water by the hands and arms to fluctuate unduly. The momentum created by one arm is largely dissipated by the time the second arm begins its pull.

It may be of some interest here to include excerpts from a report by

FIG. II–15. The Glide or "Catch-up" Stroke

This stroke was popularized in the early 1930's and probably set crawl swimming back twenty years. The reasoning behind the use of this stroke was that one arm (A) would be resting while the other arm (B) was working. Arm A has remained stationary in a stretched out or glide position while arm B has pulled and recovered. Arm A does not start to pull until arm B catches up with it. During the time either arm is recovering there is no propulsion on the water from either arm. This fluctuation in force results in a fluctuation in the speed of the swimmer and is mechanically uneconomical.

Frank Beaurepaire [5] who, following the 1932 Olympic Games in which the Japanese swimmers startled the swimming world by their outstanding successes, was commissioned to report on the techniques innovated by the Japanese. Mr. Beaurepaire himself was an outstanding swimmer of his time and competed for Australia in Games in London (1908), Stockholm (1912), Antwerp (1920), and Paris (1924).

Japanese successes at the Olympic Games, August 1932, were no mere "flash in the pan"; they were due to an intensive and scientific study of swimming technique, during the course of which it was discovered that the application of ordinary mechanics could be made to the physiological position of the body lying prone on the surface of the water. The Japanese deserved their successes, even if only because they were prepared to exploit revolutionary swimming changes which, of course, are now fast becoming the standard for the swimming world.

. . .

At first glance the outstanding feature of the Japanese stroke is the extent of relaxation in both the arm and leg movements. The greatest single feature, however, is the isolation of the arms in recovery movement from the shoulders and trunk. Other features are the shortness and speed of the recovery action, the long glide forward of each arm in turn after it has entered the water just ahead of the shoulder, the isolation of the head from

[5] Frank Beaurepaire, "The Technique of Swimming" (What We Must Learn from the Japanese), unpublished report.

the shoulders and trunk in respiratory movements, the complete independence or isolation and relaxation given to the leg movements, the comparative slowness with which pressure is applied from the catch, and the fact
that the arm in recovery has reached the water and gone well towards catch
before the arm applying pressure has reached the bottom of stroke.

. . .

. . . It is part of the true rhythm of the stroke to take the arm out of
the water short. . . . There is no trunk or shoulder roll in the true sense
of the word in the Japanese stroke and it is to help to positively eliminate
any trunk or shoulder roll that the arms are taken forward in recovery so
quickly; . . . . The independent thrash of the legs is maintained without
any relationship to any section of the arm movements.

. . .

Any swimmer—young or old—should give much attention to the culti-
vation of relaxed and independent thrash of the legs for without it the arm's
movements and trunk position are difficult to maintain.

The effect of this report and others similar to it concerning Japanese
stroke technique was profound. Coaches and swimmers styled their
mechanics after these *descriptions* of Japanese technique with little
regard as to their validity. There is little in the swimming literature of
30 years ago to tell us whether Beaurepaire's analysis of Japanese methods was correct. The Japanese published a book [6] in 1935 which indicates
that they did advocate the deep catch, but it is not clear how they felt
about independent leg action, body roll, head action, and so on. Because
of the dearth of knowledgeable information (from Japanese coaches and
swimmers of the time), those who had read the report consciously imitated its analysis; the effect was detrimental to the understanding of
proper stroke mechanics.

The antithesis of the catch-up or glide stroke would be a stroke in
which an effort was made to have a continuous application of propulsive
force from the arms. Such a stroke is the *continuous arm stroke,* as it is
termed by its proponents. In this technique a constant effort is made to
keep at least one of the hands applying force on the water at all times.
Since the first and last parts of the arm pull are less effective than the
middle portion, it would appear to be theoretically proper to attempt
to overlap these two portions of the stroke as much as possible. This is
seldom done because it can only be accomplished by rushing the recovery and, as previously mentioned, this is not desirable. The pulling
arm should be at least halfway through the pull before the recovering

[6] *Swimming in Japan* (Tokyo: International Young Women and Children's Society, 1935).

arm enters the water. If the pulling arm is in front of this point, the swimmer is probably gliding too long with his arm up front and using too much catch-up or glide. The degree to which the pulling arm has completed its pull will vary from one swimmer to the next. The amount of this variation will depend upon the efficiency of the swimmer's pull and the amount of resistance he creates. If the swimmer has little resistance or drag and a good, strong, efficient pull, the hand should have completed from 50 per cent (90° from the horizontal plane) to 60 per cent of its pull. It the swimmer has poor body alignment due to such factors as low buoyancy or a poor kick, he may have to complete more than 60 per cent of his pull before the recovering hand enters the water. This latter swimmer will have to go almost directly into his pull as soon as his hand enters the water. The former type of swimmer can delay his catch slightly or allow his hand to sink slightly into the water after its entry before starting his catch. As mentioned previously, it is important that such a swimmer not drop his elbow below his hand at this point. The hand may stop almost completely when it is in front of the shoulder waiting for the other hand to complete more of its pull. Prior to the completion of this pull, the hand that has just recovered begins its own pull so that both hands are being moved at the same time. The leading hand will travel at least 12 inches before achieving any forward propulsion. Since the swimmer is moving forward through the water, he must pull his hand backward faster than he is moving forward or his arms will not contribute much forward propulsion. It requires 12 to 28 inches before the hands reach this speed. Research at Indiana University has shown that some poor swimmers receive no propulsion from their arms until they are at right angles to the body and are directly downward.

For this reason a swimmer should make a strong catch early in his pull; that is, once he begins to pull his hand down and back, he should try to feel the pressure on his hands build up to the point where he is effectively pulling himself forward. Too often the swimmer allows his hand to drift through the first half of his pull with the result that his hand does not develop enough speed to effectively push the water backward until it is almost directly under him. At the other extreme is the swimmer who places his hand in the water and pulls it backward so fast that it does not have time to overcome the inertia of the body. The swimmer must develop the feeling in his hands for the right amount of pressure to apply during this part of the stroke. Figure II–16 shows various degrees of completion of the pull before the recovering hand enters the water.

Among the various styles of swimming the crawl stroke which are taught today, differences in the evenness of the application of force are probable.

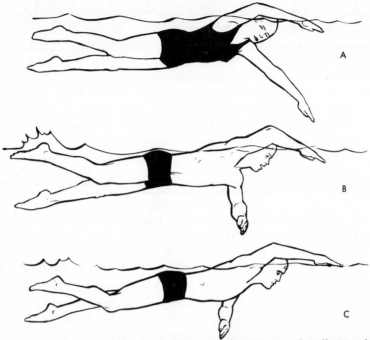

**FIG. II–16. Variations in the Degree of Pull Completed in
Three Champion Freestylers When the Recovering Arm Enters
the Water**

A. Martha Randall, World Record holder for 400-meter Freestyle in 4:38.0. Martha
uses a greater degree of catch up in her arm stroke than any other world record holder.

B. Don Schollander. Don's arm has completed half of its pull when the recovering
hand enters the water. Most good six beat crawl swimmers use this timing.

C. John Nelson, National champion at 400 meters in 4:14.1. John's pulling arm has
completed over half of its pull when the recovering arm enters the water. This timing is
used by many two beat kick crawl swimmers.

A STUDY OF THE EVENNESS OF THE APPLICATION OF PROPULSIVE FORCE.
In 1951 I conducted a study of the evenness of application of force in
two types of crawl stroke,[7] the results of which are recorded here. The
most feasible approach to analyzing the evenness of application of the
propulsive force seemed to be through the use of some form of test in
which the forward propulsive force could be measured and a graphic

[7] James E. Counsilman, *An Analysis of the Application of Force in Two Types of
Crawl Stroke*, Ph.D. dissertation, State University of Iowa, 1951.

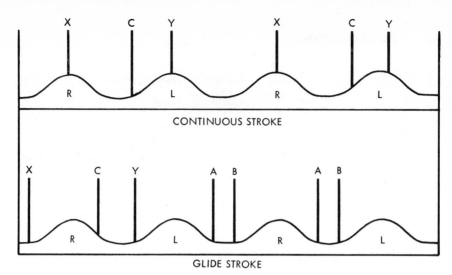

FIG. II–17. Fluctuation of the Application of Propulsive Force in Swimming Two Types of Crawl Stroke

A–B. Period during which neither arm is pulling (this occurs only during the glide stroke)

C. Point at which inhalation is made

R. Force created by right arm pull

L. Force created by left arm pull

X. Point at which left arm entered the water

Y. Point at which right arm entered the water

representation of this measurement made. It was important that this force not only be tested from a static position (in the static position the entire arm acts as a propulsive element when it is pulled backward), but also in an actual dynamic swimming situation (in the swimming situation only the part of the arm moving backward faster than the water is going past it actually creates any forward propulsion).

This study was made on the apparatus shown in Figure II–6. Instead, however, of pulling the subject toward the apparatus, the subject swam from the apparatus and the subject's forward speed was controlled by the speed with which the line (attached to the subject's belt) was released from the shaft. The force which three subjects created at two different tempos for both types of crawl stroke was measured and graphed at the following velocities: 0, 1.03, 1.95, 2.61, 3.17, 4.11 feet per second.

Figure II–17 shows the fluctuation in force at zero velocity fast tempo for both glide stroke and continuous stroke (sprinting tempo of one complete arm cycle every 1.20 seconds for subject 1). This figure reveals that the variation in propulsive force is greater in the glide stroke than it is in the continuous stroke. The glide stroke results in a constant

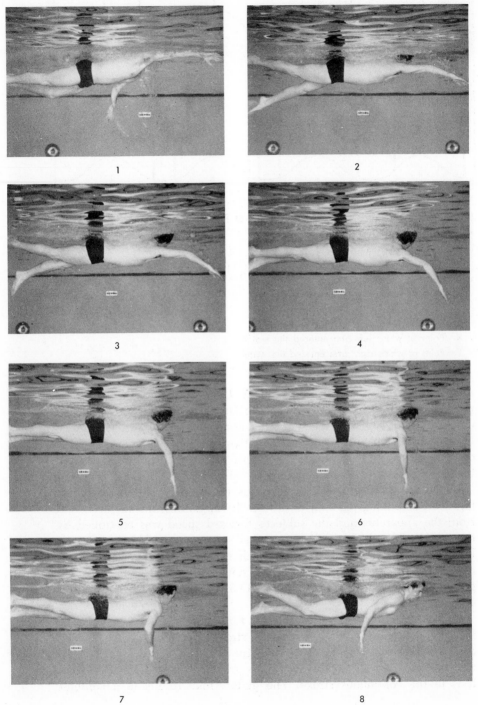

1

2

3

4

5

6

7

8

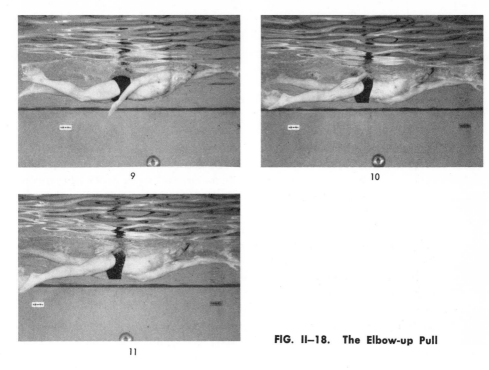

FIG. II–18.   The Elbow-up Pull

This series of pictures shows Mike Troy swimming with a near-perfect crawl arm stroke pull. Mike uses a straight two beat crawl kick, with a continuous arm pull. All crawl swimmers will do well to study these pictures and then try to imitate the arm action demonstrated here.

fluctuation of velocity—a positive acceleration during the pull and a negative acceleration (or deceleration) during the recovery of the arm, while there is no propulsive force from the arm action of the other arm.

At both tempos (the slow tempo was 1.72 seconds per arm cycle) and at all controlled speeds, with all three subjects, the continuous stroke created: (1) a more even application of force, (2) a higher average force, and (3) a faster forward velocity. The obvious conclusion is that the glide or catch-up stroke is inferior to the more continuous stroke so far as speed is concerned, and that, on the basis of mechanical principles, it is probably more desirable to teach beginning swimmers and all levels of swimmers to use a form of the continuous crawl stroke.

The Elbow-up Pull

At Indiana University we have photographed, under water, poor swimmers, good swimmers, great swimmers, beginning swimmers—swimmers of nearly every age and proficiency level. Better swimmers all used some form of the *elbow-up* pull in which the elbow is bent and held higher than the hand throughout the first part of the pull. This pull is demonstrated in Figure II–18 and is a classical representation of this pull. It may be profitably studied and imitated by all crawl and butterfly swimmers.

Poor swimmers drop their elbows as the swimmer is doing in Figure I–7, illustration A. The elbow-up pull permits maximum backward thrust of the hand during its first half and is the most efficient technique that can be used.

As the arm is pulled down and back by the three main arm depressor muscles (lattissimus dorsi, pectoralis major, and teres major—the triceps also help), it is also rotated medially by the same muscles plus the subscapularis. This action increases the strength available to pull the arm backward. Because of anatomical differences, not all swimmers are capable of swimming with their elbows as high as the swimmer in Figure II–18. The purpose of the elbow-up arm position has been said to enable the swimmer to push the water backward at a more efficient angle. The swimmer can achieve the same effect by rotating the upper arm and swinging the hand across in front of the chest so the hand is pushing the water backward at as beneficial an angle as the swimmer in Figure II–18. However, he will have to retain some concept of the elbow-up arm position and his arm may have to swing further across the mid-line of the body.

THE AMOUNT OF BEND IN THE ELBOW AND WHEN IT OCCURS. As has been demonstrated in Figure I–7, when the crawl stroke is swum properly, the elbow must bend during the arm pull in order to be able to push the water backward at an advantageous (or correct) angle. The arm pull begins with the elbow straight or almost straight. As the arm is pulled under the body, the elbow begins to bend and reaches its maximum degree of bend when the arm is approximately perpendicular to the body or halfway through the pull. The amount of bend in the elbow at this point varies slightly from one good swimmer to the next. The average, however, is close to 100°. Figure II–19 shows the maximum amount of elbow bend in various swimming champions which usually occurs when the arm is halfway through the pull or when it is perpendicular to the body.

It can be seen from these pictures that there is considerable variation in the amount of bend in their elbows, and also in the position of the arm and hand in relation to the body. The obvious question is, "Which of these positions is the best? Which should the coach try to have his swimmers imitate?" While it is obvious that we expect some differences among individuals, some limitations must be prescribed as to the maximum and minimum amount of elbow bend desirable at a given point during the arm stroke. Many persons have speculated that girls should

A   B

C   D

FIG. II–19. Maximum Elbow Bend of the Pulling Arm in Four Champion Freestylers

The four champion swimmers are shown at a point in their arm stroke at which the elbow achieves its maximum bend. This point occurs when the arm is approximately half way through the pull. In all four swimmers pictured here, the thumb is held apart from the rest of the hand.

A. Steve Clark, co-holder of the World Record for the 100-meter Freestyle in :52.9. The angle formed between the upper arm and the lower arm is 125°. Steve's hand crosses slightly past the median line of his body at this point.

B. Alain Gottvalles, co-holder of the 100-meter Freestyle World Record with Steve Clark, is pictured from diagonally underneath. This makes accurate measurement of the degree of elbow bend impossible. Head-on, underwater movies of Gottvalles show that the angle formed between his upper arm and forearm measured 92°. Alain's hand crosses past the median line of his body until his finger tips are directly under the opposite shoulder.

C. Mike Burton, World Record holder in the 1500-meter Freestyle event. A study of underwater movies of Burton's stroke shows that the angle formed between his upper arm and forearm measures 94°.

D. Terri Stickles, former National champion, Bronze Medal winner in the 1964 Olympic 400-meter Freestyle. Terri's arm pull is similar to Gottvalles. The angle formed between the upper and lower arm is 95°.

bend their elbows more than boys because they are weaker; others have used the same reasoning to justify girls' using less elbow bend.

In Figure II–19, illustration D, Terri Stickles' elbow bend is similar to that of Alan Gottvalles, while some underwater movies I have studied reveal that a few of the better girl swimmers use an elbow bend closer to that used by Steve Clark than to Terri Stickles'. Most, however, follow a pattern similar to the one illustrated.

Speculation also exists as to whether the distance swimmer should or should not bend his elbow more than the sprinter. In Figure II–19, illustrations A and B are of two all-time great sprinters, both of whom have shared the world record for the 100-meter freestyle at :52.9. In illustration A, Steve Clark is shown with an angle between his upper and lower arm of about 130°, while illustration B depicts Alan Gottvalles with a bend of about 90°. In illustration C, Mike Burton, who is primarily a distance swimmer, is shown with an elbow bend almost identical to that of Alan Gottvalles, a sprinter. There is a definite trend among the better swimmers toward a greater bend in the elbow, similar to that used by the swimmers in illustrations B and C.

It is important to remember that the elbow bend is maintained for a short time only during the pull, for, as the hand is pushed further back, the angle of the elbow increases continuously until it is almost fully extended. This type of pull has been termed the *bent arm pull*. This expression is not fully descriptive; a better name might be the *straight-bent-straight* pull.

STRAIGHT THROUGH PULL, "S" PULL, OR THE INVERTED QUESTION MARK PULL.   For years it has been advocated that the swimmer pull his arm through the water in a line straight down the center of his body. However, the body rolls on its longitudinal axis, and therefore the center line of the body also rolls from side to side. A better description of this straight line pull might be: the arm should be pulled in a straight line directly under the center of gravity of the body. Looking at this statement superficially, one would have to agree that this type of pull does indeed appear to be best. However, upon examining the path of the hand underneath the bodies of some of the great swimmers, we find that nearly all follow the same general pattern. This pattern is not a straight line, but is either in the shape of a bottom-heavy "S" or an inverted question mark. The degree to which the line of pull varies justifies categorizing the pull into three groups: (1) the "S" pattern pull, (2) the inverted question mark pattern pull, and (3) the modified straight line pull. Figure II–20 is a representation of the pull pattern used by three champion swimmers.

From a careful study of underwater movies of outstanding swimmers

FIG. II–20. The Pull Pattern of Three Champion Freestyle Swimmers

The drawings above represent the pull pattern of three Olympic champion Freestylers. The broken line represents the path described by the middle finger of the pulling hand. All three swimmers use a slightly different variation of the inverted question mark pull.

A. Don Schollander

B. Dawn Fraser, three-time Olympic Gold Medal winner in the 100-meter freestyle, and World Record holder at that distance in :58.9

C. Bob Windle, 1964 Olympic Gold Medal winner in the 1500-meter Freestyle in 17:01.7.

The pull pattern of the left hand of each of these three swimmers is not identical, but is similar to that of the right hand.

I have concluded that a majority use the inverted question mark pull pattern. One cause which may account for the desirability of the inverted question mark action of the arms during the pull is that some of the lateral action in the pull may cancel out the lateral action caused by another part of the stroke. As stated before, every linear movement (movement in a straight line) made by a human is the result of a series

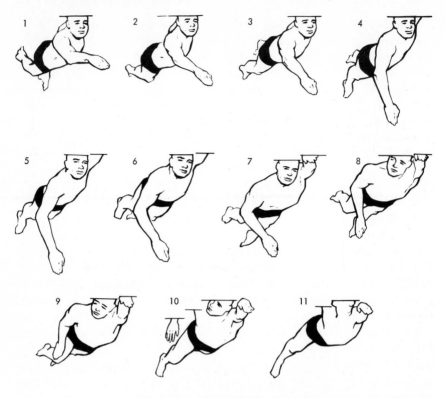

FIG. II–21.   Don Schollander's Underwater Crawl Stroke

of circular or angular movements. If an angular movement causes a distortion of the body position, it is possible for another movement of equal and opposite force to cancel out the effect of the first. I have been able to observe these opposing forces in slow motion pictures of a few swimmers, and to identify why some swimmers cross over and what other force they are cancelling out. These factors are not observable in most cases; the explanation of the pull being stronger in the inverted question mark pattern appears to be the main reason for accepting it.

Figure II–21 is a series of drawings showing Don Schollander's underwater arm pull. While Don does not use as much cross-over in his arm pull as do most good swimmers, he nevertheless does use an inverted question mark pull.

When the arm is directly under the body, the hand and the whole forearm may be effective as a paddle in propelling the body forward. Thus it is possible that, with the inverted question mark pull, the swimmer is always able to have the center of his paddle in line with the longitudinal axis of his body.

When the swimmer swings his arm across in front of his body, he is also more capable of pushing the water in a line parallel to the longitudinal plane of his body. In this case the swimmer is accomplishing the same thing he does when he keeps his elbow up as the swimmer is doing in Figure II–18. Swimmers capable of keeping the elbow-up position do not require as wide an inverted question mark pattern as do swimmers who cannot achieve this position.

Another possible explanation to justify the question mark action of the hands during the pull may lie in an application of the theoretical square law. If a hand is pulled through the water in a straight line and covers the distance of six feet per second, creating an average force of 20 pounds, this force could be increased if the hand were made to pull backward in an "S" pattern or in an inverted question mark pattern in the same length of time, because the velocity of the hand would be greater. If the speed of the hand were doubled, the force would be quadrupled. This force would not be directly backward, and the lateral component would cause distortion of the body alignment, unless this lateral component could be cancelled out by some other action, such as a lateral thrust of the kick.

The writer wishes to make clear that too much deviation of the pull from the center line or too large an inverted question mark action of the pulling hand can be detrimental. Within limits, the amount of this type of movement that is desirable varies from one individual to the next and will depend to a large extent upon other factors that have been discussed.

MEDIAL ROTATION OF THE UPPER ARM.   As the hand pulls through the water during the first part of the pull, it must be able to push the water backward at a desirable angle and also catch up with the speed of the water before it is too far into the pull. To do this the upper arm must be rotated medially (rotated inwardly toward the middle bend of the body) during the first half of the pull. This medial rotation plus an increasing flexion of the elbow is continued throughout the first half of the pull. A better understanding of this rotating action can be had by studying Chapter X on dry land exercises, specifically, the exercise called the *medial arm rotators drill*. This particular action is shown clearly in the elbow-up pull in Figure II–18. This medial rotation of the upper arm should be distinguished from medial rotation of the lower arm or forearm. The latter action merely turns the palm over, while rotation of the upper arm causes an increase in pulling strength by adding the strength of the arm rotator muscles to the strength of the arm depressor muscles to pull the arm through the water.

This use of the arms is natural to a large extent, since a person tends to use his muscles in a manner which provides the strongest action. This fact partly accounts for the zig-zag pull pattern which can be seen even in some beginning swimmers. For years this action was called *feathering* and was discouraged by both swimming coaches and teachers.

An easy way to demonstrate to the swimmer how important it is to use this action to improve the strength of his pull is to have him perform the following task: jump into the pool and hang onto the side, submerged to the shoulders. He should then place his hands on the pool deck and climb out of the pool by pushing his hands down on the deck. Most swimmers will immediately rotate their upper arms as they push downward, their elbows will go out, and they will largely imitate the movement used in the crawl arm pull.

The total effectiveness of the arm pull to achieve maximum propulsion, therefore, involves two considerations: (1) the most profitable application of force so far as the laws of motion are concerned, and (2) the most efficient application of force so far as anatomical function is concerned. Within limits, the swimmer must try to satisfy both requirements and, to do this, may have to settle for a slight deviation from the absolute observation of each principle. The variation in the arm strength of three arm positions is shown in Figure II–22. It is obvious that the swimmer is stronger in position *C* (the position advocated in the above discussion). While the scale used in Figure II–22 is only a spring scale and not of the type used in research projects to study muscle action, it has the advantage of being a simple way of showing the swimmer the difference in strength of the pull of the various arm positions. Actual research studies of the arm pull made at Indiana University, in which cable tensiometers were used instead of a spring scale, reveal the same findings.

Medial rotation of the upper arm is an important action, and the role it plays in the mechanics of all four competitive strokes will be discussed in each of the chapters involved with a particular stroke.

HOW MUCH ROLL? Shoulder and body roll varies somewhat among great swimmers, but this variation is surprisingly small and is probably due largely to variation in shoulder flexibility among the swimmers. Generally, the greater the flexibility of the shoulders, the smaller the amount of roll (this roll being on the longitudinal axis of the body and not to be interpreted as lateral movement of the body). The swimmer should roll more to the side on which he breathes. The amount of roll at this point is about 40°, plus or minus 5°.

The amount of roll of the body to the non-breathing side should be decreased by only 10° to 15° from that of the breathing side. The total amount of roll in degrees, as approximated from observing underwater movies, varies among good swimmers from 70° to 100°. The roll of the shoulders, the hips, and the body should be synchronized. It is wrong to try to hold either the shoulders, the hips, or both in a flat position.

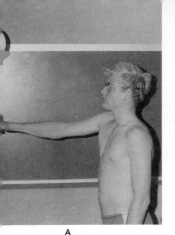
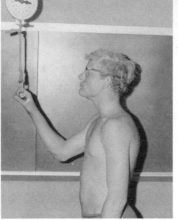
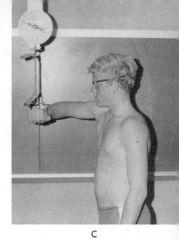

A   B   C

FIG. II–22. Variation in the Strength of Arm Pull with the Arm in Three Positions

Position A. Straight arm pull (force created, 31 pounds). When the elbow is held straight, the swimmer creates the smallest amount of force. The decreased amount of strength at this point can be credited to the great length of the lever arm and the fact that, in this position, he cannot take advantage of the additional strength of the arm rotator muscles.

Position B. The dropped-elbow pull (force created, 46 pounds). The force created by this pull is greater than that of the straight arm, and almost as great as that of the correct pull in Position C. In swimming, however, it is not possible to direct this force backward effectively in this typical pull. The strength gained here is attributed to the shortening of the lever arm and the addition of the strength of the triceps muscle to that of the arm depressors.

Position C. The elbow-up pull (force created, 48 pounds). Due to the addition of the strength of the arm rotators to that of the arm depressors, the force created by this pull is greater in good swimmers than that created by the other two types of pull. This is not the case in untrained swimmers who have not developed sufficient strength in their arm rotators.

It is also wrong to try to roll just to be rolling. When correctly exploited, the roll serves several purposes:

1. Makes the recovery of the arm easier and permits a shorter radius of rotation of the recovering arm.
2. Places the strongest part of the arm pull more directly under the center of gravity of the body.
3. Places the hips in such a position that the feet can thrust at least partly sidewards during the kick, thus cancelling the distorting effect of the recovering arm.
4. Facilitates breathing.

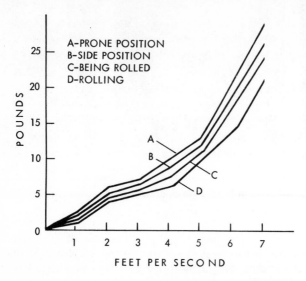

POUNDS

A–PRONE POSITION
B–SIDE POSITION
C–BEING ROLLED
D–ROLLING

FEET PER SECOND

FIG. II–23. **Drag with the Body in Four Positions**

The coach and swimmer should work together to determine the amount of roll best for that swimmer. Although the swimmer will roll naturally as he strokes, it cannot be assumed that he will always roll the right amount naturally. Frequently, such stroke defects as a dropped elbow or delayed breathing may upset this balance and cause too much roll, or these defects may be caused by excessive roll. If, at this time, the swimmer is instructed not to roll at all, the real cause of his excessive roll will not be eliminated and he may be worse off than before.

A forced, completely flat position of the body is not possible. If the swimmer tries to remain flat, he will usually find he is wiggling from side to side.

A study of the drag created by a swimmer in four drag positions reveals what a detrimental effect excessive rolling can have on the resistance a swimmer creates (Figure II–23). The swimmer created the least resistance when dragged in the prone (A—face down) position. The increasing order of drag was then: side position (B), while being rolled by an external force (C), and while rolling himself (D).

HEAD POSITION

The position of the head has already been discussed briefly in the section on body position. The question, should the head be carried high or low? cannot be answered specifically because the terms *high* or *low* are relative. The head should be carried with a slight posterior flexion of the neck. If the head is placed in the proper position, it will create a bow wave that will leave a trough or concavity in the water at the side of the head where the swimmer will be able to get his breath without having to roll too far or to lift his head too high (Figure II–24).

If the swimmer has found the proper placement of his head, he will be able to breathe below the normal surface of the water. The swimmer's mouth should be pulled toward the breathing side of his face by the facial muscles. The swimmer should experiment with different head positions in an effort to find the bottom of the bow wave (the trough) when he rolls his head to the side to breathe.

It is important that the swimmer turn his head to the side merely by rotating his neck on its longitudinal axis and not by lifting or flexing it laterally. As mentioned before, these latter two actions will cause distortion of the body alignment. The roll of the head should be timed with that of the body. The maximum roll of the head to the breathing side should be achieved at exactly the same time as the maximum roll of the body is achieved. This action also applies to the opposite side. The head does not work independently of the body or the arms, but it does travel further in terms of degrees of rotation on the longitudinal axis. *Independent head action* has been emphasized by some swimming authorities. Generally those who advocate this method of breathing believe that the head should be snapped to the side, independent of the body roll, and the breath should be taken quickly and the head snapped back to center,

FIG. II–24. Effect of Head Position on Formation of the Bow Wave

World Record holder Mike Burton is shown with his head held in an excellent position to enable him to breathe in the trough at the bottom of the bow wave.

once again independent of body roll. Coordination of the various parts of the body are tied together. If a swimmer snaps his head back quickly this will invariably cause an increase in the speed of the recovering arm, and the swimmer will develop a jerky rhythm in his stroke. A rushed arm recovery can often be corrected by elimination of this fast head action.

Once the breath has been taken, the head should return, not just to the mid-line under the body, but should roll with the shoulders, so that it rolls at least 15° past center. This assures the swimmer that he has balance in his stroke and is not swimming onesided, as do so many swimmers who do not return their heads past the center line. Stopping the head at the center line after breathing usually results in a shortened pull and a wider, more difficult recovery of the arm opposite the breathing side. A good way for the coach and swimmer to check if the head is coming back far enough is to make sure that the ear on the non-breathing side is exposed, out of the water, at some time during each arm cycle.

Bi-lateral breathing—breathing every third stroke—has been used by some coaches to correct this fault. I feel this is a poor way of correcting this mistake for several reasons:

1. The swimmer is practicing something different from what he will do in a race. He also is holding his head stationary in the center for a longer period of time than he normally would do and this may only aggravate the fault.
2. Any mistake should be corrected by having the swimmer try to do specifically what he wants to do, not something he will never do in a race. This fault can be corrected in the manner already described, that is, by getting the ear on the non-breathing side out of the water.
3. Often a swimmer will develop such firmly established bad breathing habits on one side that it is always good to have one side with a clean slate. Thus, the coach and the swimmer can start from scratch, if necessary. Hardly a season has gone by when I have not changed at least one swimmer's breathing side, primarily because it is easier to learn properly on a new side than it is to break old habits.

MECHANICS OF BREATHING

Almost immediately after the swimmer inhales and places his mouth underwater, exhalation should begin, with a steady trickle of exhaled air leaving the mouth and the nose (most will leave from the mouth). It is important to emphasize that the swimmer need not forcefully eject the air at this point. If he does so, he will have exhausted the supply of air before he turns his head again to inhale. The swimmer will usually only exhale and inhale a little over a pint of air with each breath; therefore he must distribute this amount of air over the time he will have his mouth underwater. Excessively deep ventilation does not contribute to the amount of oxygen picked up by the lungs, but does contribute to fatigue of the respiratory muscles. Excessively shallow breathing is also harmful because it does not permit adequate exchange of oxygen and carbon dioxide in the blood at the lungs.

The steady flow of air from the mouth and nose should be maintained fairly constant until the swimmer's mouth is ready to break the water. At this point exhalation becomes somewhat more vigorous. Among many swimmers this action becomes automatic and serves to blow away the water which is rolling off the face and onto the mouth and nose, and to leave the area around the mouth and nose clear for the split second required to inhale.

In the case of beginning swimmers and sometimes even competitive swimmers it is important to have practice drills on this particular skill.

I do not advocate use of the type of breathing known as *explosive breathing*. In this type of breathing the breath is held throughout most of the time the head is underwater in an effort to increase the buoyancy

FIG. II–25.   Sequence of the Crawl Stroke

This sequence of drawings shows the swimmer performing a conventional six beat crawl stroke with a continuous arm action.

1. As the right hand enters the water at shoulder width with the palm facing downward, the pulling arm has accomplished half of its pull. Air is being exhaled from the mouth and nose in a steady trickle, indicating a rhythmical breathing pattern.

2. The downward momentum developed by the hand during the recovery causes the right hand to sink downward for its catch. The pulling arm continues its pull backward with the palm still facing backward.

FIG. II–25   Continued

3. The right hand continues to move downward slowly as the pulling hand starts to come back toward the center line of the body.

4. The arm depressor muscles now start to contract actively and depress the right arm downward.

5. The left arm has almost completed its pull and the swimmer is now applying force with both hands. The force of the right hand is not as yet directed backward sufficiently to contribute any forward propulsion to the body.

6. As the left arm finishes its pull the left leg thrusts downward vigorously. This action cancels out the effect that the upward action of the arms has upon depressing the swimmer's hips.

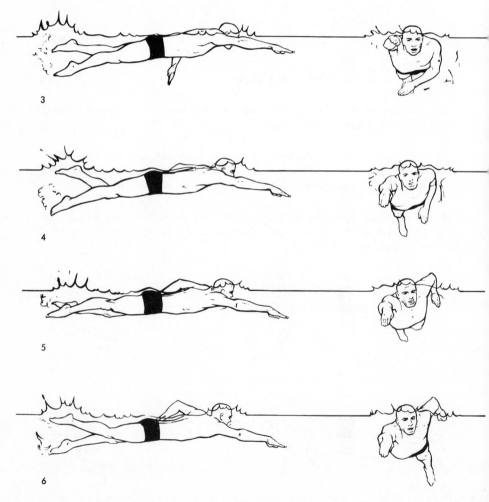

FIG. II–25.   Continued

7. As the right hand presses downward, the elbow starts to bend.

8. The elbow-up position of both the recovery arm and the pulling arm is apparent.

9. The pulling hand has accomplished half of its pull and the hand starts to rotate on its longitudinal axis. The amount of air being exhaled begins to increase.

10. The pulling hand has accomplished half of its pull and the head starts to rotate on its longitudinal axis. The amount of air being exhaled begins to increase.

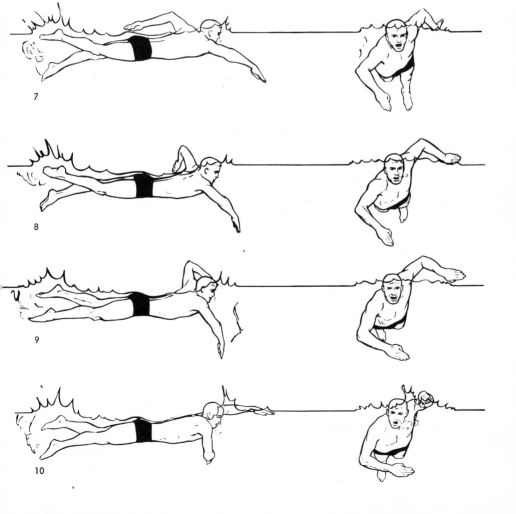

FIG. II-25. Continued

11. The head continues to turn to the side as the chin appears to follow the action of the elbow as it goes backward. The pulling hand starts to round out and come back toward the center line of the body.

12. The swimmer's mouth is opened further as the volume of air exhaled is increased.

13. The pulling hand is no longer facing directly backward, but is held at an angle of about 45°. The thumb-out position at this point is noticeable in many good swimmers, but is neither detrimental nor beneficial.

14. The downward thrust of the right leg starts as the right arm finishes its pull. The mouth finally breaks the surface of the water and the inhalation is about to begin.

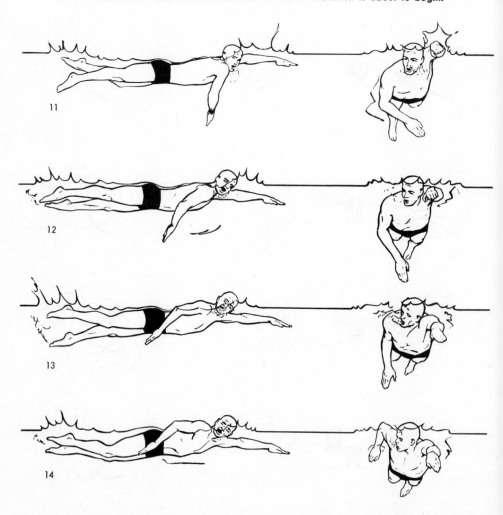

FIG. II–25.   Continued

15. Immediately before the hand breaks the surface of the water, it is turned so the palm faces inward toward the body. The swimmer opens his eyes and starts his inhalation.

16. The downward thrust of the right leg ends as the swimmer starts his right arm forward. The inhalation is almost completed.

17. The head starts to rotate back toward the center line of the body as the recovering arm swings forward.

18. The swimmer starts to exhale as the face is almost completely submerged. The left arm is about to enter the water and complete the stroke cycle.

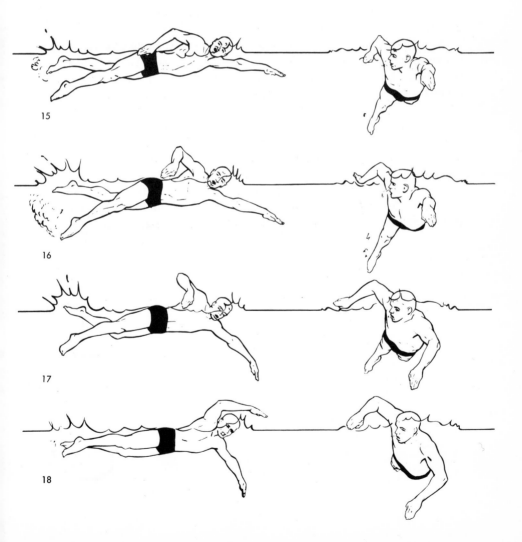

of the swimmer. I do advocate, however, a form of rhythmical breathing as described above, with a sufficient increase in air expulsion at the very end of exhalation to clear the water away from the mouth.

How Often to Breathe?

Certainly in the distance events a breath should be taken with every complete arm cycle. In sprints the breathing pattern that provides the best results on the basis of time trials and experience should be used. Some great 50-yard sprinters have swum the entire distance without breathing after they started the race. The general plan which suits most sprinters for the 50-yard distance in a 25-yard pool is to take one breath before going into the first turn and then one or two breaths on the second length. The number of breaths taken by age group swimmers should be greater than that taken by senior swimmers.

Often a swimmer with faulty breathing habits, such as a pause in the stroke when he breathes, does not correct his mistakes but tries to compensate for them by breathing less often. If the breath is taken properly, it need not cause a pause in the stroke, and many swimmers will be able to sprint as fast when breathing every complete arm cycle as they can when breathing less often. Many of the top 100-yard sprinters have achieved their best times while breathing in this manner. Once again, however, the method which gives the best results is the one which should be used.

After the dive in all freestyle races, including distance events, the swimmer should take at least two arm strokes before taking a breath. In the sprints this number can and should be increased.

III

The Butterfly Stroke

The butterfly stroke resembles the crawl stroke in that the arms and legs work similarly, with the obvious exception that both arms stroke simultaneously, as do both legs. The butterfly stroke was first introduced as a form of the breaststroke in which the breaststroke kick was used with the butterfly arm pull. In 1952 the FINA [1] separated the two strokes into two events and legalized the use of the dolphin kick with the butterfly stroke.

The speed of the new stroke has progressed to the point that some people feel it will one day supplant the crawl as the fastest swimming stroke. There is little chance of this occurring, however, since the butterfly stroke has one outstanding mechanical defect: application of propulsive force in the butterfly is fluctuating and permits a tremendous surge of power when both arms are pulling simultaneously and a correspondingly large deceleration of the body when the arms are recovering. As has been described previously, there is a disproportionate

---

[1] *Fédération Internationale de Natation Amateur*, the governing body of international swimming.

amount of energy lost in this *stop and go* type of speed fluctuation.

The rules governing the butterfly stroke state the following:

> Both arms must be brought forward together over the water and brought backward simultaneously and symmetrically.
>
> The body must be kept perfectly on the breast, and both shoulders in the horizontal plane.
>
> All movements of the feet must be executed in a simultaneous manner. Simultaneous up and down movements of the legs and feet in the vertical plane are permitted.
>
> When touching at the turn or on finishing a race, the touch shall be made with both hands simultaneously on the same level. The shoulders shall be in a horizontal position in line with the surface of the water. Note: A legal touch may be made above or below the surface of the water.
>
> Any competitor introducing a sidestroke movement shall be disqualified.
>
> When a swimmer is in the underwater position at the start, when turning or during the race, he may be allowed to make one or more leg kicks.
>
> A swimmer may change from dolphin to frog kick or vice-versa at will during a race provided other provisions of this section of Rule VI are not violated.[2]

The breaststroke kick is still permitted in the butterfly, but its use slows the stroke to such an extent that it is never used by swimmers in world class competition.

The butterfly stroke is similar enough to the crawl stroke, in terms of the muscle groups and mechanics used, for many freestylers to swim excellent butterfly with a minimum of time spent in training with the butterfly. The reverse situation is also true; most top butterfliers can switch to the crawl and perform well without great difficulty.

BODY POSITION

In the butterfly stroke there is a much greater up and down movement of the body than exists in the other strokes. This movement is not a forced undulation, but results from three main factors: (1) the action of kicking downward with the legs forces the hips up, (2) the inertia of the recovering arms tends to pull the head and shoulders down, and (3) the first part of the pull tends to make the head and shoulders rise upward. While some of this action in the vertical plane is desirable, so as to facilitate breathing, the body must remain fairly well streamlined if the swimmer is to keep the level of drag reasonable. Large undulations of the body, such as were practiced in the early days of the stroke and were

---

[2] Amateur Athletic Union of the United States, *Official Handbook for 1965*, Rules for Competitive Swimming, Section VI, p. 8.

considered to be propulsive, are now considered harmful to forward progress. Likewise, complete inhibition of this up and down movement has been shown to be detrimental, for it makes proper arm recovery, kicking technique, and breathing difficult.

Butterfliers who swim the stroke properly say they feel a flowing motion in their bodies, and a gentle but definite rhythmical rise and fall in body position. Careful observation of moving or sequence pictures of good butterfliers reveals that they do manage to time the kick, pull, and head lift for breathing in such a way that body position remains relatively horizontal. The hips of a good butterflier remain close to the surface of the water and the angle of his body in general does not approach the diagonal position pictured in Figure I–3, illustration I. The effect which the arm pull, kick, and breathing have on body position, as well as how they should be timed in the total stroke, will be discussed in other sections of this chapter.

THE DOLPHIN KICK

This kick is the fastest of those of the four competitive strokes when done in kicking drills on the kick board. The kick is difficult for some swimmers and requires, as do the front and back crawl kick, good ankle flexibility (plantar flexion). Ankle stretching exercises along with a lot of kicking drill help to increase this ankle flexibility.

Is the Dolphin Kick Propulsive?

There is a strong possibility that, in the butterfly stroke, one of the kicks may actually be propulsive, an idea which has been discarded by most experts in the cases of the back and crawl strokes. Little scientific evidence is available to substantiate the fact that the kick is or is not propulsive, or that one of the two kicks in each stroke cycle is propulsive while the other is not. The first kick downward, that which occurs immediately after the arms enter the water, is generally the larger and more vigorous of the two. It comes at a time when the swimmer is at his slowest speed in the stroke cycle, due to the fact that the acceleration he had gained during the previous arm pull has begun to be dissipated. This factor, plus the drag effect that the entry of his arms into the water has had on his forward speed, causes the swimmer to be at this slow rate of speed. The first kick, coming as it does at this point, *may* drive the swimmer forward, but it definitely serves to elevate his hips and to put his body in an almost perfectly streamlined, horizontal position when the arm pull is made. The second kick occurs during the last part of the arm pull. It is nearly always smaller than the first, and its function is to cancel the hip-dropping effect of the latter part of the pull on body position. Some swimmers do not use the second kick and, as a result, the hips are forced downward by the last part of the pull. Even some good swimmers eliminate the second kick when they get tired, or make it so small and feeble that it is nearly imperceptible. This is most likely to occur when the swimmer is tired, either near the end of a race or in practice, and cannot finish his arm pull properly, so that the time required to finish the arm pull is shortened to the point that the swimmer hasn't time to kick twice in each stroke. When the arm pull is shortened, particularly at the end of the stroke, there is less need for the second kick, whose main function is to keep the hips up. The second kick can often be kept in the stroke by having the swimmer concentrate on lengthening the stroke by pulling his arms back further.

When a swimmer with an exceptionally strong arm pull is sprinting and is using a strong finish on his pull, his two kicks per cycle will be almost identical in size. Obviously the strength or forcefulness of the finish of the pull has a great deal to do with the size of the second kick. It is my feeling that the coach need not teach nor the swimmer try to force a major and minor kick into the stroke, but, within limits, allow this to occur automatically. Just as a runner automatically starts to swing his arms more when he sprints, so perhaps does a butterflier adjust the dolphin kick (primarily the second kick) to his stroke particularly to the end of the pull.

Speculation as to whether a one, three, or even four beat kick might replace the present two beat kick as the best technique would appear to be unjustified.

Drill on a Kick Board

The mechanics of the dolphin kick are best learned on a kick board, but the mere fact that the swimmer can master the kick on the board does not mean he will be able to do it properly when swimming the total stroke. Some butterfliers even prefer to do their kicking drill without the use of a kick board; most, however, like to use a kick board because when the board is not used, the swimmer tends to undulate his body too much by alternately piking at the hips and arching the back. Since the swimmer tends to do in the whole stroke what he has practiced in kicking and pulling drills, this stroke defect can be transferred to the whole stroke with a resulting excessive up and down body movement.

When the swimmer grasps the kick board he should hold the board in such a way that his shoulders are low in the water. He should not press downward on the board in order to maintain his shoulders high in the water. The board should be kept in a flat position, that is, the front should not be tilted upward. As he kicks on the board, the swimmer's elbows should be straight or almost straight, and he should look down the board to the opposite end of the pool. The board should remain in a relatively stable condition and should not be forced up and down. As he looks at the other end of the pool, the swimmer should be aware of whether or not his head and shoulders are bobbing to any great extent, and should try to control the bobbing. He will feel his hips rise as he kicks downward and drop somewhat as he recovers his legs upward. He should not try to control this body motion rigidly, but, as mentioned before, should try to prevent excessive piking action at the hips and

FIG. III–1. The Fishtail Kick

This sequence of photographs shows the mechanics of the fishtail kick as it should be done when the swimmer is engaged in kicking drills on the kick board.

1. The legs are at the bottom of their downbeat with the heels at a depth of almost two feet. The hips are just breaking the surface of the water.

2. The legs are brought upward with no bend in the knees. This particular action is desirable and is apparent in all good kickers. No forward propulsion is derived from the upbeat of the kick.

3. The extended legs continue upward. This lifting of the legs causes a lowering of the hips.

4. The upper leg now starts downward, as the feet continue upward. This combined action is possible because of the flexion of the knees.

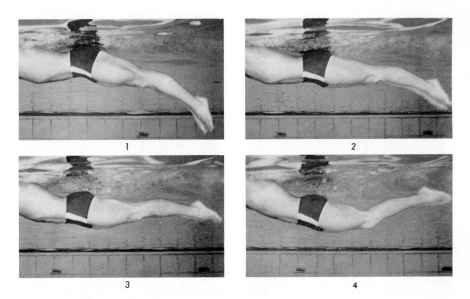

FIG. III—1.   Continued

5. The speed of the downward movement of the upper legs is accelerated, but the increased bending action of the knees raises the feet even closer to the surface. The hips are at the lowest point of submersion.

6. As the knees reach a flexion of 90° the feet, now at the top of the upbeat, begin to plantar flex in preparation for the beginning of the downbeat.

7. The propulsive phase of the fishtail kick begins as the feet are thrust downward with a noticeable hyperextension or plantar flexion of the ankles. At this point in the kick it becomes apparent why good ankle flexibility is a desirable trait.

8. The downward thrust of the feet continues without any apparent change in the position of the upper legs. This downward action of the feet has its reaction in the elevation of the hips as they move closer to the surface.

9. As the knees become extended, the feet continue downward and the upper legs start upward.

10. The downbeat of the feet is completed when the legs reach full extension at the knees. The upper legs have already started upward and some of this upward momentum will now be transferred to the lower legs. The cycle is completed.

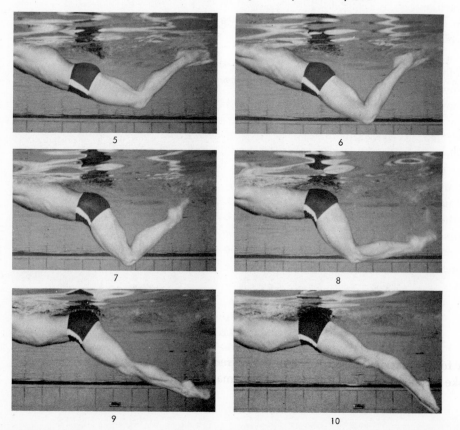

5

6

7

8

9

10

arching of the back. Uncontrolled, these conditions introduce a wasted undulating movement.

Figure III–1 depicts the correct mechanics of a good fishtail (another name for the dolphin) kick. The kick in this sequence is somewhat bigger than it will be when the whole stroke is swum and does not show the variation in size between the two kicks in a stroke cycle, of which the first is usually the bigger.

A very important point to emphasize in teaching this kick is that of having the swimmer start the recovery or upbeat of the kick with straight legs. If the swimmer starts his legs upward by merely bending at the knees, he will create a greater negative force or drag with the backs of his legs than if he starts the kick up with straight legs. He will also finish his legs in a poor position to drive downward.

The legs should remain straight for over half of the uplift. The uplift of the legs is not forceful, but is made with relatively little effort in order to minimize drag. The emphasis on the kick is on the downbeat, and this is the case to such an extent that the speed of the feet is over twice as fast as it is on the uplift. This emphasis on the downbeat is important since this element of the kick is its propulsive phase, and, if it is made with a fast motion, causes increased forward propulsion, an application of the principles involved in the theoretical square law. It is often wise to tell the swimmer who is having trouble mastering the kick to try to think of the upbeat taking a count of two and the downbeat only a count of one.

Before the feet reach the top of their lift, the upper legs start to drive downward. The bending of the knees permits this rising of the feet and downward movement of the upper legs to occur simultaneously. As the lower legs and feet start downward, the momentum developed in the upper legs is transferred to them and they get a sudden acceleration which permits a whip-like action of the lower legs and, consequently, a great terminal velocity at the feet. During this downward thrust of the feet and lower legs, the upper legs and hips are driven upward.

Many swimmers toe-in when doing the dolphin kick, particularly during the downward phase. This toeing-in should not be forced, but, if it occurs naturally, should be permitted only to the degree to which it will not make the kick illegal. The amount of toeing-in will depend upon the manner in which the femur (the bone in the upper leg) sets into the hip joint.

THE ARM PULL

A former national champion and world record holder in the butterfly stroke has described her arm pull as being made with completely straight

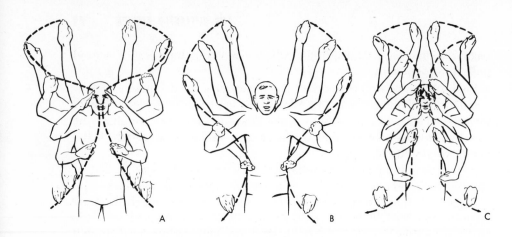

FIG. III–2. **Double S Pull Patterns of Three Champion Butterflyers**

(Dotted line indicates the path of the tip of the middle finger of each hand.)

A. Kevin Berry, 1964 Olympic champion and World Record holder in the 200-meter Butterfly at 2:06.6. (His pull is also pictured in Figure III–3, A.) Kevin's hands follow a typical hourglass or keyhole pattern in which the hands almost touch when they are directly under the chin. At this point, Kevin's elbows are dropped slightly. This is a stroke defect.

B. Fred Schmidt, NCAA and American record holder of the 200-yard Butterfly in 1:51.4. His arm pull pattern sweeps out a little wider to the side and does not come into the center as much as Kevin's does. A difference in the positioning of the hands is also apparent.

C. Sue Pitt, National champion and World Record holder for 200-meter Butterfly. Sue's arm pull pattern is typical of age-group swimmers and girl swimmers who do not have the arm strength to pull in a pattern such as in illustrations A and B. Because of this lack of strength, the swimmers drop their elbows and extend their wrists and *let go of the water.* These two actions cause a loss in efficiency of the pull.

elbows and with both arms pulling directly down and back. A study of underwater movies, however, revealed that she swam in a manner similar to that of all world class butterfliers, which is with an arm pattern described variously as a key hole, hour glass, or double S pull. At one point in her stroke she bent her elbows as much as 90°. She is not an exception, however; as I have said before, many great swimmers do not know exactly what they are doing strokewise.

Figure III–2 shows the double S pull pattern of three champion swimmers. The explanation for the effectiveness of this type of pull pattern would be similar to that used in the previous chapter (Chapter II, page 52), that is, it provides a use of the arms in the strongest line of pull, so far as the muscular power of the arms is concerned, and permits a good application of propulsive force backward.

If the arms were pulled directly downward, with the elbows straight during the first half of the stroke, the upper body would be forced up and the swimmer would virtually climb out of the water. If the arms are continued in this pattern with no elbow bend, they will achieve a good application of force only when directly under the body, but will cause the body to be pulled downward at the end of the pull.

A good way to demonstrate the effect of the straight arm pull is to have the swimmer lie in the water in a prone position with his feet supported by a tube or water polo ball. His arms should be extended straight up and over the shoulders. The swimmer should then be instructed to pull vigorously, in the manner described previously until his arms are in the vertical position. The effect of the first half of this type of pull will become apparent immediately, for the body will rise high in the water. The effect of the second half of the pull can also be evaluated by having the swimmer lie in the water in the same position as before, with his legs supported, except that he will start with his arms held straight downward from the shoulders in a vertical position. As the swimmer pushes back and up vigorously, the effect on his body position becomes apparent as he is forced forward and downward.

The swimmer has now been shown what not to do and why not to do it. He must be shown what to do and also told why he should do it in the prescribed manner. A demonstration similar to the one used to show the swimmer why he should not use the straight-through arm pull with the straight elbow can also be effective in showing the swimmer the proper pull. The swimmer should lie in the water in the prone position with his feet supported as before and his arms over head as before. He should then pull his right arm backward and halfway through the pull, but in the manner pictured in Figure III-7, that is, not by pushing directly down and back, but rather diagonally down and outward in such a way that the hands separate on the horizontal plane. The result of this action of the right arm will cause him to move forward and to the left, but only slightly upward. He should then repeat the same action with his left arm only. The action of the left arm will be similar to that of the right arm except that it will push the swimmer to the right. When two forces are equal and opposite, they cancel one another out; thus, when both arms are pulled simultaneously, the lateral thrust of each arm is cancelled out by the effect of the other and the body remains in longitudinal alignment with no lateral deviation.

The swimmer who is bobbing up and down excessively may often be corrected by being directed to pull wider during the first quarter of his

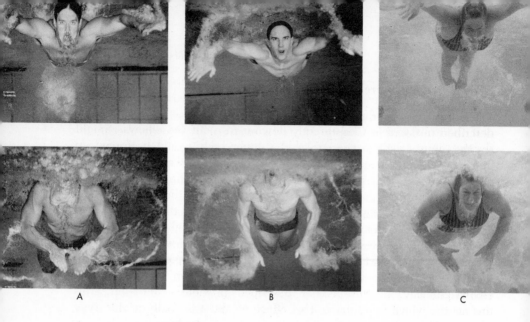

A   B   C

FIG. III–3. Underwater Photographs of Three Champion Butterfly Swimmers

These pictures show the widest and the narrowest spread between the hands during the pull in three champion swimmers.

A. Kevin Berry's pull is widest after the arms have sunk about 12 inches under the surface of the water. His hands nearly touch when they are directly under his chin.

B. Fred Schmidt's pull reaches its greatest width when the arms are almost two feet beneath the surface. The hands are closest together when they are under the hips.

C. Ada Kok of Holland, World Record holder in the 100- and 200-meter Butterfly. Her pull is at its widest spread at almost the same point as that of Kevin Berry, that is, at a depth of 12 inches. She swims with a one beat kick. In the top photo she is shown completing the down beat of her single kick. Her hands come closest together at a point farther back than Berry's, but not as far back as Schmidt's.

pull. The straight downward press of the arms should be avoided, but an excessively wide pull puts the arms in a position in which the muscles begin to lose their strength. The effect of the latter part of the proper type of arm pull can also be noted in a demonstration similar to that devised for the straight arm pull, in which the swimmer once again repeats the arm movement shown in Figure III–7. He can see that this action does not drive him downward as much as did the action of the second half of the straight arm pull.

The "Over-the-Barrel" or Elbow-up Position

The arm position during the first part of the butterfly pull has been described in detail in Chapter II, *The Crawl Stroke*, since its mechanics are the same. As the arms are pulled obliquely downward and outward, the upper arms are rotated medially (see Chapter II, page 50) as the elbows are bent. This particular action causes elevation of the elbows, giving the swimmer the sensation of reaching *over the barrel*. It permits the arms to push the water backward at an advantageous angle. A *dropped elbow* (Figure I–7, illustration A) during this phase of the pull would result in the force being directed downward more than backward.

After the hands and arms press outward, they begin to come together until they almost touch. This action is accomplished by bending the elbows plus increasing the medial rotation of the upper arms. Once again, this action, which is similar to that of the crawl arm stroke at the same point, is accomplished for the same reason as the one given in the case of the crawl: (1) to make the arm pull stronger by adding the strength of the arm rotators to that of the arm depressors (Figure II–21), and (2) to assure a more efficient application of propulsive force backward. Figure III–3 shows two key positions in the arm pull of three champion butterfly swimmers.

The mechanics used in the crawl arm pull and the butterfly arm pull, as well as the justification for this particular action, are so similar that it would be needless repetition to detail them again here. For this reason I recommend a study of the material on pages 40 to 42 of Chapter II.

The Arm Recovery

Preparation for the arm recovery is made before the arm pull finishes. There is an overlap of these two phases, for the upper arms and elbows are already being recovered as the hands continue their push backward. The hands at the end of the pull do not push directly backward, but sweep outward in a rounded out motion. This rounding out conserves most of the momentum of the arms and hands which has been developed during the pull, and permits it to be· used in aiding the recovery of the arms.

The arm recovery begins with a slight elbow bend and, as the hands leave the water, the arms start to swing forward in a low, flat parabola, becoming completely extended due largely to the centrifugal force generated by their circular motion. The arm recovery should be considered primarily a ballistic movement. The force applied to establish such a movement is applied for only a short period at the beginning of the movement. The momentum developed during this period then carries that part of the body through the rest of the movement. In the butterfly arm recovery, the recovery muscles (primarily the deltoid and trapezius mus-

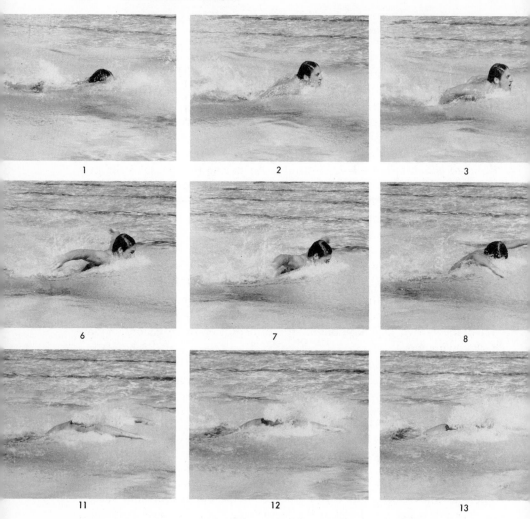

FIG. III—4. Kevin Berry's Arm Recovery and Breathing Pattern

Kevin Berry uses good mechanics in his arm recovery and breathing pattern. As the sequence begins, the head has broken the surface. Before the arms have completed their pulling action, the mouth breaks the surface and starts the inhalation. As the arms become completely clear of the water, the inhalation is almost completed. As the arms approach the shoulder level in their recovery, the mouth is submerged and the neck begins to flex. As the arms swing past the shoulders, the hands are pronated (turned so the palm is down). As the arms enter the water, the neck is flexed and, shortly thereafter, the head becomes submerged slightly beneath the surface.

4   5

9   10

cles) contract vigorously during the first part of the arm swing, then relax, and allow momentum rather than their sustained contraction to carry them forward. One way of conveying this idea to the swimmer is to tell him to concentrate on relaxing his arms once recovery has begun.

The palms of the hands are facing almost directly upward as they leave the water. If this *palm-up* position were to be maintained for any length of time, the recovery of the arms would be very difficult because this position decreases the mobility of the upper arm in the shoulder joint. This is particularly true in the case of the swimmer with limited shoulder and upper arm flexibility. Almost as soon as the hands leave the water the swimmer should make a conscious effort to rotate the upper arm laterally in order that the palms may be facing downward as the hands swing forward past the shoulder. The hand should enter the water at a point only slightly outside the shoulder line, with the palms facing downward and slightly outward in order that the thumb will be lower than the rest of the hand. (Figure III–4 shows the out-of-water arm recovery of Kevin Berry, 1964 Olympic champion.)

Transition from Recovery to Pull

A common mistake made by many swimmers occurs immediately before the arms enter the water. If the swimmer slows down the movement

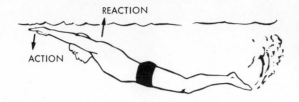

FIG. III–5.   **High Catch Causing Climbing Action**

FIG. III–6.   **Low Catch with Elbows Up Permitting Greater Forward Propulsion**

of the arms at this point, the downward momentum of the arms is transferred to the body and the swimmer sinks further underwater than he should. Too many swimmers place their arms in the water with too much control at this point.

The downward momentum of the arms and hands should be absorbed by the water and not cancelled by muscle action. This action not only causes the body to drop lower into the water, it also causes the hands to stop near the surface. If the pull is begun at this point, the force of the first part of the pull is directed downward too much and the swimmer *climbs upward* as a result (see Figure III–5).

If the swimmer allows the momentum of the arms, developed during the recovery, to cause the arms to sink slightly without pulling the head and shoulders down to the low position shown in Figure III–5, he will be in a better position to apply the force of his pull more backward and less downward (Figure III–6). Much of the excessive up and down motion of the butterfly swimmer can be attributed to this defect.

BREATHING ACTION AND TIMING

Swimmers not accustomed to swimming butterfly often complain of sore muscles in the back of the neck when they do begin to swim the stroke. The posterior neck muscles (splenius capitus, splenius cervicus) are used to lift the head by hyper-extension of the neck, thus permitting the shoulders to remain lower in the water while the swimmer is breathing than he otherwise could. The butterfly is the only one of the four strokes in which these muscles are used in this way and they are not conditioned in swimmers of the other strokes. If the swimmer does not hyper-extend his neck, he will have to breathe with his face looking downward, and his body position will be elevated during the breathing phase. I tell such swimmers to lift their heads to breathe by concentrating on hyper-extension of the neck. The head-lift action should raise the head high enough to get the mouth clear of the water, but not enough to allow the chin to be too far above the surface. Some swimmers lift their heads so high that the chin is five to six inches above the water level. Kevin Berry, 1964 Olympic champion of the butterfly event, states that when he is swimming well in a calm pool, he tries to plow a furrow in the water with his chin. In rough water this low chin position is difficult and the swimmer may get a few mouthfuls.

After the breath has been taken, these muscles should be relaxed and the head should drop until it is almost in straight alignment with the body. This head action is apparent in the sequence series of the butterfly stroke in Figure III–7.

FIG. III–7.   Butterfly Sequence

This sequence displays the correct mechanics of the butterfly stroke. Two complete arm stroke cycles are shown here; the first is one in which the breath is not taken and the second one in which the breath is taken.

1. The stroke cycle begins as the arms enter the water at shoulder width. The legs, with the feet plantar-flexed, are ready to begin the downbeat of the kick. The head is not facing directly toward the bottom of the pool, but is tilted slightly forward.

2. As the momentum of the arms, developed during the recovery, causes the hands to sink downward, muscular effort is also applied to direct the pull diagonally outward. The downward thrust of the feet has begun.

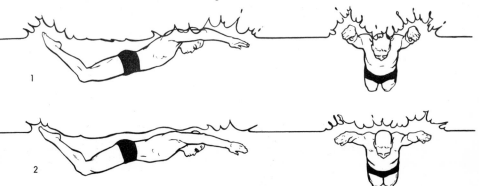

FIG. III–7.   Continued

3. The pull continues as the kick is almost completed. The reaction of the downbeat of the kick has caused the hips to come up to the surface.

4. The feet dorsi flex at the ankles as the legs begin their upbeat. During the first part of the pull, even when the swimmer does not take a breath, he lifts his head as though he were looking forward. This action occurs naturally.

5. The arms now at their maximum spread are pulled down and backward in the elbow-up position. The legs have completed the first leg beat and are positioning themselves to begin the second beat.

6. The arms start to come closer together. The line of air bubbles indicates the general pattern of the pull.

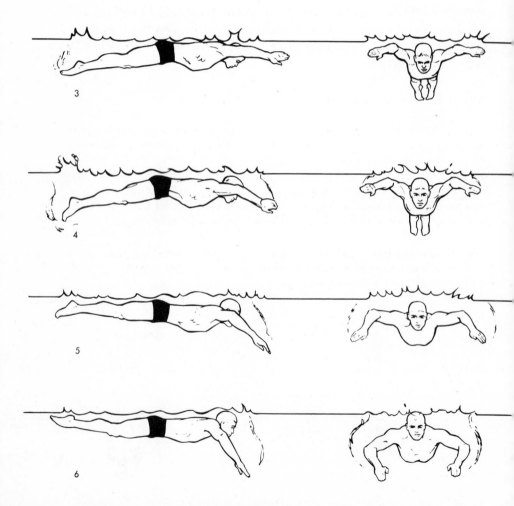

FIG. III–7. Continued

7. The hands come close to touching one another as they pass directly under the shoulders. The elbow bend, still held out away from body, is approximately 90°.

8. The elbows are adducted or brought closer to the body as the hands pass under the shoulders. The downward thrust of the legs begins as the hands start upward during the last part of the pull. At this point the swimmer begins to flex his neck and to drop his head slightly.

9. As the arms near the end of the pull, they start to swing outward to prepare for the recovery. The neck continues to flex.

10. The legs complete their downbeat slightly before the hands leave the water. The purpose of the second kick is to keep the hips near the surface so the body is in a streamlined position.

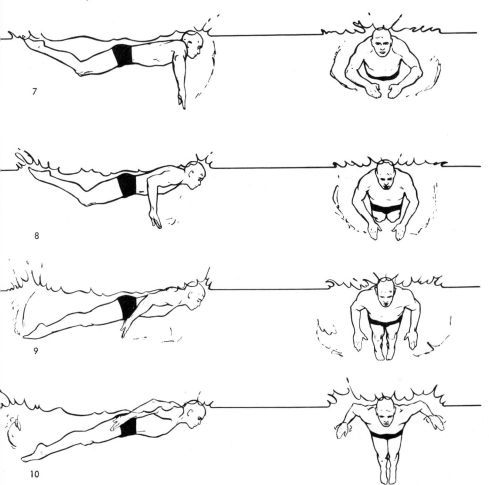

FIG. III–7.   Continued

11. As the arms leave the water and begin their recovery, the legs are brought upward with no bend in the knees. The head is lowered so the face is almost parallel with the bottom of the pool. This action of the head facilitates an easier arm recovery.

12. As the hands swing past the shoulders, the palms are facing downward. The elbows are completely extended. The feet start to plantar flex as they near the top of the upbeat.

13. The upper arms start to hit the water, as the hands prepare to enter.

14. The hands become submerged as the upper legs start their movement downward. Flexion of the knees is increased. The feet almost break the surface as they start their downbeat.

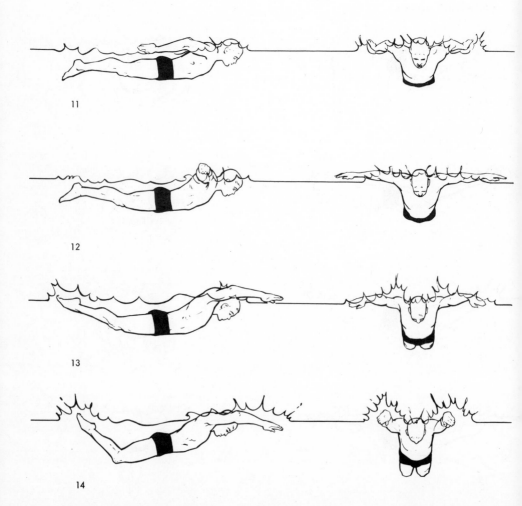

FIG. III–7.   Continued

15. The downbeat of the kick nears completion during the first part of the pull. The swimmer who has been holding his breath during the previous arm cycle begins his exhalation upon the beginning of the arm pull. The rotation of the upper arms causes the elbow-up arm position.

16. The swimmer continues his exhalation as he lifts his head upward.

17. The exhalation continues as the pull changes direction sharply and the hands are brought close together.

18. The head is lifted primarily by the flexion of the neck and the inhalction begins before the arms complete their pull. The downbeat of the kick again coincides with the finish of the arm pull.

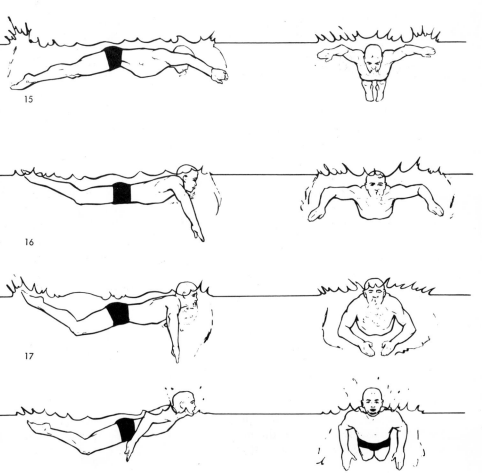

FIG. III–7.   Continued

19. As the arms start to recover, the inhalation is completed (see Figure III–4) and the downbeat of the second kick is also completed.

20. After the inhalation, the face is dropped back under water and the arms complete their recovery as the legs start upward.

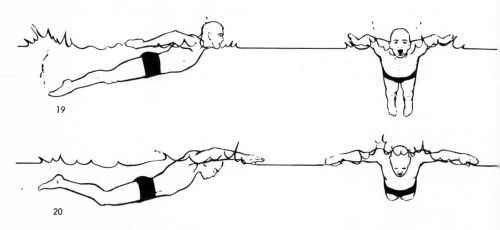

The swimmer should time his head lift so that his inhalation coincides with the time at which his shoulders are at their highest elevation. Too often the swimmer will use a *late* breathing pattern; that is, he will be lifting his head to breathe after his shoulders have reached the peak of their climb and are on their way down. This late-breathing pattern causes the swimmer to arch his back and rush his arm recovery. Such swimmers should begin the head lift immediately after the catch—or the beginning of the pull—is made. During the first half of the pull the shoulders should rise as the neck continues to flex and, when the arms are past a line perpendicular to the body, the face should be almost completely out of the water and the inhalation should begin. The inhalation continues until the arms have completed their pull and begun the recovery. As the recovery is made, the head should be lowered into the water by flexion of the neck.

As the arms pass by the head on their forward swing, the face should be completely submerged underwater, at least to eye level (see Figures III–6 and III–7). If the arms pass by the shoulders on their recovery and the swimmer is still breathing, he can be considered to be using late breathing.

If the lift of the head is timed properly, it can serve to keep the body position relatively flat. Since the arm pull causes the body to rise in the water and the head lift causes the body to drop lower into the water, these two forces combined tend to cancel one another. Since the arm pull has a greater lifting force than the head lift has a lowering force, the body does rise at this point in the stroke. In fact, the head is lifting and the neck is flexing during most of the arm pull. The head drop is a fast movement and takes approximately half of the time the head lift takes. It is important for two reasons that the head be lowered: in order that the water may support its weight, and to facilitate arm recovery.

If the swimmer does not drop his head, his body position will be detrimentally affected, for he will drop his hips lower, thereby increasing frontal and eddy resistance. On the other hand, if he drops his head excessively, he will introduce an additional up and down motion in the stroke which will also cause increased drag. Excessive dropping of the head occurs most frequently among swimmers who have a poor kick insufficient to keep their hips up. The action of the head is used to compensate for the poor kick, since it does cause a slight elevation of the hips.

Diving of the head and shoulders can also result from the piking action of the body at the hips. This action should be discouraged.

Breathing to the Side

Few world class swimmers have had success with breathing to the side. There are valid reasons to show why this technique is not as satisfactory as forward breathing: (1) there is no lift to cancel some of the upward rise caused by the arm pull, and (2) when the neck is rotated laterally, the vertebrae are placed in such a position that the neck can scarcely extend, much less hyper-extend. The swimmer, in order to get his mouth clear of the water, even though he is breathing at the side in the trough formed after the bow wave, will have to climb upward with his shoulders more than he would if he were breathing straight forward.

The deceptive feature of this type of breathing is that, because the head remains in a static position in relation to the body, it appears that the swimmer is not actually climbing as much as he does when he uses forward breathing.

How Often Should a Swimmer Breathe?

The normal procedure for a swimmer is to breathe less often in the sprints, that is, once every two or three strokes on the 50-yard, 100-yard, or 100-meter distances, and more often during the longer races, breathing perhaps once every one or two strokes in the 200-yard or 200-meter events. Some swimmers have experienced success while breathing every stroke, even during the sprints.

The breathing pattern a swimmer finally adopts must be determined by experimentation, but to serve as a guide, the patterns of swimmers who have done outstanding times are noted in the particular races where their performances were outstanding:

Mike Troy—his breathing pattern in winning the 1960 Olympic title in the 200-meter butterfly at Rome was as follows: in the first 100 meters, once every two strokes; in the second 100 meters, a two and one pattern in which he would take two strokes and breathe, then one stroke and breathe.

Kevin Berry—in winning the Olympic 200-meter event in Tokyo in 1964, breathed once every stroke throughout the entire race.

Walt Richardson—in winning the NCAA 100-yard butterfly and setting a record at :50.3, he also breathed every stroke.

Fred Schmidt—in setting the NCAA 200-yard butterfly record of 1:51.3, he breathed a two and one pattern throughout the race.

It appears that for distances over 50 yards, a swimmer is foolish not to breathe at least every two strokes.

IV

The Back Crawl Stroke

The practice of swimming on his back has a very obscure beginning in the history of man and his aquatic adventures. As early as 1794, Bernardi,[1] albeit inadequately, described what was apparently a form of the elementary backstroke.

For a perfectly horizontal position of the body lying on its back and parallel with the surface, the head must be under water up to the ears—the legs are crossed along the tibia and over the instep, to make them figure as pointed an extremity as possible. If they were kept apart or widely stretched, when advancing head forward, they would meet the water's resistance proportionately with the angle of their opening, thus impeding or at least retarding the pace.

In 1871, in London, the Marquis Bibbero [2] reportedly swam a mile on his back in 39½ minutes, the exact style that he used not being mentioned.

[1] Oronzio de Bernardi, *L'arte ragionata del nuotare*, parts I and II, Vol. II, 99, in Ralph Thomas, *Swimming* (London: Sampson, Low, Marston & Co., Ltd., 1904), p. 217.
[2] Thomas, *op. cit.*, p. 365.

Before leaving London 13 Nov '71 he was "prevailed upon" to take a benefit, when he was described as of Manchester and "Inventor of the Life-saving dress." He then swam a mile on his back in 39½ minutes (they did not trouble with fifths of a second in those days).

Backstroke was popular but saw limited use as a competitive stroke until 1906, when swimming races were divided into three classes in national and international competition: breaststroke, backstroke, and freestyle. From this time until about 1912, when the back crawl was introduced, the elementary backstroke or the double overarm backstroke with either the frog or scissor kick was used in races. After the introduction of the back crawl stroke, the other forms of backstroke slowly disappeared from competitive swimming and are now taught and used only as utility strokes.

The present rules concerning the backstroke are outlined below:

The competitors shall line up in the water, facing the starting end, with the hands resting on the end or rail of the pool or starting grips. It shall be the Starter's duty to see that the competitor's feet, including the toes, shall be under the surface of the water and that no competitor is standing in or on the gutter or curling his toes over the lip of the gutter.

The competitor in a backstroke event must not turn over beyond the vertical toward the breast before the hand has touched the end of the pool or course for the purpose of turning or finishing. It is permissible to turn over beyond the vertical after the foremost hand has touched, for sole purpose of executing the turn, but the swimmer must have returned past the vertical to a position on the back before the feet have left the wall.[3]

Within the limits of these rules any form of backstroke could be used, but the back crawl stroke with its alternate arm action and flutter kick is so superior that no other stroke is seen swum by good competitive backstroke swimmers. There have been definite trends in the teaching and coaching of the mechanics of the backstroke, but even today there is little unanimity of opinion regarding the general principles of swimming the backstroke. Some swimming authorities and most of the books on swimming advocate a straight arm pull with the shoulders held in a level position allowing little or no body roll. One of the factors which has contributed to the confusion surrounding the use of the straight arm pull or the bent arm pull is that many of the top backstroke swimmers do not know *how* they pull their arms through the water, and have made statements in clinics and interviews unintentionally misinterpreting what

[3] "Rules for Competitive Swimming," *Official Handbook of the AAU* (1965), Sec. VI, p. 8.

they do when they swim. To test my belief that this last statement is true, I have interviewed world class backstrokers and have found that not one could reasonably describe the action of his arm pull. This lack of ability to know exactly what they are doing, so far as their stroke mechanics are concerned, is not restricted to backstroke swimmers, but also applies to swimmers of the other strokes.

A careful study of underwater movies of the 1965 National AAU men's finalists in the 200-meter backstroke revealed that all eight swimmers were using a bent elbow pull. The straight elbow pull is still taught and used by many swimmers, however, and perhaps, although I doubt it, some world class swimmers are still using it. One of the greatest backstroke swimmers of all time, Adolph Kiefer, who won the 100-meter backstroke event in the 1936 Olympic Games in a time of 1:05.9, used this pull. Truly a person of great natural talent and a competitor who had the ability to rise to the challenge of a big race, Kiefer set the standard for backstrokers for many years. In some rare underwater movies of him which I have he clearly does not bend his elbows in the slightest degree.

Kiefer pulled his arms through the water in an almost perfect half-circular motion. Other swimmers, when using a straight arm pull, frequently zig-zag the arms in an S pattern as they are pulled through and the swimmer pushes downward at the end of the stroke. Since Kiefer's time, however, the world record for the 100 meters has been lowered many times by swimmers using the bent elbow pull, until it is now under one minute.

Trends in stroke mechanics often are more a result of the opinions of coaches and swimmers of what they think their swimmers are doing than of what the swimmers actually are doing. I am confident that most good crawl backstrokers since the stroke was introduced over a half century ago have used the bent elbow pull, although most of them would not have been aware of it. In the past decade or two we have become increasingly aware of what swimmers actually are doing, and can therefore assume that the back crawl stroke has not changed much since its inception; only our understanding of it has changed. Improvement in backstroke times will continue as we continue to improve our understanding of these mechanics.

The mechanical principles which govern the swimming of the back crawl stroke are the same as those that apply to the other strokes. For that reason, you will notice a recurrence of the opinions which were stated for the front crawl and the butterfly, and which will appear again in the description of the breaststroke. Since I feel it is important to see these relationships, I have made no attempt to avoid repetitions in the discussion of mechanical principles of the various strokes.

BODY POSITION

The effort to streamline the body in the backstroke by getting it into a completely horizontal position must be moderated by the consideration that this would put the legs in a position too high to perform their job effectually. Upon looking at underwater movies of themselves for the first time, most backstrokers are surprised at how low their body position is in the water. They—as do all swimmers—swim through the water, not on top of it. There is a tendency, however, among most swimmers, far from swimming too high and flat, to be in just the opposite position of tending to sit down in the water. This particular placement is the result of an excessive piking or jack-knifing action at the hips, often coupled with a forward flexion of the neck. Low hip position is referred to as *sitting up* in the water (Figure I–3, illustration G) and has actually been advocated by some people. However, it causes an increase in drag and should be avoided.

Proper body position is related to the other phases of the stroke and will also be discussed in other sections of this chapter.

THE KICK

The back crawl kick is similar to the flutter kick used in the front crawl stroke with the obvious difference of being inverted. In the crawl stroke (Chapter II) it has been postulated that the function of the kick is primarily that of a stabilizer, which keeps the body in good horizontal position and decreases lateral movement of the body caused by the action of the arm recovery. It is likely that the kick serves a similar role in the backstroke, with the main exception lying in the fact that the lateral movement being cancelled is due to movement occurring at the end of the pull, not to the arm recovery. This action is shown clearly and discussed in the backstroke sequence pictures (Figure IV–5).

It is well known that the *part* of a total skill, such as the kick as a part of the total backstroke, when learned separately, will transfer more easily when it closely emulates the exact movement as it occurs in the whole stroke. Unfortunately, as in the case of the front crawl stroke kick, the swimmer, when kicking drills on his back, uses a slightly different kick from that he uses when swimming the whole stroke, in which his body rolls and the kick is not always in the vertical plane. Up to this time we have found no way the swimmer can imitate this roll when he is engaged in kicking drills.

That is not to say that backstroke kicking drills are unimportant. They remain the best way to condition the legs, as well as to provide the opportunity for the coach to emphasize certain movements in the kick which do not always develop naturally.

The swimmer can best do his kicking drills on his back with both arms held overhead. This method helps him develop good body position. As he holds his arms overhead, he should extend his elbows without lifting the shoulder blades in a stretching movement. The hands may be held together or slightly apart. As the swimmer lies in the water and kicks, he should try to let his feet just churn the surface on the upbeat without actually breaking it. When the feet are at their greatest depth, they should reach 18 to 24 inches below the surface of the water. He should keep his head back in the water to the point that his ears are submerged, but his face is not. His head position should be adjusted by flexing or extending the neck in order that, depending on his buoyancy and the strength of his kick, he will be doing his kicking drill in a position approximating that which he should be in when he swims. When the swimmer does his kicking drills with his hands at his sides, he tends to drop his hips, and this tendency may transfer into his stroke. Kicking with both arms overhead can be difficult for a person with poor shoulder flexibility or with a poor kick; although it is not preferred, it is permissible in such cases to practice the kick with one arm held overhead and one arm held at the side.

When the kick is integrated into the stroke, it varies in size, with two of the six beats per complete cycle being larger than the other four. For this reason it may be profitable for the swimmer to practice alternately using two widths of kick.

The primary propulsive force of the kick in the backstroke occurs on the upbeat, which is the reverse of the case of the front crawl stroke. The knees bend on the upbeat and are kept straight for a major part of the downbeat. It is apparently difficult for most swimmers to keep their legs straight long enough on the downbeat. They tend to kick from the knees, failing to bring the thighs sufficiently into action. Swimmers who kick in this fashion find their knees breaking the water's surface on the upbeat and their bick being less effective.

Figure IV–1 shows the backstroke kick as it should be done in kicking drills.

THE ARM PULL

The previously mentioned disagreement over the bent versus the straight arm pull for the back crawl stroke will continue for several reasons. The term *bent arm pull* is not really descriptive since merely bending the arm does not assure a proper pull.

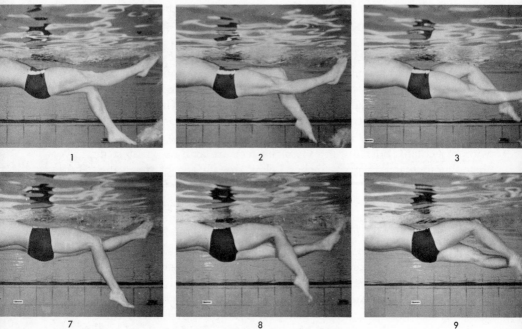

FIG. IV–1.   Backstroke Kick Sequence

This sequence of pictures shows the mechanics of the backstroke flutter kick as it should be done when the swimmer is doing kicking drills.

1. The sequence begins with the right foot at the top of its upbeat, the left foot at the bottom of the downbeat.

2. As the left leg starts downward with no bend in the knee, the foot is dorsi-flexed. As the upper part of the left leg starts upward, the bend in the knee is increased slightly and the ankle is plantar flexed, enabling the top of the left foot to press the water backward at an advantageous angle.

3. The left leg continues downward. The right knee appears to break the surface of the water, but this illusion is caused by the concavity in the water created by the left leg. It is important that the knees never break the surface of the water.

4. The upbeat of the left leg continues, due to the extension of the knee. The right leg still shows no sign of flexion at the knee.

5. The left leg, nearing the completion of the upbeat, is almost completely extended. The right leg starts to bend at the knee.

6. The upper half of the left leg has already started downward while the left foot

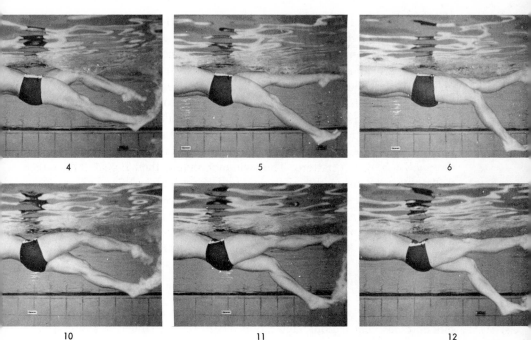

4   5   6

10   11   12

continues upward, with the toes just churning up the surface of the water. The upper part of the right leg starts upward while the foot continues downward. This combined action is made possible by flexion of the knee.

7. The knees pass one another, but the feet remain 24 inches apart. The right knee bend nears its maximum. The angle formed between the upper thigh and the lower leg is around 95°.

8. The left leg is thrust downward with no bend in the knee, as the right knee leads the action of the right leg upward. The right foot is extended or plantar-flexed as it is driven upward.

9. The blurred appearance of both feet indicates that the feet are at their maximum speed when they pass one another. At this point the instep of the right foot passes by in a line parallel with the ankle of the left foot.

10. The right knee reaches its maximum height, just an inch or two below the surface of the water.

11. The feet show a noticeable deceleration as all signs of blurring disappear in this photograph. The left knee has already started upward, with the left foot continuing to move downward.

12. As the legs approach their maximum spread, the leg kick cycle is completed.

A good method of demonstrating the ineffectiveness of the *straight arm pull* is to have the swimmer put his feet in a tube and float on his back in the water with one arm at his side and the other overhead. Using the arm that is overhead, he should take several back stroke arm pulls with the elbow held completely straight. He will find he is pulling himself around in a small circle. This can be compared to a canoeist using a sweep stroke to turn his canoe. He should next swim a length of the pool with the tube still around his legs and stroke alternately with his arms using the straight elbow pull. He will find he is moving down the pool in a zigzag pattern. The swimmer should then repeat the same drills, this time using the bent arm pull described in this chapter. He will find that the lateral effect of the pull will be reduced to less than half of that of the straight arm pull. The illustration of the canoeist using a sweep stroke and its effect upon the canoe can be carried further by showing how the canoeist can use the J stroke to keep his canoe straight. In many respects the backstroke pull is comparable to this J stroke action of the canoeist.

A little parable can make my point in the case of the ineffective bent arm pull. An age-group swimmer, who had been using the straight arm pull and was near national age-group record time, changed her pull after hearing my affirmative reply to the question of whether I believed in the bent arm pull. Her times proceeded to get slower and slower. Upon observation of her swimming style, it became immediately clear that, although she was indeed swimming with a bent elbow, she was failing to rotate the upper arm. In effect, she was now swimming with a dropped elbow, one of the cardinal sins, just as the crawl swimmer is doing in Figure I–7, illustration A. Correction of her stroke to follow the prescribed pattern of pull resulted in a great improvement in times and she went on to place in the National AAU Championship Meet.

This experience indicates that a little caution is appropriate when you contemplate changing a backstroker's arm pull. Make certain there is complete understanding of the complex movement involved in swimming correctly with the bent elbow. As I have mentioned, the term itself is a misnomer since it is not fully descriptive. The pull begins with the elbow straight, its bend increasing progressively as the arm is pulled backward until the pull is about half completed. After this point, the elbow begins to straighten until it reaches full extension at the end of the pull.

The arm, with the elbow straight, enters the water in a line directly over the shoulder. When the hand enters, it is turned in such a way that the palm is facing outward, the small finger entering first and the thumb last. Upon entry into the water after the recovery, the arm does not stop at the surface, nor immediately underneath the surface; the momentum developed during the recovery should be permitted to sink the arm to a depth of six to twelve inches. At this point the pulling muscles take over and there is a smooth transition from the end of the recovery to the beginning of the pull. Shortly after the pull begins, the elbow starts to bend as the hand and arm continue to sink lower into the water. This lowering of the arm and hand is due to the roll of the body. The elbow bend is accompanied by a rotation of the upper arm which prevents the elbow from dropping. The rotation of the upper arm, as it has been described in the chapters concerned with the crawl and butterfly strokes, is the exact action that the backstroker wants to emphasize during the first half of his pull, and it occurs as the elbow bend is increasing. When the hand is in a position directly opposite his shoulder, his elbow will be bent aproximately 90°.

Figure IV–3 shows the elbow bend at this point as it occurs in the strokes of three outstanding backstroke swimmers. The hand comes within a few inches of the surface of the water. If it breaks or comes within an inch or two of breaking the surface, it will drag air bubbles down with it, and this will decrease the efficiency of the pull. After this point of maximum elbow bend has been reached, the hand pushes backward and downward in a quarter circle motion with the palm pushing toward the bottom of the pool at the end of the arm pull. The last half of the pull is achieved by extension of the elbow, a continued medial rotation and adduction of the upper arm.

The downward push at the end of the pull causes the body to roll on its longitudinal axis. If the palm is not facing downward as the arm ends the pull, the hand will have to go deeper in order to achieve its goal of causing the swimmer to roll. In many cases the hand finishes a foot below the hips because the palm is facing inward toward the thigh as it pushes downward.

The pull, from beginning to end, has described the pattern of a flattened "S." Figure IV–4 shows the pull pattern of three good backstroke swimmers. Notice the depth of the hand at the end of the pull and also the position of the hand at this point. The push downward is a fast movement and is close to a throwing motion in terms of its acceleration. Because of this fact and its close similarity to the motion used in cracking a whip, it has been referred to by some backstrokers as the "buggy whip" pull.

I have photographed this pull among good age-group swimmers as young as six years of age who have never had a lesson or any coaching instruction. I assume, therefore, that it must come naturally, at least to some swimmers.

In order to fully exploit this downward press of the hand towards getting the shoulder up, the swimmer must allow only one shoulder to rise as he pushes the hand downward. If the swimmer tries to hold the

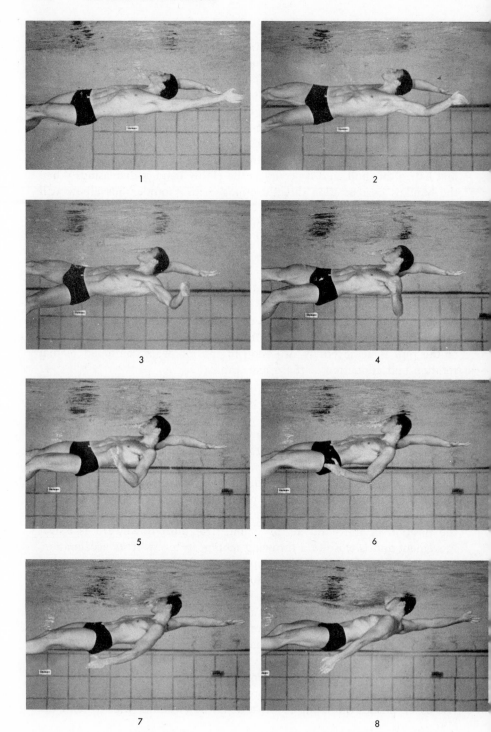

1

2

3

4

5

6

7

8

9

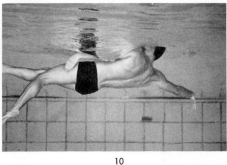

10

11

FIG. IV—2.   Tom   Stock's   Arm Pull

This series of photographs shows Tom Stock, former World Record holder for 100-meter Backstroke at :60.9 and 200-meter Backstroke at 2:10.9, in an excellent demonstration of the correct mechanics of the backstroke bent arm pull. The arm stroke shown here is the first stroke taken after a turn and push-off. This stroke is used in the series of photographs because this is the only stroke in which air bubbles created by the arm entry do not obscure the hand action.

Stock starts with the arm straight. As he pulls backward, the elbow starts to bend and reaches maximum flexion (around 90°) when the hand passes by the shoulder. As the hand continues backward past this point, the elbow starts to extend and reaches full extension at the end of the downward push.

On the arm recovery upward, the palm is turned in toward the median line of the body. The wrist is flexed as the hand leaves the water.

body flat, he can, through muscle tension, cause the downward thrust to have its effect on the whole body—not on just one side. Since this is undesirable and the rolling motion is desirable, such muscular tension should be avoided.

The roll of the body at this point achieves three purposes: (1) it causes the shoulder on the side of the pulling arm to become elevated with the result that it will not create unnecessary drag during the arm recovery, (2) it places the opposite arm at a better angle for obtaining a stronger pull, and (3) lacking a proper amount of roll, the swimmer

| A | B | C |

FIG. IV–3.   Arm Pull of Three Champion Backstrokers

These photographs reveal the two key positions in the arm pull of three champion backstrokers. The top photo in each case shows the arm stroke when the elbow has its maximum bend. The lower photo shows the arm pull when the hand has reached its deepest submersion beneath the surface of the water. This point generally comes at the end of the pull after the palm has been turned in toward the body, and prior to the arm being recovered upward.

A. Judy Humbarger, National champion.

B. Gary Dilley, National champion and Silver Medal winner in the 1964 Olympics.

C. Charles Hickcox, National champion.

would not be able to bend his elbow to the desired angle without having his hand break the surface of the water.

The reason the backstroke is not as fast as the crawl or butterfly strokes is that the arms must pull from a very disadvantageous position. The further the arms are placed in back of a line parallel to the side of the body, the weaker their depressor action becomes. By rolling the body, the angle between the pulling arm and the shoulder can be decreased, thus strengthening the pull.

As in the crawl, the swimmer should not roll just to be rolling. He can easily roll too much, if he is not careful. The amount of roll to each side is usually slightly less than 45° among swimmers with normal shoulder flexibility, and somewhat higher among those with less than normal shoulder flexibility. The shoulders and hips should roll simultaneously. If the swimmer allows his shoulders to roll, but tries to keep his hips flat, he will find himself *wiggling* or getting a lot of lateral movement in his legs. When the hips roll properly, the legs are in position at the right time to kick diagonally up and across the center line of the body, cancelling the distorting effect of the second half of the arm pull upon body alignment. The head should remain stationary as the rest of the body rolls around it. Among good backstrokers the head appears neither to roll nor to have any lateral movement.

After the hand pushes downward, the pull ends and the arm recovery begins with the hand at a depth of approximately one and a half feet below the surface or deeper. The underwater recovery phase of the arm stroke should be accomplished with a minimum of resistance created by the hand as it moves upward. Most swimmers achieve this either by flexing the wrist (as pictured in the backstroke sequence, Figure IV–5) or by rotating the forearm so the palm of the hand is facing inward toward the thigh and almost touching it. To convey the proper impression of how the hand should be recovered out of the water the swimmer should be told that, as his hand leaves the water, his thumb should come out of the water first. Lifting the arm during this period can cause the body to be pulled downward into the water, merely as a reaction to the lift. It is very important that the swimmer kick downward with the leg on the same side as the recovery arm at this point of the arm's recovery. The downward thrust of the leg will cancel the effect of the upward lift of the arm. This is but another example of equal and opposite forces cancelling one another, and it usually occurs automatically.

The arm recovery should be made up and forward in a perfectly straight and vertical line. Any deviation from this line may result in a lateral reaction in the body. If the arm is swung wide in a low, flat, circular movement there will be a reaction in the legs in the opposite direction. To observe this, a swimmer need only float in the water on his back with his feet supported by a tube and his arms held at his sides. As he recovers one arm sidewards, in the manner described above, he will notice the sideward movement of the feet in the opposite direction. If he repeats the same recovery motion, but with the arm recovery made in the prescribed manner on the vertical plane, he will find there is no lateral movement of the legs.

During the recovery the elbow should be straight, but not held rigid through muscle tension. The recovery should be a relaxed, ballistic movement with a minimum amount of muscular control.

As the hand breaks the water, the palm will be downward or facing the thigh. Between this time and the time the hand passes by the head (or halfway through the arm recovery), the hand should have been turned so that the palm is facing almost directly sideways. The hand will remain in this position until the recovery has ended.

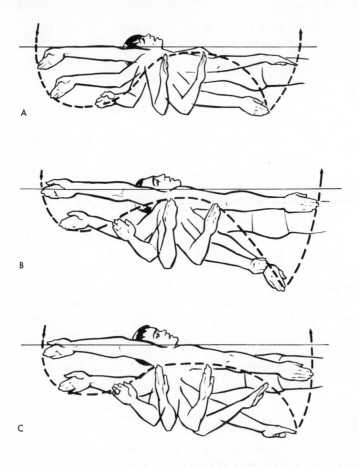

FIG. IV–4.   Arm Pull Pattern of Three Champion Backstrokers

These figures depict the arm pull pattern of the same three swimmers pictured in Figure IV–3. The dotted line indicates the path of each swimmer's middle finger.

A. Judy Humbarger finishes her pull with the arm rotated so the palm is facing inward toward the body. As she lifts her arm upward to the surface of the water, she turns the palm downward.

B. Gary Dilley pushes downward with his palm at the end of his pull and then, prior to lifting his hand upward out of the water, rotates his arm so the thumb is up and the palm is facing his body as the water surface is broken by the hand.

C. Charles Hickcox pushes more directly downward with the palm of his hand at the end of his stroke than does Humbarger or Dilley. In recovering his arm out of the water, he rotates it in a manner similar to Dilley's.

The speed of the recovery arm should correspond almost exactly to the speed of the pulling arm, in order that there may be almost complete arm opposition during the whole stroke. This arm opposition is more complete in the backstroke than in the front crawl stroke. In the crawl stroke it has been shown that it is possible for one arm to start its pulling action before the other has finished. This action is not possible in the backstroke. Some backstrokers have tried to accomplish it by rushing the recovery and have only succeeded in achieving a disconnected stroke which lacks any semblance of rhythm. One of the most beautiful sights in swimming is to see this flowing rhythm between the two arms, such as that used by Frank McKinney, Jr., who, even when he set his world records, looked effortless and rhythmical.

A few years back, a number of swimmers were putting their arms in the water at the end of the recovery at an angle away from the shoulder line. It was said that the arms should be put in the water at 10 and 2

FIG. IV–5.   The Back Crawl Stroke

This sequence of drawings shows the swimmer doing the bent arm back crawl stroke with a six beat kick. When trying to judge the depth of the arm pull, use the side view. The head-on view has greater distortion so far as the true position of the water surface is concerned. This is due to the convergence error in the pictures this series of drawings was taken from.

1. The sequence begins as the left arm enters the water directly over the shoulder, with the little finger entering the water first. The right hand has finished its pull and is starting to move upward in its recovery.

2. The downward momentum developed by the left arm during the last half of the recovery phase causes the arm with the elbow still extended to sink downward into the water. The right hand moves upward at the same time as the left foot. This timing is seen in most good backstrokers.

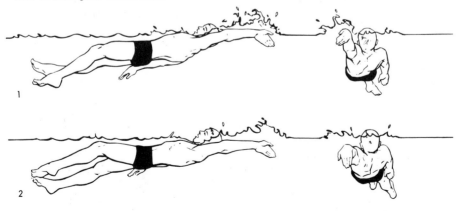

FIG. IV–5.   Continued

3. Muscular effort takes over control of the right arm as it is pulled downward. The right arm starts to break the surface, while the hand flexes at the wrist.

4. The left elbow begins to flex as the arm is pulled downward and sideward. The right leg which is at the bottom of its downbeat is ready to begin the upbeat at a slightly diagonal angle.

5. The left arm pull continues as the flexion in the elbow is increased. The palm of the pulling hand faces almost directly backward. The right arm is recovering directly upward. The right leg starts to kick upward at a diagonal angle.

3

4

5

FIG. IV–5.   Continued

6. As the left hand passes by the shoulder, the elbow reaches maximum flexion of 90°. The recovering arm starts to rotate, turning the palm outward away from the body. This action facilitates the arm recovery.

7. The elbow on the pulling arm starts to extend as the hand goes past the shoulder. The recovering arm, directly over the shoulder, is rotated so that the palm of the hand faces directly outward. The swimmer closes his mouth to keep out the drops of water falling from his recovering arm. At this point in the stroke cycle the body reaches its maximum roll of 40° to 45°.

8. The left hand position is changed, bringing the palm of the hand closer to the body, and ready to begin its push almost directly downward. The recovering arm continues in its vertical path.

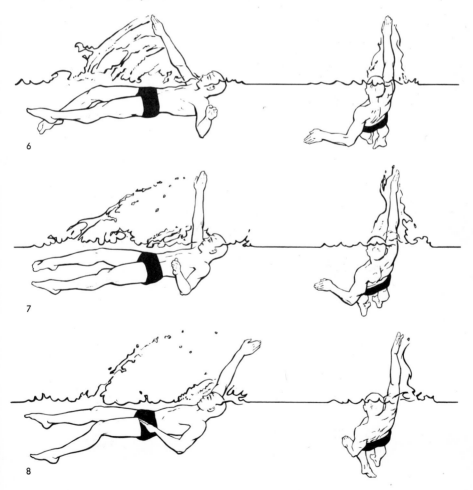

FIG. IV–5. Continued

9. The left arm finishes its pull with the elbow completely extended and the hand palm down at a level of three to six inches below the hips. This downward push of the hand helps to elevate the right shoulder.

10. As the right hand enters the water, with the palm facing outward, the left arm starts its upward recovery. The swimmer pictured here is lifting his arm upward, with the palm facing downward. Many swimmers rotate this arm so that the palm of the hand faces inward toward the median line of the body (see Figures IV–2 and IV–4). Both techniques are acceptable. At this point in the stroke neither hand is applying any propulsive force.

11. The left shoulder breaks the water prior to the out-of-water recovery of the left arm. The right hand sinks into the water, getting ready for its catch.

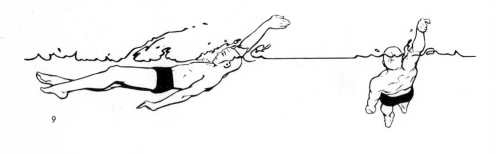

9

10

11

FIG. IV–5.   Continued

12. The catch of the right hand is made with a straight elbow as the left hand starts its out-of-water recovery. The left leg is kicked diagonally downward. Once again, the upbeat of the leg on the opposite side coincides with the final lift of the arm from the water.

13. The bend of the right arm becomes apparent as the arm is depressed sideward.

14. The right hand directly opposite the shoulder is applying its force directly backward. The left shoulder is lifted up and over the water, due primarily to the roll of the body.

FIG. IV–5. Continued

15. The pulling arm has completed half of its pulling action. From this point on the hand will come in toward the body, tending to pull the hips in the opposite direction and destroy lateral body alignment. This action can be cancelled by the diagonal and upward thrust of the left leg.

16. As the right arm starts its downward thrust, the left leg continues to thrust diagonally upward.

17. The left hand, palm outward, continues its recovery action, as the right hand pushes back and downward.

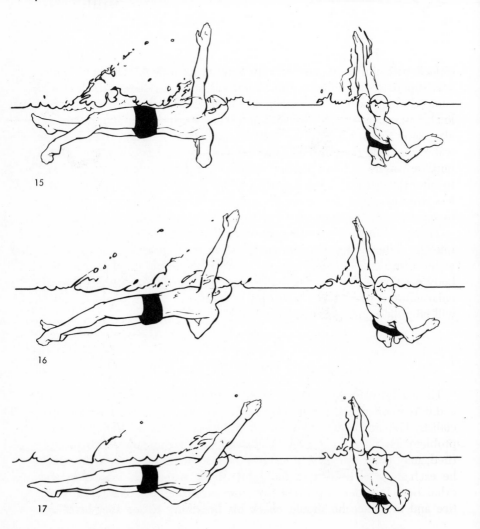

15

16

17

FIG. IV–5.   Continued

18. The right arm finishes its pull, while the left hand has almost finished its recovery. The full stroke cycle is now complete.

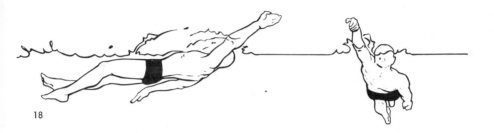

18

o'clock with the head position representing 12 o'clock. This wide entry was supposed to eliminate the lateral thrust of the arms which would come during the first 12 inches of the pull. The idea contained some logic, but, since it takes the hand some time to sink to pulling depth and also some time to accelerate until it catches up with the speed of the water, the wide entry did not assure the swimmer of any propulsive force until he was almost half finished with his arm pull. By allowing the hand to enter the water in a line directly over his shoulder, the swimmer creates less resistance and also gives his arm time to sink to pulling depth and to accelerate to an effective speed before he is too far into his pull.

The speed of the recovering arm should not be changed before it goes into the water. If the momentum of the recovering arm is dissipated by water resistance, it will have no appreciable effect on the swimmer's body position. If, however, the momentum is slowed down through muscular effort, it will be transferred to the body and the head and shoulders will be pulled downward (Figure I–15).

BREATHING

The backstroker, because his head is out of the water at all times, has a different breathing problem from that of the other three stroke specialists. He can breathe when he wants to, and this in itself presents a problem. He may breathe too shallowly and, particularly when he gets tired, may enter into a *panting* or very fast breathing pattern in which he exchanges as little as a half pint of air with each inhalation and exhalation. In order to prevent this from occurring, occasionally in practice and in a race he should check his breathing to see that he is not breathing much more than one inhalation and exhalation per arm cycle. In practice he can work on his breathing pattern by inhaling during the recovery of one arm and exhaling on the recovery of the other arm. Since the inhalation takes less time than the exhalation, this method may not seem to be sound; however, it serves as a guide in establishing a general pattern.

Backstrokers who swim a lot of crawl do not have as great a problem with shallow breathing, but in any case it is one that is easy to correct. Most breathing mechanics are reflex in nature and need very little adjustment from us.

The Breaststroke

The breaststroke is the oldest of the competitive strokes and is one of the oldest swimming styles. However, it was preceded by several methods, notable of which are the human and the animal strokes. Although there were isolated cases in which people used more advanced strokes, during the early periods these two strokes were in popular use throughout western civilization. The human and animal strokes, however, are very tiring and inefficient. Moreover, they do not provide a stable position in the water. The need must have been felt for a more effective stroke which would provide a stable position even in rough water and yet would maintain the head out of the water. As late as 1690 a Frenchman, Thevenot, wrote the following:

> To swim with the head towards heaven—to look upwards, and if we knew how to use it there would not be as many drowned as there daily are, for that happens because . . . they look downwards and embrace the water as it were with their arms.[1]

[1] Melchisedech Thevenot, *The Art of Swimming*, 3rd ed., pp. 18-19. English translation printed for John Lever, Little Moorgate next to London Wall, near Moorsfield, 1699.

At the beginning of the sixteenth century first mention was found of a method which seemed to embody the requirements of the people of that time. In this style the simultaneous action of the arms made its appearance and, although the legs were still kicked alternately in the manner of the human kick (that is, with the propulsive force of the kick from the instep of the foot), this method may be regarded as the initial step in the evolution of the breaststroke.

During the eighteenth century the breaststroke became known as the frog stroke, which seems to indicate that there was a spread in the legs. Even though the frog kicks backward in a straight line, it does spread its knees.

Guts Muth, 1798, states that swimming on the breast was the style then used all over Europe. He says the upper surface of the feet are used not the soles of the feet and he says it is quite wrong to compare breaststroke with that of the frog.[2]

It is believed that the next development which occurred soon after Muth wrote his description was the change of the forward thrust from the instep to the sole of the foot. In 1842 R. H. Horne [3] concluded that the power derived from the wedge was greater than the power derived from the soles of the feet, and thereby started a controversy which is still unsettled.

Toward the last half of the nineteenth century a great deal of interest was developing in competitive swimming, especially in England. The breaststroke was the first stroke used in races, but it is not to be thought that it was the only stroke being swum. Other strokes were being used and new ones evolved which were later to take the popularity of the breaststroke. Notable among these were the sidestroke, the overarm sidestroke, and the trudgen crawl stroke.

On August 24 and 25, 1875, Captain Matthew Webb swam the English channel from Dover to Calais in 21 hours and 45 minutes and thus gave a great impetus to swimming. He used the breaststroke method. In spite of this great feat by a breaststroke swimmer there was a trend away from use of the breaststroke and towards speedier strokes. The turn of the century found nearly all competitive swimmers using the overarm side and the trudgen crawl strokes, and the advent of the Australian crawl around 1900 to 1905 brought a further loss of interest in the breaststroke. This might be attributed to the fact that races during the period were

---

[2] Kleines lehrbuch der Schwimmkunst zum selbstunterrichte, p. 99, cited in Ralph Thomas, *Swimming*, p. 99.
[3] Ralph Thomas, *op. cit.*, pp. 98-99.

not divided into the various stroke classifications they now possess. A given distance was established and the first swimmer to reach the finish —regardless of style—was declared the winner. The breaststroke race was often featured in the program of swimming meets as a novelty race and it was not until 1906 that races were divided into three classes in national competition. These were the breaststroke, backstroke, and free-style. During that year A. Goersling won the 200-yard breaststroke race in 2 minutes and 52.6 seconds.

The emphasis in competitive swimming, however, was placed on the freestyle events and, as a result, most of the good swimmers did not enter the breaststroke event.

The breaststroke underwent constant experimentation by swimmers in their attempts to increase its speed. Notable among the early adaptations was the underwater stroke, in which the swimmer submerged and took one to four strokes underwater. The arms were pulled in a long sweeping pull and all the way down to the sides. The kick and pull were together and not alternate. This stroke helped swimmers who had poor kicks and relied on the arm pull for most of their propulsion.

The greatest innovation in the breaststroke was the introduction of the butterfly stroke, in which the arms were recovered out of the water. This new stroke which continued the use of the breaststroke kick was first used in competition on December 16, 1933. On this occasion it was used by Henry Myers in a meet at the Brooklyn Central YMCA.[4] Myers lost the race but other swimmers were intrigued by his innovation and began using the stroke with more success. The 1936 Olympics saw the orthodox Japanese breaststroker, Detsuo Hamuoro, win in the time of 2:42.5 seconds. The best a butterfly swimmer (John Higgins) could finish was fourth. He, however, had recorded a time of 2:41.1 prior to the meet.

During the period between 1933, when the butterfly stroke was intro-duced, until after the 1952 Olympics, when the breaststroke and butterfly were made separate events, it was not uncommon to see the butterfly stroke being swum by some swimmers and the breaststroke by others in the same race. Swimmers would often switch back and forth between the two strokes in the same event. In 1942, when I won the National AAU Outdoor 200-meter butterfly event, I swam the first 100 meters butterfly, the next 50 meters orthodox breaststroke, and the last 50 meters butterfly. The men butterfliers so overwhelmed the orthodox swimmers in the 1948 and 1952 Olympic Games that the two strokes were divided into separate events and the dolphin kick was legalized for butterfliers. If the events

[4] Personal correspondence between the author and Henry Myers, December 4, 1957.

had not been separated, the historical breaststroke would have been dropped as a competitive stroke.

Underwater swimming was permitted in the breaststroke, not only for one stroke after the turn as the rules presently state, but at any point in the race. In 1956 the Olympic Games breaststroke event was won by Masura Furukawa in a time of 2:34.7. Following these Games the rules were amended to exclude underwater swimming except for one long pull and kick after the turn and dive, and to require that the head break the surface of the water at all other times during the race. Using this style of swimming, Terry Gathercole set the world record at 2:36.5. Gathercole's technique included holding the head in a flexed position at all times and, while he had an excellent kick, his pull was relatively weak. He was said to receive 80 per cent of his propulsion from his kick and only 20 per cent from his arms. The 1960 Olympics were won by Bill Mulliken in a time of 2:37.4.

In the summer of 1961 a new style of swimming breaststroke was introduced by Chet Jastremski of Indiana University, with which he lowered all world records: the 100 meters from over 1:11 to 1:07.5 and the 200 meters from 2:36.5 to 2:29.6. Chester's relatively poor kick made it necessary to customize his stroke in an effort to streamline the body to get more effective propulsion from his arms.

A great many breaststrokers have imitated Jastremski's stroke with success, but while many of the stroke innovations introduced by him may help the average breaststroker, it must be remembered that each swimmer must use his abilities and aptitudes to their best advantage. For example, a swimmer with a good propulsive kick can expect a longer glide up front than the one used by Jastremski. Chet was an *arm* swimmer, not a *kick* swimmer. He pulled 100 meters breaststroke with his legs in a tube in 1:19, while he could only kick the same distance on a kick board in 1:29. Many breaststrokers, particularly women and age-group swimmers, kick breaststroke faster than they can pull it.

Jastremski's stroke featured a faster turnover, more emphasis on the arm pull, a relatively narrow whip kick, and an up and down motion of the head for breathing.

The present rules governing the breaststroke state:

> Both hands must be pushed forward together from the breast on or under the surface of the water and brought backward simultaneously and symmetrically.
>
> The body must be kept perfectly on the breast and both shoulders in the horizontal plane.
>
> The feet shall be drawn up simultaneously and symmetrically, the knees

bent and open. The movement shall be continued with a round and outward sweep of the feet, bringing the legs together. Up and down movements of the legs in the vertical plane are prohibited. Breaking water surface with the feet shall not merit disqualification unless caused by movement of the legs in a vertical plane.

When touching at the turn or on finishing a race, the touch shall be made with both hands simultaneously on the same level. The shoulders shall be in a horizontal position in line with the surface of the water. Note: A legal touch may be made above or below the surface of the water.

Any competitor introducing a side-stroke movement shall be disqualified.

Swimming under surface of the water is prohibited except for one arm stroke and one leg kick after start and turn.

The starting position of the breaststroke shall be with the arms together and extended forward and with the legs together and extended backward. The instant the hands leave the extended position a new stroke shall have been started. Either complete or incomplete movement of the arms or legs from the starting position shall be considered as one complete stroke or kick. On the breaststroke, from the moment when a swimmer, after the start or turn, begins the second stroke, one part of the head shall always break the surface of the water.[5]

BODY POSITION

As in the cases of all strokes, the body should be as streamlined or horizontal as possible and still permit the arms and legs to perform their function of creating propulsion. Underwater photographs of beginning swimmers and poor competitive breaststroke swimmers reveal that they swim with their bodies at a sharp angle, thereby creating a lot of frontal and eddy resistance (Figure I–3, illustration C).

Good streamlined body position is related to other mechanics of the stroke and will be discussed in its relation to these mechanics.

THE KICK

The controversy which has centered around the breaststroke kick has been particularly concerned with the source of its propulsive power. There are two theories which have dominated the thinking about the kick: the wedge action theory and the whip action theory.

[5] "Rules for Competitive Swimming," *Official Handbook of the AAU* (1965), Sec. VI, pp. 7-8.

The Wedge Action Theory

The oldest and perhaps most common explanation of this kick, as described by Davis Dalton in 1907,[6] states that the swimmer must keep "the legs straightened out[,] bring them together . . . the water thus compressed between the legs pushes the body forward." That many people continue to hold to this belief is proved by the fact that publications are still published which advance the opinion that the wedge is the best source of power for the breaststroke kick. Water, however, is a yielding substance and it is not reasonable that water would be forced backward, but rather that, upon leaving the space between the legs, it would assume an upward and downward direction as it flows around the legs.

The wedge action theory of propulsion has also been offered as an explanation of the source of power of the flutter kick. Experimentation with wedge eliminating kicks has proven that there is no justifiable evidence to show that the wedge increases efficiency of the flutter kick.[7]

The recovery of the legs in the wedge is accomplished by abduction (or spreading) of the upper thighs as the hips flex. The heels are held together throughout the entire recovery phase. The hip flexion continues until the upper legs are perpendicular to the line of the body. The angle formed between the thighs is approximately 100°. When the hips reach their maximum flexion, the legs are thrust outward and backward and then squeezed together. The knees reach full extension immediately after the legs begin to come together, so that the last two-thirds to three-fourths of the kick consists merely of squeezing the water between the fully extended legs. Thus, there is little or no backward pushing of the water with the soles of the feet once the legs are extended. After the legs become extended, the feet maintain, as nearly as possible, the same plane in the water as during the kicking phase. The feet are inverted (turned inward) during the last part of the kick.

Whip Action Theory

Proponents of the second theory state that the power derived from the wedge is negligible and that the forward thrust is obtained almost exclusively from pushing the water backward with the soles of the feet.

---

[6] Davis Dalton, *How to Swim* (New York: Knickerbocker Press, 1907), pp. 24-26.
[7] Thomas K. Cureton, "Mechanics and Kinesiology of Swimming (The Crawl Flutter Kick)," *Research Quarterly*, I, No. 4 (December 1930), 97-98.

In the whip kick recovery there is less flexion of the hips and greater flexion of the knees. The angle formed by the plane of the body and the upper leg is around 45°, as compared to 90° in the wedge kick. The heels are brought up until they almost touch the buttocks and there is less spread of the knees. The heels are kept slightly apart during the recovery.

As the kicking phase begins the knees are brought inward and the feet are thrust outward. This action is obtained by an inward rotation of the upper legs which is not apparent in the wedge type of kick. If the legs are rotated inwardly, it is impossible for the toes to point outward as they do in the wedge kick. The upper legs are rotated outwardly as the legs come together until the legs are in normal alignment. The knees do not reach full extension until the legs are almost touching. The feet finish the kick by pressing backward with a slight upsweep. The power of this kick is derived mainly from the extensor muscles of the knee and the extensors of the hip. The adductor muscles enter into the action, but their importance is usually overstressed, since it is believed that the muscles which rotated the leg inwardly are more important than the adductor muscles.

The width of the whip kick is smaller at the knees, but at the feet is not much narrower than the wedge kick.

Experimental evidence concerning the effectiveness of the two kicks has been presented in two separate studies. One, by Frances Cake, concluded that: "When the two kicks are mastered, it [the whip kick] is superior in force, speed, and economy of movement to the wedge action kick." [8]

In 1947 I studied the two kicks experimentally and concluded:

The results of the tests proved conclusively that the whip style kick was superior to the wedge kick in every respect—speed, propulsive force, economy of movement—and that it was capable of a faster tempo than the wedge kick.

The whip kick seemed to have an additional advantage in the recovery phase since the legs were not drawn forward as much, and did not create as much resistance as the recovery in the wedge kick. The main difference between these two kicks was the point at which extension of the legs was reached. In the wedge kick the legs reached full extension immediately after the legs began to come together (a spread of thirty to fifty inches at the heels). The legs did not reach extension until the last part of the whip kick (six to twelve inches spread between the heels). In the whip kick there was a definite inward rotation of the legs as the feet were thrust outward to begin the kicking phase.

[8] Frances Cake, "The Relative Effectiveness of Two Types of Frog Kick Used in Swimming the Breaststroke," *Research Quarterly*, 13 (March 1942), 201-4.

The theory of the squeeze action as a source of propulsion was shown to be erroneous by tests with the wedge eliminating kick and by observation of water currents. It was believed the propulsive force of the kick was derived from pressing the water backward with the lower legs and the feet.

The following generalizations could be made as a result of the study concerning the most efficient manner of performing the breaststroke kick. The recovery should use a minimum amount of muscular effort and create as little resistance as possible. Yet it should place the legs in a desirable position to begin the kicking phase. The knees should not be spread too much. As the kicking phase begins, the heels of the feet should almost touch the buttocks. . . . The kicking phase should begin with an outward thrust of the feet as the knees begin to come together. This is accomplished by inward rotation and adduction of the upper legs. . . . The legs should not reach full extension until they are almost touching. When the kick is finished, the legs should be plantar flexed (pointed) to create as little resistance as possible. The swimmer should, however, try to relax them since undue strain in stretching only results in fatigue.[9]

A good position of the legs after the leg recovery has been completed (so far as streamlining of the body is concerned) would be at an angle of flexion of approximately 30° at the hips. This would not place the legs in a strong position to drive backward, however. The legs are relatively weak at this point and the drive of the feet backward must be accomplished primarily by the knee extensor muscles (the quadricep extensor muscle group). If the hips are flexed to an angle of 50° to 60°, there will be more drag created, but this will be more than compensated for by the greater strength of the kick, which can be attributed to increased use of the hip extensor muscles (primarily the gluteus maximus muscles). (See Figure V–1.)

When the leg is flexed to a 90° angle, the increased drag will more than compensate for the increased leg drive. Hip flexion of this extent is accompanied by a sudden rise of the hips out of the water and a consequent drop during the backward drive of the legs. Evidence of this type of stroke defect is up and down motion of the hips. The optimum desirable angle of hip flexion appears to be somewhere between the two previously stated angles of 50° to 60°.

As the legs are thrust backward, it is very important that the swimmer concentrate on extending his hips in order that the upper legs can be driven upward toward the surface. If this is not done, the path of thrust of the feet will be diagonally downward and the feet will describe a "V" pattern as they come together. This latter action is undesirable, for it causes the thrust of the feet to push the hips upward too much, rather

[9] James E. Counsilman, "A Cinematographic Analysis of the Butterfly Breaststroke" (Masters Thesis, University of Illinois, 1948), pp. 101-2.

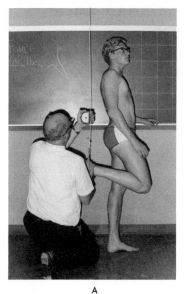 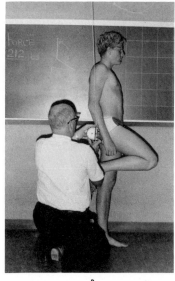

A   B

FIG. V—1.   Variation in Leg Strength with the Leg in Two Positions

The two figures above demonstrate the variance in strength of the leg thrust between two different positions, as tested on a tensiometer. Position A shows the knee bent maximally, but with little flexion at the hips (an angle of 150° between the trunk and the upper legs). Position B shows the knee bent maximally, but with greater flexion at the hips (an angle of 130° between the trunk and the upper legs). Position A created an average force of 62 pounds, whereas Position B created an average force of 212 pounds, or over three times as great a force.

than straight forward, and leaves the feet at the end of the kick in a position in which they will create excessive drag. It also does not permit maximum use of the hip extensor muscles at the end of the kick. Some swimmers with poor mechanics have their heels as deep as two and a half feet or more under the surface.

An important aspect of the breaststroke kick is the progressive acceleration of the speed of movement of the feet as the kick is accomplished. The beginning of the kick should be made with a firm but not fast motion that will enable the swimmer to feel the water pressure on the soles of his feet. As his legs thrust backward he should increase the speed of his feet to the point that maximum speed is reached during the last quarter of the kick. The biggest mistake a swimmer can make is to accelerate his kick so greatly in the early part of the kick that, during the last quarter, the feet almost drift together. The speed of this thrust is directly associated with the extension of the knees. This is another reason the knees should not reach full extension until the feet are almost together.

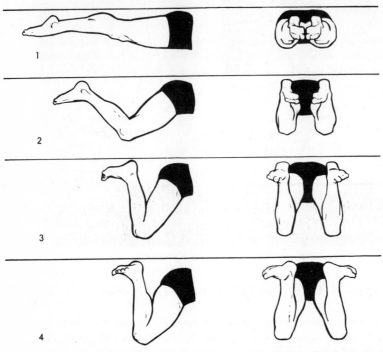

FIG. V–2.   The Breaststroke Whip Kick

This sequence of drawings depicts the correct mechanics of the breaststroke whip kick, as it should be done when performing kicking drills on the kick board. When actually using the kick in the whole stroke, the feet will drop lower under the surface of the water at other times in the stroke than shown here. This is due to the reaction from the pull and the head lift.

1. When the feet are not engaged in the kicking motion, they should be held in a fully extended, streamlined position close to the surface of the water. The feet should be plantar-flexed.

2. The leg recovery begins with a flexion of the legs at the hips and at the knees. Most coaches, including myself, attempt to have the swimmers keep their heels together as they are brought upward. The better kickers keep their heels close together as shown here, but very few of them touch heels at this point.

3. As the heels approach the buttocks, the feet begin to dorsi-flex and the heels and the knees to separate slightly.

4. The knees and hips reach their maximum flexion as the toes are turned outward and the ankles dorsi-flexed. The angle formed between the trunk and the upper leg is 125°.

FIG. V–2.   Continued

5. The first few inches of the backward leg thrust are non-propulsive and are used for the legs to accelerate and to permit the feet to position themselves for a good backward thrust with the sides and the bottoms of the feet. At this point, the feet have engaged the water and are becoming effective.

6. The feet are pushed outward and backward as the knees extend. The upper legs are driven upward toward the surface of the water through the action of the strong hip extensor muscles. The feet, still dorsi-flexed, engage the water with the soles of the feet.

7. As the legs continue to extend at the knees, they are also brought together. The upper leg continues to be driven upward.

8. The knees almost reach full extension when the feet are only a few inches apart.

9. As the kick finishes, the feet are plantar-flexed. The swimmer will hold this glide position for a short time during which his feet will rise a few inches until his heels almost break the surface.

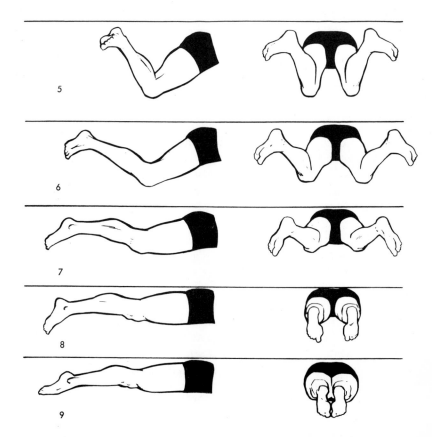

The ankle action is very important in the breaststroke kick. Breast-strokers need good ankle flexibility, particularly for dorsi flexing the feet (that is, for bringing the top of the feet up toward the knee). Good dorsi flexion of the ankles as the kick begins permits the bottom of the feet to engage the water for the backward push. As the feet are drawn upward during the recovery phase, the ankles are relaxed and the feet merely trail the knees upward. As the feet start to spread, dorsi ankle flexion begins, and by the time the backward thrust of the feet has begun, the ankles should have achieved maximum flexion. This ankle dorsi flexion is maintained until the kick is almost completed and, as the kick nears completion, the ankles are plantar flexed to enable the bottom of the feet to face upward in a streamlined position. Frequently the soles of the feet are pushed together, but this action is more easily achieved in the wedge kick than the whip, since it cannot be accomplished unless the upper legs are rotated outwardly.

A simple test to measure the dorsi flexion (ankle flexibility) of a swimmer is to have him stand erect with his hands grasped in back of his neck. His feet should be held directly together with heels and toes touching. Without raising his heels, he should try to do a complete squat, letting his buttocks touch his heels. If he can't get all the way down, or if he raises his heels or falls backward, he has poor ankle dorsi-flexion flexibility and needs ankle stretching exercises. These exercises are discussed in Chapter X, *Dry Land Exercises*.

Knee Injuries

A number of breaststroke swimmers complain of knee trouble and, in some cases, the pain has reached the point that the swimmers have had to switch to another stroke. This pain can be due to muscle injury, but is most frequently due to injury of the ligaments or the muscle tendons. Such injury can be avoided by the swimmer in three ways: (1) by stretching his legs with appropriate exercises before going into the water (the experience of my swimmers has shown me that dry land exercises which strengthen and also stretch the muscles of the legs help prevent injuries because the supporting muscles of the knees, when they are strong, help to prevent injuries to the knee ligaments and tendons), (2) by doing his kicking with only moderate effort until his legs are warmed up, and (3) by the elimination of early extension of the knees during the backward thrust of the feet. This wedge action causes strain on the medial ligaments of the knees along with possible injury to the adductor muscles of the upper leg that squeeze the legs together.

While some people have reported sore knees due to use of the whip kick, we have had no injuries to the knees of our swimmers who use the

| A | B | C |

FIG. V–3.   Elbow-up Pull of Three Champion Breaststrokers

These pictures show the arm pull of three champion breaststrokers when their hands are at the widest spread in their strokes and when they are in a good position to push the water backward.

A. Chet Jastremski.

B. Tom Trethewey, former National champion and NCAA Record Holder for 200-yard Breaststroke at 2:10.4. Trethewey's arm stroke is shown from a diagonal view.

C. Catie Ball, National champion and World Record holder for 100-meters and 200-meters.

All three of the above swimmers have good arm stroke mechanics, particularly Jastremski and Ball. Trethewey tends to drop his elbows slightly. Figure V–4 diagrams the complete pull pattern of Jastremski and Trethewey.

whip kick properly. Proper mechanics of the whip kick can more easily be learned when practicing this kick while lying on the back with the arms held overhead. At Indiana University we begin every season doing about half of our kicking drills in this position.

THE ARM PULL

The arm pull on the breaststroke begins with a deep catch at a depth of six to eight inches below the surface. If the swimmer begins his pull at the surface there will be a tendency to climb too high and energy will be wasted in up and down movements. During the glide the hands have been held in such a way that they are almost touching, with the elbows completely extended and the palms of the hands turned diagonally sideways in preparation for the pull. After the kick has finished and the swimmer feels his forward speed dissipating somewhat, he allows his hands to begin spreading without applying much muscular effort. As the hands separate—with the elbows still extended—they begin to move

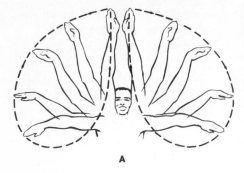

A

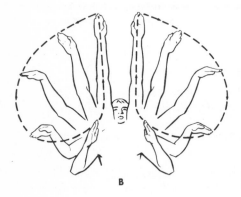

B

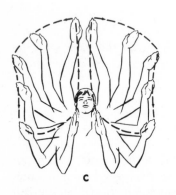

C

FIG. V–4. Pull Pattern of Three Champion Breaststrokers

These illustrations show the pattern described by the middle finger as the arms are pulled and then recovered.

A. Chet Jastremski shows almost perfect mechanics in the arm pull. Chet does not drop his elbows or bring them in close to his ribs, as in illustration C.

B. Tom Trethewey loses some effectiveness in his pull by dropping his elbows. His arm recovery is made with the hands pushed forward at shoulder width instead of almost together.

C. Claudia Kolb, Silver Medal winner in the 1964 Olympic Games in the 200-meter Breaststroke. Claudia lacks the arm strength to pull properly, as do most girls and, consequently, drops her elbows and pulls them into her ribs. This action causes a loss of effectiveness. As a result, Claudia relies on her kick for the main source of propulsion, as must most girls.

diagonally outward and downward. When they are about 12 inches apart, the elbows begin to bend slightly and the upper arm to rotate medially, as in the crawl and butterfly pull. The breaststroke swimmer also wants to achieve an elbow-up pull in order that he may push the water backward at the most effective angle. This high elbow position is apparently not a natural movement for most swimmers and must be taught to them. As the swimmer pulls backward, he should try to feel the pressure on his hands build up as he continues to accelerate his arms throughout the pull. The elbows should never be higher than the shoulders, but should always be higher than the hands during the pull (Figure V–3).

As the swimmer pulls backward, he forms a heart shaped pattern with his hands. Figure V–4 shows this pattern in three good breaststrokers, as seen from directly below. The elbows should never go beyond the shoulder level during the pull; if they do, the swimmer is dropping his elbows. Once the pull is completed and the swimmer starts to recover his arms, the lateral rotation plus the adduction of the upper arms may cause the elbows to come in back of this line.

As the arms finish the pull and start their recovery, there is a big temptation for the swimmer to make a stop in his arm action before he begins his recovery. The checking of the arms at this point is referred to by the swimmers as "getting stuck," and should be avoided. The arm motion developed during the pull should be rounded out, as shown in Figure V–4, and the arms should go directly from the pull into the recovery without stopping their motion. This will assure the swimmer of having his arms in an extended position when the propulsive phase of the kick begins.

BREATHING AND THE HEAD LIFT

Many persons have advocated that the breaststroker's head be carried in a high position at all times, in order that the swimmer might be able to swim in a constant position. This head position has been used by many swimmers, some of whom have been successful (Terry Gathercole, for example). Other swimmers have held their necks in this hyperextended position and dropped their heads low in the water by piking at the hips, as does Claudia Kolb, 1964 Olympic silver medal winner.

As far as back as 1896 the importance of not keeping the head continuously elevated was noted:

. . . you will see every good swimmer in the world swimming with his mouth under the water till the arms separate. . . . It is practically what I have insisted on throughout this book that the more the head is under water the better, as the swimmer then has less to support.[10]

A good demonstration to show the reason for dropping the head by flexing the neck after the breath is taken is to have the swimmer swim one length of the pool with his head kept high enough to be out of water. He should count the number of strokes and record the time it takes him to swim one length. His hip position and feet position should also be noted. They will be low in the water. He should then swim the same test length, this time using the proper head movement, as previously described. If it is done in the prescribed manner with the correct timing, he will find it takes fewer strokes, is faster, and that his hips and feet will be higher in the water.

[10] Sydney Holland, *The Badminton Magazine of Sports and Pastimes,* edited by A. E. T. Watson (London, New York & Bombay: Longmans, Green & Co., 1896), in Thomas, *Swimming,* p. 400.

A   B   C

FIG. V—5.   Head Action in the Breaststroke

The head in the breaststroke should be lifted just high enough to permit the swimmer to take a breath (illustration A—back view, and illustration B—front view), then it should be lowered (illustration C—front view) by flexion of the neck until it is almost, but not quite, submerged. The swimmer should make a conscious effort not to pull the shoulders and head up high above the water level.

The timing of the head lift is also easily demonstrated by having the swimmer do the following experiment. Lying in the water with his face down, his arms extended overhead, and his feet supported by a tube or a water polo ball, he should first perform the breaststroke arm pull without lifting his head, and observe the effect on his shoulders. He will find that shortly after he starts his pull the shoulders will rise upward, and will reach their maximum climb toward the end of his pull. He should then assume the same position, this time leaving his arms extended over his head, but stationary rather than pulling, and lift his head to see what effect this action has upon his shoulders. As the head is lifted, the shoulders will drop. If these forces are combined, since they are opposite, they will tend to neutralize one another and the shoulders will remain relatively flat. This timing is considered to be *normal breathing*.

There are two other types of breathing which are in some use in the breaststroke. One is *early breathing*, in which the head is lifted during the recovery of the arms and the inhalation is taken when the arms are extended out front in the glide position. I have noticed this style of swimming to be particularly prevalent among Canadian and English swimmers. This breathing pattern reduces the effectiveness of the kick since the head is up during part of the kicking phase. In the *late breathing* style of swimming, the head is not started upward until the arm pull has almost been completed, and the inhalation is taken after the body has reached its maximum elevation due to the arm pull. There is usually a pause in the stroke at this point, while the inhalation is taken, which causes the forward inertia to be detrimentally affected.

In the recommended method (the normal breathing pattern, Figure V—5), since the head lift takes less time than the arm pull, the head lift starts slightly after the pull begins and the inhalation is taken as the pull is finished. As the arms are pushed forward in their recovery, the neck is flexed and the face is placed underwater. The neck should be flexed sufficiently to tilt the face to an angle of about 45° from the horizontal. It is unwise to flex the neck so much that the eyes are looking directly downward at the bottom of the pool. This exaggerated head action can cause the head to drop under the surface of the water and, instead of merely cancelling the up and down movement of the shoulders, will contribute to it.

The head lift should be made at a steady rate, comparable to the rhythm of the arm pull, with the drop of the head occurring at a faster speed than the head lift. It is also in rhythm with the arm recovery, which is made at a faster speed than the pull.

TIMING OF THE STROKE

The Glide Stroke

When using the glide timing in the breaststroke, the propulsive phases of the arms and legs are alternated. The arm pull is begun while the legs are fully extended. Before the arm pull is completed, the swimmer should have started to recover his legs. During the early part of the arm recovery the legs continue their recovery and, immediately before the arms reach full extension and after the face is submerged, the backward thrust of the feet begins. It takes the feet approximately six inches to accelerate to the speed at which they will contribute forward propulsive force. When this point is reached, the swimmer's arms should be completely extended overhead, his face submerged in water, and his body in good horizontal position so that the force of the kick will push him forward against a minimum of drag. A common stroke defect is for the swimmer to push his arms forward in their recovery phase as the legs are thrusting backward in their propulsive phase. This timing eliminates much of the forward drive of the kick. The precise timing of the arms, legs, and head is critical and in most swimmers does not always occur naturally in its correct form, as it does among most swimmers for the other three strokes. The coach should watch the timing of the swimmer's head lift, head drop, leg recovery, and other phases of the stroke, for deviations from the pattern.

When the kick is completed, the arms should be held overhead briefly in a fully extended position with the hands touching; the body should be kept as streamlined as possible with the back held straight by contraction of the abdominal muscles. The stronger the kick, the longer the swimmer will be able to hold this position. If the swimmer is not buoyant and has a poor kick, he may not be able to hold the glide

FIG. V—6. **The Breaststroke Sequence**

This sequence of drawings shows the swimmer performing good mechanics in the breaststroke, using a whip kick and an elbow-up pull.

1. The swimmer is in the glide position with his body relatively horizontal. His head is about 80 per cent submerged, with his face tilted slightly forward. His arms are extended overhead with his palms facing diagonally outward.

2. The hand catch is made at a depth of seven to nine inches and his pull begins with his hands pulling laterally. His exhalation begins at this point and air bubbles start to come from his nose and mouth.

3. The arms, with no apparent bend in the elbows, continue to pull out to the side. The exhalation of air continues to increase.

FIG. V–6.   Continued

4. The elbows start to bend and the upper arms to rotate as the swimmer's head starts upward slightly, due to extension of the neck.

5. As the arms reach their maximum spread, the elbows are bent so the angle formed between the upper arm and the forearm is 110°. The high elbow position becomes apparent at this point. The arm position is similar to that used by butterfliers at one point in their stroke (see Figure III–3).

6. The head continues to lift upward as the neck continues to extend. The final exhalation of air is made as the mouth begins to break the surface of the water. The hands start inward, finishing the last effective propulsive part of their action.

FIG. V–6. Continued

7. The inhalation is made as the arms are ready to be pushed forward. The elbows are not pulled into the ribs, as most swimmers want to do. The knees start to bend and the leg recovery is started.

8. The inhalation is completed and the mouth is closed. The hands start to move forward as the leg recovery continues.

9. The neck flexes in order to lower the head back into the water. The feet are brought up toward the buttocks, as the arms continue to move forward due to the extension of the elbows.

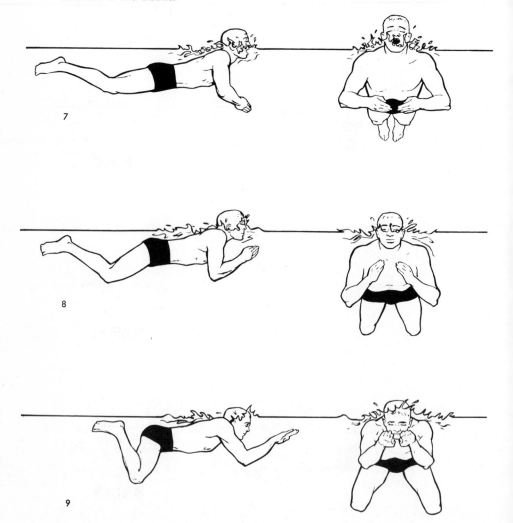

FIG. V–6. Continued

10. The head continues to be tilted downward by flexion of the neck. The feet are plantar-flexed as the backward thrust of the legs begins and the arms near completion of their recovery.

11. The feet are driven backward and start to come together. The swimmer is holding his breath and will not begin his exhalation until the next arm pull starts.

12. The arms are now fully extended with the hands slightly lower than shoulder level. The legs are near completion of the kick.

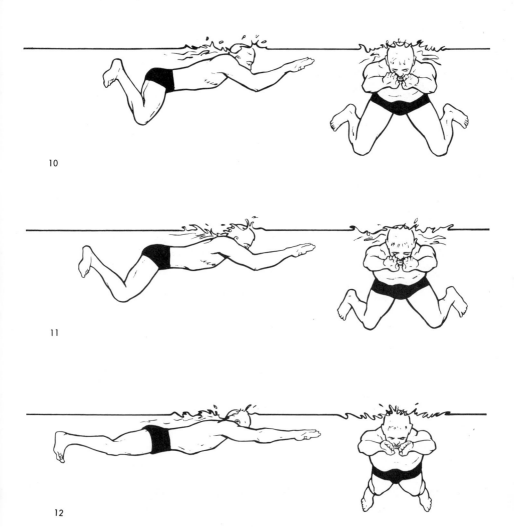

10

11

12

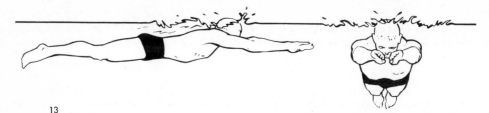

13

FIG. V–6. Continued

13. The swimmer completes his kick and concentrates on getting his body into straight horizontal alignment. He will hold this glide position for a split second and then, when he feels himself slowing down, will begin the stroke cycle again.

for more than a split second before he must begin his pull. It is very important, however, that all breaststrokers, regardless of the effectiveness of their kick, feel this complete body extension for at least a fraction of a second.

The Continuous Stroke

Many great breaststrokers use no glide in their strokes, particularly when sprinting, e.g. Catie Ball, Chet Jastremski, Ken Merten, Brian Job. With this continuous timing the swimmer begins his pull before his legs have completed their backward thrust. This is advantageous because it permits the overlapping of the end of the propulsive phase of the kick and the beginning of the propulsive phase of the arm pull. It also requires the swimmer to take more strokes per length and to use more energy. This stroke is definitely faster for many swimmers and as the speed of the breaststroke event increases may prove to be the best method of continuing improvement. I direct our swimmers to try both glide and continuous timing and to eventually settle for the technique that provides the fastest times. In most cases a slight glide is used for the 200-yard or 200-meter distance; no glide is used for the 100-yard and 100-meter distance. When using the continuous stroke, a slight raising and lowering of the head should be perceptible, but since the swimmer has less time in which to perform this action he should not flex and extend his neck as much as when using the glide stroke.

Regardless of what timing he will be using in races, it is good practice in early season to work on body position and stroke timing by doing some swimming drills in which there is an exaggeration of the glide position. A swimmer can hold the glide after each stroke for as long as three seconds and try to swim his practice lengths in as few strokes as possible; for example, each 25 yards in 5 strokes or less, or each 50 meters in 15 strokes or less.

VI

Swimming Starts,
Turns, and Pace

Opinion is widely diverse concerning the mechanics of the swimming start from a dive. Few swimmers know exactly how they perform their start, but after swimming competitively for a few years most manage a fairly good start. The mechanics of a start, when fully understood, can be taught to even age-group swimmers in a few practice sessions.

The most common misconception concerns the right and wrong ways of performing the arm movements. Most swimmers try to keep their arm swing to a minimum. They have read books and received advice recommending that the arms be swung directly backward and then forward. The logic behind this start is that the backward swing of the arms moves the center of gravity of the body forward, the swimmer loses his balance, and starts to roll forward into his start. According to Newton's third law of motion (action-reaction), as the arms are swung backward, the torso does move forward. The flaw in the reasoning is that the center of gravity of the total body (torso and arms) remains at the same point. A person could stand on the edge of the Empire State Building doing this motion and never fall off.

As the sequence pictures in Figure VI–1 reveal, the arms should make a circular swinging motion before the swimmer leaves the starting block. As the arms make the circle, they accelerate and build up tremendous angular momentum. When they are stopped, their momentum is transferred to the body and pulls it in the direction the arms were going at

FIG. VI–1.   Forward Swimming Start

1. The swimmer should take care to wrap his toes around the front edge of the starting block. He looks straight forward and begins concentrating on his preparations for a good start. His feet are placed from 6 to 12 inches apart.

2. "Upon the command 'Take your mark' he shall assume any desired starting position provided he holds a steady balance for an appreciable length of time. When the starter sees that the contestants are ready, he starts the race with . . . a pistol shot."

Upon the command "Take your mark" the swimmer bends forward at the trunk and *bends his knees slightly,* his arms placed almost straight down with the palms facing back. His head is held high enough so as to permit his line of sight to be about half of the way down a 25-yard pool. He should feel that the center of gravity of his entire body is over the balls of his feet and that he is delicately balanced and not rigidly stable. He should concentrate on listening for the gun and reacting fast. He should not try to analyze critically the entire complex movement, but should think of getting his center of gravity forward.

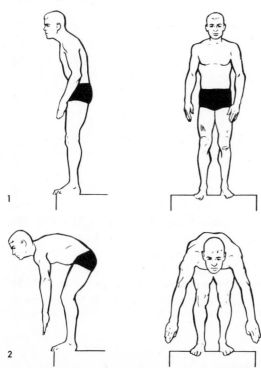

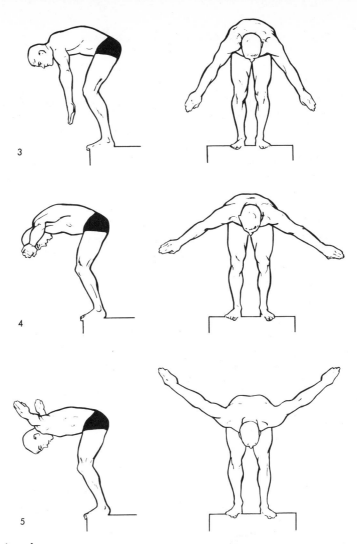

FIG. VI–1. Continued

3. As the gun fires, the swimmer begins to move his arms upward, outward, and forward. The head begins to drop by flexion of the neck. His knees have moved forward due to dorsi flexion of the ankles. This action of the ankles is the real cause of the center of gravity moving forward and is caused by contraction of the anterior muscles of the lower leg (primarily the tibialis anterior) and relaxation of the calf muscles.

4. The arms continue to move forward, upward, and outward as the head continues to lower. At this point most swimmers begin to open their mouths and start to exhale before inhaling.

5. The elbows are kept almost completely extended during the arm swing. At this point the head starts to lift upward. The movement of the head, just as does the action of the arms, imparts momentum to the body in the direction the swimmer wants to go.

FIG. VI–1. Continued

6. The arms reach the peak of their swing and the heels lift from the starting block as the head continues upward. The center of gravity of the body is well in front of the toes, the body continues to bend at the hips and to go into a tight crouch.

7. The swimmer is in a position to begin his final forward drive with his legs. His back is rounded or flexed slightly forward. The extension of the back from this point on will give him additional distance in the dive. His head continues to lift.

8. The knees and ankles begin to extend as the arms start down and forward. The hands are brought in closer to the body with the palms facing the knees. From this point onward the swimmer will have the impression that all movement is forward. The swimmer with a poor start often already has his arms extended forward at this point.

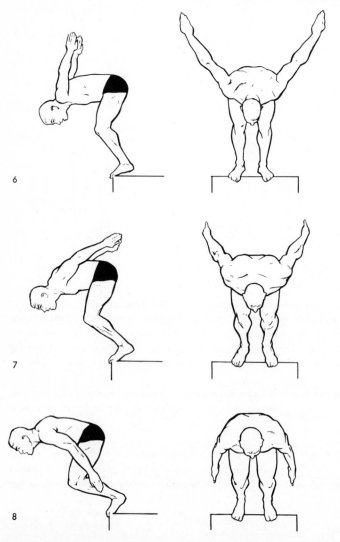

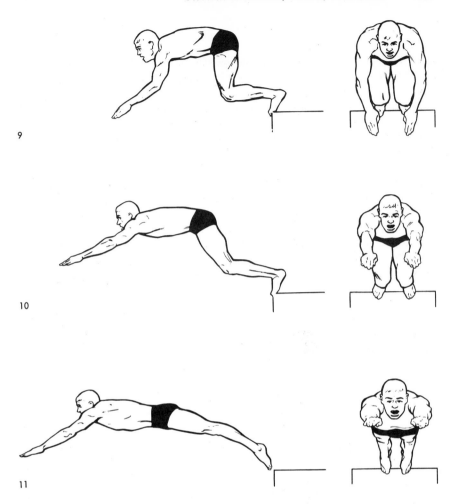

FIG. VI–1. Continued

9. The body continues to extend and the legs to drive the body forward by extension of the hips and knees. As yet the ankles have not started their final drive. The swimmer starts inhalation of his breath at this point.

10. The movement of the head is stopped at this point (inertia) and the arm swing stops simultaneously, with the arms held diagonally downward. The momentum developed by the head and arms is transferred to the body and pulls the body upward and outward away from the starting blocks. The ankles prepare for the final drive.

11. Just as the legs become completely extended, the ankles are, plantar-flexed and give the final forward thrust to the body. The center of gravity of the body is only 14 to 18 inches higher than the top edge of the starting block.

FIG. VI–1.   Continued

12. The swimmer's inhalation continues and his back continues to arch as his head begins to lower. The action of his arms begins again as they start to come up.

13. As the swimmer lowers his head, his arms continue upward. The back tends to arch slightly. Excessive arching should be avoided by contraction of the forward flexors of the trunk (primarily of the rectus abdominus). The inhalation of the breath ends at this point.

14. The body has now rotated forward sufficiently so that, when the swimmer contacts the water, his hands, which are held together, touch first, followed by the rest of the body. His head is lowered slightly upon entry. The abdominal muscles are contracted and the knees and ankles extended with the result that the body is as streamlined as possible. The swimmer should think of stretching and not tend to relax as he enters the water.

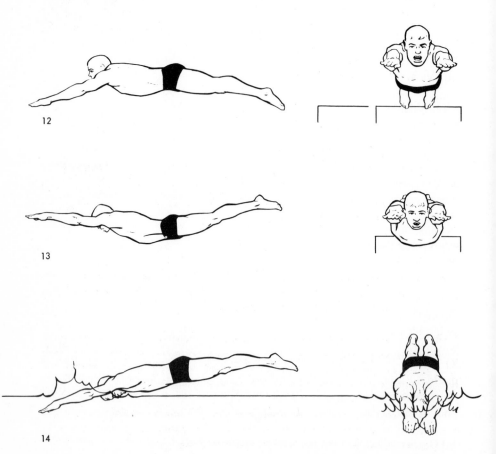

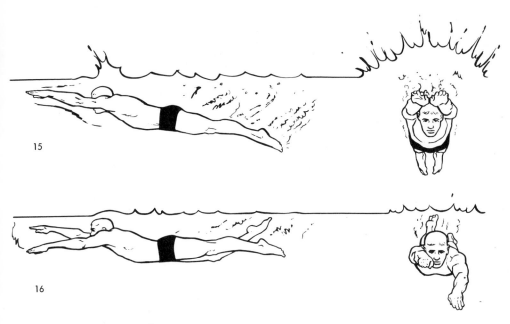

FIG. VI–1.   Continued

15. Following his complete submersion in the water, the swimmer's body will tend to continue to drop and will go too deeply unless he lifts his head slightly and lets his hands serve as a rudder to direct the path of his body slightly upward.

16. When the head is within a few inches of the surface and as the swimmer slows down to swimming speed (and no sooner), he starts his arm pull and kick simultaneously. If he is excessively deep he may have to kick once or twice in order to raise himself to the surface. He should not make an effort to kick down with one leg and pull with the other arm, as shown here, but should let the timing work in by itself. The number of strokes he will take before breathing will depend upon whether he is swimming a sprint or a distance event.

the time they were stopped. Does the circular arm swing delay or slow down the take-off? The answer to this question is no. In the time the swimmer's center of gravity takes to move from the point at which it was as the swimmer was standing on his mark (Figure VI–1, illustration 2) until it is at the point at which it will be when his final leg push is made (Figure VI–1, illustration 10), he has enough time to complete the circular wind-up. Gravity alone determines how fast the person's body will fall this distance ($\frac{1}{2}GT^2$).[1]

[1] G = gravity, T = time, acceleration of gravity is 32 feet per second, per second.

AN ANALYSIS OF THE FORWARD SWIMMING START

"In all swimming races with the exception of the backstroke each contestant shall stand erect with both feet on the starting mark in readiness to assume a starting position." [2]

Variations in the Start:
Breaststroke versus Freestyle and Butterfly

The starts for these three strokes are nearly identical except for the angle of entry into the water. In the butterfly and crawl strokes the angle of entry into the water is approximately 15°, as shown in Figure VI–1, illustration 14. In the breaststroke start the angle of entry is slightly steeper, around 20°. This permits the swimmer to go deeper in the water and to be in a better position to take his long arm pull and kick before surfacing.

Common Mistakes in Starting

I. Starting position mistakes:
   A. Arms held back too far; some swimmers actually hold their arms behind the hips.
   B. Head held down too much, as though looking at the feet.
   C. Head held up too high, as though looking at the far end of the pool.
   D. Body tucked up too tight, knees almost touching chest.
   E. Knees not bent.
   F. Feet spread too far apart; 6 to 12 inches of spread is the normal range.
   G. Sitting back on the heels; the weight of the body should be forward over the toes.
   II. Failure to take full advantage of the arm swing. Girls in particular use very little arm action and miss a half foot to a foot of the ·extra distance they might get from the start.
   III. Starting to swim too soon. Some swimmers begin to swim as soon as they hit the water, some even begin to kick in the air. *Remember to wait until you slow down to swimming speed before beginning to swim.* Learning this technique takes time and practice. Occasional stopwatch research on short dashes (12½ yards) may be necessary to help the swimmer evaluate his progress.
   IV. Landing too flat or jackknifing upon entry (Figure VI–2). Both of these faulty actions can be caused by the same two things: (1) stop-

[2] *National Collegiate Athletic Association Rule Book,* 1966, p. 10.

FIG. VI–2. Jackknifing upon Entry

ping the arms at the horizontal or higher after the arm swing. This action tends to pull the front of the body upward, causing the swimmer either to land flat on his chest or, more commonly, to avoid this by piking or jackknifing. (2) Pushing off the starting block at too high an angle, that is, before the center of gravity has had a chance to roll forward and downward sufficiently. This *high-angle* diving results in the same action described above.

Jackknifing is a fault commonly seen in age-group swimmers, but is also occasionally done by swimmers in the finals of the Olympic Games. Such a swimmer is guilty of either of the two faults and should be told to: (1) stop his arms after the swing in a position diagonally downward, as shown in Figure VI–1, illustrations 10 and 11, or (2) postpone the push of his legs until his body has rolled further forward, or (3) a combination of the two.

Practicing the Start

The start is one of the easiest skills to teach; it can be likened to jumping for a basketball. The arm action and the timing of the arms and legs can be practiced by having the swimmer stand on the deck and jump upward vertically, reaching as high as he can with his arms.

The arm action can also be practiced as the swimmer stands on the edge of the pool without actually doing the dive. Simple drills designed to give the swimmer a general idea of the skill are helpful.

What Qualities Make a Good Starter?

Not every swimmer can be a good starter, because two of the three qualities needed are largely inherent. Almost any swimmer, however, can improve on his start so he gets off the mark faster and out further.

The three qualities needed to be a good starter are good reaction time, power, and good mechanics.

1. Good reaction time is one of the qualities that is largely inherent. A swimmer can learn to get off the mark faster by learning to assume the correct starting position and working on mechanical corrections.

2. Strength is the ability of the muscle to create tension. Power differs from strength in that it also involves *time rate* of work, that is, speed of muscular contraction. A person with good explosive power and poor mechanics can often outdive a person with the opposite combination. Do not be misled by a person who has good reaction time and power, but lacks good mechanics. He may be getting out faster and further than anyone of your team, but he will do even better if he acquires all three qualities. Power can be improved, within limits, by weight training and isometric contractions.

3. Good mechanics can be taught and poor mechanics can be improved with practice, good coaching, and understanding of the principles involved in a good start.

THE CRAWL STROKE TURN

"A hand touch is not required at the turn, it is sufficient if any part of the body touches the end of the pool on each turn." [3] This rule imposes little restriction on the swimmer in the execution of his turn. The efficiency of the turn becomes the primary criterion for accepting or rejecting its use. The *open* or *grab* turn is so slow that it is virtually never used in competitive swimming unless a swimmer wants to hear or see the counter to determine the number of lengths he has swum. There are several types of crawl turns and they, or slight variations of them, are used by most swimmers. The *flip crawl turn,* as described here, is the one most commonly used by nationally ranked swimmers and appears presently to be the fastest turn. There are slight variations of this turn, and Figures VI–3 and VI–4 depict the two mainly used variations.

The swimmer is confronted with three problems as he does his turn: (1) he must change his forward linear motion to angular motion; in other words, let his forward speed be used to spin him around, (2) he must perform a half twist as he is doing his flip turn in order that, as he pushes off, he will be on his chest and not on his back, and (3) he must complete his turn in such a way that his feet and legs may be in good position for a push-off.

[3] *National Collegiate Athletic Association Rule Book,* 1966, p. 11.

AN ANALYSIS OF THE CRAWL FLIP TURN

Common Mistakes in Executing the Crawl Flip Turn

I. Failure to twist the body around as the turn is made. Too many swimmers flip directly over, with the result that the push-off comes while the swimmer is partially on his back. The half twist during the turn must be practiced.

FIG. VI–3.   The Crawl Stroke Turn

1. When the swimmer's head is about four to seven feet from the end of the pool, depending on his size and the effectiveness of his arm pull, he begins his last pull, in this case with the left hand. His right hand continues to push back as he looks forward at the wall.

2. The swimmer looks at the wall and must make his decision to turn at this time or wait until the next stroke.

3. At this point the decision to turn is made, and instead of recovering the left hand he stops it at his side and continues to pull back with the right hand. His legs start to go upward together preparatory to doing a slight fishtail kick. Some swimmers prefer to continue to lift one hand, in this case the left one, and to recover it half the way forward and then suddenly stop it in the air. In this way the momentum of the arm is transferred to the body and is effective in helping the body flip over. The arm is then returned to the overhead position. This arm action in the air is similar to a flag-waving motion.

FIG. VI–3.   Continued

4. The head is thrown downward by flexion of the neck. The palms of both hands are turned so they are facing downward; the legs and feet are together with the knees bent.

5. The body is thrown out of straight alignment as the head continues downward and the body flexes at the trunk. Simultaneously, both hands, palms down, are pushed downward as if preparing for a surface dive. The feet are kicked downward in a fish-tail kick in order to help drive the hips upward.

6. The body continues to bend forward at the hips. The resistance created by the head and body at this point tends to stop the inertia of the top part of the body. The forward inertia of the lower trunk and legs is not affected as much by this resistance and continues to move forward and over the upper trunk. If the swimmer is going fast enough, as in the sprints, this source of turning may be virtually all he needs to turn himself around. In this illustration the left hand is starting to bend at the elbow and pull toward the head.

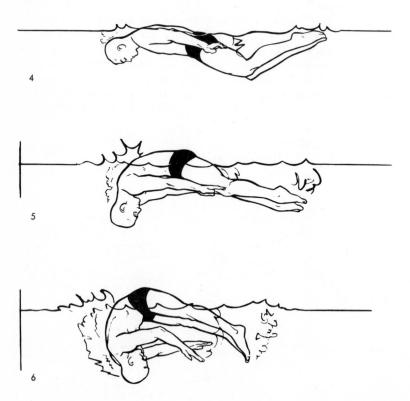

4

5

6

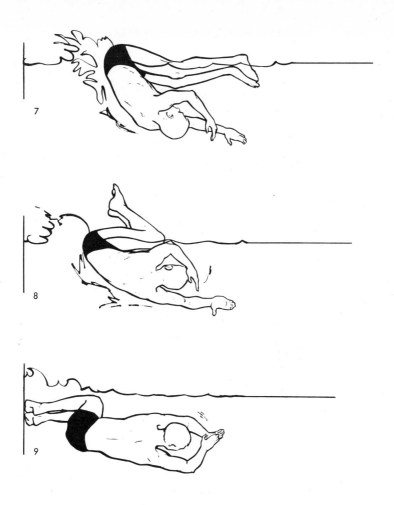

FIG. VI–3. Continued

7. As the hips pass over the head, the left hand continues to push water toward the head. This action helps accomplish the flip. The right hand, palm facing inward, sculls in a slight circular motion to turn the swimmer's body on its longitudinal axis. The feet are not brought directly over the head, but slightly to the right of the median line of the body.

8. As the feet are completely out of the water, the legs are tucked and thrown backward to the wall as the hands finish their sculling motion. The swimmer should consciously turn his head and shoulders and should try, without breaking the rhythm of his movement, to turn over on his side.

9. The swimmer's turn is completed and he must get his body in position for the push-off. His hands are almost touching as they start forward. He continues to rotate his body in order to be on his side.

FIG. VI–3. Continued

10. As his legs start to drive him forward by extending at the knees, the arms continue to extend.

11. The shoulders are almost completely level when the final leg push occurs. As the feet leave the wall with the extension of the ankles completing the final drive, the arms are stretched outward with the head between them in a streamlined position.

12. The swimmer should regulate his depth by using his hands as rudders. He should also lift his head to help raise him to the surface. If he is too deep, he may have to kick once or twice to help him rise to the surface. If his depth is right, he can start his kick and pull together.

10

11

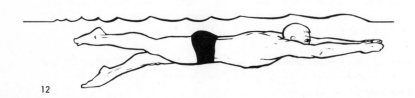

12

FIG. VI–3. Continued

13. The swimmer sets up his stroke and gets back into stroking tempo. He may breathe after the first arm stroke off the turn (this technique is particularly good in the longer races) or he may take at least two arm strokes before breathing (as he should in the sprints).

II. Turning too far away from or too close to the wall—only alertness and practice can prevent this mistake.

III. Failure to streamline the body during the push-off—the swimmer should practice this skill by practicing push-offs for distance and concentrating on stretching. His sequence of thinking should be: hands together, arms squeezing the head; abdomen in; legs extended; toes pointed.

IV. Failure to drive hard enough off the wall with the legs and ankles. The swimmer must learn to push hard and work each turn in practice for maximum thrust. Swimmers too often use their turns to rest.

FIG. VI–4. Variation of the Flip Turn

1. The leading arm is kept forward as the other arm finishes its recovery.

2. Both arms start to pull backward with the leading arm just slightly ahead of the other arm.

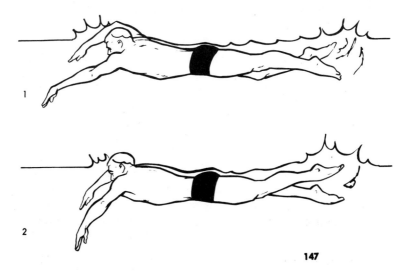

FIG. VI–4. Continued

3. Both arms continue backward, pulling together. The swimmer feels as though he were using a butterfly pull. From this point on the turn is identical to that in Figure VI–3, illustrations 4 to 13.

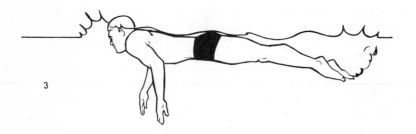

3

THE BUTTERFLY START AND TURN

When touching at the turn or on finishing a race, the touch shall be made with both hands simultaneously on the same level, and with the shoulders in the horizontal plane. Once a legal touch has been made, the contestant may turn in any manner desired, but the prescribed form must be attained before the feet leave the wall in the push-off.

When a contestant is in the underwater position after the start, when turning, or during the race, he is allowed to make one or more kicks.[4]

The butterfly swimmer should use a start and dive similar to that of the freestyler. After he has entered the water, as in Figure VI–1, illustration 15, as well as after the turn and immediately before he slows to swimming speed, the swimmer should start to recover his legs by bending the knees and bringing his heels up toward the surface. This will put his feet in a position to thrust downward as he begins his arm pull. Some swimmers try to kick two or three times before beginning their arm pull. This technique is not recommended unless the swimmer is too deep and needs to use the kicks to help him get to the surface.

In turning, the butterfly swimmer should touch the wall with both hands simultaneously and on the same level. Once he has touched the wall, he should not pull in close to the wall, but should let his elbows bend just slightly as his momentum pushes his body in toward the wall. The hand on the side toward which he will turn should pull away from the wall shortly after it has touched. It is pulled in toward the chest, while the other hand pushes against the wall in an effort to help the upper part of the body turn away from the wall. While this is occurring, the legs are tucked up tightly and pulled under the body. When the

[4] *National Collegiate Athletic Association Rule Book,* 1966, p. 12.

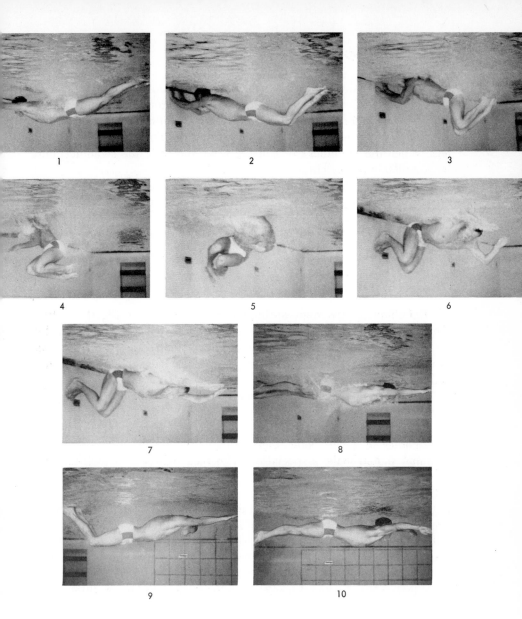

FIG. VI–5. The Butterfly Turn

Lary Schulhof, National AAU champion and former holder of the 110-yard Butterfly World Record, is pictured doing the butterfly turn. Lary uses good mechanics on his turn. It will be noticed that, as many other swimmers do, he crosses one foot on top of the other as he tucks his legs and pulls them in to the wall. This action may decrease the resistance his feet create. He returns his feet to a normal position as he plants them on the wall for the push-off. After letting go of the wall with his trailing hand, it is recovered over the water. Following his push-off and when he has slowed to swimming speed, he brings his feet up for his first kick. As the downward thrust of the legs is made he begins his arm pull.

149

trailing hand finally leaves the wall, it is pulled into the chest (it can be thrown over the water, as in Figure VI–5, illustrations 5 and 6, or merely placed underwater immediately) and joins the other hand before they are both pushed forward in preparation for the final push-off with the legs. When the swimmer's feet finally leave the wall, the swimmer must be completely on his chest.

A flip turn in the butterfly is legal, provided the rules stated at the beginning of this section are not violated. Bill Barton, former Indiana University swimmer and National champion, used the butterfly flip turn in the National AAU meet as early as 1957 without being disqualified. Fred Schmidt also used it with mild success.

Common Mistakes in the Butterfly Turn

I. Pulling up too high during the turn. After grasping the gutter, some swimmers pull themselves in close to the pool edge and then lift their shoulders and head high out of the water as they turn. All this extra effort is tiring, makes the turn slower, and puts the swimmer in a bad position for a push-off.

The swimmer should keep his shoulders almost completely in the water and never get his mouth more than a few inches above the water level.

II. Failure to tuck the legs tightly enough. Many swimmers keep their bodies in a very loose tuck position as they do their turns. The swimmer should make a special effort to tuck tightly, as it will increase the speed with which he can complete the turn.

III. Finishing a length either on a half stroke or a half stroke short. Butterfliers frequently make poor turns because they fail to space their strokes out, finishing a bit short on a stroke and literally eating the wall of the pool if they take another stroke. The swimmer must learn to look for the wall two to three strokes before he gets to it. In this way, he can space his strokes in such a way that he never gets stuck on a half stroke. With experience he can learn to take two long strokes or three short strokes when he is at a given point.

Some swimmers try to kick in if they are a little bit short on a stroke, while others prefer a short half arm stroke. An alert swimmer will seldom be caught in this predicament.

THE BREASTSTROKE START AND TURN

. . . Following the take-off and each turn, one arm-pull and one leg-kick may be taken underwater, but some portion of the contestant's head must break the surface of the water before another stroke is started. . . .

When touching at the turn on finishing a race, the touch shall be made with both hands simultaneously on the same level, and with the shoulders in the horizontal plane. Once a legal touch has been made, the contestant may turn in any manner desired, but the prescribed form must be attained before the feet leave the wall in the push-off.[5]

The breaststroke swimmer, because he is permitted and benefits from a long arm pull and a kick underwater before surfacing, should have a steeper angle of entry into the water following the dive than the freestyler or butterflier. Once the swimmer has entered the water he should let himself slow to swimming speed and then start his underwater stroke. This stroke is identical to the technique used after the turn (see Figure IV–6, illustrations 1 to 12).

The breaststroker must turn in much the same manner as the butter-flier (Figure VI–5, illustrations 1 to 8). He must touch with both hands simultaneously and on the same level. The proper manner for executing the turn is almost identical to that described for the butterflier.

When the breaststroker pushes off, however, he must angle downward somewhat so he will be deep enough to take his underwater stroke. Figure VI–6 pictures Chester Jastremski doing the long stroke after a turn and push-off.

Common Mistakes in the Breaststroke Turn

I. Pulling up too high during the turn. This mistake is similar to that described in the butterfly turn. It has the same causes and is corrected in the same manner.

II. Holding the turn too long or not long enough. Some swimmers rush their turns and come up almost immediately, while others prolong their turns so much that they lose time. The length of time a swimmer should hold his turn from the time he touches the wall until his head breaks the surface after the long stroke should be between 3.2 and 4.2 seconds.

Chet Jastremski, who had one of the best breaststroke turns of all time, is pictured in the sequence in Figure VI–6. He held his turns 3.6 to 3.8 seconds when setting the American record of 58.5 seconds for the 100-yard breaststroke, short course, and 3.8 to 4.2 seconds when setting the American record for the 200-yard breaststroke of 2:09.0.[6]

The length of time a swimmer holds his turn depends on the distance he is swimming—in a sprint he will not hold it as long as in a 200 race— on the power of his push-off, and on the effectiveness of his long stroke.

---

[5] *National Collegiate Athletic Association Rule Book,* 1966, p. 11.
[6] Records set at the National AAU Championships, Yale University, New Haven, Conn., 1962.

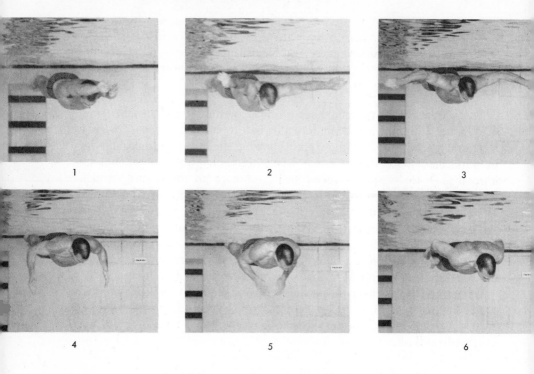

FIG. VI–6.   The Long Pull and the Kick after the Breaststroke Turn

1. After the push-off the head is held down between the arms and the swimmer is two to three feet beneath the surface of the water.

2. The arm pull begins with the arms almost completely straight and pulling directly sidewards in a line parallel with the surface of the water.

3. The arms start to bend at the elbows as the hands come down slightly. The arms and elbows are almost at shoulder level.

4. The elbows bend as the hands come closer together. The head is kept low in an effort to keep the body from rising to the surface.

5. The hands are almost touching one another as the elbow bend exceeds 90°. From this point backward the hands will accelerate in a fast whip-like action as the elbows are extended.

6. The elbows are almost completely extended and the swimmer is ready to push the water directly upward with the palms of his hands.

FIG. VI–6. Continued

7. The hands have completed their pull and the palms are facing directly upward. This upward thrust of the hands helps to keep the body under water and leaves the hands in a good streamlined position.

8. The swimmer holds the gliding position for one to one and a half seconds. He can adjust his depth by using his hands and head as rudders. If he wants to be closer to the surface, he lifts his head slightly. If he feels he is too shallow, he lowers it.

9. As the swimmer feels his speed drop off, he begins to recover his arms and legs simultaneously. The hands and elbows should be kept close to the body as he recovers them in order to reduce drag.

10. The elbows are kept close to the ribs as the hands are brought up under the chest. The swimmer should try to *sneak* the arms up at a steady, but not fast, rate. The legs continue to recover slowly by flexion at the knees.

11. The arms are almost completely extended and the head is just a few inches under the surface of the water. The legs are ready to begin their backward thrust.

12. The leg kick drives the swimmer forward as his head breaks the surface of the water. The swimmer now is legally able to begin his next stroke. From here on, however, his head must break the surface of the water at all times until he starts his next turn.

7

8

9

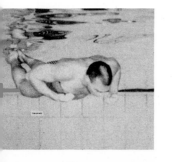

10

11

12

III. Going too deep during the push-off. If a swimmer pushes off too deep, he will have to delay his second stroke while he floats up. He cannot begin the second stroke until his head breaks the surface after the first stroke. This rule is violated frequently with impunity.

THE BACKSTROKE START AND TURN

The rules governing the start and turn for the backstroke vary somewhat between those of the AAU and those of the NCAA. The NCAA Rules, which apply to collegiate and high school swimming, are:

> *a.* The contestant shall push off on his back and continue swimming on his back throughout the race.
> *b.* The contestant may not turn over beyond the vertical toward his breast before his foremost hand has touched the end of the pool.[7]

The AAU and international rules (FINA) are as follows:

> The competitors shall line up in the water, facing the starting end, with the hands resting on the end or rail of the pool or starting grips. It shall be the Starter's duty to see that the competitor's feet, including the toes, shall be under the surface of the water and that no competitor is standing in or on the gutter or curling his toes over the lip of the gutter.
> A competitor in a backstroke event must not turn over beyond the vertical toward the breast before the foremost hand has touched the end of the pool or course for the purpose of turning or finishing. It is permissible to turn over beyond the vertical after the foremost hand has touched, for sole purpose of executing the turn, but the swimmer must have returned past the vertical to a position on the back before the feet have left the wall.[8]

The collegiate rules concerned with the starting position have been interpreted as permitting the swimmer to wrap his toes around the lip of the pool gutter, so long as part of his feet are in the water. The AAU and international rules specifically forbid this practice. It is hoped that the AAU and international rules will be changed to conform with the NCAA rules. Figure VI–7 pictures Tom Stock performing a start that conforms with the AAU rules. It is similar in mechanics to the start used in compliance with the NCAA rules with the exception that the latter type of start permits the performer to get greater height and, consequently, greater distance in the plunge after the start.

After the swimmer is completely under water, he must make a correc-

---

[7] *National Collegiate Athletic Association Rule Book,* 1966, p. 12.
[8] *Amateur Athletic Union Official Swimming Handbook,* 1965, Section VI, p. 8.

1

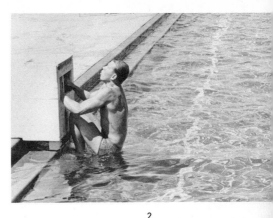

2

3

4

FIG. VI–7.   The Backstroke Start

1. Upon the command, "Take your mark," the swimmer flexes his elbows and pulls his chest in close to the starting block, lifting most of his body out of the water.

2. At the pistol shot the swimmer starts his head upward and backward. He drives his shoulders and upper body upward and away from the starting block by pushing downward and inward with his arms against the hand grip bar. Inhalation begins at this point.

3. The swimmer continues to pull his head backward as he lets go of the hand grip. At this point he starts to swing his arms forward in a flat, horizontal path, similar to the recovery action of the butterfly stroke. His legs start to extend vigorously.

4. As the arms swing forward past the shoulders, the legs continue to extend and the ankles (now shown here) are about to begin their drive. From this point on the swimmer must guard against excessive arching of the back. This is done by contracting the abdominal muscles (rectus abdominus and external oblique muscles).

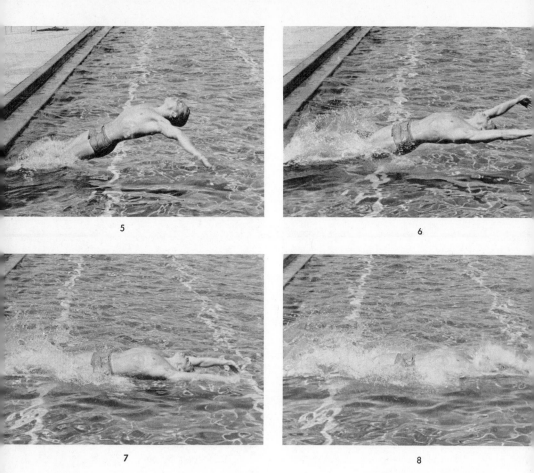

5   6

7   8

FIG. VI–7. Continued

5. The swimmer's feet are just leaving the wall with the final thrust coming from the extension of the ankles. At this point the arms should be in a position slightly above the head, but not all the way overhead. If this picture is viewed upside down, the swimmer appears to be in a swan dive position.

6. The swimmer continues to fall toward the water surface as he continues his arm movement upward. At this point the swimmer begins to think of streamlining his body in order that he may get an effective glide after he submerges.

7. As the swimmer hits the water, his head is still back and his arms are almost together with the hands touching. The swimmer's inhalation ends at this point. The swimmer must now start to adjust his body position so that he will not be too shallow or too deep during the plunge.

8. The swimmer is almost completely submerged. He is now in a good streamlined position and will sink to a depth of slightly over a foot and a half shortly after his body becomes completely submerged.

tion in his body position in order to prevent himself from going too deep. This correction usually consists of a forward flexion of the neck and a corresponding forward movement of the arms. The swimmer holds the glide position until he slows to swimming speed. If he is at the proper depth, he begins his arm stroke and kick simultaneously. If he is too deep, he will have to kick two or more times to help raise his body closer to the surface.

The swimmer begins his arm stroke by pulling one arm at a time. Some experimentation with world class swimmers with the double arm pull on the first stroke after the start or turn has proven it to be of doubtful value. Such a pull causes a dead spot in the stroke between the finish of the double pull and the beginning of the stroking when there is no application of force on the water.

Common Mistakes in the Backstroke Turn

I. Throwing the arms directly upward after they let go of the hand grip. The arms should be swung sidewards, not upward.

II. Getting the arms overhead too fast. Some swimmers try to extend their arms fully overhead before their feet leave the pool edge. As the feet leave the wall the arms should be at shoulder level or a little higher. This permits the momentum developed during the arm swing to help pull the body outward, away from the mark.

III. Pulling up too high immediately after the start. The swimmer should try to push out horizontally as far as he can and not upward at too high or vertical an angle.

The Backstroke Flip Turn

The backstroke flip turn is not truly a flip turn, since the body never flips completely over to the front. It could more accurately be called a *pivot turn,* executed on the back with the legs being flipped out of and over the surface of the water. The swimmer, once he has touched the wall, can legally get off his back, but he must be on his back again before he pushes off.

There are two types of backstroke flip turn being used today. The normal flip turn, which is that pictured in Figure VI–8, and described in this chapter, and the rolling backstroke flip turn. In the latter type the swimmer rolls almost completely over during the actual flip, but finishes on his back before the push-off. This turn is fast, but hazardous because the swimmer must start the roll onto his front side before he touches the wall. If he misjudges or anticipates the turn slightly, he invariably rolls too far and thus violates the rule forbidding him to turn off his back before touching.

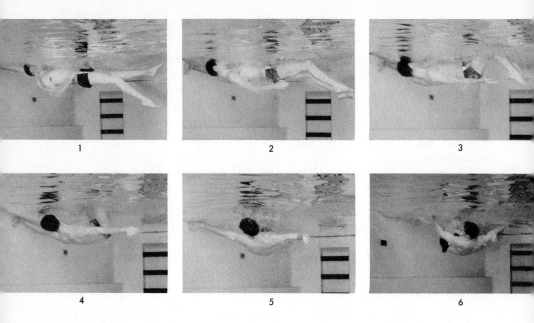

FIG. VI–8.   Backstroke Flip Turn

1. The swimmer's hand touches the edge of the pool in a line directly over his head with his finger tips pointed inward. His right hand continues to finish its pull.

2. The swimmer bends the touching arm and starts to tuck up his legs by bending his knees. His right hand has completed its pull and now begins to turn so the palm is facing inwardly.

3. The knees are pulled out of the water as the legs are lifted upward. The elbow on the touching arm continues to bend and allow the body to come close to the wall. The right arm continues to rotate so the palm is facing directly upward.

4. The legs from the knees down are out of water and are thrown sidewards, not directly overhead. The swimmer never gets off his back, but pivots around as if lying on a turntable. The touching arm now starts to extend and push the top of the body away from the wall, thereby helping the swimmer to turn.

The right hand, palm in a vertical position, has positioned itself so that it is now ready to take over the job of aiding the turning action.

5. The right hand now pulls backward toward the head as the touching hand finishes its final push-off from the wall.

6. The right hand continues to pull toward the head as the left arm, with the hand out of water, now starts upward and forward. The legs are about to become submerged as they approach the wall.

FIG. VI–8.   Continued

7. As the right hand finishes its pull, it appears to almost pat the head with the palm. The left arm with the hand still out of the water continues to move upward to a point where it will meet the other hand prior to the final leg push-off. The feet begin to submerge as the turn is almost completed.

8. The legs sink until the feet are about 14 to 18 inches under the surface. Both arms continue upward.

9. The hands are now together and the elbows are almost completely extended. The feet are firmly planted on the wall and the legs are ready to begin their drive. The heels of the feet never touch the wall.

10. The swimmer's arms are extended overhead as the leg drive begins. The swimmer concentrates upon streamlining his body by stretching his arms overhead and by pulling in his abdominal muscles to keep the back straight.

11. The swimmer finishes his final leg drive by extending his ankles vigorously. He uses his head and arm position as well as the amount of bend at the hip joints to adjust his depth in the water.

12. The swimmer holds his push-off position until immediately before he slows to swimming speed. He then starts to spread his legs preparatory to beginning a kick.

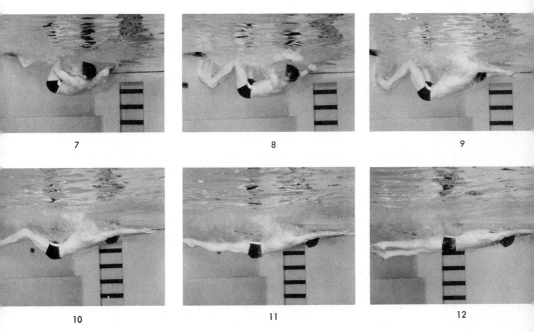

7   8   9

10   11   12

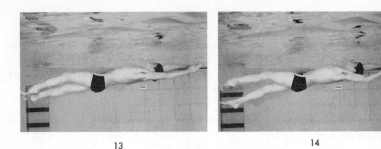

13   14

FIG. VI–8.   Continued

13. and 14. Immediately before the swimmer breaks the water surface, he begins his arm pull. If the reader wants a further look at how the swimmer completes this arm pull and breaks the surface afterward, he should refer to Figure IV–2.

Figure VI–8 pictures Charles Hickcox, National champion and record holder, performing a normal backstroke flip turn and one arm stroke after the turn.

RELAY TAKE-OFFS

The AAU rules concerning relay take-offs are as follows:

> In relay races a competitor other than the first swimmer shall not start until his team mate shall have concluded his leg. . . . In relay races the team of a competitor whose feet have lost touch with the ground (or deck) before his preceding partner touches the wall shall be disqualified, unless the competitor in default returns to the original starting point at the wall but it shall not be necessary to return to the starting platform.[9]

The swimmers in a relay should employ the normal racing start with a full arm swing. Relay swimmers should practice relay take-offs, specifically with the swimmers comprising their relay team and in the order in which they will swim.

The swimmer should begin to move his arms into their swing and allow his body to move forward soon after the preceding swimmer's head has passed the turning "T" target marked on the bottom of most pools, that is, when the head is three to four and a half feet from the end of the pool. During the time he is completing his arm swing and forward roll

[9] *AAU Official Swimming Handbook,* 1965, Competitive Rules, Section VI, p. 9.

and his final leg thrust, the swimmer in the water will have had time to cover the remaining distance.

Only through practice can this technique be perfected and the swimmers acquire the timing necessary for good relay take-offs.

The swimmer must also be able to anticipate which hand the swimmer will touch with. The incoming swimmer must drive in hard and give the next swimmer a good fast touch. Frequently, the "jumping" or illegal take-off can be blamed on the incoming swimmer who does not finish properly, as when he drifts in to the wall.

PACING THE RACE

The following discussion of pace applies to races in all four competitive strokes, but not to the individual medley event. Once a swimmer goes past the shorter distances which are swum at sprinting speed (50 up to 100 yards or meters), in order to achieve his best performance, he must learn to distribute his effort economically throughout the race. He can achieve this best by performing at a relatively constant speed over the entire distance.

Pace in the 100 Yards/Meters Distance

It is rather doubtful that a swimmer can swim the entire 100 yards or meters distance at an all-out speed. At this distance even the best-conditioned swimmers will stroke the first 50 yards or meters slightly slower (and will breathe more often in the case of the freestyler) than they would in an all-out 50 yards or meters effort.

In swimming the 100 yards/meters distance, the best policy is to swim the first 50 within .5 to 1.0 second of the time the swimmer is capable of doing in a maximum effort 50. Since the swimmer completing the 50 on the way to a 100 is not driving in to touch the finish, but is delaying his hand touch (or not touching at all in the crawl turn) so he can turn more effectively, the 50 will necessarily be slower than an all-out 50 effort.

Steve Clark's American record for the 100-yard freestyle (short course) of :45.6, set in 1965, is an example of a well-swum event:

Steve Clark's		
American record	:21.8	:45.6
Time for each 50	:21.8	:23.8

Steve's best time from a flat start for 50 yards is :20.9, or .9 of a second slower than his split on the way to the 100.

Swimmers not in top condition may have to slow their first 50 so that it is more than one second over what they are capable of doing in an all-out effort. They will otherwise experience too great a drop-off in the last 50. Occasionally a swimmer will perform better times on his 50 split time on the way to a 100 than he will on an all-out 50 effort. This is usually because he is trying too hard on the all-out 50 and is literally "spinning his wheels." Such a swimmer can profit from time trials and races in practice sessions in which he is instructed to keep his stroke long and to slow his tempo so he feels he is swimming slightly slower than all-out speed.

Principles Involved in Pacing Middle and Longer Races (200 and over)

There are three principles which demonstrate the need for careful pacing in the middle distance and longer events:

1. A swimmer should try to prevent the build-up of a high oxygen debt early in the race. If the swimmer starts out at too fast a pace and uses up energy to the extent that he begins to accumulate a high level of oxygen debt early in the race, he will experience an almost immediate drop-off in his efficiency and speed. The swimmer, depending on the distance he is swimming, should try to swim in a steady state so far as oxygen consumption is concerned. That is, he should take in almost as much oxygen as he is consuming in his performance. He should build the oxygen debt slowly as he completes the race. For short distances or periods of time, as in sprint events, a swimmer can tolerate a relatively high level of oxygen debt. When swimming the longer events, however, the swimmer does not want to achieve a high level of oxygen debt except toward the end of the race.

The second and third principles involve the disproportionately high rate of energy expenditure at the faster speeds.

2. The theoretical square law governing air and water resistance is in operation: air and water resistance vary approximately with the square of the velocity. When a swimmer doubles his speed from three feet per second to six feet per second, he does not merely encounter twice as much resistance, but four times as much.

3. The energy costs of a muscle contraction vary with the cube of the speed of contraction. If, in the illustration above, when the swimmer doubled his speed, he also had to contract his muscles twice as fast, he would not merely increase his energy expenditure and oxygen consumption by double or even four times, but by eight times.

The following is an application of these two principles: a swimmer who swam his 200-yard event in two minutes by swimming his first 100 in 53 seconds and his last 100 in 67 seconds would create more total resistance, use more energy, consume more oxygen, and be more fatigued than a swimmer who paced his race more evenly, swimming his first 100 yards in 58 seconds and his last 100 in 62 seconds for the same total time.

Factors Affecting Pace and Split Times

In Tables VI–1 and VI–2, *Even Pace Charts,* it will be noted that the first 50 yards or 50 meters of each pace is three seconds faster than the succeeding fifties. Immediately following the start, during the time the swimmer is in the air and for a short time after he is in the water, he is traveling at a speed greater than his swimming speed. (In track, the opposite is true, for the runner is slowed down by the start.) For this reason, the first length of a swimmer's race, *even though it may be swum at the same pace* (so far as the actual swimming speed for the length is concerned) *as the rest of the race,* will always be faster, usually by two to three seconds, depending on how the split time is taken. In the freestyle event, if the swimmer does a flip turn without touching the pool edge with his hand, a foot touch must be timed. This will add to the time of the first length and subtract from the time of the last part of the race.

While a fairly even pace throughout the race is desirable, it is not my intention to advocate that every swimmer's race be identical. Other factors enter into swimming a race than the mechanical and physiological principles already mentioned. *There is no constant pattern or rigid blueprint for pace that a swimmer must follow to achieve his best time.* There are individual differences which may change a swimmer's strategy and his plan of pacing in a race. Some swimmers who are what I call "agonists" seem to enjoy the pain caused by physical exertion and don't mind hurting themselves. Such people can take a race out hard and keep going hard all the way. Others who are more timid physically must swim well within their pain threshold and are only willing to hurt themselves during the last part of the race. The former, everything else being equal, will become the greater distance swimmer of the two.

Some swimmers are front swimmers and swim much better when they are leading the others in the event. They are able to relax more and swim better mechanically when not constantly being harassed by someone swimming along with them. Others are incapable of sustaining a constant pace unless someone is there with them, either pushing them or pulling them along. Some swimmers are capable of performing in one of the ways described above on one occasion and an entirely different way at another time. This inconsistent pattern is due more to psychological than to physiological factors.

A swimmer may begin a race faster than an ideal pace in an effort to get out in front of the pack and avoid the choppy water. In some well-designed pools the water does not get as rough as in some other pools, thus the strategy of a swimmer's race may take this factor into consideration.

Some swimmers like to swim *strategy races* and, in some cases, have won National and Olympic titles by swimming races in which their pace varied considerably. Notable among these have been Murray Rose and Roy Saari. These swimmers almost seem to disregard pace and swim the opponent in a race planned not particularly to produce a good time, but primarily to win the race. This type of race has its merit, depending on the personality of the swimmer as well as on the consideration he may have to give to resting himself for another event. In a race of this type, it is highly unlikely that a great performance will be achieved or new records set.

How to Use the Even Pace Chart

The even pace chart demonstrates what time a given pace in seconds per 50 yards or 50 meters will give a swimmer at the various distances. At all paces the first 50 yards or 50 meters are three seconds and the second 50 yards or meters are one second faster than the pace thereafter. This is for the reasons already stated concerning the faster speed for any length starting with a racing dive or any with a no-touch turn. Experience has shown that this is true, attributable to the causes stated above and not just to the fact that the swimmer is not yet tiring. In the middle distance or long races, the swimmer should be on pace after the first 100 yards or meters and try to hold his speed almost constant after this point.

In the freestyle a swimmer's split time will vary depending on whether he is using a touch turn or a no-touch turn. In the backstroke a swimmer does not gain as much from the backstroke start as do the swimmers of the other strokes from a diving start. His first 50 will therefore be somewhat slower than the time listed in the above charts.

While there are variations of how any individual should pace himself, depending on such factors as have already been discussed, the above chart serves as a guide to help the swimmer and coach determine the pace a swimmer should try to match in order to achieve a certain time.

If a swimmer wants to swim the 1650-yard freestyle, short course, in 18:05, he locates this time under the column labelled 1650 in Table VI–1. He then works backwards to find that he must maintain an average pace of 33 seconds per 50 yards after the first 100 yards. To swim the race most economically, he would have to approximate the split time listed in the chart.

TABLE VI–1. Even Pace Chart * (Split Times for 25 and 50 Yard Pools)

Pace per 50 Yards in Seconds	Distance: 50	100	150	200	250	300	350	400	450	500	1000	1500	1650
43	:40	1:22	2:05	2:48	3:31	4:14	4:57	5:40	6:23	7:06	14:16	21:26	23:35
42	:39	1:20	2:02	2:44	3:26	4:08	4:50	5:32	6:14	6:56	13:56	20:56	23:02
41	:38	1:18	1:59	2:40	3:21	4:02	4:43	5:24	6:05	6:46	13:36	20:26	22:29
40	:37	1:16	1:56	2:36	3:16	3:56	4:36	5:16	5:56	6:36	13:16	19:56	21:56
39	:36	1:14	1:53	2:32	3:11	3:50	4:29	5:08	5:47	6:26	12:56	19:26	21:23
38	:35	1:12	1:50	2:28	3:06	3:44	4:22	5:00	5:38	6:16	12:36	18:56	20:50
37	:34	1:10	1:47	2:24	3:01	3:38	4:15	4:52	5:29	6:06	12:16	18:26	20:17
36	:33	1:08	1:44	2:20	2:56	3:32	4:08	4:44	5:20	5:56	11:56	17:56	19:44
35	:32	1:06	1:41	2:16	2:51	3:26	4:01	4:36	5:11	5:46	11:36	17:26	19:11
34.5	:31.5	1:05	1:39.5	2:14	2:48.5	3:23	3:57.5	4:32	5:06.5	5:41	11:26	17:11	18:54.5
34	:31	1:04	1:38	2:12	2:46	3:20	3:54	4:28	5:02	5:36	11:16	16:56	18:38
33.5	:30.5	1:03	1:36.5	2:10	2:43.5	3:17	3:50.5	4:24	4:57.5	5:31	11:06	16:41	18:21.5
33	:30	1:02	1:35	2:08	2:41	3:14	3:47	4:20	4:58	5:26	10:56	16:26	18:05
32.5	:29.5	1:01	1:33.5	2:06	2:38.5	3:11	3:43.5	4:16	4:49.5	5:21	10:46	16:11	17:49.5
32	:29	1:00	1:32	2:04	2:36	3:08	3:40	4:12	4:44	5:16	10:36	15:56	17:32
31.5	:28.5	:59	1:30.5	2:02	2:33.5	3:05	3:36.5	4:08	4:39.5	5:11	10:26	15:41	17:15.5
31	:28	:58	1:29	2:00	2:31	3:02	3:33	4:04	4:35	5:06	10:16	15:26	16:59
30.5	:27.5	:57	1:27.5	1:58	2:28.5	2:59	3:29.5	4:00	4:30.5	5:01	10:06	15:11	16:43.5
30	:27	:56	1:26	1:56	2:26	2:56	3:26	3:56	4:26	4:56	9:56	14:56	16:26
29.5	:26.5	:55	1:24.5	1:54	2:23.5	2:53	3:23.5	3:52	4:21.5	4:51	9:46	14:41	16:09.5
29	:26	:54	1:23	1:52	2:21	2:50	3:19	3:48	4:17	4:46	9:36	14:26	15:53
28.5	:25.5	:53	1:21.5	1:50	2:18.5	2:47	3:15.5	3:44	4:13.5	4:41			
28	:25	:52	1:20	1:48	2:16	2:44	3:12	3:40	4:08	4:36			
27.5	:24.5	:51	1:18.5	1:46	2:13.5	2:41	3:08.5	3:36	4:03.5	4:31			
27	:24	:50	1:17	1:44	2:11	2:38	3:05	3:32	3:59	4:26			
26.5	:23.5	:49	1:15.5	1:42									
26	:23	:48	1:14	1:40									

* The first 50 is listed as 3 seconds and the second 50 as 1 second faster than the pace or time for each 50 thereafter.

TABLE VI–2. Even Pace Chart * (Split Times for 25 and 50 Meter Pools)

Pace per 50 Meters in Seconds	Distance: 50	100	150	200	250	300	350	400	800	1200	1500
50	:47	1:36	2:26	3:16	4:06	4:56	5:46	6:36	13:16	19:56	24:56
49	:46	1:34	2:23	3:12	4:01	4:50	5:39	6:28	13:00	19:32	24:26
48	:45	1:32	2:20	3:08	3:56	4:44	5:32	6:20	12:44	19:08	23:56
47	:44	1:30	2:17	3:04	3:51	4:38	5:25	6:12	12:28	18:44	23:26
46	:43	1:28	2:14	3:00	3:46	4:32	5:18	6:04	12:12	18:20	22:56
45	:42	1:26	2:11	2:56	3:41	4:26	5:11	5:56	11:56	17:56	22:26
44	:41	1:24	2:08	2:52	3:36	4:20	5:04	5:48	11:40	17:32	21:36
43	:40	1:22	2:05	2:48	3:31	4:14	4:57	5:40	11:24	17:08	21:26
42	:39	1:20	2:02	2:44	3:26	4:08	4:50	5:32	11:08	16:44	20:56
41	:38	1:18	1:59	2:40	3:21	4:02	4:43	5:24	10:52	16:20	20:26
40	:37	1:16	1:56	2:36	3:16	3:56	4:36	5:16	10:36	15:56	19:56
39	:36	1:14	1:53	2:32	3:11	3:50	4:29	5:08	10:21	15:32	19:26
38	:35	1:12	1:50	2:28	3:06	3:44	4:22	5:00	10:04	15:08	18:56
37	:34	1:10	1:47	2:24	3:01	3:38	4:15	4:52	9:48	14:44	18:26
36.5	:33.5	1:09	1:45.5	2:22	2:58.5	3:35	4:11.5	4:48	9:40	14:32	18:11
36	:33	1:08	1:44	2:20	2:56	3:32	4:08	4:44	9:32	14:20	17:56
35.5	:32.5	1:07	1:42.5	2:18	2:53.5	3:29	4:04.5	4:40	9:24	14:08	17:41
35	:32	1:06	1:41	2:16	2:51	3:26	4:01	4:36	9:16	13:56	17:26
34.5	:31.5	1:05	1:39.5	2:14	2:48.5	3:23	3:57.5	4:32	9:08	13:44	17:11
34	:31	1:04	1:38	2:12	2:46	3:20	3:54	4:28	9:00	13:32	16:56
33.5	:30.5	1:03	1:36.5	2:10	2:43.5	3:17	3:50.5	4:24	8:52	13:20	16:41
33	:30	1:02	1:35	2:08	2:41	3:14	3:47	4:20	8:44	13:08	16:26
32.5	:29.5	1:01	1:33.5	2:06	2:38.5	3:11	3:43.5	4:16	8:36	12:56	16:11
32	:29	1:00	1:32	2:04	2:36	3:08	3:40	4:12			
31.5	:28.5	:59	1:30.5	2:02	2:33.5	3:05	3:36.5	4:08			
31	:28	:58	1:29	2:00	2:31	3:02	3:33	4:04			
30.5	:27.5	:57	1:27.5	1:58	2:28.5	2:59	3:29.5	4:00			
30	:27	:56	1:26	1:56	2:26	2:56	3:26	3:56			
29.5	:26.5	:55	1:24.5	1:54							
29	:26	:54	1:23	1:52							

* The first 50 is listed as 3 seconds and the second 50 as 1 second faster than the pace or time for each **50 thereafter.**

If a swimmer wants to swim the 200-meter breaststroke in 3:04, he looks on Table VI–2 under 200 and follows it down until he finds the time closest to the goal for which he is striving. Reading across he finds his splits should approximate :44 at the 50, 1:30 at the 100, 2:17 at the 150, and 3:04 at the 200.

Few swimmers ever pace an event perfectly; however, as improvements in times become more difficult to make, it is apparent that even pacing will play a more important role.

Following are several actual record breaking swimming performances as compared with the Even Pace Chart times:

	100	200	300	400	500
Mike Burton (April, 1967, National AAU Meet)	:51.7	1:47.8	2:44.2	3:41.4	4:37.0
Time per 100		:56.1	:56.4	:57.2	:56.6
Proposed Even Pace Chart Time Schedule for a Time of 4:36.0	:52.0	1:48.0	2:44.0	3:40.0	4:36.0
Time per 100		:56.0	:56.0	:56.0	:56.0
Difference [10]	−.3	+ .1	+ .4	+ 1.2	+ .6

Don Schollander's 200-yard short course American record of 1:41.2 was set with a more even pace than that advocated in the charts.

	50	100	150	200
Don Schollander (April, 1967, National AAU Meet)	:23.8	:49.4	1:15.1	1:41.2
Time per 50		:25.6	:25.7	:26.1
Proposed Even Pace Chart Time Schedule	:23.5	:49.0	1:15.5	1:42.0
Time per 50		:25.5	:26.5	:26.5
Difference	+ .3	+ .1	− .8	− .4

Fred Schmidt's NCAA record in the 200-yard butterfly was set in a close race with Carl Robie. Both swimmers wanted the advantage of the lead at the 100-yard mark and swam the first part of the race harder

---

[10] Burton used no-touch turns, thus the differential might have been slightly less if he had touched (not significantly, however).

than they had planned. The big drop-off can be seen on Schmidt's last 50 yards. Schmidt's time would probably have been faster had his pace been more even.

	50	100	150	200
Fred Schmidt (March, 1965, NCAA Meet)	:24.5	:52.6	1:21.1	1:51.4
Time per 50		:28.1	:28.5	:30.3
Proposed Even Pace Chart Time Schedule [11]	:25.8	:53.5	1:22.3	1:51.1
Time per 50		:27.7	:28.8	:28.8
Difference	−1.3	− .9	−1.2	+ .3

Pam Kruse's American record for the 500 yards, set in April, 1967, comprised split times that were very close to the even pace times.

	100	200	300	400	500
Pam Kruse (April, 1967, National AAU Meet)	:58.7	2:01.3	3:04.3	4:07.2	5:06.9
Time per 100		:62.6	:63.0	:62.9	:59.7
Proposed Even Pace Chart Time Schedule for a Time of 5:06.0	:58.0	2:00	3:02	4:04	5:06
Time per 100		:62.0	:62.0	:62.0	:62.0
Difference	+ .7	+ .6	+ 1.0	+ .9	− 2.3

Learning Pace

A swimmer learns pace both in practice and in actual races. As in all learning, a swimmer learning pace forms an association between cause and effect (or as is mentioned in Chapter VII, between stimulus and response). The cause is the amount of effort he puts into swimming a given distance and the effect is the resulting speed, or time it takes to cover the distance. In fact, the swimmer must learn to memorize the sensations that result from application of a given amount of effort. These

[11] Interpolated from the charts since the time of 1:51 falls between two listed times.

sensations arise from the muscles and from the sensations of stress upon the various parts of the body. The water pressure upon the hands and legs as they perform their movements, and the other sensations of the movement of the body through the water, also serve as guides to help the swimmer determine his speed.

These mechanisms must be trained to the end that, when the swimmer calls on his built-in speedometer to tell him how fast to swim, he should not be more than 1 to 2 per cent off. It often happens that good pacers can swim 100 yards and state their time within a matter of a few tenths of a second. Such drills are helpful to the swimmer in teaching him pace. During every day of practice, he should learn something about pace. He should take careful note of each time he swims in the interval training, repetition training, and time trial phases of his program. They serve the dual purpose of conditioning him and of teaching him pace.

Mechanical pacing devices and pace clocks, as well as times taken by the coach, all help the swimmer evaluate his speed and, consequently, learn pace. Races and all-out time trials are a necessity for a swimmer's complete training in pace. In training for races of 100- and 200-yard or -meter distances, he should swim eight to twelve such races or time trials during the last two months of the season to assure maximum learning. In training for the longer races, he may want to swim in fewer, perhaps only four to six, all-out efforts over the racing distance, since all-out efforts over the longer distance may interrupt his training schedule. Pace for a 1650-yard or 1500-meter race can also be learned by swimming shorter races such as 1000-yard or 800-meter swims.

Various methods of teaching pace by breaking the race into segments are discussed in Chapters VIII (on training methods) and XII (on organization of practice). These techniques, whether they be *broken swims* or *simulators*, all contribute to the swimmer's complete understanding of how the race should best be swum.

A swimmer may go to a big meet and improve his best time in a 200-yard freestyle event by as much as three seconds, let us say from 1:58 to 1:55. He swims a well-paced race, yet has never swum near this time before. It is hard to understand how he trained for this pace if he had never swum as fast previously. The fact is that the swimmer, when working on pace, is learning *how much effort to exert*. All season he has been training hard and is nearly always tired, even on the days of meets. The amount of effort he exerts on these occasions gives him enough speed to swim the 200-yard distance in 1:58. Prior to his big meet of the season he tapers off for two weeks and becomes rested. Under these conditions the same amount of effort exerted by the swimmer now gives him a time of 1:55.

This illustrates the fact that, in learning pace, the swimmer must learn to analyze the amount of effort he must exert, not just be able to predict the various split times he will achieve during the race.

Pacing the Individual Medley

One of the most interesting of all competitive races is the individual medley. The relative positions of the various swimmers usually changes after the leg of each stroke is swum. In this, more than any other race, it is impossible to come up with a theoretical pace that is perfect for all swimmers because each swimmer excels in one or more strokes over some others. In this event the swimmer must truly swim his own race and largely disregard his opponents' race patterns.

A study of the split times of the various legs of the 200-yard individual medley of ten nationally ranked men swimmers compared with the best times they achieved in an all-out 50-yard effort in each stroke is presented below. It is not intended as the ideal pattern for swimming the race, but as a guide for the aspiring individual medleyist to compare with his own race pattern.

	50 Butterfly	50 Backstroke	50 Breaststroke	50 Free
1. Average of totalled elapsed time	:25.4	:55.3	1:31.2	1:59.2
2. Average split time per 50 yards in the 200-yard individual medley	:25.4	:29.9	:35.9	:28.0
3. Average best time for all-out effort for 50 yards	:24.0	:26.4	:30.4	:22.6
4. Difference between 2 and 3	+1.4	+3.5	+5.5	+5.4

An individual medley swimmer must be more critical of his split times than any other swimmer since he has more chances to commit errors. He must constantly work on improving his ability to switch from one stroke to the other and still maintain essentially the same amount of effort, even though his rate of speed may vary, and he must experiment in both practice and races with different pace patterns.

Such trial and error practice is the only way any swimmer can learn the best way to swim the various distances.

VII

The Teaching and Learning of Swimming Skills

The teaching of swimming skills is an often rewarding and challenging, but, at times, frustrating experience. While discussing the problems with a group of fellow swimming coaches and teachers, I made the statement that a great deal of confusion exists about the teaching of swimming skills. I was challenged by a fellow instructor who felt this was not true, and that it was beautifully simple. "You just drill the swimmers on the part of the stroke you are trying to teach until it becomes automatic, then you go on to the next part and do the same until you have all of the parts taught; after that you put them together."

The part-whole method of teaching seems logical and does have certain merit. Later in this chapter the whole method, the part-whole method, and the progressive-part method will be discussed on the basis of some principles and theories of learning. In many instances, however, the traditional part-whole method of teaching, as used by many teachers and advocated by many groups, is vastly inferior and even detrimental to the learning process.

Just as a swimmer must learn to swim by swimming, so a teacher must learn to teach by teaching, and a coach to coach by coaching. One administrator's evaluation of a teacher who had been teaching for 30 years was not that she had had 30 years of experience, but that she had had one year of experience 30 times. It is easy to fall into a pattern; to teach exactly the same methods and the same teaching progressions, and to make the same mistakes year after year. For fear of stubbing our toes by trying new ideas, we teachers and coaches often become so static that we lose our flexibility in thinking and resist new concepts.

If a coach or teacher is hopeful of doing a good job of teaching swimming skills, he must have more than a superficial knowledge of the principles of good stroke mechanics and of the motor learning process to guide the process effectively. The need for the first kind of knowledge is obvious because the stroke and swimming skill mechanics he teaches are literally his course content; the need for the latter kind is not so obvious but, after some deliberation, most people will agree that some knowledge of the motor learning process is essential. To sum up: the former is *what* we teach, and the latter *how*.

While this chapter is not an attempt to explore in great detail all of the factors involved in motor learning, it may serve to introduce the reader to a few principles of learning which may help him to a better understanding of the process as it relates to swimming.

PRINCIPLES OF MOTOR LEARNING

Trial and Error Learning

Many great swimmers know very little about the mechanics of their specialty, and have apparently learned their stroke mechanics with little assistance from their coaches and no accurate evaluation of their own. They are said to have learned to swim *naturally*. Belief in this phenomenon has been the basis for a permissive philosophy among many teachers and coaches. This philosophy and subsequent behavior—"there is no *one* correct way of swimming a stroke, leave the swimmer alone and he will find the pattern that is best for him"—can justify the straight arm pull, the wedge kick in the breaststroke, or almost any violation of the principles discussed in the first five chapters. It is true that there are minor variations in stroke mechanics, but these variations are based on anatomical differences in shoulder or ankle flexibility, buoyancy, and so on, or on physiological differences in such factors as speed of muscular contraction.

Great swimmers, however, never seriously violate basic mechanical principles, while poor swimmers almost always do, even though neither group may be aware of the principles or of what they are doing to observe or defy them. I have often been surprised at the answers I have received from great swimmers upon questioning them about their stroke mechanics. They are particularly unaware of what they are doing during the underwater phase of their strokes. Some freestylers have said they pull with a straight arm, when underwater movies have shown them to be bending their elbows as much as 90°. In some cases, their coaches have told them to keep their elbows straight. The obvious discrepancy between the way they have been coached, the way they think they perform, and the actual way they do perform is not exclusive to swimmers, but must include divers, baseball players, and athletes in all sports.

The baseball player, for example, when throwing a ball, feels and thinks he lets go of the ball when his hand is forward in front of him; he actually releases it at a point when his hand is almost even with his shoulder. As the ball leaves his hand, it continues in the direction it was going at the point of release. If he had let go of it in front and forward, as he believes he did, it would have proceeded downward on the path begun before release. If he had let go of the ball too soon, it would have continued to go upward. When learning to throw a ball as a child, through trial and error, he learned to associate a successful throw with certain sensations within his body (kinesthetic sensations) which were further associated with a given point of release of the ball. As these kinesthetic sensations became associated with throwing the ball properly, he established a cause and effect relationship without understanding the mechanical principles involved. Visually he was able to analyze each attempt as acceptable or unacceptable, for he could see the direction the ball went. He came to associate certain kinesthetic feelings with an acceptable throw. This is the beginning step in learning a motor skill. Most of our simple motor (physical) skills are learned by this trial and error method. However, there are limits to how far this method can take an athlete in the acquisition of more complex motor skills: in pitching a curve, drop ball, and other skilled pitches. It cannot be assumed that he will be able to learn these skills automatically.

When a child sees another person swimming the crawl stroke, he may try to imitate the general movement of the stroke. Many times, if left alone, with no instruction, he will eventually develop an effective stroke pattern. He may even, as has been suggested, develop an effective stroke if he is taught and coached improperly. Such people, who develop good stroke mechanics in spite of poor or no instruction, have been singled out by coaches as individuals who are great natural swimmers, and have been used as evidence that a swimmer either has *it* or doesn't have *it*, and that no amount of coaching or teaching will give it to him.

It is true that some people learn motor skills faster than others, but it cannot be assumed that any person, by dint of his efforts alone, will develop a perfect stroke, any more than it can be assumed that a bright college student will develop a tenable understanding of Einstein's theory of relativity without instruction or guidance. There appears to be a limit to the acquisition of motor skills without guidance. The limit may vary from one person to the next, and the guidance the person receives may be self-administered, from his coach, from visual aids, or from watching other swimmers, but it can help him acquire better or worse techniques depending upon the quality of the guidance.

How Motor Learning Occurs

Motor learning may be defined as a change in movement pattern due to reinforced practice. The nerve-muscle mechanisms involved in this change are not precisely known, although there is enough information available to make certain assumptions. When a skill is learned, a series of neuro-muscular pathways is established. These pathways include neurons or nerve cells in the brain, the spinal column, motor neurons (those going to the muscles), and the motor units of the muscle affected by these neurons.

The neuro-muscular pattern determines exactly what muscles or portions of muscles will contract and in what sequence, and in this manner determines the whole pattern of movement. It is obvious that we do not carefully think out every movement that we make and the neuro-muscular patterns for such simple motor skills as standing, walking, running, and even swimming may become so well established that nerve impulses can travel over them without much control from the higher brain center, the cerebral cortex.

Franklin Henry [1] has espoused a theory referred to by him as the *memory drum theory* in which he states that unconscious neural (nerve) patterns acquired from past experiences are stored in the central nervous system in what may be thought of as a *memory storage drum.*

When a skill is first performed, it is under the conscious control of the individual. At this stage it lacks efficiency and may be awkward and tense. As the skill is learned, through a process of repetition, it becomes

---

[1] Franklin Henry, "Increased response latency for complicated movements and a 'memory drum' theory of neuromotor reaction," *Research Quarterly,* XXXI (1960), 448-457.

a part of the person's repertoire of skills and becomes more and more automatic. It can then be thought of as stored in the memory drum where it remains available for recall.

During the initial learning stage the person must use the higher centers of his brain (the cerebral cortex) to perform the movement. He literally thinks out his task, much as a person who is learning to drive a stick shift car must think about shifting and using the clutch, or as a beginning swimmer learning the crawl stroke must think about getting his arms out of the water and kicking his legs. At this stage, dependence upon the higher centers of the brain to think out these movements makes them slower and lacking in precision. There is unwanted tension in the body due to unnecessary muscle action. As the skill being practiced becomes more automatic, muscular tension decreases and the movement becomes more refined and efficient. Parts of the complete movement pattern seem to be made without conscious awareness on the part of the performer. This part of the movement pattern has become, at least temporarily, the property of the lower central nervous system. The possibility of a memory drum of motor patterns, therefore, exists at both the cortical and the lower levels.

The Three Levels of Control of Movement

When the person wants to perform a skill he has previously learned, he calls upon the already established patterns to begin to function. The impulses that initiate the movement originate in the motor area of the cerebral cortex. The cortex is the top, covering layer of the brain which is generally considered to be the seat of memory, association, and perception, and, in fact, the center of all of our higher mental processes. This part of the brain might also be considered the master control center of our movements. As described previously, when an individual first learns a skill or changes a skill, this part of the brain thinks out the movement. This level of control of movement can be termed the *conscious level.*

As the movement is repeated over and over, the cerebral cortex begins to assign more of the control of the movement to the lower or sub-cortical centers—possibly the reticular formation and the cerebellum—the former generally considered an activating center, while the latter coordinates and refines movement. This level can be termed the *automatic level.*

A third level of control of movement, which is lower than the other two, is the *reflex control of movement* at the spinal level of the central nervous system. The part of the movement attributable to this type of control is considered nearly always right and generally results from reflex actions that protect the individual or that are predetermined by our basic nervous responses to simple stimuli. These movements are usually localized and are only part of the total movement. For example, if a swimmer is told to recover his arm in some manner which would place an abnormal stretch on a given muscle, the proprioceptors in that muscle send impulses to the spinal column, where impulses in turn are sent to the muscle in order to contract it and help it to resist injury through being overstretched.

No one can really think out a complex movement. He must rely on all three levels of control. The swimmer standing on the edge of the pool dives into the water. The cerebral cortex portion of his brain makes a decision as to which stroke will be swum. It then assigns part of the job of controlling these swimming movements to the other two levels, but, due to the fact that this section alone possesses conscious perceptivity, retains the option to take over control of the movement at will. If, for example, the cortex receives stimuli from the eyes, via the optic nerve, telling it that the turn is coming up, it can then assume control of the legs from the automatic level, direct them to stop kicking and to tuck up for the turn.

Trial and error learning is believed by most motor learning authorities to occur only at the conscious level of control. If this were true, it would appear that most people would be able to provide a reasonable verbal analysis of their movements when performing a skill. This, however, is not the case. It is my contention that much trial and error learning occurs at a sub-conscious level, and that we frequently learn to perform skills efficiently without any awareness on the part of our conscious level.

The action of the two lower levels assures us that most of our simple movements will be correct. Constant over-teaching and over-coaching of minor details or of improper mechanics can replace automatic and reflex action or naturally correct movements with movements that are completely artificial, voluntary movements. The learner should be guided through a learning experience in such a way that what is going to occur naturally in a correct manner will have an opportunity to develop without inhibition. Forcing a learner into a rigid blueprint pattern of movement can override these natural processes and permanently affect the person's learning.

This does not mean that I advocate the *laissez-faire* attitude toward teaching and coaching. I would like to state, however, that I believe the teacher should not expect the entire control of the movement to issue from careful and close control of the movement by the cortex, but that the sensations which come from the muscles and other sources should be allowed to help determine the proper movement. If there is too much conscious awareness of the movement, these impulses may be ignored and the movement will become less efficient than if less cerebral control were exercised. Stated simply: when a person is first learning a skill, complex descriptions may be harmful; conversely, lack of any guidance may also be harmful and time-wasting so far as the learning process is concerned.

If the nerve-muscle patterns lie in the memory drum too long without being used, they may fail to retain all of their ability to make the body perform in the manner it did before; in other words, part of the pattern may be lost and we say that we have forgotten exactly how to perform the skill as we did it before.

The term *retention* refers to the ability to recall previously established patterns, which, if they are practiced a few times, begin to be recalled in their previous form. People have varying ability to recall these patterns. If any of the previously learned nerve-muscle patterns either interferes with or facilitates the formation of new patterns, it is said to have *negative or positive transfer*.

Thorndike's Stimulus-Response Theory of Learning [2]

While the memory drum theory does provide a concept that can be used in forming an idea of how learning occurs, it is admittedly a superficial approach to a very complex subject. Its main purpose, originally, was to describe the specificity of learning skills and the transfer of identical elements underlying the skills. Another approach to understanding the learning process which may be of assistance to the aspiring teacher/coach is consideration of Thorndike's S-R theory of learning. A generally accepted theory of learning and one that has had a profound effect on the educational system of today, Thorndike's stimulus-response laws of learning were first developed in the 1890's. The theory hypothesizes that all learning consists primarily of the strengthening of bonds between stimulus and response.

Applications of Thorndike's laws can be made in class and workout every day of a coach's career. While the laws have been refined, and certain of the original premises have been qualified, it is my hope that the readers will gain some insight into their application (or function) to his own situation.

In developing his concept, Thorndike proposed three laws:

1. LAW OF READINESS.   This law states that learning is dependent upon the learner's readiness to act. This readiness to act is generally considered to be a *mental set* which facilitates learning or the strengthening of bonds between stimulus and response.

[2] Ernest R. Hilgard, *Theories of Learning*, 2nd ed. (New York: Appleton-Century-Crofts, Inc., 1956), pp. 15-45.

In applying this law to the teaching of swimming, the swimmer who is in this condition of readiness is more receptive to learning a new skill. Two of the functions of the teacher/coach are to create this state in the individual and team, and to recognize the state of readiness when it exists. Too often the coach does not attempt to do either of these things. A swimmer who is highly motivated and eager to learn, and is physically fresh and relatively free from tension, is more likely to be receptive to learning than the swimmer who is physically tired, poorly motivated, and in a state of emotional stress.

2. LAW OF EXERCISE. This law states that repetition strengthens the association between stimulus and response. In applying this law to motor learning, it can be said that the more often a given movement or skill is repeated, the more firmly established it becomes. Drills in which the proper movement is repeated many times are an example of an application of this law.

Since Thorndike first formulated his laws of learning, it has been shown that other factors besides mere repetition are important for strengthening the S-R bonds. Two of the contributing factors are knowledge of the results and the motivational level of the learner. Therefore, the more times a swimmer repeats a given movement, influenced by his belief that he is doing the movement correctly and is supported by a high degree of motivation, the better he will learn the swimming skill.

3. LAW OF EFFECT. This law states that the effect of the act, whether it is pleasing or displeasing, influences the chance of recurrence. Thorndike felt that a person tends to repeat a pleasant experience and to avoid an unpleasant one.

This is a very important law for the swimming coach to remember. It explains why he should try to make a learning experience a pleasant and enjoyable one, for, if a swimmer enjoys the workout and the learning experience, he will want to repeat it and will look forward to the next one. If he finds it to be unpleasant in the sense that it is unprofitable or does not gratify his desire for accomplishment, he will tend to avoid future experiences of a similar nature.

Thorndike also felt that learning was specific, and that there was transfer of learning only when the elements in the task already learned were identical to those in the task being learned.

Perceptive Ability and Learning

A human is a complex organism capable of receiving multiple stimuli, screening these stimuli, and selecting the appropriate response.

A person learning a swimming skill goes through a series of experimental observations and, on the basis of them, begins to associate stimulus with response. The ability to impart meaning to stimuli, which affect the response accordingly, is called *perception*. Individuals vary in their perceptive ability. Cratty writes,

> A more recently devised categorical system to describe individual differences in perception is the *visual* and *haptic* framework. In general, it has been found that some individuals characteristically perceive more easily through visual impressions, while others (the haptics) add the most meaning to their experiences primarily through touch and kinesthesia.[3]

While a baseball player would necessarily have to receive most of the stimuli which govern his response from visual sources, the swimmer, when he is in the water, has to rely primarily on the sensations of touch and kinesthesia.[4] A swimmer is virtually enclosed by the medium in which he works. A track man, although he is surrounded by the air, does push against the ground, can see movement, and can hear sounds clearly, thus relying on a combination of many environmental factors to tell him if he is responding properly, and interpreting these factors to keep him aware of pace and to measure the effectiveness of his responses.

The swimmer, since the amount of clearly distinguishable stimuli he receives from his eyes and ears is limited, must rely on three main sources for his stimuli. These are the feelings of touch or pressure, the vestibular sensations that inform him of his body position, and the kinesthetic sensations that arise in his muscle tendons and joints. Years ago, Ernst Bachrach said that, when he first saw Johnny Weissmuller swim, he knew Johnny had "feel" for the water and would someday be a great swimmer. Many coaches have had this impression when they have felt they could identify a swimmer with this "natural feel" for the water. I experienced this impression when, while teaching at a teachers college, I saw a college freshman in my swimming class who had never swum competitively, but who had this nebulous attribute. I was so convinced that he had this *feel* that I told him, if he wanted to work for it, he could some day set world records in the freestyle events. Three years later George Breen made this prediction come true by setting three world records in the distance freestyle.

[3] Bryant J. Cratty, *Movement Behavior and Motor Learning*, Health Education, Physical Education, and Recreation Series (Philadelphia: Lea & Febiger, 1964), p. 133.
    [4] Kinesthesia is defined as the sense by which motion, weight, and the position of the various parts of the body are determined. Kinesthetic sensations arise from stimulation of sensory nerve endings in muscle tendons and joints. Kinesthetic sense helps to determine the degree of contraction in a muscle, the degree of bend in a joint, and the relationship of one part of the body to the other.

At one point, I personally felt that the trait that distinguished a good natural swimmer from an average or poor swimmer was the sensitivity of his hands to pressure changes of the water when he was pulling his hands through the water. A few years back I used a test which measured the ability of the person to perceive these changes of pressure on his palms by testing them with varying weights. The subject would express whether each subsequent weight was lighter, heavier, or the same as the preceding one. The first subjects I tested were two Olympic team members and their scores were compared to the scores achieved by two beginning swimmers who were having difficulty learning to swim. I was encouraged by the results of the tests, since the scores of the two good swimmers were much higher than those of the two non-swimmers. Subsequent testing has not borne out these findings and, while there may be more ability among good natural swimmers to distinguish pressure changes on their hands, further research will be necessary to learn if this is true.

It is important that a swimmer be able at any time to evaluate the effectiveness of his stroke by determining how fast he is going. In this manner he begins to associate certain kinesthetic sensations throughout the body with certain external stimuli which tell him he is swimming effectively. Once again, this illustrates the association of cause and effect. The swimmer is able to perceive how fast he is going by:

1. Water pressure on his head, shoulders, and other parts of his body; the faster he goes, the greater the water pressure.

2. Visual cues, which are used more by some swimmers than by others. Such people might like to swim in the end lane, next to the wall, in order to gain an impression of how fast they are going by the speed with which they see the side of the pool going by or by other visual cues. These swimmers might not like long course or outdoor swimming because there are fewer visual cues by which they can evaluate their performances.

3. Auditory cues; the importance of sound in giving the swimmer an idea of his speed represents an unknown element. In discussing the subject with a number of swimmers, I have had their subjective opinion that they can distinguish a variation in sound as they swim at different speeds.

Perhaps a great natural swimmer, possessing this nebulous quality of *feel for the water,* is simply a person able to perceive these multiple sensations, impart meaning to them, and adjust his stroke pattern accordingly. He may or may not be consciously aware of this process of discriminate learning. He may be swimming entirely on impressions and sensations without knowing what he is doing in terms of actual stroke mechanics. This theory could explain the fact that so many great athletes do not know much about the mechanics of their performances.

Natural Swimming Ability

Any person who has taught swimming knows that people vary widely in their ability to learn swimming skills. Other factors than the natural ability of general perception or *feel for the water* enter into the ability to learn them, the psychological set of the learner being one. It is clear, however, that the role of natural ability is important in determining how far a swimmer can progress with or without instruction. Just as a person with below-average intelligence could not hope to earn a doctoral degree in atomic physics, so a person with a low level of natural swimming ability cannot expect or be expected to set world records. We do not know how to evaluate *feel for the water,* but we do know that this trait, plus the others of strength, flexibility, and power or speed of muscular contraction are needed in high degree to make world class swimmers.

While this natural ability to learn swimming skills is an important factor, there are others in the learning situation that play an important role in how fast and how accurately a swimmer can learn these skills. Cratty states:

> . . . some individuals seem able to learn quickly any skill to which they are exposed. At present, the subject is a controversial one. There is an indication, however, that these quick learners are highly motivated, possess above average strength, are able to analyze quickly and accurately the mechanics of a task, and are relatively free from excess tension which might impede performance. The isolation and identification of a single general motor educability factor, however, seems to be a tenuous experimental undertaking.[5]

This natural swimming ability is primarily an inherent factor, beyond the influence of the coach or teacher. The latter can design his program and conduct the teaching situation, however, in such a way that maximum learning occurs. Some of the factors that affect the learning process are the degree of motivation, anxiety, stress and tension, and the manner of presentation of the skills to be learned.

MOTIVATION. The coach and teacher must set the stage in such a way that those who are learning the skills are highly motivated. Motivation may be defined as a general state of *arousal to action,* and, in all learning, determines the receptivity of the individual to learning.

It has been referred to by some as the catalyzer in the learning process, since a high degree of motivation usually speeds up the process. While some individuals are highly self-motivated (to use a term in common use by coaches, they have drive!) to learn new skills or to improve on

[5] Cratty, *Movement Behavior and Motor Learning,* p. 235.

the ones they have, the coach cannot assume that the entire class or team will have this arousal to action attitude in high degree. He must, therefore, be ready to present his material in such a manner that the entire group will be motivated to act or, in this case, to learn.

Motivation is not an isolated factor and should always be considered in day by day planning of the program. Its association with the other factors of learning will be given consideration as they are discussed in this chapter. Methods of motivating learning are discussed in greater detail in Chapter XII.

ANXIETY, STRESS, AND TENSION.   These three states may be deterrents to learning and performance or, depending on their degree, the learner, the skill, and the situation, may be facilitators. For example: two swimmers are being taught a new skill, a flip turn, by a highly demanding and critical coach. Both may experience similar degrees of anxiety, but the speed of learning of one may be aided while that of the other may be detrimentally affected.

Anxiety is defined as the state of being uneasy, apprehensive, or worried about what might happen—misgiving.[6] It is hard to predict precisely what effect the various levels of anxiety will have on the learning process of any one individual. Generally, however, extreme anxiety will detrimentally affect the learning rate of most individuals, as well as their general motor performance, while a slight degree of anxiety seems to improve their rate of learning. In the example set forth above, both swimmers want to perform well, but in the presence of extreme anxiety, tension and apprehension may prevent the slower learner from coordinating his movements properly.

The intelligent coach/teacher is able to analyze the level of anxiety of the team or class or even the individual and to reduce or increase the pressure he imposes, in order that the class members may not be too relaxed and indifferent or too tense to learn properly. The coach or teacher who expects and demands too little or the one who expects and demands too much will both finish short of optimum results.

A certain amount of muscular tension is also desirable when a person is learning or performing a motor skill. The desirable amount brings about a readiness for the muscle to contract and, according to some investigators, raises the level of excitation in the muscles via cerebral cortex action. As a swimmer stands on the starting mark, waiting for the sound of the gun, he holds his arms down and, while the muscles in the arms are not held tensely, they are also not completely relaxed. Rather, they have enough controlled tension to be ready to move quickly at the sound of the gun.

---

[6] *Webster's New World Dictionary of the American Language* (Cleveland and New York: World Publishing Company, 1951), p. 67.

The kind of tension that is detrimental to learning and performing is that in which there is so much unnecessary contraction that it interferes with the correct movement.

Muscles work in pairs or in groups; when one muscle performs a given action, there is another muscle or combination of muscles which can supply precisely the opposite action. Thus, when one muscle or muscle group contracts, its antagonistic muscle or muscle group tends to relax. The coordination of contraction and relaxation, a function of the central nervous system, is referred to as *reciprocal innervation*,[7] and occurs automatically. This trait, as do all traits in humans, varies in degree from one person to the next. Those having this trait in high degree move with economy, and it is this particular trait which, as an aspect of coordination, is important to all athletes, particularly swimmers.

Excessive tension indicates that state in which the person lacks good reciprocal innervation. Certain conditions contribute to it: a person suffering from extreme anxiety may be excessively tense, and, as a result, less receptive to learning correct swimming skills. Tension and anxiety are increased by a stressful situation, particularly in high anxiety persons. The coach/teacher should try to avoid placing the learner in a condition of extreme stress. A tense coach, who repeatedly reprimands his swimmers for their performance in practice or competition or reduces their self-esteem, creates so much tension and anxiety in the learner that the subtle sensations he receives from his kinesthetic sensory receptors and from his pressure receptors are completely overridden by the tension created in the muscles. Learning under these conditions becomes as impossible as in the other extreme condition in which the coach/teacher is so indifferent and casual that he provides no motivation for the swimmer. The parents of the learner or competitor can also cause this stressful condition. When too much is expected of the person, either by the coach or his parents, in learning or performing, the results can be negative, depending once again upon the individual and his reaction to stress.

Presentation of Material

Before adopting a plan of action or a method of presenting his material, the coach must evaluate the learners, the situation, and himself. Such factors as the maturity level of his swimmers, their attention span, and their level of skill are important considerations in evaluating them. A different approach must be used with young age-group swimmers than with college swimmers; young swimmers can be shown the general pattern of the crawl arm pull by the method of having them lift themselves

---

[7] The term, *reciprocal inhibition*, can be used interchangeably with this term.

out of the pool by pushing down on the edge of the pool with their hands, rotating the humerus as they bend their elbows, and then extending the elbows. A college swimmer may be shown the same movement accompanied by a more sophisticated description and the use of a spring scale to show that the pull is stronger when the proper mechanics are used. The short span of attention of the younger group usually prevents more detailed explanations and, often, lengthy technical descriptions by the coach to swimmers of this age hurt more than they help.

TWO METHODS OF DESCRIBING MOVEMENTS.   There are two methods of describing a given movement to a learner. The movement may be described to the individual in terms of the *feelings* or *sensations* he will feel. For example, in describing the crawl arm pull using this technique, the swimmer might be told to place his hands in the water, then to feel a strong catch, and proceed to keep a relative, constant pressure on the water as he tries to push it backward toward his feet. This brief description conveys an idea to the swimmer of the general sensations he should feel as he pulls his arm backward, but does not tell him how he should do the movement mechanically. At the other extreme, an analytical description of the skill may be offered, along with a detailed mechanical analysis of the stroke, such as the following: place the arm in the water with an angle of 165° between the lower arm and the upper arm; after the hand becomes submerged in the water, the elbow should reach complete extension. As the catch is made at a depth of six to eight inches below the surface, the elbow begins to bend until it reaches an elbow bend of 90°, when the hand is directly under the body, and so on.

Objective assessment of mechanical techniques has become so exact that there is a danger of moving so much toward the latter technique that complete disregard of the teaching of sensations and impressions results. Coaches who had formerly been swimmers, but have no technical knowledge of stroke technique, are able to help some swimmers by using the *impression* approach. It often happens, however, that interpretations of terms among different people vary, and confusion occurs when such a coach attempts to communicate verbally. One backstroke swimmer, while describing his impressions when swimming well, has said, "I feel I am riding real flat and high in the water like a canoe, with my head completely out of the water and my legs thrusting me through my arm pull." This statement would be hard to interpret to a learning swimmer who might do everything wrong in trying to recreate these impressions in himself. The subjective impressions of the learning swimmer may have been very real to him, but they lack real substance to other people. We might study this swimmer when he was swimming well and, through the use of underwater photography, determine objectively that the swimmer's body was rolling 45° to each side and that his arm reached a maximum bend of 90° at the elbow. There is no disagreement as to what is meant by 45° of roll or an elbow bend of 90°. The swimmer, however, cannot carry a protractor with him and measure the degree of roll or the degree of elbow bend. To help him visualize exactly what the movement should be like, this type of description helps, but it does not give him much of an idea of how the movement will feel to him. Coaches and teachers often use either of these techniques to the exclusion of the other, and can be classified as *impression* coaches or *analytical* coaches. The foregoing explanation of the weaknesses and strengths of both methods makes it clear that I favor a method that is a combination of the two.

In Chapters II through V of this book most of the space has been devoted to an analytical evaluation of the stroke mechanics of the four competitive strokes. Some effort has been spent on impressions but, since a statement of impressions is likely to be interpreted in so many different ways, this particular method of teaching is being left to the individual coach so that he may establish a common acceptance of terms with his swimmers. When attempting to convey an impression through the medium of language, the spoken word is far superior to the printed one.

If the coach has not experienced these sensations himself, he can ask his swimmers, particularly the good ones, to express the impressions and sensations they experience when they are swimming well. I have frequently asked this of my own swimmers and their opinions and impressions have enabled me to better understand them, not only by improving our ability to speak the same language, but also by increasing their awareness of their ability to identify their sensations and impressions.

At times, a coach can combine an analytical description of a stroke with an impression of it in the same coaching period. He can tell the backstroker to finish his arm pull by pushing his palm toward the bottom of the pool at the end of his arm pull until his hand is approximately six inches below his hips. As he pushes downward, he can be told to try to get the impression that this action causes the shoulder on the same side to lift up and over the water during the recovery.

The Skill Impression Method of Teaching

When a person is first exposed to a new physical skill such as a new swimming stroke, he need not be given a complex description of the skill. All he needs at the beginning is a general impression of the skill. He may receive a sufficiently good impression to start the learning process by merely watching someone perform the skill for only a few moments.

The teacher might introduce the butterfly stroke to a group of swimmers in the following manner: 1. by demonstrating or having someone demonstrate the butterfly stroke, 2. by presenting a brief description such as the following, "recover the arms out of the water by throwing them out, wide to the side and then forward, keep the legs together and kick them up and down."

After the swimmer has learned the general pattern of the movement, the teacher can introduce the details of the movement. If there are parts of the movement or some aspects of its timing that occur naturally, perhaps the timing of the kick, there is no need for the teacher to even mention this in his description or discussion.

The swimmer now is engaged in cumulative learning; that is, he is accumulating knowledge of and ability to perform accurately many of the small skills that make up a more efficient total stroke.

Presentation of a Swimming Skill

When a swimmer is first introduced to a new skill, assuming he has little idea of it or a wrong impression of how it should be done, he must be made to understand how it should be performed. The idea can be presented to him in four ways.

1. ACTUAL VISUALIZATION.   This can be done through moving and still pictures, charts, gestures, or demonstration of the actual skill. For the more advanced swimmers the use of slow motion or stop projection movies is particularly effective since movies at normal speed, or even the actual movement, may occur at a speed the eyes are not capable of analyzing critically. The use of charts, sequence pictures, or drawings is helpful at all levels of swimming proficiency and they are not used enough by most coaches. Pictures in any form, gestures or attitudes of the body or a limb of the body can often be more meaningful than words, particularly to a young child or in a pool area where the teacher's or coach's words are muffled by poor acoustics.

2. VERBALIZATION.   The importance of good verbalization or a mutual understanding of a given word or phrase has already been mentioned. The learner, however, should not always be on the receiving end of the verbalization, but should be able to communicate his own thoughts in words. This encourages the thinking process and fortifies learning, since all of us want to verbalize our experiences and will go to a lot of thought and effort to do so effectively. In this manner the movement can be better visualized analytically and the sensations better identified during actual swimming.

The coach cannot always listen to each swimmer describe his stroke or the impressions he has as he swims. However, he can arrange a teaching session in order that each swimmer may have this experience with another swimmer. The coach can describe the mechanics of a certain movement (for example, the crawl arm pull) to the entire group in a regular instructional period. He can then divide the group into pairs. One swimmer in each pair is designated as an assistant coach and the other as the swimmer. All the swimmers assigned to be assistant coaches put on underwater face masks or goggles, go into the water, and submerge themselves. The persons designated as swimmers swim directly toward the assistant coaches, while the latter watch for such things as the pattern of arm pull and the degree of elbow bend. Back on the deck, they try to describe the stroke as it should be swum. The process is then reversed, with the assistant coach becoming the swimmer, and the swimmer the assistant coach. This particular technique of stroke instruction is not meant to supplant the head coach's stroke correction, but is useful in promoting the learning process for the reasons already mentioned. The person who learns the most is often the one assuming the role of the assistant coach, because he must analyze critically and then verbalize his conclusions. This process of group interaction stimulates the persons involved into an exchange of information. It also facilitates learning because of the stimulus of social interplay.

It is important for the coach to discuss stroke technique with each swimmer as often as possible, in addition to sessions with the swimmers in a group. This discussion should involve verbalization on the part of the swimmers as well as the coach, again in order to expedite the learning process. Both the coach and the swimmer may learn together—the swimmer learning something about the technique his coach wants him to acquire, and the coach learning where any confusion on the part of the swimmer may lie, as well as something about the sensations the swimmer has had as he swims.

3. GETTING THE "FEEL" OF THE MOVEMENT. As has been mentioned, a person interprets his movements in the water largely through sensations which arise within his body (kinesthetic sensations). A person is able to swim a good stroke with his eyes closed, so it can be assumed that the eyes are not always needed to help analyze movements.

A swimmer can simulate or practice movements and positions out of water that will help him develop a *feel* for what he should do in the water. This practice can take the form of exercises or drills which are as close to the actual movement as they can be made. These exercises or drills can be made against no resistance, or against such resistance as barbells, stretch cords, and pulley weights. The latter method is best since the sensations which will occur during the actual swimming movement are more closely related to sensations which occur when the person works against resistance.

Isometric contractions can also be used effectively in helping the swimmer acquire the *feel* for a given position of the body or limbs at a particular point in the stroke. An isometric contraction permits the learner to focus his attention on a specific point in the movement. Isometric contractions are also a teaching device useful in conveying visually such factors as the specific degree of elbow or wrist bend at a given point in the stroke. Isometric contractions are helpful, but they should not be used exclusively; some methods using movement should always be included in teaching the swimmer to recognize these sensations.

Manipulation by the instructor or another person of the learner's arms, legs, or head in a manner that imitates the proper movement may be helpful in learning that movement. The person teaching the movement may direct the learner to exert some force as he imitates the movement in order that the sensations of muscular effort which arise within the body may more closely imitate the sensations that occur when the swimmer will be working against the resistance of the water.

The use of mirrors, or of films made during actual swimming, or the above mentioned drills help the swimmer to associate kinesthetic sensations with his actual performance. I have placed a mirror underwater and have had swimmers wearing goggles watch their own underwater stroke mechanics as they swim toward the mirror. This technique has also proved to be helpful in the acquisition of better understanding of what the swimmers are doing. Perhaps some day our pools will have these mirrors built into their walls as standard teaching devices.

4. MENTAL PRACTICE OR CONTEMPLATIVE ANALYSIS.   It is possible for a person to learn something about the mechanics of movement through contemplative thinking or mental practice. A coach might tell a swimmer to think over a movement they have been discussing during a skull session, and to ask any questions he may have about that movement the next day. This kind of physically inactive, but mentally active, contemplation can aid in the learning of a complex motor skill. The learner may draw from his experiences of observing others perform, watching himself and others in movies, or himself in a mirror. His discussions with the coach and other experiences, some of which have been mentioned, provide him with the material needed to make his contemplation meaningful.

THE APPLICATION OF MOTOR-LEARNING PRINCIPLES
TO TEACHING STROKE MECHANICS

The preceding part of this chapter has been devoted to the motor learning process; the last portion will be confined to the application of this process to learning and teaching swimming skills. Although the description in the first section may seem an over-simplification of the process to a specialist in motor learning, to many people, uninitiated in the area, it may be complex and hard to apply to the actual class or team situation.

It has already been shown that too much formal guidance in teaching skills can be harmful, while too little or no guidance can be equally undesirable. Herein lies the great challenge for coaches and teachers. The coach must strive to introduce the optimal amount of and the right kind of guidance at the appropriate time. The logical pattern of teaching a skill would be to offer the maximum amount of guidance during the initial stages of learning and to provide the learner with more opportunities to try unguided practice during the later stages, the instructor being on hand only to correct mistakes.

This principle applies not only to learning new skills, but also to the correction of wrong movements. One of the criticisms of swimming coaches heard most often is that they don't work enough on stroke mechanics. Once the actual training season has begun, the coach is busy conducting practice with the emphasis on conditioning his swimmers, rather than improving their stroke mechanics. If he takes too much time from practice to work on stroke mechanics, he will not have his swimmers in top shape. True, he can drop a few words here and there, but he and the swimmers are primarily concerned with how they are swimming their repeats, and so on. The ideal time for the major portion of the stroke work in terms of motor learning and of time available is early in the swimming season, before hard swimming training has begun.

A complex movement such as a swimming stroke, a racing start, or a turn is difficult to change. This change results in a delay of response, and major changes generally should not be made during the actual competitive season. As an example, we might take a swimmer who has a very poor arm movement in making his start. He always gets off a little slower than the rest of the swimmers. When his arm movement is corrected during the height of the season so that it is mechanically correct, he will doubtless get off the mark even more slowly because of this delay in response. The new movement must be thought out and will be tense and unnatural, and will remain so for several weeks. If he were able to continue to use it for this length of time, he would eventually master it and be able to get off much faster than when he was using the incorrect arm action.

Unfortunately, both the coach and swimmer often come to the conclusion that, since the new method does not give better results immediately, it should be discarded. *Corrections in mechanics, even though they are correct, do not always give better results immediately.*

At Indiana University our swimming classes and swimming teams follow similar patterns of learning new skills or correcting already acquired skills.

Early Learning Stage—Pre-Season or Early Season Period

In the case of our competitive swimmers, this period occurs at the very beginning of our training period in September and October, when we are on a heavy program of dry land exercises and are not doing a great deal of training in the water. The purpose of this period is to make the swimmer familiar with the terminology we will be using, mechanical principles and their application to swimming strokes and starts and turns, and to give the learner a general and, at times, specific idea of what is expected of him. During this time the swimmer will begin to visualize, verbalize, and get the feel of the desired movements.

We approach the accomplishments of this program in several ways; we have classroom sessions in which:

A. we discuss mechanical principles and their application;
B. we discuss the desired mechanics to be used in the skill;
C. we show slow motion and stop projection movies of both desirable and undesirable movements;
D. we discuss sensations and impressions that occur during the performance of the correct and incorrect movements;
   1. we use dry land exercises, particularly isometric contractions, to help the swimmers visualize and feel certain positions which are desirable or undesirable;
   2. we have swimmers work with one another in the water in order that they might help each other achieve proper movements.

Discussions of mechanical principles may often have to be on a very elementary level during the first sessions. If a teacher tries to give an immature learner a mechanical explanation of all the principles underlying performance of a complex motor skill, more confusion than enlightenment may result. The coach must take into consideration the maturity level of his swimmers, as well as the level of information they already possess. As the swimmers begin to understand the mechanical principles underlying their task, they will be more highly motivated and cooperative in correcting their skills.

Judd [8] found that when boys who were shooting at an underwater target with bows and arrows were instructed in the principles of light refraction, their accuracy was little affected when depth of the water was changed. A second group which had had no instruction in the principles of light refraction experienced difficulty in adjusting to changing conditions.

[8] C. H. Judd, "Movement and Consciousness," *Psychological Review,* VII (1905), 199-226.

However, the mere fact that a person has knowledge of the mechanical principles of a skill does not mean that he will be able to apply this knowledge. It is up to the teacher to help the learner do this in a meaningful way. His understanding will help him see what his teacher means when he says certain stroke mechanics are correct or incorrect. He will often become able to make certain stroke corrections himself in the same way the knowledgeable archers made corrections in Judd's study.

The use of simple demonstrations of the applications of these principles will help the learner to understand the principles, as well as to depict the applications. In the first five chapters of this book demonstrations of this kind have been discussed.

During classroom sessions the movies and discussions should be designed to be interesting as well as informative. The sessions set the stage for the swimmer to be in the *state of readiness to act or learn* of which Thorndike speaks. The coach cannot force the learner to accept an idea or technique against the learner's wishes. He must help the learner prepare for learning, and the early season sessions help to do this.

Since the swimmer often regresses in his performance after changing a movement pattern, major changes in stroke mechanics should be made early in the season. If we could study the skill learning curve of an individual, it would probably reveal that, when working on a new skill, an immediate improvement is often followed by a plateau on which there is no further improvement or even decreased improvement. Coaches should prepare their athletes for this possibility in order to avoid the frustration which usually accompanies this plateau period.

Reel, in referring to this phenomenon in connection with coaching track athletes, states:

> When an athlete first comes out and starts practicing, the tendency is for him to worsen rather than improve. As the training proceeds, additional stress is placed upon the specific muscles needed to perform the movements of the athlete's particular event or activity. The muscles will at first break down under the demand of the additional work. Then as the need for improvement is realized, the muscles will gradually strengthen and the athlete's performance will improve.
>
> An example of how the learning curve works might be as follows: A boy comes onto the athletic field and starts to high jump. He clears 5′ 2″ without previous conditioning or training. This indicates he has some potential and might become a good high jumper, so he reports to a coach and begins scientific workouts. He conditions his legs, takes exercises, works on form and at the end of the first week, clears 5′ 4″. Thus encouraged, he sets about training in earnest, and before long jumps for height again. This time, after repeated trials, he clears no better than 5′ 0″. This is the critical point in the embryonic athlete's life. After working out for a month with experi-

enced help from a coach, he fails to better his initial effort—achieved without training or coaching. Why work? Why train? Now, according to the psychologists, is when he should really go to work. He will begin to have "plateaus of learning" and "degrees of improvement." Gradually he will improve, and once improvement begins, it will continue until he has reached his physiological limit. The degree of improvement is large at first, but as progress continues gets smaller and smaller. Time plateaus, conversely, are short at first and gradually lengthen. The important point to get across to the young athlete in this connection is that in ALL fields of learning there comes a point where you perform with less achievement after practicing than you did before practicing. This is natural and happens to EVERYONE in all physical learning situations. The champion is the one who works through this momentary delay in improvement, and goes on to achieve greater performance and approach his personal absolute potential.

Curves of motor learning are characterized by spurts of improvement and by plateaus appearing as periods of no improvement.

Learning is characterized by rapid initial improvement.

Learning plateaus often represent periods during which a new set of habits is being formed, and these new sets of habits probably are the basis for later improvement.

Following a plateau the learner normally makes further improvement at a slower rate than the initial improvement.

A plateau signifies the learner has mastered the lower-order habits, but they are not yet sufficiently automatic to leave the attention free to attack the higher-order habits.

Lack of motivation, faulty training methods and the limitations of poor technique account for some plateaus.

The beginner must understand that all champions have passed through similar periods where progress seems at a standstill.[9]

Every individual learns at a different rate and responds differently to the various methods of presenting the skill. The slow learner obviously takes more time to learn, and this requires more patience on the part of the coach, who must remember that his ultimate swimming potential may be as great or greater than that of the fast learner. Whereas one swimmer may learn a great deal from the movies he studies and little from manipulation of his arms, legs, or head by the coach in a pattern similar to that of the desired swimming stroke movements, the reverse may be true of another swimmer. For this reason it is recommended that many various forms of instruction, as suggested earlier in this chapter, be tried.

During the early season period at Indiana University sessions are

[9] S. F. Vincent Reel, "Learning and the Learning Curve," *Track Theory and Technique,* Asian Track & Field Coaches Assoc. (Richmond, Calif.: Worldwide Publishing Co., 1963), pp. 74-75.

held for the entire group of swimmers when principles that apply to all strokes are discussed. Such sessions deal with starts, turns, general mechanical principles, and so on. When a specific stroke is being discussed only those swimmers whose specialty it is and the individual medley swimmers attend the session. The plan for practice sessions during a typical week in October is outlined below.

Monday, 3:00 to 3:50 P.M. Entire team does exercises together, these exercises imitating the swimming movements as closely as possible, in order that the transfer of learning to the actual stroke movement in the water will be optimum.

3:50 to 4:10 P.M. Entire team looks at movies of swimming starts—both good and poor starts, but with the emphasis on good starts. Discussion of mechanical principles involved in racing starts.

4:10 to 4:30 P.M. Practice of starts. Each swimmer does a start which is discussed by the entire group as to flaws and good points. Next step is to have the group, working in pairs, help one another. A few dry land drills in practicing the arm swing can be used early in the practice to familiarize the group with a given movement.

4:30 to 5:00 P.M. Swimming workout. Swim one mile using fartlek (speed play) method.

Tuesday, 3:00 to 3:50 P.M. Entire team does exercises together.

3:50 to 4:30 P.M. Breaststrokers meet in a classroom to look at both out of water and underwater movies of good breaststroke swimmers, as well as recent movies of the swimmers themselves in order that they may note the good points and defects. The movies are followed by a discussion of mechanical principles and stroke movements, conducted in an informal manner; with remarks by both coach and swimmer on sensations and impressions which the swimmers should be aware of along with an analytical approach to these sensations. Gestures should be used to indicate arm, leg, or head position. On a given day, emphasis can be on one part of the stroke only, such as focussing on the mechanics of the breaststroke kick.

4:30 to 5:15 P.M. Coach and breaststroke swimmers go to underwater window for the purpose of watching one swimmer at a time. Discussion should ensue in which the coach helps the swimmers analyze one another's stroke mechanics. If an underwater window is not available, individual face plates and masks can be used. After watching each swimmer underwater, the group should go into the pool to practice the skills it has just discussed.

While the coach and breaststrokers are in the classroom, the other swimmers of the team should be doing the swimming workout of 1 to 1½ miles total distance under the direction of the assistant coach, team captain, or manager.

Wednesday, 3:00 to 3:50 P.M. Exercise period for entire group as usual.

3:50 to 4:30 P.M. Skull session for all freestylers and individual medley swimmers, following the same procedure as for breaststrokers on Tuesday.

During the skull session the remaining team members will work in the pool for ten minutes on the mechanics as discussed on Monday. They might then do their workout of 1 to 1½ miles, thinking of the points discussed in the last skull session, this group to be supervised as before by the assistant coach, captain, or manager.

Thursday. Same procedure as during the previous workout except that the skull session will be devoted to the backstroke.

Friday. Same procedure as that followed on the four previous days except that the skull session will deal with the butterfly and the problems of the individual medley swimmers.

During the week following the week just described, the coach might want to meet with one or another group once or twice in the classroom situation to discuss such factors as turn, dry land exercises, or conditioning. As long as the coach can present effective material in this manner, he should do so. It makes his job of teaching and coaching much easier. Football skull sessions are considered indispensable, and there is no reason why they should not become an integral part of most competitive swimming programs.

Mid-Season Period

In November and December, as the tempo of workouts increases and more emphasis is placed on conditioning, less time can be devoted to skull sessions and the teaching of new skills. As the swimmer swims, kicks, or pulls his practice lengths, he should be aware of whether he is performing his stroke movements properly. The coach can still make major corrections, if they are necessary, but most of such corrections should have been completed by this point in the season.

This period should be considered as the time when the swimmer begins to stabilize his stroke patterns and begins to develop the polish of his techniques that he will need in order to perform almost automatically. His attention can be focused on the defects he has, while little attention need be devoted to the movements he is doing correctly.

As the swimmers are working out, the coach can make stroke corrections. This will be easy or difficult depending on how effective the skull sessions were during the early season stage. Often just a phrase from the coach during the rest interval between repeat swims will be enough to let the swimmer know what correction he needs to make. Some use of movies, discussions, pictures, and isometric contractions can also be made during this period in order to effect the refinements of stroke technique.

Another kind of learning begins to become important during this period. The strategy, pace, and effort which are essential to swimming the various competitive races must be learned.

Competitive Season Period—January, February, March

During this period major changes in stroke mechanics should be avoided unless the swimmer is performing very poorly. As has been explained, such changes frequently result in poorer performances for a considerable time. Minor changes, however, may be made, and it is important that the coach and swimmer remain alert to the appearance of stroke defects which might detrimentally affect performance. Underwater and out of water moving pictures should be taken of the swimmers when they are at their best in order that they may be used as a standard in the event that defects do develop.

The final touch on learning strategy, pace, and effort should be made during this period of time. This can be done through races, time trials, repeat swims, and general pace work. The coach and swimmer should discuss the races, study the split times, and critically analyze them in order to decide how the swimmer's performance can be improved.

Learning never ceases during the entire season—the emphasis on different phases of the performance, however, does change.

Part-whole, Whole, and Progressive-part Methods

The *part-whole* method of teaching swimming strokes has been used by a majority of swimming programs over the past 50 years or more. It has become so firmly entrenched as the best method that, despite research projects which have shown the *whole* method to be superior for most learners, the use of the part-whole method continues to dominate.

One of the difficulties in differentiating between the whole and the part-whole methods of teaching skills is in distinguishing and designating what is a *whole* and what is a *part*. In swimming, the whole method is that used by most people who learn to swim by themselves. They try the whole stroke without breaking it into its various parts, i.e., kick, pull, breathing, and so on. Most of the motor skills that people acquire such as walking, running, and throwing, have been learned by the whole method. In interviewing the members of the U.S.A. Olympic Swimming Team of 1964, it was interesting to discover that only a few of them had been taught to swim in classes. Most had had no formal instruction until they began swimming competitively.

It is possible to use the whole method of teaching and still work on various parts of the stroke. These parts, however, are not practiced in isolated drills; the swimmer's attention is focused on the particular part of the stroke he is working on, while he also continues to perform the rest of the stroke. When the part-whole method is used, the various parts of the stroke are taught separately and practiced in isolated drills, i.e., kicking drills, arm drills, breathing drills, and so on. When all of the parts have been learned separately, they are combined into the whole stroke.

At Indiana University we have alternately taught beginning and advanced swimming classes with the whole and the part-whole methods. The classes taught by the whole method have progressed at a faster rate than those taught by the part-whole method.

Niemeyer's [10] study also showed the superiority of the whole method over the part-whole method. The subjects in his study who were taught the whole stroke as a unit were able to swim the stroke with better form, sooner, faster, and further than could the group taught with the part-whole method. The group taught with the whole method swam an average of 845 yards, while those taught the other method only averaged 442 yards.

There are two apparent reasons to explain the inferiority of the part-whole method to the whole method for most learners. First, it is wasteful of time because time has to be spent in learning all of the parts and then in integrating the parts. Second, it is almost impossible to imitate the exact movement as it will be used in the whole stroke when the swimmer isolates the part and drills on it alone. An example of this difficulty is the kick in the crawl stroke. When a swimmer uses the whole crawl stroke, the kick does not move straight up and down, but thrusts diagonally sidewards when the body rolls on its longitudinal axis, thus fulfilling its role as a stabilizer. When the kick is practiced by itself the feet kick up and down in the vertical plane at all times.

It can be seen that the swimmer is practicing a different movement than he will use in the whole stroke.

It is significant to understand that *transfer of learning* will only occur in the elements of a task that are identical to elements in a task already learned. Since the kick when practiced alone contains some elements which are identical (such as plantar flexion of the feet) and some which are not (such as the diagonal thrust of the feet, already mentioned), only part of the kicking skill will transfer to the whole stroke. I do not mean to imply that kicking drills have no value, only that the value is confined to conditioning and over-learning. These drills have little place in isolated or part drills in the initial phase of learning a motor skill where they may harmfully affect the learning process.

Another method of teaching, called the *progressive-part* method, consists of practicing the initial two parts of a skill separately, then putting them together and progressively adding skill parts until the skill is complete. An example of this type of teaching is to have the swimmer learn

[10] Roy K. Niemeyer, "Part versus whole methods and massed versus distributed practice in the learning of selected large muscle activities." Proceedings, College Physical Education Association, 1958, pp. 122-25.

the crawl arm stroke and leg kick separately, then to combine them, followed by learning the breathing, and so on.

The method of teaching a skill should be dependent upon the complexity of the skill and the motor educability of the learner. In learning simple skills the whole method is superior to the other two. In learning more complex skills the part-whole method and the progressive-part method are superior to the whole. Is a swimming stroke a simple or a complex skill? For some swimmers with a high degree of motor educability it is a simple skill, for others with low motor educability it is a complex skill. Poor learners might have to be taught the swimming strokes with many part drills, while these seem unnecessary for fast or average learners. Research findings are not in complete agreement, but it would appear that for teaching swimming skills to the average and above-average learner, the whole method would be superior to the other two. For the poor learner the progressive-part or the part-whole methods would probably be superior to the whole method.

Over-learning and Over-correction

When teaching a skill it is better to emphasize what to do, rather than what not to do. For example, it is better to tell the learner to swim with a high elbow during the first part of the crawl arm pull than to tell him not to drop his elbow. Positive description is superior to negative even though it sometimes becomes necessary to tell the swimmer exactly what he is doing incorrectly in order to tell him how to do it correctly.

When a swimmer has a bad stroke defect, such as too little bend in his knees on the downbeat of the fishtail kick, he can usually only correct this fault by practicing with an exaggerated action in the opposite direction (or too great a knee bend). When he practices this over-correction, it is better to isolate the part of the stroke he is working with, in this case to practice with the leg kick only while hanging onto a kick board. In other words, it is preferable to use the part method of learning. When this swimmer adapts the kick he has been practicing on the kick board to the whole stroke, he will find it virtually impossible to retain the exaggerated knee bend, but will probably retain enough of it to be closer to a satisfactory degree of bend than before.

Another example of the value of over-correction might be in the placing of the arms in the water in the back stroke. A swimmer tends to place his arms in the water too far across the center line of his body in front of his head. The coach tells him to place his hands in the water directly over his shoulders or out to the side about eight inches from the former point of entry. The swimmer tries to move his hands outward, and feels that he has succeeded in placing them about eight inches outward, but his coach can see no change in the hand entry position. The swimmer has probably moved them out about an inch, although to him it feels like eight inches. His coach may feel he is being uncooperative and uncoachable, but he has tried to comply with the coach's direction to the best of his ability. The coach should now tell him to feel as though he is putting his arms diagonally out to the side as they enter the water. The swimmer tries this and feels that he is doing it, but his arms might now go straight overhead in the correct position. This form of overcorrection is not used for the team as a whole but for individual cases such as the two just described. I use this form of correction with one or more swimmers in nearly every workout.

Skills which are over-learned are less easily forgotten. For this reason it is often worthwhile to spend considerable time and emphasis on drills that teach a swimmer a skill in which he is not naturally proficient. For example, Chester Jastremski had a natural breaststroke arm pull, but a relatively poor kick. To improve his kick, more time was spent on over-learning the kick than on drills for his arm stroke.

The emphasis on kicking drills may seem incongruous in light of the statements made earlier in this chapter concerning the preference of this writer for the whole method of teaching a swimming stroke. In this case, however, the swimmer has already learned the whole stroke and is doing a specific part of the stroke as a drill designed to perfect that part.

In applying this method of over-learning, it might be appropriate to say that an advanced or competitive swimmer was using the whole-part-whole method. He first learned to swim the whole stroke as a single unit. Later he broke the stroke into its components and tried to correct the mistakes that existed in each, then tried to carry these corrections into his whole stroke.

VIII

Training Techniques
in Competitive Swimming

Training techniques in any sport develop slowly and follow trends set by the training methods of the outstanding sportsmen of the time. In this respect the sport of competitive swimming has been no exception. As various coaches and swimmers have tried new techniques, the more successful have been retained and the less successful discarded. Thus the science of training swimmers (if it can be called a science) has progressed by trial and error, as do most sciences at their inception. In the past century it has advanced from training by merely swimming a small volume (one half to one mile daily) of relatively slow, almost continuous swimming to the presently popular method used by today's champions of swimming large amounts of high quality or relatively fast swimming (four to six miles daily) in a method of training generally called *interval training* or *repetition training*.

The introduction of interval training and its associated techniques probably marks one of the most important single factors in the continuing improvement of competitive swimming times in the past several decades.

Many people believe that interval training is based on simple and uncomplicated concepts, but, while a general idea of what an interval training workout is like is understood by most people associated with competitive swimming, not all understand these concepts. The obvious purpose of any training program is to condition the athlete to perform his activity more efficiently, with greater speed, and with less fatigue.

The term *conditioning* is used by most sportsmen and has the same general meaning for nearly everyone. It might, however, be worthwhile to define the term: the process of conditioning for a sport's activity is the sum total of all of the physiological, anatomical, and psychological adaptations made by the organism to the stress of the training program.

The stress factor in a training program is of course the exercise in which the individual engages during his training routines. It is a physiological law that the body attempts to adapt to the specific stress placed upon it by changing itself in order that it might be better able to cope with this specific type of stress the next time it is imposed. It is important to note the word *specific*. If a physician wants to immunize his patient against a specific disease (smallpox, for example), he will not vaccinate the patient with just any kind of vaccine (polio or measles, perhaps); rather he will use a specific vaccine (in this case, smallpox vaccine) as the stress factor. The body will adapt to this specific stress factor by producing a specific type of antibodies, which will help ward off that particular disease when the person next encounters it. These antibodies will not help him against other diseases.

In training swimmers we vaccinate the swimmer with some moderate work of a specific nature, and the swimmer's body adapts in such a way that it can do similar work, but of greater intensity. The amount and intensity of the work is then increased and the swimmer's body again attempts to adapt, with the result that the swimmer becomes conditioned progressively. If the work load is too great, the swimmer will not adapt and will go into the *failing adaptation* condition. This will be discussed in Chapter XIII and is mentioned here only to show that the following statement is a partial truth: hard work improves the organism's ability to do harder work.

In illustration of the specificity of training, if a person swims long distances at a slow pace, the body adapts physiologically through certain changes that enable it to tolerate swimming long distances at a slow pace. There will not be significant adaptations to toleration of the stress of sprinting.

In a swimmer's training program he must be exposed to the same or, at least, to a similar stress to the one he will encounter in the race in order to make the proper adaptations. In swimming, the interval training method has been oversimplified to the extent that most people believe it is merely the practice of doing a series of repeat swims near race speed with a controlled amount of rest between swims (that is, perhaps 20 × 50-yard swims with 30 seconds rest between each swim). In this manner the body adapts to the stress of swimming at race speed.

It is unlikely that full understanding of a training system for a swimmer can be comprehended without knowledge of how training has developed to its present point, and without a study of the research which has led to the development of the concepts. A brief outline of the historical developments of swimming training techniques as well as a discussion of similar trends in training trackmen might, therefore, be useful at this point.

A discussion of the history of the development of training methods will invariably bring dissenting opinions concerning who developed what method and when. The purpose of the following discussion is not to serve as a detailed list of credits to every coach or swimmer who has contributed to our knowledge of training methods, but merely as a general guide to show how the various training techniques and trends evolved. A particular method usually evolved slowly over a period of one or more decades; only rarely has there been a sudden change in these techniques.

THE PROGRESSION OF TRAINING TECHNIQUES IN SWIMMING

When competitive swimming was first introduced prior to the middle of the nineteenth century, there is every evidence to indicate that little hard training existed as we think of it today.

Ralph Thomas writes in his 1904 classic of the history of swimming:

> The quicker time in which distances are now swum is a sign of improvement. It arises from more careful attention to details, stroke, and training. C. Steadman informed me that he never trained and there is little doubt that the other champions of his day (1850) did not either, though training for swimming was then becoming popular.[1]

Some time obviously was devoted to perfecting the techniques used in races, and most of the actual swimming in training was done at a relatively slow pace.

An improvement in training techniques occurred when swimmers be-

[1] Ralph Thomas, *Swimming* (London: Sampson, Low, Marston & Co., Ltd., 1904), p. 149.

gan kicking on a flutter board and pulling with the legs tied or supported. These methods permitted improved conditioning of those particular parts of the body being used, due to the increased work they had to do. The exact origin of these techniques is claimed by various people. Its introduction, however, did not change the general concept that a swimmer should train by swimming relatively long distances (400 yards to two miles) at a slow pace, even though he might be training for a race of only 50 or 100 yards distance. This method, known as *over distance training*, dominated the sport for many decades, even into the late 1920's.

It was at this time that a few coaches and swimmers became discontented with merely swimming long distances at slow or moderate speeds and began to add some fast swimming, usually at the end of their daily workouts. This frequently took the form of four to eight 50-yard sprints. In the 1930's a technique of training, variously referred to as *pyramids* or *locomotives,* became popular; such great swimmers as Adolph Kiefer, the Spence brothers, and others used this improved technique of training with resulting great improvements in times.

In this type of training a swimmer might swim a long distance continuously, but he would vary the speed with which he swam the lengths. An example of this type of workout as used by Adolph Kiefer (mid-1930's) in a 25-yard pool follows: swim four lengths very hard, four lengths slowly, three lengths hard, three slow, two hard, two slow, one hard, and one slow; then back up the ladder, one hard, one slow, two hard, two slow, and so on.

A variation of this type of workout, as given the writer in 1938 by his coach, Ernst Vornbrock of the St. Louis YMCA, was as follows: swim two lengths fast, two lengths slow, one length fast, and one length slow; repeat ten times. This workout demonstrates how close to interval training many coaches of three decades ago came and illustrates the ability of such coaches as Kiefer's coach, Stan Brauninger, Vornbrock, and others.

This type of workout is still sometimes used and, in fact, closely compares with the *fartlek* (speed play) system of training used by trackmen.

From the 1930's through World War II few advances were made in swimming training techniques, and no mention can be found of the term *interval training* in swimming literature. In track, however, the first mention of the term appears in the literature immediately prior to World War II.

During the two decades of the thirties and forties (and even in the late twenties) such coaches as Matt Mann III, Robert Kiphuth, and others improved their training methods by placing more emphasis on speed in the form of wind sprints, such as ten to fifteen 50-yard sprints at the end of their workouts. In the late 1920's Arne Borg, Swedish world record holder in the 1500-meter freestyle, is said to have trained by doing eight 200-meter swims in a single workout at almost top speed. In preparing for the National AAU Championships in 1942 this writer swam four 200-meter time trials in one day, six 100-meter time trials the next day, and then two days of locomotives before returning to 200 and 100 repeat swims.

Despite these efforts to explore new methods, which were made in a tentative way with only a vague notion of why they might become effective in improving conditioning, there cannot be said to have been a systematic search for increasing physiological conditioning until the mid-1950's. Isolated instances of individuals swimming repeat time trials in a single workout were a long way from the present concept of interval training. This type of training, in which the rest between the repeat swims is long enough to permit almost complete recovery of the heart rate to normal, is called *repetition work.*

In 1952 the following workout was used in preparing Bowen Stassforth [2] for the Olympic Games:

1. Warm up 300-meter crawl swim.
2. Kick 600 meters, sprinting every third length.
3. Pull 400 meters, sprinting every third length.
4. Butterfly swim 800 meters, sprinting every fourth length and last 200 meters.
5. Time 300 meters kick.
6. Time 300 meters pull.
7. Rest five minutes; time 150-meters butterfly all-out.
8. Time three times 50-meters butterfly almost all-out.
9. Rest ten minutes; time 300-meters butterfly.

While this also cannot be called a true interval training workout, it does represent an attempt to emphasize the quality of the work over the quantity. This type of workout might still be used occasionally in a training program with good results, inasmuch as it combines many of the qualities still considered desirable by present day standards.

In this way swimming training techniques were advancing toward a form of interval training, with an increasing regard for higher quality work appearing in training programs everywhere.

In the mid-1950's swimming people became aware of what trackmen were doing and of the research that had been done in interval training.

[2] Stassforth was the second place winner in the 1952 Olympic Games held in London. His event was the 200-meter butterfly-breaststroke (butterfly arm pull with breaststroke kick).

At first, it was cautiously introduced into the swim programs. In many cases the inertia of the old techniques was hard to overcome as older coaches resisted the trend. Even today some coaches continue to resist. In preparation for the 1956 Olympic Games, the Australians used interval training to such advantage that they startled the swimming world with their successes and gave a tremendous impetus to the development of interval training methods throughout the swimming world.

The experience of the Australians was all that was needed to send American and foreign coaches into the *battle of the training schedules.* Some figured if a little bit of interval training was good, and a lot was better, a tremendous amount would be best. Unfortunately, this attitude displayed more enthusiasm than discretion. During the late 1950's and early 1960's the battle ensued, with more and more emphasis being directed toward the number of repeats rather than to their quality. Such workouts as sixteen 440's with one to two minutes' rest were reportedly used by some world class swimmers; forty 100's with one minute rest between efforts by the German swimmer, Gerhard Hetz; and one hundred 50's with 30 seconds' rest by Hetz and others. In the summer of 1961 the writer tried the latter workout with his team on two occasions and, although two trials do not constitute a fair trial, decided that if it took this kind of workout for a swimmer to get in top shape, his team would have to remain mediocre. It did not seem logical that in order to train for a 100-, 200-, or 400-meter race, a swimmer should have to swim such workouts as 100 × 50. This workout, aside from being monotonous, could not be tolerated over a long period by athletes of normal intellect or above. It also seemed to violate one of the basic premises of the concept of interval training, which is that the swimmer should swim his practice lengths at or near the speed he is training to swim in the race.

Not every coach and swimmer became involved in the battle of the training schedules, sometimes because of the lack of time in the pool, sometimes because they did not subscribe to the theory, or simply because they were unwilling to pay such a price for a drop in swimming times. It did, however, represent a popular trend which has, fortunately, been dropped by most coaches and swimmers.

Once again, it was the more successful coaches, such as George Haines, Forbes Carlile, Don Talbot, Don Gambril, and Don Sonia, who showed that volume should not be the prime concern in an interval training oriented program. They are now leading the trend toward high quality in repeat work at the expense of quantity. Instead of using 50 to 100 × 50 repeat swims, they might use only sixteen to forty 50's. By requiring fewer repeats they could stress higher quality.

In summarizing the events described above, it seems fair to say that the over-zealous enthusiasm with which interval training was accepted has been moderated by experience and the opportunity to think over the actual purpose of training. Prevailing opinion is that it is the quality of the work done that is of prime importance, and that the emphasis should remain on swimming at racing speed. However, these opinions may once again be moderated by a new tendency which is resulting from a better understanding of the body's specialized response to different kinds of conditioning methods. This writer feels it would be a great mistake to limit a training program exclusively to high quality work. Many of the errors that have been made in developing training programs could have been avoided if coaches and swimmers had profited from the earlier experience of sportsmen in other sports, particularly in track, as well as the results of research in this area.

The history of our training methods shows that from the beginning we have been concerned with the problems that continue to bother us today in setting up our training programs. They are: (1) the distance to be swum, and (2) *how fast* the swimmer should swim that distance or *how much effort* he should put into each repeat swim. With the introduction of interval training and repetition training into our programs two new considerations have been added. The four together are often expressed as D I R T: (1) D for *distance* to be swum (at what distances should repeats be swum—50's, 100's, 200's, etc.), (2) I for *interval* (what should be the interval of rest between repeat swims—30 seconds, 60, etc.), (3) R for *repetitions* (how many repetitions of a given distance should a swimmer do—10, 20, 30, etc.), and (4) T for *time* (in what time should a swimmer cover the repeats—31 seconds per 50, etc.).

TRAINING TECHNIQUES IN TRACK

The following discussion of training methods developed in track and of some of the research in this area may help the reader form some conclusions which will, in turn, give him a better understanding of the principles upon which scientific training methods for swimmers are based. It should also help to answer the four questions represented by the word D I R T.

Since there are important differences between the sports of swimming and track, some pitfalls are apparent in applying the methods of one sport directly to the other. For example, running is a weight-bearing activity, while in swimming the body is supported by the water. In track the legs are the source of propulsion, while in swimming the arms serve as the main source of propulsion (except in the breaststroke). These differences require that the systems be adapted to the particular activity. In track top male sprinters run 50 yards in under 6 seconds, 100 yards in 9 to 9.5 seconds, and 200 meters in 20 to 21 seconds; in swimming sprinters swim the distances in 20 to 23 seconds, 45 to 53 seconds, and frequently must swim the 200-yard distance in 1:41 to 1:50. Thus, the runner of the 200 meters might not need to develop the cardio-vascular endurance required by the swimmer over the same distance.

There is also the fact that a swimmer can dissipate the heat his body generates at a much faster rate than can the track man. One of the important limiting factors in running is the inability of the runner to dissipate this heat fast enough. For this reason and the first of those stated above, a swimmer might be able to train profitably more hours per day or at a more intense level than can a trackman. In comparing training schedules of champions in the two sports, this is apparently true.

In spite of these differences, there has been a parallel development in the training methods of the two sports which is the result of some important similarities between the two, and which makes it possible to apply some general concepts of training to both. Some attention to the evolution of track training methods will serve to emphasize the similarities.

Advancement in Training Techniques in Track

The history of track training systems has followed a pattern similar to that described for swimming. There was the same gradual transition from the practice of running most of the workout at a slow pace with only a small part being run at a fast tempo, to the present method of running in which much of the work is done in the interval training and repetition training methods. The main difference in the development of the two sports lies in the fact that the introduction of new track techniques has always preceded the introduction of the same techniques in swimming by at least ten years. Obviously, the swimmers have learned a great deal from the trackmen and have accepted precedents set by them. Many swimming coaches will disagree with the belief that training techniques in swimming have been copied from track athletes. Perhaps it is true that these techniques have evolved in a natural pattern and would have arrived at the same point without help from the trackmen, but the fact remains that most of the training methods were adopted much earlier by the people in track than by those in swimming. Consequently, they have lived with them longer and have had more time to experiment with them in a methodical and scientific manner.

In track as in swimming the various training techniques evolved slowly and their beginnings are not clearly documented.

"Speedplay" or the Fartlek Method

One of the first methods which began to evolve and which is still used in training programs today, particularly by middle distance and distance runners, was the *fartlek method*—translated from the Swedish as "speedplay"—of training. It consists of covering relatively long distances of two to ten miles or even longer at varying speeds. This running is not usually done on the track, but in the countryside over varying terrain.

Doherty [3] believes it had its inception as early as the 1870's, when an English champion runner, Walter G. George, trained by running over the hills and dales of England at varying speeds. Much of the credit for developing this method must go to the Finnish and Swedish runners who used a modified form of it in the first 30 years of this century. Such Swedish runners as Hagg and Anderson, world record holders in the mile run in the early 1940's, helped this method gain popularity.

Doherty [4] gives credit for naming this system and publication of the first material concerning it (in the late 1940's) to the Swedish coach, Gosta Holmer.

As the training program progresses and the runner's conditioning improves he may add more and longer fast runs. This fast-slow running has an obvious correct physiological basis for conditioning middle distance and distance runners. The fast running permits athletes to run at paces equal to or faster than the speed they will want to run in the race, and thus conditions them for fast pace. The continuous nature of the effort even with the jogging at a much reduced pace or the fast walking has a beneficial training effect, particularly on the cardio-vascular system, thus enhancing endurance.

The main quality developed by the fartlek system, however, seems to be general endurance, and it is particularly important to note that this method of training is not generally recommended for sprinters.

The fact that the runner is away from the track in a continually changing environment has a good psychological effect and helps relieve the boredom of continuous running around an oval track.

The fartlek method is still used as a part of the training program by many (perhaps even by the majority) of the world's top rank middle distance and distance runners. It is used especially during the early part of the training program to develop stamina (general endurance). Herb Elliott's coach, Percy Cerutty, uses the technique of training runners by

[3] J. Kenneth Doherty, *Modern Track and Field*, 2nd ed. (Englewood Cliffs, N.J.: Prentice-Hall, Inc., 1963), p. 167.
[4] *Ibid.*

having them run over sand dunes, a form of fartlek, even though Cerutty is reluctant to admit it.

Runners want to build endurance early in their training and stress speed work later in the training program and during the actual competitive season. This principle of building endurance before going into speed work also appears to be applicable in training swimmers.

The fartlek method is very permissive in that nothing is timed with a watch and, while the runner does run on a plan, it is flexible enough to permit variations depending on how the individual feels. Its informal nature makes it difficult for the person who is not strongly motivated, is weak-willed, or does not understand it thoroughly to profitably engage in it. A more formalized program may be more practical for such persons.

Fartlek has been used in swimmers' training programs and, while the swimmer is not able to enjoy a continually changing environment as can the runner, he nevertheless gets a respite from interval training and repetition training methods. Precisely how it can be used in a swimmer's program will be discussed later in this chapter.

Repetition Training in Track

As has already been mentioned in the description of the development of training techniques in swimming, at various times, even early in the developmental stage, *repetition work* was used to a minor degree by many athletes, both in track and swimming. The real credit for popularizing the use of repetition work in United States track training belongs to Billy Hayes, who was training his runners with this type of training as early as 1923 at Mississippi State College. Later, while at Indiana University, Hayes developed such great middle distance runners as Lash, Decker, and Wilt.

In repetition work the athlete runs or swims a given distance at a fast speed, usually close to racing speed, then rests long enough to permit almost complete recovery—at least of the heart rate—and a return to normal of the respiratory rate before swimming or running again. While this may sound like interval training, the principal difference between the two is that in the latter method the rest period is controlled so the heart rate may make only partial recovery. Fred Wilt describes the difference between these two types of training:

> *Repetition-running* is a refinement in interval training which has been described by Franz Stampfl as running a given distance at a pre-determined speed a specified number of times with complete rest after each such fast run. In actual practice repetition-running differs from interval training in

terms of the length of the run, and the degree of recovery after each fast run. Repetition-running is concerned with running comparatively longer distances (such as 880 yards to 1¼ miles) with relatively complete recovery (often by walking) after each. Interval-running involves running relatively short distances (110 to 440 yards) at fast pace (near racing speed or faster) with a recovery something less than complete after each. The recovery in interval-running usually involves jogging a distance equal to the fast run in a speed 2 or 3 times as long as required to complete the fast run. Repetition-running is more exhausting than interval-running, and continues to become more so as the fast runs approach the final racing distance. For this reason, repetition-running over longer distances should be at considerably less than racing speed. When repetition-running reaches racing speed, the length of the fast runs should not exceed more than half of the actual racing distance.[5]

Repetition work is a very important part of the training program for trackmen, both middle distance runners and sprinters, and for all swimmers. It attempts to simulate a stress more like that the runner or swimmer will encounter in his race than the stress imposed on the athlete by the fartlek or interval training methods.

Repetition training, as used by trackmen, introduces more speed into the training program than does fartlek or interval training. It may be considered to be *special speed and endurance* running, devised to help the runner acquire the specific speed and endurance he will need in his race. The relative speed of the repetition runs are increased as the training progresses.

Interval Training Introduced Into Track

The first athlete trained in the *interval training* method to receive international acclaim was Rudolph Harbig,[6] who in 1939 astounded the sports world by setting the then unbelievable world's records of :46.0 for 400 meters and 1:46.6 for 800 meters. Harbig was coached by Woldemar Gerschler, who was then developing the modern technique which he called the *controlled interval method.* To Gerschler must go the credit for devising this system, used entirely or in part by most middle and long distance runners in the world today. Gerschler had felt that there was a lack of sufficient control in the Swedish fartlek system. He decided to control carefully the distance, interval, repetitions, and time (D I R T). Although introduced in Germany before World War II, this method was

[5] Fred Wilt, *Run, Run, Run* (Los Altos, Calif.: Track and Field News, Inc., 1964), p. 259.

[6] Doherty, *op. cit.*, p. 177.

scarcely heard of, despite Harbig's successes, until after war's end, specifically in 1952, when Gerschler's protégé, Josey Barthel, won the Olympic gold medal in the 1500-meter run. The interval training method then became tremendously popular as most middle distance and distance men began to subordinate or exclude entirely the fartlek phase of their training in favor of interval training. The subsequent triumphs of such runners as Kutz, Pirie, and particularly Zatopek contributed such impetus to the use of interval training that it might be said to have caused an over-emphasis on this type of training with a corresponding under-emphasis of the other phases of training. Zatopek is reported to have run as many as sixty 400-meter runs in one training session.

THE GERSCHLER-REINDELL LAW.[7] Interval training has various meanings for different people. In swimming, unfortunately, it has come to mean any type of training in which a series of repeat swims is done with the interval of rest held constant. If this were the case, it would also embrace repetition work. To illustrate what interval training means to the scientist who developed it, we must go to the research on which the method was based. After experimenting with 3,000 cases, studied during an actual track training program over a period of three weeks, Gerschler came up with the following guiding principles for setting up a training program designed to develop maximum cardiovascular fitness or endurance.

A typical interval training routine and the manner of conducting it, as recommended by Gerschler: [8]

1. Before beginning the series of repeats (50 × 100, for example) the athlete should increase his pulse rate to 120 beats per minute by preliminary warm-up.

2. The next step is to run the first of his repeats—a 100, 150, or 200 meters—in a given time (or effort) which will bring his heart rate to 170-180 beats per minute.

3. After running the distance the athlete will walk or jog until his heart rate returns to approximately 120 to 140 beats per minute. When this point is reached the athlete will begin running again (second effort). The time required for the heart rate to drop from 170-180 to 120-140 should not exceed one minute and 30 seconds. As the athlete improves his conditioning, recovery time will shorten.

Gerschler believes that the primary stimulus for cardiovascular improvement occurs during the recovery phase when the heart rate is being reduced from 170-180 to 120-140 beats per minute.

Endurance is related to the amount of blood the heart can pump in a

[7] P. Sprecher, "Visit with Dr. Woldemar Gerschler," *International d'Athletisme,* translated by Brother G. Luke, F.S.C., in *Track Technique,* No. 9 (September 1962), 282.
[8] *Ibid.*

given period. Endurance athletes, such as marathon and distance runners, have relatively larger hearts and greater ability to pump large amounts of blood than have sprinters.

The ability of the heart to pump a large volume of blood can be increased by conditioning in the following ways:

1. By running long distances, as in the marathon training advocated by Peter Snell's former coach, Arthur Lydiard.

2. By using the fartlek method of training.

3. By using interval training methods.

The advantage of interval training appears to be that it can improve this ability of the heart in a much shorter time than can the other two methods. Hollmann [9] determined that, with the use of an interval training program, in a period of less than two months the heart volume was increased by more than 100 cc. With former training methods this great an improvement might have taken several months to achieve.

The German track coach, Toni Nett, says of interval training:

> Today interval training is no longer universally the all important and "only" training method. It is merely one of many methods, but, it will continue to exist. It was a valuable addition to the number of training methods already known. Enthusiastic to have found the "jewel of wisdom" the shot went over the target. Today we use interval training for specific purposes. For example, there is no better method than interval training to enlarge the heart in the shortest possible time, but, this has its misgivings too—"easy come, easy go." The effect is not as stable as the enlarging process of the heart by means of consuming long distance running. There is no doubt though that in certain cases (to overcome accidental loss of training time, before big meets or championships), a quick method to enlarge the heart (raising the endurance level) is needed.[10]

Apparently the increased amount of blood pumped per heart beat (heart volume) is greatest during the interval of rest immediately following the bout of exercise. This maximal heart volume provides the optimal stimulus for the increased hypertrophy of the heart muscle. According to many of the German track coaches and researchers, the real training of the heart occurs during the interval of rest and not during the actual exertion. If this interval is held too long, there is a pooling of the blood in the venous system and less chance for optimum heart volume during both the next exertion and the next period of rest.

It cannot be assumed that there is unanimity of opinion about interval

---

[9] Med. W. Hollmann (Dr.), "Der Arbeits—und Trainingseinflues auf Kreislauf und Atmung" (Darmstadt: Dr. Dietrich Steinkopf Verlag, 1959) in Wilt, *Run, Run, Run,* p. 185.

[10] Toni Nett, "Complex Training," in Wilt, *Run, Run, Run,* p. 229.

training, its application, and values among track coaches and runners. Arthur Lydiard,[11] coach of Olympic champions Halberg (5000 meters, 1960) and Peter Snell (800 meters, 1960—800 and 1500, 1964), claims he uses no interval training in his program. He says that marathon training and repetition training are all any middle distance or distance runner needs. He further claims that the marathon training gives the runner the increased endurance he needs, while the repetition work provides the speed and pace work. A close examination of Lydiard's training schedules for 880-yard runners, however, reveals the following workout, which might be considered by some to be an interval training workout and by others to be a form of fartlek.

> Run two miles of fifty-yard dashes separated by sixty-yard floats and follow with three practice starts, running each out to fifty yards.[12]

The disagreement between track coaches on many issues concerning training may be due to a large extent to the lack of a common acceptance of the terminology of training. Without such agreement it is easy to see why confusion exists. It might be simpler to classify both interval training and repetition work as interval training, but this solution would contribute nothing to real understanding of the different purposes which lie behind each of these methods.

As Lydiard's sample workout so well points up, even with a common terminology there is a certain overlap in the methods which makes for further confusion. For example, in an interval training workout, as the period of rest is lengthened between a series of swims or runs, and the heart rate is allowed to return almost to normal, the training approaches repetition work. Precisely where one type of training ends and the other begins may always be a matter of individual interpretation. However, acceptance of a common terminology will undoubtedly help coaches and swimmers to a conceptual mastery of training principles.

DEFINITION AND DISCUSSION OF TRAINING
TERMINOLOGY IN SWIMMING

Fartlek Training (Speedplay)

Fartlek training consists of swimming relatively long distances of one-half mile and over continuously, using a variety of speeds. It can be done

---

[11] Arthur Lydiard and Garth Gilmour, *Run to the Top* (Wellington, New Zealand: A. H. and A. N. Reed, 1963).
[12] *Ibid.*, p. 94.

in a pool, lake, or river. It can be loosely organized and consist of swimming at a relatively slow pace for most of the distance, interspersed with occasional sprints; or it can be highly organized with a very rigid plan. Below is an example of a highly organized fartlek training session:

1. Swim at a slow speed for five minutes, then time a 400-yard sustained effort in a predetermined time.
2. Swim a steady, moderate effort for five more minutes, then time a maximum effort for 50 yards.
3. Continue in this manner for one hour until 4 × 400 and 4 × 50 have been swum.

The fartlek method and all other training methods discussed can also be applied to training on a kicking board or pulling with the legs tied or suspended. The main quality developed by this method is stamina (endurance), but it also develops some speed depending on how much speedplay is introduced into the training session. The cardio-respiratory endurance of the swimmer is favorably affected by this type of training. There is also an increase in the capillarization (number of functional capillaries) of the muscle.

This type of training should be used extensively early in the season by middle distance and distance men, and perhaps even by sprinters.

Over Distance Training

As the name implies, the swimmer trains at distances greater than the distance of the event for which he is training and, naturally, at a speed slower than that he will use in the actual race. If, for example, the swimmer is training for a 200-meter event and he swims 1500 meters continuously in training (with or without being timed), or if he swims a series of repeat swims such as 4 × 400 meters, he can be considered to be using this method.

It cannot be assumed, however, that the swimmer will always be swimming these distances slowly. He may possibly swim them as an all-out effort or time trial. The purpose of these extended efforts is threefold: (1) to improve stamina or endurance and, as mentioned in the case of the fartlek method, the cardio-respiratory endurance, and to increase the number of functional capillaries in the active muscles, (2) to permit the swimmer to swim at a steady but somewhat slower than racing pace in order to concentrate on stroke mechanics, and (3) to develop more confidence, based on the theory that a person who occasionally swims efforts greater than racing distance will feel more capable of handling the shorter distance.

Over distance training should be used during the early part of the season and, to a lesser degree, throughout the entire season. After the introduction of interval training and repetition training, many coaches unfortunately neglected this type of training, particularly in age-group programs. Fartlek and over distance training develop endurance in terms of cardiac efficiency more slowly than does interval training, but the endurance attained by the former two methods is more stable and longer lasting.

Interval Training

This method consists of swimming a series of repeat efforts at a given distance with a controlled amount of rest between efforts. The rest interval is long enough to permit partial, but not complete, recovery of the heart rate to normal. In interval training the optimal stimulus for improvement of the cardio-vascular system occurs during the interval of rest, at which time the volume of blood pumped by the heart per beat is at its greatest.

The distance swum in the repeat efforts is never longer than the distance the swimmer is training for. Once again using the 200-meter swimmer's program as an illustration, he will swim his interval training sessions at the following distances: 50, 100, 150, and 200 meters. These efforts are nearly always timed, and an attempt is made to keep the speed constant on each effort.

Interval training can be subdivided into two types:

1. Slow interval training. This consists of swimming repeat swims at a speed slower than race speed with a short rest interval and incomplete recovery of the heart rate. The rest interval is always shorter in time than the time it takes to swim the distance.

The following is an example of a slow interval training workout as used by Kevin Berry in 1963 (winner of the 1964 Olympic 200-meter butterfly event with a time of 2:06.6): 30 × 50-meter butterfly swims with 10 seconds rest between each effort. Average time of each effort—34.6 seconds. This time is slower per 50 than the pace Berry used to set the world record of 2:06.6, in which his average was :31.6. His average heart rate at the end of an effort was measured at 178, and dropped only to the average level of 148 at the end of the ten second interval of rest.

This type of interval training is used to develop cardio-vascular reserve and does not contribute much to the swimmer's speed. It would not be recommended for a swimmer training for a 100-meter event and probably would not be used during the final preparation phase of even a 200-meter swimmer.

2. Fast interval training. This method is different from the type of interval training just discussed in that it permits longer rest intervals and,

consequently, greater recovery of the heart rate to normal as well as faster speed at which the repeat effort can be swum.

The sample workout of the same 30 × 50 set of repeats used by Berry when modified a few days later to become a fast interval training type of routine is: 30 × 50 with 40 seconds rest interval. Average time—31.2 seconds. Average heart rate at the end of repeat swim was 181; average heart rate at the end of rest interval was 126. It should be noted that by increasing the rest period from 10 seconds to 40 seconds Berry could maintain an average speed (:31.2) faster than the speed he averaged (:31.6) when he set the world record. The obvious advantage of this fast type of interval training over the slow type is that it places more emphasis on speed.

Fast interval training may be considered to be beneficial for both cardiac muscle and skeletal muscle. It improves the endurance of the heart muscle and the resistance of the skeletal muscle, the latter being its ability to withstand the accumulation of fatigue products and to operate anaerobically (without oxygen).

Repetition Training

Repetition training consists of swimming a series of repeats of a shorter distance than and at a greater speed than that swum in the race. The rest interval is long enough to permit almost complete recovery of the heart and respiratory rate. The recovery is so complete that little physiological adaptation value is gained during the rest interval, such as that described in the case of interval training.

Whereas slow interval training is primarily endurance or heart work and fast interval training introduces more elements of speed or muscle work into training, repetition work goes even further in this direction and becomes primarily speed or muscle work with the quality of endurance subordinated to a secondary position. An example of a repetition training workout as used by Tom Stock in the summer of 1962, when he set the world record of 2:10.9 for 200 meters backstroke, is: 6 × 100 meters with rest interval of four to eight minutes. Average time—64.4 seconds (faster than the average of his 200 world record); average pulse rate after each repeat swim was 186; average pulse rate after each rest interval was 99 (his resting pulse rate in a basal state was 64). It should be observed that Stock's heart rate does not approach the basal rate even though the rest interval has been lengthened considerably. It is possible that the heart rate might stay slightly elevated for hours after a hard workout. This phenomenon has been noted in Stock and many other swimmers trained by this writer, particularly early in the season.

The interval of rest should be long enough for the swimmer to feel no acute discomfort from the effort of the previous swim (he should, for example, experience no respiratory difficulty such as labored breathing). His pulse rate should have decreased to below the level of 110-100, although it may not always be possible to get it below this level. The interval of rest should be at least three times as long as the time it takes to swim the distance. This would hold true on the shorter repeat swims (50 through 200 meters), but not necessarily on the longer repeats (such as 300, 400, or longer). As the swimmer becomes progressively fatigued, a longer rest interval may have to be allowed.

The number of repeat swims at a given distance accomplished in a repetition training session will usually be fewer than the number used in a comparable interval training workout. Thus a swimmer may use a *straight set* of 100's for an interval training workout of 15 × 100 with one minute rest interval; a comparable standard or straight set of 100's in a repetition training workout might be 6 or 8 × 100 with three to six minutes rest interval.

In this type of training the swimmer does not sprint or use an all-out effort. He does, however, swim at a fast, controlled speed, and this speed will be determined by the distance he is swimming and the race pace to which he is attempting to adapt his body and mind. In this respect this type of training can be considered to be *pace* or *tempo* work. The swimmer will learn how to swim his race in this type of training as well as in time trials and actual competition.

Sprint Training

Sprint training consists of swimming all-out efforts at top sprinting speed, either in a series (6 × 50 all-out efforts with a long rest) or as isolated efforts (1 × 75, 1 × 50, 1 × 25). These sprints must not exceed 100 meters—it is even doubtful if anyone can maintain a top speed at that distance. They usually consist of distances of 25 and 50 yards or meters.

A relatively long rest period should be allowed between each all-out sprint. The recovery of the heart and respiratory rate should be to a level more closely approaching the basal level than that used in repetition training. In an all-out sprint the swimmer is not able to take in oxygen as fast as he uses it, with the result that he builds up an *oxygen debt*. He must repay this oxygen to his muscles and blood, from which he has "borrowed" it, after he ceases swimming. Following a sprint he will feel some respiratory difficulty and will experience labored breathing for a while. This period of distress no doubt accounts for the term *wind sprints,* frequently applied to this type of training.

One of the chief differences between a sprint race and a distance race is that in the sprint event the swimmer swims most of his race in oxygen debt (using oxygen at a faster rate than he can absorb it), while in a distance race he operates on a pay-as-you-go basis, only entering the area of high oxygen debt at the finish of the race when he may sprint. Thus the sprinter must adapt his body to tolerate high levels of oxygen debt while the distance man must adapt his body to absorb large quantities of oxygen during the actual swim.

Sprint training may also be considered, along with dry land exercises, to be the best method of improving the strength of the swimmer's muscles. The increased resistance caused by the increased speed of the movements serves as the stimulus to cause hypertrophy (increase in size) and a consequent increase in the strength of the muscle. Everything else being equal, swimmers on a sprint program will have stronger muscles than will swimmers on an over-distance program, but their muscles will have poorer qualities for endurance swimming. While the programs of all competitive swimmers, regardless of the distance for which they are training, should include some sprint work, indiscriminate or excessive use of it can cause excessive fatigue, and can also result in poor stroke mechanics. Emphasis on sprint training should come late in the training program; little should be done in the early weeks.

Definition and Description of Sets of Repeat Swims

The term "a set of repeat swims" refers to the series of swimming, kicking, or pulling efforts done during a workout. There has already been a description of the ways a set of repeats may be used in the various training methods (interval training, repetition, and sprint training). The amount of effort that a swimmer puts into each repeat swim can be held constant, increased, decreased, or varied in a combination of these methods. Just as one method of training should not be used exclusively throughout the season to condition a swimmer, so should just one type of set of repeats not be used exclusively. Although most training will be confined to the use of "straight sets" or "progressive sets," there are times when the use of other types of sets is desirable.

STRAIGHT SET OF REPEATS. When doing a straight set of repeat swims (such as 10×100 with approximately one minute of rest between each and holding each one at 56 seconds), the swimmer is trying to keep the time of each repeat swim relatively constant, as well as the rest interval. This will mean that as he progresses into the set and becomes tired, he will have to exert more effort in order to maintain a constant speed. This type of set is the backbone of most training programs, particularly the interval training phase. After the first few repetitions the heart rate may reach a level of only 150 to 160. As the set progresses and the swimmer becomes more fatigued, his heart rate after the repetition will be higher to the point that, after the last one, it may reach a level of 170 to 180. It is helpful to use this type of routine as a means of motivation and of measuring improvement in conditioning.

DECREASING DISTANCE REPEATS.   Recent experiments with swimmers at Indiana University and also with trackmen in Germany have shown that a relatively unexploited method of training may offer new opportunities for improving the conditioning of our athletes. This method is based on doing a set of repeat efforts in running or swimming in which, as the set progresses, the distance of the repeat effort is decreased, while the speed of the repeat is increased (Table VIII–1). This type of set can be done as interval training (with a short rest interval and incomplete heart rate recovery) or as repetition training (with a long rest interval and almost complete heart rate recovery).

Such sets have been found to be superior when used as a form of repetition training, but the method is still undergoing experimentation as a form of interval training.

An example of this type of set of repeats as done by a good distance swimmer follows. When swimming each repeat swim, the swimmer's time *on the way* (at the distance of the succeeding repeat swim) is recorded. When he swims that next repeat swim, he tries to improve on this time.

	Rest Interval	Distance	Time	Split on the Way
1st repeat		500-yd.	5:10	400 on the way was 4:06
2nd repeat	6-12 min.	400-yd.	4:00	300 on the way was 3:01
3rd repeat	5-10 min.	300-yd.	2:59	200 on the way was 1:57
4th repeat	4-8 min.	200-yd.	1:55	100 on the way was :55
5th repeat	3-6 min.	100-yd.	:53	

We use the above set as a standard decreasing-distance repeat for our distance men, and one of these sets is done every week or two during our hard-training phase. Straight sets are also used for sprinters and middle distance swimmers and are charted in Table VIII–5.

We have also tried reversing the procedure and have begun with the shorter distances, each subsequent distance being longer. This method has been abandoned for several reasons: first, it did not appeal to the swimmers and thus seemed to be a poor method psychologically (that is, to swim slower as the set progressed); second, the total accumulated time of the set was slower; third, the pulse rate, as well as the oxygen debt, was greatest at the beginning of the set. When distances are shortened and the intensity increased as the set progresses, there is a steady increase in stress and the heart rate and oxygen debt increase with each set; this type of distribution of stress seems physiologically more sound than the other arrangement. More research is definitely needed in this area before accurate decisions can be made about the value of this kind of repeat.

TABLE VIII–1. Examples of Decreasing-distance Sets of Repeats

Dis.	R. I.	Dis.	R. I.	Dis.	R. I.	Dis.	R. I.	Dis.	Category of Swimmers
150	3-6 min.	100	3-6 min.	75	3-6 min.	50			Sprinters & mid. dist.
200	4-8 min.	150	3-6 min.	100	3-6 min.	75	3-6 min.	50	Sprinters & mid. dist.
300	5-10 min.	200	4-8 min.	150	3-6 min.	100	3-6 min.	50	Sprinters & mid. dist.
400	5-10 min.	300	4-8 min.	200	3-6 min.	150	3-6 min.	100	Mid. dist.
500	6-12 min.	400	5-10 min.	300	4-8 min.	200	3-6 min.	100	Mid. dist.
800	6-12 min.	500	6-12 min.	400	5-10 min.	300	4-8 min.	200	Distance
1650	10-20 min.	800	6-12 min.	400	5-10 min.	200			Distance

SIMULATORS.   In the discussion of interval training it has been shown how the swimmer tries to increase his heart rate to a given level (160–170) and how, during the short interval of rest between repeats, it drops to a level of 120–150. The drop in heart rate is dependent on the length of the rest interval, the intensity of the previous repeats, and the state of conditioning of the swimmer. Repetition training increases the intensity of the effort used in the repeat, and, as a consequence, obtains a higher pulse rate (170–180). The subsequent rest interval in repetition training is longer and the heart recovery more complete.

A type of training introduced at Indiana University in 1964, which varies somewhat from these methods but which also uses the pulse rate rise and recovery as a guide, is the *simulator*. I have felt for some time that neither interval training nor repetition training techniques simulated the physiological stress the swimmer encountered when he swam a race to a close enough degree to bring about the exact conditioning wanted in the swimmer. The actual maximum effort time trial swims over the dis-

TABLE VIII–2. Examples of Simulators

Simulator Total Distance	1st Seg.	R.I.	2nd Seg.	R.I.	3rd Seg.	R.I.	4th Seg.	R.I.	5th Seg.
100	50	5 sec.	25	5 sec.	25				
100	75	5 sec.	25						
200	100	5 sec.	50	5 sec.	25	5 sec.	25		
200	125	5 sec.	50	5 sec.	25				
400	200	10 sec.	100	5 sec.	50	5 sec.	50		
400	250	10 sec.	100	5 sec.	50				
500	200	10 sec.	100	5 sec.	100	5 sec.	50	5 sec.	50
500	250	10 sec.	100	5 sec.	100	5 sec.	50		
800	400	15 sec.	200	10 sec.	100	5 sec.	100		
800	300	15 sec.	200	10 sec.	150	10 sec.	100	5 sec.	50
1500	600	15 sec.	400	10 sec.	200	10 sec.	200	10 sec.	100
1500	500	15 sec.	400	10 sec.	300	10 sec.	200	5 sec.	100

tance should do this, but too-frequent 100 per cent efforts (particularly over the 200-yard distance or more) exhaust the swimmer and are not good for him psychologically.

If, in a practice situation, the swimmer's heart rate can be elevated to the level it will reach in the race and he can then be permitted a periodic rest just long enough to repay some of his oxygen debt and let the heart rate recover slightly (perhaps from 180 to 170) and then continue the swim, the swimmer can nearly duplicate the stress he will encounter in the race. This method would not be as exhausting as an all-out time trial. An example of this type of swim for a butterflier who swims the 200-yard butterfly in 1:51 would be as follows: swim 100 yards from a dive in the time you want to go out in in the race (:53.0 seconds); rest 5 seconds, then swim a 50 butterfly in 29 seconds; rest 5 seconds, then swim a 25 in :13.5; rest 5 seconds, then swim another 25 in 13.5. The total swimming time is 1:49.0, with a total elapsed time of 2:04. If there are pace clocks on both ends of the pool, the swimmer can time himself. By starting on 45 he can cancel out his resting time and he can read his total swimming time directly from the clock. In this respect it is like a broken swim set of repeats.

These are the very important considerations in using simulators: (1) The rest should not be long enough to let the pulse rate drop more than 15 beats. We never use more than 15 seconds rest or less than 5. (2) The distance of each succeeding segment of the simulator gets shorter than the preceding segment or stays the same. (3) The first segment of the simulator should be approximately half of the total distance of the race. This applies only to races of 400 meters or shorter. In the case of the longer races a smaller segment can be used (for example, for a 1500, the first segment might be 500). (4) The total elapsed swimming time should be close to or better than the best time the swimmer can swim this event in a race.

Near the end of the simulator the swimmer may have to swim 25's because this distance accommodates to a short course pool. Simulators may be used in a 50-meter pool by eliminating the 25's or by directing the swimmer to stop in the middle of the pool, rest 5 seconds, and then push off the bottom to swim the next 25.

The mistakes made by swimmers in pacing their races are most commonly made in the first half of the race. If a butterflier wants to learn how to pace a 53-second time for the first 100 yards on the way to his 200-yard race, he can practice swimming isolated 100's in this time. Experience has shown that this type of practice does help somewhat, but an isolated 100 is not the same as a 100 on the way to a longer race. Through the use of simulators in which the swimmer knows he will get only a short rest before he must continue, he can come closer to creating the same mental as well as physical (or physiological) approach he will want to have in the race. *Except for the race itself, simulators are the best method of teaching pace to swimmers.* In this respect they are even superior to practice time trials. Similar precaution is necessary in using simulators as should be used in all-out time trial, that is, they should be used sparingly. There is the chance that their continued use may cause undue fatigue. They should be introduced into the training program after the swimmer has had some basic conditioning; therefore, they best fit into the hard-training and tapering phases of the training schedule.

MIXED SET. When doing a mixed set of repeats neither the distance nor the interval of rest are held constant. A favorite mixed set of Kevin Berry's, when he was preparing for his world record swim of 2:06.9 for the 200-butterfly in February, 1964, consisted of the following distances and rest intervals:

Swim	400	300	200	100	50	100	200	300	400
Rest interval in mins.	5	3	2	1	1	2	3	5	

Another kind of mixed set as used frequently by the Indiana University distance swimmers is as follows:

1. 1 × 800 meters——5   minutes rest
2. 2 × 400 meters——5   minutes rest
3. 2 × 200 meters——3   minutes rest
4. 4 × 100 meters——1½ minutes rest

This variation permits the swimmer to get away from the high pressure of straight sets. He can vary these sets in almost limitless patterns. It gives him a variety of paces and can help prevent the grooving of his stroke tempo into one swimming speed. This set of repeats is not to be confused with the decreasing distance repeats discussed earlier.

PROGRESSIVE SET.   In this kind of set the distance is held constant; the swimmer starts at a controlled speed, and will swim progressively faster with each repeat. In order to do so, he will have to exert a perceptibly greater effort with each repeat swim. An example of such a set might be to begin 10 × 100 with approximately 1 minute rest between each, with the first 100 to be swum in 1 minute, dropping steadily until the last repeat is swum in 53 seconds.

In addition to having a good psychological effect upon the swimmer, this type of set may also be better physiologically in some respects than a straight set. It permits the swimmer to begin at a relatively low level of effort and physical stress and to finish with almost maximum stress.

The inherent shortcoming of this type of set is that the swimmer will swim his first repeats so slowly that they will not provide enough stress to affect his conditioning. The coach and the swimmer must set reasonable goals, insofar as time is concerned, to prevent this occurrence. In this kind of set it is not always important that the rest interval be held constant. As the swimmer becomes more fatigued from the steadily increasing exertion, his recovery between repeats will be prolonged. The swimmer, however, may want to hold the rest period constant in order that he might standardize the set. That is, he might swim a given progressive set similarly each time and thus use this set to test his conditioning.

An example of a progressive set of 8 × 200-meter swims with a rest interval of about 5 minutes, as used by Don Schollander in preparing for the 1964 Olympic Games, is given as follows:

Number of repeats	1	2	3	4	5	6	7	8
Time for 200 meters	2:16.7	2:14.1	2:11.6	2:10.0	2:10.1	2:09.0	2:08.2	2:06.7

REGRESSIVE SET.   Regressive sets of repeat swims, in which the swimmer intentionally swims more slowly with each successive repeat, probably have a detrimental psychological effect as well as doing little for him physiologically. Each successive repeat of a swimmer in poor condition may be slower, but this diminishing speed is due to fatigue and should not be intentional.

ALTERNATING PROGRESSIVE-REGRESSIVE SET.   An amusing and challenging method of swimming a series of repeats, particularly of the shorter distances (such as 20 × 50) is that of having the swimmer go a set of alternate progressive-regressive repeats. In such a set the swimmer will try to increase his speed progressively on the odd numbered repeats and decrease his speed on the even numbered repeats. This kind of routine introduces variety into the workout and allows the swimmer to learn a little about pace. It teaches him to "shift gears," that is, to swim at various speeds. However, it should not be used too often since it probably does not introduce a physiological stress factor that is constant enough to bring about optimum conditioning. It is useful, however, when the swimmers are a little too tired for either a straight or progressive set. This writer likes to use this kind of set with his team during the tapering period or, as has been mentioned, when he wants to give the swimmers a change from their normal workout routines.

ALTERNATING SLOW-FAST SET. When swimming this type of set the swimmer will alternate a hard, fast repeat with a slow, easy one. Such sets are used extensively in track. The slow repeat can be swum with or without timing, and is used primarily to aid recovery. This type of set has not been popular with most swimming coaches and swimmers, and its use has generally been confined to early season, to rest the swimmers when they are tired, or during the tapering period.

BROKEN SET. This set is a very interesting and strongly motivating method of training. In it the swimmer will swim only a small number of repeat swims, such as 4 to 8 × 50, using a short rest interval of 10 to 30 seconds, but keeping the speed of these swims faster than pace speed. After doing such a set, the swimmer will take a long rest, then do another set. An application of this type of routine, as used by Dick Roth, Olympic champion at the 400-meters individual medley (1964) in 4:45.4, follows: swim 8 × 50 meters in individual medley sequence (2 × 50 fly, 2 × 50 back, 2 × 50 breast, and 2 × 50 free) with a rest interval of 10 seconds and with only a record of the actual swimming time being kept (a more detailed description of this method can be found on page 252). Repeat this series 3 times, allowing adequate rest (5 to 8 minutes) between each series. Roth's times were 4:45, 4:42, 4:41, all of which were as fast or faster than his world record.

This type of routine can also be adapted to fit the needs of sprinters (4 to 8 × 25, rest interval of 10 seconds), 200-meter men (4 to 6 × 50, rest interval of 15 seconds), and so on.

This set obviously combines interval training and repetition training. While it may seem to be more a form of interval training than of repetition training because of the short rest interval between each repeat, nevertheless it more closely conforms to the tenets of repetition training since the intensity or speed of the swim is so high (faster than actual racing speed) and since almost complete recovery is allowed between each set of repeats. The short rest between each fast repeat swim permits the swimmer to repay some of his oxygen debt and also allows the heart rate to return more nearly to normal. This type of training can be considered to be both speed and endurance work and perhaps better simulates the actual stress conditions the swimmer will encounter in his race than any other type of training except time trials or the actual race.

Time Trials and Competitive Racing

Important parts of any swimmer's training program are the time trials and actual races he engages in to prepare for his top performances. These efforts provide the swimmer with an opportunity to learn how to swim his race. They are of little value if he repeatedly makes the same mistakes. To a degree they permit experimentation with such variables as pace, breathing patterns, and turns. Their purpose, however, is not to serve as a means of trying every "crack-pot" idea that enters the swimmer's mind.

According to Nikolai Kriukiv,[13] Secretary of the Russian Swimming Federation, the Russians feel, on the basis of research in the area, that a swimmer should swim his race either in a time trial or a race at least 10 to 12 times during the last three months of training. Only in this way can he consistently count on swimming his best possible race as far as pace is concerned.

The use of all-out efforts (other than short sprints) either as time trials or in actual races should be discreet, however. As a daily training routine, maximum efforts may be harmful, resulting in a depletion of what Hans Selye[14] calls *adaptation energy*. When Austrian scientists exposed hamsters to a daily training program consisting of bouts of extended maximum efforts (swimming and running were the activities used), they soon showed signs of exhaustion and, after a few days, their performance levels dropped sharply.[15] Many coaches and swimmers find this phenomenon also occurring in humans when too much high quality or near maximum efforts are introduced into their workouts.

---

[13] Interview by the author, February, 1964.
[14] Hans Selye, M.D., *Stress of Life* (New York: McGraw-Hill Book Co., 1956), pp. 65-66.
[15] Ludwig Prokop, "Adrenals and Sport," *The Journal of Sports Medicine and Physical Fitness*, III, Nos. 2-3 (June-September 1963), 117.

THE FORMULATION OF
SOME PRINCIPLES OF TRAINING

On the basis of the various types of training methods that the coach assigns to the swimmer, specific physiological adaptations are made and the swimmer proceeds to become *conditioned*. The generally held concept that interval training develops endurance exclusively, that sprint training develops speed exclusively, and that repetition training develops some of both is again an over-simplification of the actual situation. A swimmer who trains on nothing but sprints will not be able to swim a mile as fast as a person of equal ability who is training on interval training methods, but he certainly will be able to swim a mile faster than a person of equal ability who is not doing any training at all. Interval training and fartlek do develop endurance primarily, but they also develop some elements of speed; the reverse is true of sprint training. Figure VIII–1 attempts to convey the concept that the various methods contribute varying amounts to speed and endurance.

Many physiological changes occur as a result of these different types of training—some are subtle, some apparent. Controversy exists on many of the issues involved in training, and the area of physiological adaptations is no exception. Many of these adaptations will not be discussed in detail since they are not of general interest. Where it is felt that a better understanding of the concepts of training will result, they will be undertaken (see Chapter XIII on the general principles of training).

Regardless of what training method or combination of methods the swimmer is using at a given time, there are certain questions which must be answered. Interval training and repetition training present the swimmer with more questions than do the other methods. The questions asked earlier in this discussion were represented by the word D I R T: distance to be repeated, interval of rest, number of repeats, and time required to swim the distance. To this list of questions must be added another two: what should be done during the rest interval (swim easily, get out of the pool and rest, or rest in the pool), and how the various methods should be combined so as to achieve maximum performance at the proper time.

The Distance to be Repeated

The distance of the repeat swims which are to be done in either interval training or repetition training should generally be less than or the same as the distance the swimmer is training for. In both interval training and repetition training the repeat swims should be done at faster than,

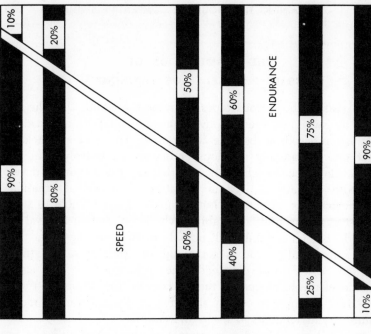

Sprint Training: 6 x 50 all-out effort. Rest Interval: 5 min. Maximum pulse rate: 185-190, recovery to less than 95. Average time: :22.5.

Repetition Training: 6 x 100 at 90-95 per cent effort. Rest Interval: 3-7 min. Maximum pulse rate: 180-185, recovery to less than 100. Average time: :51-:52.

Fast Interval Training: 15 x 100 at 85 to 90 per cent effort. Rest Interval: 1 min. Maximum pulse rate: 175-180, recovery to 120-140. Average time: :55-:56.

Slow Interval Training: 20 x 100 at 80-85 per cent effort. Rest Interval: 15 to 30 sec. Maximum pulse rate: 170-180, recovery to 150-160. Average time: :62.

Fartlek Training: Alternating slow-fast swimming for 1 mile. Maximum pulse rate: 170-180, minimum pulse rate: 130.

Marathon Swimming: Swimming continuously at a moderate speed. Average pulse rate: 140-155.

FIG. VIII–1. Relative Percentage Contribution of the Various Methods of Training to Speed and Endurance

TABLE VIII–3. Summary of Total Number of Various Distance Repeats Swum, Kicked, and Pulled by Mike Troy in One Year of Training, 1959-60*

Swimming	25's	50's	100's	220's	440's	880's
November	86	252	29	7	6	0
December	32	214	43	6	7	1
January	26	289	76	19	9	2
February	173	434	79	14	5	0
March	38	384	72	19	13	1
April	0	25	2	3	1	0
May	1	112	29	6	26	4
June	12	491	180	43	42	8
July	150	403	98	56	31	3
August	61	226	55	23	16	1
Totals	379	2831	663	196	156	20

Kicking (flutter board)

	25's	50's	100's	220's	440's
November	20	41	11	0	5
December	6	30	17	0	4
January	6	33	30	4	4
February	0	45	40	4	2
March	0	31	17	2	3
April	0	0	1	0	0
May	0	10	8	0	8
June	0	58	46	3	9
July	16	58	32	9	4
August	0	10	24	2	1
Totals	48	316	226	24	39

Pulling (with seven-inch tube wrapped around ankles)

	25's	50's	100's	220's	440's
November	20	39	11	0	2
December	6	33	17	0	2
January	6	34	30	4	1
February	8	44	41	4	2
March	0	28	15	2	2
April	0	0	0	0	0
May	0	10	8	0	8
June	0	58	47	3	9
July	6	58	27	9	5
August	0	10	16	2	1
Totals	46	314	212	24	32

TOTAL MILES †

	Miles Swum	Kicked	Pulled	Total
Winter	162.1	53.4	49.0	264.5
Summer	170.0	51.0	45.5	266.5
Total	332.1	104.4	94.5	531.0

* Only the interval training part of the workouts are included in this summary. The lengths swum but not timed are not included.

† The total miles in workout are included, not just those lengths that were timed.

near, or at racing speed. If the distance swum is much greater than the racing distance, the swimmer will have to swim at a speed considerably slower than racing speed. While some combination of over distance, interval training work (such as 4 × 440-yards swim for a 200-yard swimmer) is desirable, particularly in early season work, it contributes little to the speed of the swimmer over the shorter distance.

The following distances are recommended for use with interval training and repetition training:

	Distances to train at
Sprinters (training for 50- and 100-yard events)	25, 50, 75, 100
Middle distance (training for 100- and 200-yard events)	25, 50, 75, 100, 150, 200
Distance swimmers (training for 200-, 500-, and 1650-yard events)	25, 50, 100, 200, 400, 800, 1500

Over distance repeats contribute to the endurance of the swimmer and, while they may help him psychologically, in that they give him confidence at the shorter distance, they must be used with discretion during the final phase of the swimmer's preparation for the big meets. They should not be substituted for under-distance repeats. Table VIII–3 shows the number of repeat 25's, 50's, 100's, 200's, 440's, and 880's done by Mike Troy in the 12-month period just prior to winning the 1960 Olympic trials and also the Olympic championship in the 200-meter butterfly event. Approximately 60 per cent of these repeats were swum using the butterfly; the other 40 per cent were freestyle. From this table it can be seen that in Troy's case maximum emphasis was placed on the 50's, 100's, and 200's.

The Interval of Rest Between Repeat Swims

The length of the interval of rest between repeat swims depends upon what quality the swimmer is working to develop. In a research project conducted at Indiana University three groups of swimmers were given the same workouts over a period of five weeks with varying amounts of rest between repeat swims. The workouts were as follows: Monday— 20 × 50; Tuesday—10 × 100; Wednesday—5 × 200; Thursday—10 × 100; Friday—20 × 50. Each group was assigned different rest intervals, as outlined below.

	Rest Between		
	50's	100's	200's
Group A: Short rest group	10	30	60
Group B: Medium rest group	30	60	2:00
Group C: Long rest group	60	2:00	4:00

All groups were timed over the distances of 50, 100, 200, and 400 yards at the beginning and end of the experiment. The improvements in times at the various distances are ranked on the chart below.

		400	200	100	50
Ranked in order of the	1	A	C & B	C	C
greatest improvement	2	B	C & B	B	B
in times	3	C	A	A	A

The results of this experiment plus the practical experience of working with interval training and repetition training seem to permit the formulation of the following conclusions. *When the interval of rest is shortened and the quality of the repeat is reduced, there is a shift away from the development of speed and towards the development of endurance. When the interval of rest is lengthened* (within reasonable limits, since too long a rest period may be detrimental to the effect of warm-up and the other adjustments of the body to exercise), *the quality of the repeat swims can be improved and it is thereby possible to emphasize the development of speed.*

Below is a chart suggesting approximate rest intervals for the various distances when using slow interval training, fast interval training, and repetition training.

	Slow Interval Training	Fast Interval Training	Repetition Training
50's	10-20 sec.	25-1:30	1:45-up
100's	10-45 sec.	50-2:30	3:00-up
200's	30-60 sec.	1:30-3:00	3:30-up
400's	30-120 sec.	2:30-5:00	6:00-up

The Number of Repeat Swims

The number of repeat swims accomplished by a swimmer in a workout depends upon several factors, including the time available and the event for which the swimmer is training. There are, however, some general principles that can guide a coach in setting up the straight or mixed sets of repeats to be done in a workout.

The shorter the race a swimmer is training for, the fewer the number of repeats he should swim at a given distance. For example, when using interval training, a distance man might do 20 × 100, others 15 × 100, and sprinters 10 × 100.

The faster a series of repeats is swum, the fewer should be the number of repeats; for example, when using the interval training method with a short rest of one minute and low quality (60 seconds per 100 yards), the swimmer, being a 200 man, might go 15 × 100. If he were using the repetition training method, he might go only 8 × 100, with a long rest of three minutes, but would swim each one in 55 seconds or faster.

It is a good policy to set up straight sets of repeats for slow interval training, fast interval training, and repetition training. Some suggested straight sets are shown in Table VIII–4.

TABLE VIII–4. Suggested Straight Sets for Slow Interval Training, Fast Interval Training, and Repetition Training

	Sprinters			Middle Distance			Distance		
	S.I.T.	F.I.T.	R.T.	S.I.T.	F.I.T.	R.T.	S.I.T.	F.I.T.	R.T.
50	20	20	8	40	30	16	40	30	16
100	15	12	5	20	15	5	25	20	8
200	8	6	2	10	8	4	16	10	4
400	4	3	1	6	4	2	8	5	3
800	2	1	0	2	2	1	4	3	2
1650	0	0	0	1	1	0	2	1	1

The Time It Takes to Cover the Distance

Two other ways of treating the same topic are to say "the amount of effort" or "the pace at which a repeat is to be swum." A swimmer doing a series of repeats in either interval training or repetition training methods may either try to swim all of them in approximately the same time, vary their speed in order to get progressively faster, begin fast and regress in times as he proceeds through the set, or alternate slow repeats with fast ones. The first two methods are recommended over the last two, as has been stated in the description of these various sets. In the present discussion the writer will refer to the first method and to sets in which the times are held constant. The reference to times will be to the mean average times. As has been mentioned, the longer the rest (within limits), the faster should be the repeat swim.

PERCENTAGE EFFORT. Frequently, swimmers and coaches will discuss the effort a person should exert in a given swim as percentage effort. Percentage effort is a nebulous term and is relative to so many factors that it has little meaning. A specific and common understanding might be attained by merely asking each swimmer to think of 10 per cent slower than the best time of which he is capable for a given distance as being 90 per cent effort, 20 per cent slower as 80 per cent effort, and so on.

For example, a swimmer who is capable of swimming 100 yards in 50 seconds would have the following percentage efforts:

	100%	95%	90%	85%	80%	75%	70%	65%	60%
Seconds	50	52.5	55	57.5	60	62.5	65	67.5	70

An actual analysis of propulsive forces in swimming the crawl stroke [16] revealed that in one of the swimmers tested the average propulsive force needed to maintain the speed of six feet per second or 100 per cent all-out effort (50 seconds for 100 yards) was 19.6 pounds. Ninety-five per cent speed is, therefore, equivalent to 18.6 pounds of propulsive force. The actual measurement of what speed this amount of propulsive force gave the swimmer is given in the bottom column of Table VIII–5.

TABLE VIII–5. Percentage of Efforts

Percentage effort	100%	95%	90%	85%	80%	75%	70%	65%	60%
Average propulsion in pounds	19.6	18.6	17.6	16.6	15.6	14.6	13.6	12.6	11.5
Achieved time for 100 yards	50.0	51.1	52.3	55.1	57.7	60.4	63.5	69.5	78.0

The preceding discussion makes several generalizations feasible: (1) when a swimmer swims his repeats at a very fast pace (see Figure VIII–2) and builds up a large oxygen debt, he is developing speed and muscle resistance, (2) the slower he swims his repeats, the less speed he is developing; if he swims them too slowly, he is not even building a significant amount of endurance, and (3) the description of the differences between repetition training and interval training in itself explains what is to be gained from swimming the repeats at the various speeds.

What To Do During the Rest Intervals

In track the runner will generally run a series of repeat efforts, and between these runs will jog or walk a given distance (perhaps a slow 220 or 440). During this period the pulse rate will decrease [from 180–170 to 120–140 if the Gerschler-Reindell Law (page 210) is being followed]. Some runners, notably those in East Germany, have tried resting by sitting down, and have found their pulse rates returned to normal faster than when they jogged. In swimming the same phenomenon has been noted by this writer. If the swimmer stops immediately following a repeat swim, his pulse rate will reach a lower rate in a given time than if he swims slowly for the same period of time. Recovery of the heart is not the only physiological consideration, however. It is possible that under certain conditions it is advisable for the swimmer to swim slowly and remain at least mildly active for a short period of time, perhaps after a very hard effort in which a large oxygen debt has been built up

[16] James E. Counsilman, "An Analysis of the Application of Force in Two Types of Crawl Stroke," Ph.D. dissertation, State University of Iowa, Iowa City, August, 1951.

and there is an accumulation of metabolites in the muscle (lactic acid, carbon dioxide, and so on). Mild exercise will have a massaging effect on the muscles which will help flush out the metabolites and bring oxygen and blood sugar to the muscles.

In the summer of 1962 this writer decided to train his team by doing a major part of the repeat work by alternating fast-slow sets in a manner similar to that of many track athletes; that is, by having them swim an easy 50 or 100 yards between each repeat swim whether they were training with interval training or repetition training. The swimmers might swim 40 × 50 with one 50 being swum hard in an effort to raise the pulse rate to 180, the next swum slowly with no time recorded. After the slow 50 the pulse rate would usually be down to the 120–130 range. The third 50 would then be fast, the fourth slow, and so on through the 40 repeats. The same procedure was used in all repeats, with the exception that between 100, 200, and 400 repeat swims 100 meters was swum easily. No control group was used in this experiment, and any evaluation of this training method over that used in previous years must be based on the subjective judgment of the coach and the swimmers involved, in addition to the best competitive times recorded by the swimmers who took part. In the opinion of the swimmers and the coach and from the evidence of best times, this method of easy swimming between each repeat swim was inferior to merely resting in the water between each swim.

This does not mean that this writer believes it is never advisable to swim easily between repeat swims. When using repetition training, some easy swimming after the repeat swim is recommended. The following procedures are recommended for a general plan concerning what to do between repeat swims:

Interval training (slow or fast)	Stay in water—remain inactive or merely loosen up by shaking arms or legs loosely. Start each repeat from a push-off.
Repetition training	Swim easily after each hard effort the following distance: for a 50—25, for a 100, 200, or 400—50, for a 400 or over—easy 100. Get out of pool and dry off, rest in sitting or lying position. Start each repeat from a dive.
Sprint training	Same as for repetition training. Start each repeat from a dive.

Combining the Various Training Methods

From the foregoing discussion of training methods, it becomes increasingly obvious that there are many effective methods of training for competitive swimming. No single method holds all of the answers for a *complete training program.* It is, in fact, impossible to develop a swimmer's full potential with a single method. At some time during the season a complete or balanced program possibly should include most of the methods discussed. The relative proportion of each type to be used in a workout will depend on: (1) what distance a swimmer is training for—a distance man's program should have a different emphasis than a sprinter's, and (2) what phase of the program the swimmer is in—there should be a different emphasis at different times of the season. It is possible that a coach might use a particular combination of systems with his team one year and an entirely different combination with the same group the next and get essentially the same results. That is not to say that any combination of systems will give the same results. These opinions should not, however, deter the coach or swimmer from experimentation within the systems, since it is important that neither of them becomes static and inflexible in planning the swimmer's program.

A swimmer uses not only his body, but also his mind while swimming. If he leaves his career in competitive swimming prematurely, it is usually for one of two reasons: lack of success or boredom. Many swimmers train and compete for as long as ten years or more. However, if a swimmer is exposed to the same type of routine day after day, year after year, he will not always be challenged either physically or intellectually. A coach should not be merely a person who assigns the difficult work that brings about maximum physiological adaptation; he should also be a person who educates and challenges his swimmers. He may be considered to be a teacher who always has a bag of tricks, and can approach the problem of training with intelligence and enthusiasm.

A coach may use over distance work for early season training one year, fartlek the next year, slow interval training the third year, and a combination of any of the two or three methods the fourth. If he has planned well, he will have good results with all four and will probably have increased the longevity of the swimmers' careers by giving them variety. If, in addition, he has explained the various techniques and their purpose to his swimmers, he has challenged them intellectually and perhaps educated them insofar as a scientific knowledge of conditioning is concerned.

Planning a Season's Swimming Training Program

THE INDIANA SYSTEM

Before a swimming training program can be set up, many factors must be considered: (1) the amount of time available in the pool, (2) the number of swimmers who will be training at a given time, (3) the level, age, sex, and proficiency with which the coach is working, (4) the kind of general condition the swimmers are in at the time, (5) the length of the season, (6) the attitude of the group toward hard work, and (7) the events and distances for which the swimmers are training. There are, however, certain easily understood concepts which must be considered also, the understanding of which should give direction to the planning of any swimming training program. They are: (1) maximum adaptation stress, (2) progression, and (3) motivation.

The Maximum Adaptation Stress Concept

It was stated in the previous chapter that the conditioning of an athlete involves the sum total of all physiological, anatomical, and psychological changes made by the individual in adaptation to the stress of the training program. It is obvious that, if the swimmer trains too little, he will fail to reach maximum conditioning; if he trains too much, the stress of the training program will be so great that the swimmer will not be able to adapt and will experience failing adaptation. This is the point of diminishing return, beyond which hard training will do him more harm than good.

It follows that an intelligent coach is aware of these facts and is constantly striving to reach the delicate balance between too much and too little training. At the present time there is no specific, easily administered and evaluated predictor of when this point has been reached. Coaches and researchers are looking for such tests, and while such measurements as the pulse rate, ECG, hemoglobin level, and blood pressure do contribute to our knowledge of the physiological status of the swimmer, the best and most practical judgment of the point at which the swimmer has had exactly enough training is exercised by the coach. Perhaps the ability to do this effectively marks the difference between a good and a poor coach. Certainly the swimmer himself cannot always evaluate when he has had enough or not enough training. He should not always quit training when he feels fatigued; in fact it is very important that, at times, the swimmer train through a period of fatigue. During the training program a swimmer should not always feel "fresh as a daisy," but should at times experience a feeling of general fatigue for a period of days.

This concept of placing a maximum adaptation stress on the individual for a period of days and then reducing the work level for a short period of time is best shown by Figure IX–1. While this graph is not an attempt at a scientific evaluation of the stress and adaptation concept, it does provide a general idea of the principles behind the Indiana system of training.

The swimmer should train hard enough in most practice sessions in order to finish the workout with an acute feeling of fatigue. Some coaches feel the swimmer should recover completely from this feeling of fatigue from one workout to the next. If the swimmer does not do so, he is permitted a rest period or, at least, a period of reduced work to permit recovery. The experience of this writer in training swimmers has not shown this type of training to be the most effective. The best results have been obtained when the swimmers have been pushed to the point at which there is a constant level of general fatigue superimposed upon the temporary or acute fatigue which the swimmer feels immediately after practice.

In other words, the swimmer should be worked hard enough so he does not recover completely from one workout to the next. He becomes forced down into what the swimmers call *the valley of fatigue*–this point

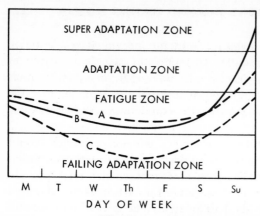

How hard should an athlete work and how much fatigue should he condition himself to endure in order to build maximum endurance? Should he work hard and, when he becomes fatigued, rest, so that he will be fresh for the next practice? Or should he impose a work load on himself that is so great that he will not completely recover from one practice session to the next? Should he always feel slightly fatigued? Can he push himself too hard?

These are questions that all intelligent coaches ask themselves when training athletes for such sports as middle or distance running, walking, swimming, and bicycling. The chart above is an attempt to show the basis for the Indiana University Swimming Program. The terms and the chart are not scientific, but are a subjective evaluation used to help present a concept.

"A" represents the progress of a swimmer who worked moderately hard Monday through Friday. With reduced work on Saturday and Sunday he started to recover from the fatigue, and his level of adaptation went above normal.

"B" represents the progress of a swimmer who worked hard enough to bring him close to the edge of the failing adaptation zone. With reduced work he was able to achieve super adaptation.

"C" represents the progress of a swimmer who was worked so hard that he was forced into the failing adaptation zone. Even with rest or reduced work he did not return to the normal level.

This chart shows that to get the maximum adaptation (which here is called super adaptation) the athlete must work very hard, pushing himself to the verge of failing adaptation (B), before he reduces his work load.

corresponding to the dip in the line in Figure IX–1. When he has been pushed just far enough and not too far, he is then given a reduced amount of work or a period of rest, and should experience the recuperation referred to as *super-adaptation* in Figure IX–1. This short period of rest or reduced work permits the body to renew its adaptation energy and ready itself for another cycle of work of a more intense nature. Keeping the swimmer in this valley of fatigue too long may result in failing adaptation, and the swimmer may have difficulty recuperating. The reverse practice, however, of never pushing the swimmer into the valley of fatigue will not result in maximum conditioning, particularly for the endurance swimmer.

Figure IX–1 indicates that there are times when a swimmer should work hard and times when the work should be reduced—either in intensity, duration, or both. This does not mean that the coach must provide an entirely different routine for each swimmer for each workout, although he should be aware of individual differences among his swimmers in their capacity for work and their ability to adapt to this work. He can introduce variation into the general workout pattern that will match the pattern of the average swimmer, and this, coupled with the natural inhibition of the individual to work hard when he is excessively tired, will provide a good program for most of the swimmers.

The highly motivated swimmer may tend to maintain too high a performance level in practice, and may push himself into the failing adaptation stage with the same workout that the less highly motivated swimmer will not do hard enough to get near maximum adaptation. Some great swimmers can feel when they are pushing themselves just the right amount and thus know when to work harder and when to throttle back. These swimmers are few and far between; a coach should feel lucky when he has *one* such swimmer. He must watch his swimmers and study each individual in order to be able at one time to encourage them to work harder, and at another to work less hard or perhaps drop out of practice temporarily. If the team is handled properly, its members' progress will follow a general pattern, and most of them will be fatigued at the same time and correspondingly rested at the same time.

SIGNS OF EXCESSIVE FATIGUE.   There are specific signs of excessive fatigue or failing adaptation, such as loss of appetite and a consequent loss of weight, or swollen lymph glands, which will be discussed in detail in Chapter XIII. Before these symptoms become manifest, however, the work load should have been reduced because the coach had observed certain other preliminary symptoms. These first signs might be a decreased level of performance by the whole team in all phases of their workouts. The times on repeat swims, kicks, and pulls would all begin to slow down. Even when called upon to make a fast effort, the team members would not have been able to come near top performance. They would have complained more than usual and have shown signs of emotional irritability, such as becoming unduly upset when they bumped into someone while swimming a repeat. A general statement which would be helpful throughout a training program might be: as long as the swimmers keep swimming fast in practice, doing good repeats and good efforts, work them hard or harder. *Even after they begin having the feeling of general fatigue, they will continue to swim well in practice, so keep them working hard up to the point at which their performances in practice begin to suffer.* At this point they should be watched carefully and the coach should be ready to reduce the work load by:

1. Decreasing the total amount of distance done in workout,

2. Decreasing the quality of work, such as going to over distance or to slow interval training, or

3. Allowing a period of rest, such as a day or a day and a half.

It is difficult for a coach to anticipate exactly when his team will reach the point at which the work load must be reduced. For this reason flexibility in the training program is desirable. This writer is opposed to a training schedule which consists of a completely predictable pattern of workouts, such as every Monday—30 × 50 repeats, Tuesday—20 × 100 repeats, and so on. A general pattern must be adopted. The following weekly general pattern is used at Indiana University when the swimmers are not peaking for a big meet on the weekend. Monday, Tuesday, and Wednesday the workouts are very hard and the coach expects good performances in the workouts. The Thursday and Friday workouts are adjusted in intensity and duration based upon how the swimmers performed on the two previous days. By Saturday the swimmers should be fatigued and the workout is usually decreased, not in terms of total distance, but in intensity. If the swimmers have trained hard for six consecutve days, the seventh day or Sunday can be taken off completely, or the swimmer can do some easy distance swimming such as a continuous mile or two-mile swim untimed.

By the next day (Monday), the swimmer should be ready to begin another bout of training and should be ready for good performances in his practice sessions. If he is still so fatigued that all of his repeat swims are slower than usual and he feels exhausted, it can be assumed that the previous work load was too great. Other stress factors such as poor diet, lack of sleep, or breaking of other training rules can also cause poor performances in practice. Their effect upon the swimmer's conditioning process must also be considered.

VARIATION OF HIGH-PRESSURE–LOW-PRESSURE WORKOUTS. It is a mistake for any coach or swimmer to feel that every part of every workout every day should be of a high-pressure or intense nature. It is also a mistake to permit so much variation of effort in practice that the swimmer never reaches top condition. The coach may assign only part or parts of the workout to be done at a high-pressure or intense level of effort, and the rest of the workout may be of only moderate intensity. One method of providing a cyclic variation in routines is to vary workouts of straight sets of repeats with workouts of mixed or progressive sets of repeats. This type of variation has already been discussed in the previous chapter. It may be considered a variation in terms of high-pressure and low-pressure workouts. The straight sets of repeats can be considered as the high-pressure type of workout because the swimmers are setting goals that they must exert extreme effort to reach, and will generally try to improve over their best previous time average for the year for that particular set.

When training with a low-pressure type of routine, the individual may swim just as far and work almost as hard, but the goals may or may not be difficult depending on whether the coach feels the swimmers need hard work or just work of moderate intensity. The high- or low-pressure factor is introduced into the workout as much by the coach's attitude and the goals he sets as it is by the type of set he assigns to the swimmers. It is also possible for this variation of pressure to fluctuate within the workout.

If, as it appears, there is a rhythm of training in which, whether they know it or not, swimmers alternate hard work with diminished work and rest, then it should be possible for this cyclic variation to be expressed within the framework of the team's method of training, particularly if the high-pressure—low-pressure pattern is used in workouts.

Progression

A swimmer who is out of shape must get into shape progressively. In other words, he should not try to begin with long, hard workouts, but should use workouts of reduced intensity in duration and effort. While this fact would seem fairly obvious, it is amazing how many programs or swimmers disregard it and try to start with a bang, beginning hard training from the first.

The Indiana System is based on a steady progression throughout the training season until the tapering period. This progression can be introduced in the form of: (1) an increase in the total distance swum in each workout, (2) an increase in the intensity with which the distance is swum, or (3) an increase in the total number of workouts per week.

For example, in early season a senior swimmer may train in the water only three days a week, averaging one and a half miles per day and training primarily with over distance or fartlek methods; later he may train five days a week, once a day, increasing the distance to two and a half miles per day in a slow interval training pattern; then, at the peak of his training season, he may come in six days a week, twice each day, averaging a total of four and a half to six miles per day and training with an integrated program which introduces more work of an intense nature. Too often, the swimmer will try to rush his training and not lay a good foundation on which to base a season's program. *It is important to remember to build endurance first in the training program and to superimpose speed later in the season.* Introducing too much speed work early in the season may produce early drops in times over the distance for which the swimmer is training, but it will increase the chances of an early season peaking and a subsequent plateau or leveling-off of improvement.

Motivation

For a swimmer to engage in a strenuous training program, he must be strongly motivated. Sometimes this motivation to succeed comes from within the individual; more frequently, however, it must be directed from without. This is the job of the coach, and the general organization of the program should be such that the program itself motivates the athlete to train conscientiously and intelligently. It is not always the coach who knows the most about training techniques whose swimmers succeed in attaining top condition; the coach who is a good psychologist, other factors being equal, will have a distinct advantage. Methods of motivating swimmers during practice sessions will be discussed in a later chapter (Chapter XII).

The Place of Dry Land Exercises in the Program

A stronger and more flexible swimmer will be a faster swimmer. It requires a lot of strength to pull the arms through the water, to push off, and to kick properly. The fastest way to build this strength, as well as to increase flexibility, is through dry land exercises. This does not mean that indiscriminate weight training and exercising will result in the building of strength and flexibility in the right places. A carefully planned program must be followed in order to obtain optimum results. A poorly planned program can bring about negative results. Chapter X discusses in detail the use of dry land exercises in the swimmer's program.

Dividing the Team into Three Groups for Practice Sessions— Sprinters, Middle Distance, and Distance Swimmers

Figure VIII–1 illustrates various training methods and the approximate percentage of speed and endurance each method contributes to total conditioning. It is obvious that all swimmers need both endurance and speed, but a sprinter needs to emphasize the development of speed, while the distance man must emphasize development of endurance. The middle distance swimmer must be concerned with developing both qualities in almost equal amounts.

A swimmer may be the best on his team in many or all events, and it may be necessary at times to have him swim events at the various distances. As the season progresses, this or any swimmer will experience better results in his special event if he trains for that specific event. Because of limited time and space in the pool, it may be impossible for a coach to organize three separate workouts for the three categories. It is possible to vary the workouts, within limits, to permit the distance men to do longer repeats and the sprinters to do more sprints. If, for example, the majority of the team members (the second category above) are doing a series of 30 × 50-yard repeats for the major part of the workout, the distance men may take one or two lanes and swim repeat 500's, while the sprinters may do only 15 of the 50's, but add 15 × 25-yard sprints. In this way all the swimmers would finish their workouts in the same amount of time. A well-organized team practice contributes to team morale and assures the coach that every team member has a good workout.

An experienced age-grouper may use workouts identical with those in any of the three groups, depending upon his ability to handle the work. Other age-group workouts are discussed in Chapter XI, devoted to age-group swimming.

CLASSIFICATION. 1. Sprinters—those who swim the 50 and 100, and occasionally the 200.

2. Middle distance—all breaststrokers, backstrokers, butterfliers, individual medley swimmers, and freestylers concentrating on the 100 and 200 freestyle events. This group makes up the bulk of most college or AAU swimming teams.

3. Distance—those training primarily for the longer freestyle races, 200 yards through 1500 meters.

Throughout the rest of this chapter the workouts for a single day will be divided into these three categories. A coach may frequently have all three groups do identical workouts. *Age-group teams do not have the wide spread in distances that college or senior swimmers must prepare for, and the coach may not want to specialize his swimmers at an early age.* It may also not be desirable to divide the swimmers at any age level into the three group patterns until the basic endurance conditioning phase is completed.

THE INDIANA SYSTEM OF INTEGRATING OR COMBINING
VARIOUS TRAINING METHODS INTO WORKOUTS

By combining various training methods into a single workout, the swimmer may build speed during one phase and endurance during another. The basis for the Indiana System of training is integration of the

TABLE IX–1. Integrated Workout Chart

Workout Phase	Type of Training	Average Time	Quality Developed	Range of Heart Rate
1. Swim 16 × 50 leaving on 45 sec.	Slow interval training	:28.5 sec.	Primarily cardio-respiratory endurance, also increase in number of functional capillaries in active muscles. Minor emphasis on speed.	Pulse rate after each 50, av. 182; before starting next 50, av. 143.
2. Swim 500-yd. pace	Over-distance training	5:21.6	Endurance—same as above, except the continuous nature of the swimming gives a longer lasting effect than interval training.	Pulse rate at start, 98; after finishing, 174.
3. Kick 500 yds. continuously	Over distance training (kicking)	No time	This phase is designed to overload the leg muscles and to develop their endurance, the actual number of capillaries being increased. Also has favorable effect on cardio-respiratory endurance.	Pulse rate at start, 108; after finishing, 152.
4. Kick 8 × 50 starting a 50 on each min.	Interval training (kicking)	:38.2 sec.	This drill introduces some speed work into the kicking practice and will help adapt the leg muscles to working at a more intense level.	Pulse rate after each 50, av. 179; before starting next 50, av. 144.
5. Pull 500 yds., two lengths at steady pace, every third length at fast pace	Fartlek or speedplay	No time	This phase overloads and builds endurance in the pulling muscles. Cardio-respiratory endurance is also favorably affected.	Pulse rate maximum of 176 after fast length; lowest level, 134.
6. Pull 3 × 100, rest 3 min. between each repeat	Repetition training	:61.5 sec.	The ability of the arm depressor muscles to resist the onset of fatigue, when the arms are working at an intense rate. This phase has a more favorable effect on speed than on endurance, but develops an element of both.	Pulse rate after each effort, av. 181; before starting next 100, av. 97.
7. Swim 4 × 150 yds., 95 per cent effort. 3–5 min. rest	Repetition training	1:19.3	This phase of the workout is speed and pace work. The ability of the muscle to resist the specific fatigue of working at intense level is favorably affected.	Pulse rate after each 150, av. 186; before starting 150, av. 94.
8. 4 × 25-yd. all-out sprints	Sprint training	:10.8 sec.	This phase is almost strictly for speed; it helps a swimmer learn to pick up his tempo and break out of slower stroking pattern he has been doing during most of workout.	Pulse rate after each 25, av. 176; before starting next 25, av. 96.

various training methods into a single workout. Just as a mixed diet of proteins, fats, carbohydrates, minerals, and vitamins is essential for good health, so a mixed or integrated program of the various types of training methods is essential for the top conditioning of swimmers. Table IX–I illustrates an integrated or mixed workout, shows how the various training methods are integrated into a single workout, and charts the quality that each phase of the workout develops.

This particular workout was used by a middle distance freestyler during the height of the indoor season. He was swimming the 100 freestyle in competition in :48.2, the 200 in 1:45.8, and the 500 in 4:55.4 at the time he swam this workout.

No one particular method of training can develop all of the qualities desirable in a swimmer, that is, speed, muscular endurance, cardiovascular endurance, and so on. The exact proportion of each of these qualities desirable in a swimmer at a given time depends primarily upon two factors: the time of season and the distance for which he is training. For this reason the relative amount of each type of training that should be included in an integrated program will also depend upon these two factors.

In order to illustrate best the different physiological changes which occur with the use of the different methods of training, let us turn to animal research. The superiority of animal research to determine the effects of various types of training programs over using only human subjects is obvious, inasmuch as we can dissect the animals to measure and observe physiological changes. Prokop, in experimenting with hamsters swimming with varying loads of 18 per cent, 36 per cent, 70 per cent, and 100 per cent, discovered that an experimental animal's heart developed to its maximum size when as little as 36 per cent of maximum training load in terms of intensity was applied to the animal in an interval training manner.[1] When the load was increased to 70 per cent and then to 100 per cent (repetition training) there was no additional hypertrophy of the heart (see Figure IX–2). In applying this animal research to human training for swimming, it would indicate that, so far as conditioning the swimmer's heart is concerned, a series of short swims at a moderate speed, such as the 24 × 50-meter swims with 10 seconds rest between each, described above, would condition the heart as well as would swimming the 50's at 70 per cent effort or at an all-out pace.

Incidentally, when experimental animals are placed in a training program of 100 per cent or all-out training effort (either by running on a tread mill or swimming with a load attached to their bodies), they soon

---

[1] Ludwig Prokop, "Adrenals and Sport," *The Journal of Sports Medicine and Physical Fitness,* III, Nos. 2-3 (June-September 1963), 117.

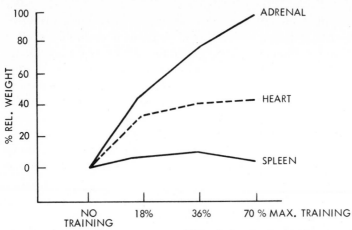

FIG. IX–2.   Prokop's Chart on the Suprarenal

begin to show signs of exhaustion and, after a few days, their perform-ance level begins to drop. Even neophyte coaches discover this fact very soon. Other than all-out efforts in short sprints, such as of 25- or 50-meters duration, very few 100 per cent efforts are required in a swimmer's train-ing program. A coach may ask his swimmers to go all-out only in a race or a time trial, perhaps once or twice a week.

In Prokop's study, the experimental animals developed some hyper-trophy of the suprarenal glands (apparently the cortex tissue is re-sponsible for the major part of the increase in size) when the interval training load was at 36 per cent intensity level. This hypertrophy was even more pronounced when the training level was increased to the 70 per cent intensity level. Under certain conditions of training, particularly when the intensity is maintained at the 100 per cent level for a period of time, the suprarenal glands apparently deplete their reserve and are incapable of supplying the hormones needed to handle the stress imposed on the body by the exercise. This is one of the first signs of failing adapta-tion of the athlete, and has been measured with some success by testing the level of ketosteroids in the urine. When this failing adaptation occurs, the athlete must be given a rest or a decreased work load. Pushing the athlete hard during this period may cause a serious setback in his train-ing schedule.

From the preceding animal research it becomes apparent that, if the adrenal gland is to be conditioned to its optimum level for exercise, some training must take place at approximately the 70 per cent level of in-tensity. This is exactly what the swimmer was doing in the last part of the workout (the repetition training phase) used as an example in Table IX–1.

While only two of the physiological aspects that are affected by training (heart changes and adrenal gland changes) have been discussed here, it is apparent that there are many other physiological changes that must be effected before a swimmer can be said to be in top condition. Some of these changes must occur in the muscles themselves. I feel that kicking on the board and pulling with the arms only are very important for the conditioning of specific muscle groups. These actions place a localized stress on that part of the body being used, and probably cause vestigial capillaries to open and other important functional changes to occur. Such capillarization would improve the muscle's ability to transport oxygen and glycogen to the muscle tissue and carbon dioxide and lactic acid away. For these reasons it is important to have a mixed training program that uses varying intensities of effort.

To summarize: The lower levels of intensity (such as the 24 × 50) condition the heart and body for endurance. Hard kicking and pulling condition the muscles locally to resist localized muscle fatigue. The moderately hard repetition work at the end of the workout conditions the body—particularly the suprarenal glands—for harder work. Too much work at the higher levels of intensity causes excessive stress on the body and, instead of adapting to the work program, the body may begin to show signs of a breakdown in this adaptation phase.

Just as nutritionists agree that a mixed diet is needed for proper nutrition, so I am sure that eventually most swimming coaches will agree that a mixed training program is necessary for proper conditioning of swimmers. But, just as nutritionists might disagree on exactly what proportion of any given food substance is essential for proper nutrition, so I am sure there will always be some disagreement among coaches on the amount of emphasis that should be placed on each type of swimming training.

General Format of an Integrated Workout

The question of whether one general pattern or format of workout is better than another is difficult to determine. In the workout outlined in Table IX–1 the main part of the speed work is done at the end of the workout. Is this always desirable? In studying the workout pattern of different champions, it can be seen that there is a great deal of variation among them (see Chapter XIV, *The Training Schedules of Some Champions*).

Perhaps no one general format is vastly superior to all of the others. The format a team uses may depend largely on the available time in the pool or the number of kick boards and pulling tubes.

The following pattern is used frequently by Indiana University swimmers when they are working out twice a day during the summer season.

FIRST WORKOUT (usually in the morning). At Indiana no single format is used for all workouts for reasons that will be explained later. The writer and swimmers, however, do have a general preference that is followed a good deal of the time, particularly for morning practice in the summertime and for the workout when only one session a day is being held.

1. Five to ten minutes of stretching exercises out of water.
2. A moderate set of repeats (usually slow interval training with a short rest, such as three to four broken 400's, ten seconds rest interval after each 50 or 100—progressive).
3. Kicking $\Big\}$ these can be reversed.
4. Pulling
5. A hard set of repeats (either fast interval training or repetition) such as 4 to 6 × 400, 6 to 12 × 200, or 8 to 20 × 100.
6. Some sprints.

The logic behind this format of workout is that the swimmers have just gotten out of bed or at least have not been in the water, and are not fully loosened up. During the night their muscles have shortened and must be stretched out properly. The easiest way to do this is to do stretching exercises and some easy to moderate swimming, starting at a relatively easy pace, and then progressively getting faster. This preliminary work conditions the swimmers to do their kicking and pulling and then the faster repeats. The weakness of this kind of format is that the swimmers become so familiar with it that they feel they need all of the preliminary swimming to warm up properly before they can swim fast. Sufficient time in the pool is not always available for a long warm-up before a meet, so it is important that a swimmer often be called upon to swim fast early in the workout in order that he may be able to do so in actual competition.

CHANGING FORMAT TO SIMULATE COMPETITIVE CONDITIONS.   It is very important that the conditions under which the swimmers will have to swim in competition be simulated in practice. Swimmers may encounter rough water, high chlorine level, poor lighting, or little warm up time. They may have to swim in several difficult races within a two-hour period. By the continued use of only one format of workout, the swimmer may become conditioned to swimming fast only after a lot of preliminary work. The reverse may also be true, and he may be so accustomed to only swimming fast early in the workout, when he is fresh, that he will not know how it feels to swim fast when he is tired, a situation he is likely to be confronted with in an actual meet after two or three hard races. For this reason it is important to occasionally change the pattern, and to have several formats in reserve:

1. One in which the speed work is done early in the workout and in which a minimum amount of warm up precedes it.
2. One in which the speed work is done late in the workout, after the swimmer is fairly tired.
3. One in which the speed work is done in the middle of the workout, after a good warm up, and before the swimmer is very tired.
4. One in which the speed work is split up and interspersed throughout the workout, such as:
   A. early and late in the workout.
   B. early, middle, and late in the workout.
   C. middle and late in the workout.

SECOND WORKOUT (usually in the afternoon). The format for the second workout of the day (or even the third) can be very flexible. If the coach feels the swimmers need a good set of repeats to elevate their morale, or if he wants a hard effort to learn exactly how the swimmers are progressing, he can plan and use the following format:

1. Warm up, as for before a meet, with an easy 400 swim and some progressive 50's (four to eight). Rest for five to ten minutes.
2. A set of hard repeats of either fast interval training or repetition training, or time a 95 per cent effort over the distance being trained for, or further, such as 200 or 400.
3. Kicking.
4. Pulling.
5. Some sprint work or another set of repeats.

The second workout permits a great variety of patterns because less warm up is needed.

THIRD WORKOUT. Several formats will be noted in the following workouts. The use of different formats helps the coach avoid the boredom factor and is mentally stimulating to both coach and swimmer.

If plenty of pool time and space is available, there may be no need for a third practice session. Unfortunately, this condition does not often exist and three workouts are necessary to get enough time in the pool. Three workouts a day present a problem, commuting time and possible loss of interest. If they are used, it should be only during the big push for the championship meets.

1. Warm up with 200 yards of swimming.
2. A set of repetition training repeats, such as 8×50 or 4×100, or a simulator 500 or 200.
3. A few sprints, 50's or 25's.

Method of Kicking and Pulling

The use of drills in which the leg kick or the arm pull is done separately serves several purposes. They provide variety in the swimmer's workout and they permit the swimmer to place an overload on the muscles being used to a greater extent than when the whole stroke is used. When a swimmer is doing a kicking drill, there is more blood available for the leg muscles than when he is using his total stroke, and the legs must share the blood flow with the arms. For this reason a swimmer can place greater localized stress on a given area when doing these drills. This stress causes increased capillarization (opening of vestigial capillaries), as well as general increased conditioning for both speed and endurance in these muscles.

Kicking and pulling drills place almost as great a conditioning stress on the cardio-vascular system as do the whole stroke drills. It is possible for a swimmer who has a temporary injury to his arms, which prevents him from using them in swimming movements, to condition his cardio-vascular system for swimming by doing only leg drills; the reverse is also true, in which a person with a leg injury can keep his cardio-vascular system in shape by using only pulling drills. Pulse rates in the range of 160 to 180 are attainable when doing all-out efforts on isolated drills.

These drills also allow the swimmer to isolate that specific part of his stroke which needs work and to concentrate on learning its proper movements. The shortcoming of this method of stroke correction, as has been discussed previously, is that it is impossible to imitate in these drills the precise movements that the swimmer will use when swimming. Since repetition is such an important factor in learning a skill, excessive use of imprecise, isolated kicking and pulling drills might be detrimental. The swimmer should try as fully as possible to duplicate the body position as well as the exact stroke mechanics of the whole stroke.

Kicking and pulling drills can be done in many ways. Kicking drills are commonly done while the swimmer holds onto a plastic kick board. Care should be taken that the swimmer not try to ride too high in the water. If he presses the board down and rides on top of it, he may succeed in holding his body too high and arching his back excessively. The board should be held out in front of the body with the arms extended and the shoulders relatively low in the water. When kicking on the back, either one arm or both should be held overhead; if both hands are held at the side, there is a tendency for the hips to drop too low.

When doing pulling drills, the swimmer should avoid dragging his feet too low in the water. One of the best methods to prevent this is to use a support, such as a small tube, partially inflated, wrapped in a figure eight around the ankles. A small implement or tractor tube with a six-inch inside diameter is the right size for age-group swimmers, while a tube with a seven-inch inside diameter is correct for older swimmers. The tube should be inflated only enough to support the feet, neither allowing them to ride unnaturally high nor to drag too low. Plastic supports and inflated bladders may also be used, if care is taken that the above precautions are observed. Many swimmers prefer to let their legs drag or to kick slightly. I, personally, do not like this method. The use of a kick board between the legs is not recommended, and it should never be used by crawl and backstroke swimmers. It causes the swimmer to ride too high, creates less drag than would be the case when he is swimming, and prevents the crawl and backstroke swimmer from rolling naturally.

Warm Up before the Race

The value of warm up before performing a physical activity has been questioned by some people, principally by researchers with little practical experience. Most coaches, however, believe it to be beneficial to the swimmer's performance, and their belief is based upon experiences with and without warm up.

Major-league pitchers have found that without sufficient warm up they tend to develop sore arms from pitching hard, they lack control, and cannot throw as good a curve ball as normally. The pitcher knows that without the warm up he has not stretched out his muscles and may possibly injure them. The warm up also gives him the opportunity to adjust or tone up his neuromuscular system in order that his coordination may be at its best. The pitcher must concentrate primarily on warming up his arm; the swimmer must warm up his entire body. The purposes of the warm up for the swimmer are:

1. To stretch out the muscles.
2. To adjust the body physiologically for the race (the heart rate rises slightly, the blood reaches the active muscles more quickly, and so on).
3. To tune up the neuromuscular system or, as the swimmers say, "to feel out his stroke."
4. To get used to the water temperature, adjust to the pool starts, turns, and so on.
5. To make final adjustments to the pace to be swum in the race.

While the warm up requirements of each individual may vary somewhat, it is good policy for a team to have a standardized warm up from which to work. An adequate warm up presupposes ample opportunity to get into the pool before competition begins. In case insufficient time or no time at all in the pool prior to competition is available, a period of stretching and warm up through the use of dry land exercises may be of some value.

A SUGGESTED WARM UP ROUTINE.   The following routine has been used by many swimmers with good results:

1. Warm up with a 500-yard swim at a moderate pace. If the swimmer begins to get winded, he should stop for a short period of time and then continue.

2. Kick 200 to 400 yards at a moderate pace.

3. Swim 8 × 50, swimming every other 50 at a moderate speed and the others at a hard, controlled speed about four to five seconds slower than best time. Rest 30 to 60 seconds after each 50.

4. Swim 4 × 25-yard sprints with a start and turn. Distance men pace 2 or 3 × 100.

5. Swim some easy lengths and then try a few starts and turns.

The warm up outlined above is designed for college swimmers in good condition. Age-group swimmers may want to reduce the distance by half or even more.

In championship meets in which there are preliminaries and finals in one day, this warm up does not have to be repeated before the finals. Once the swimmer is warmed up the effect will last for most of the day. The second time the swimmer has to swim he may find he only needs to swim a few lengths, with one or two paced 50's, or some hard 25's.

Each swimmer should try different warm up routines before such events as time trials or small meets in order that he may discover what warm up is best for him.

THE INDIANA SYSTEM OF
CHANGING EMPHASIS IN THE INTEGRATED WORKOUTS
AS THE SEASON PROGRESSES

The pattern of workouts changes as the swimming season progresses. The relative amount of endurance work in an integrated workout early in the training season will be greater than it will be later. Conversely, as the season progresses, more speed work in the form of repetition training, sprinting, and simulators will be introduced. In the plan of a year's training program that follows, the reader should note this change. While many swimmers will be unable or will not want to follow this program exactly, they should try to introduce similar changes in emphasis as their own programs progress through the season.

Workout Terminology

When the coach prescribes verbally or posts his workouts on a board, there should be agreement on the abbreviations and terminology. When such an abbreviated form as "30 × 50 swim on the minute" is used, this would, of course, mean that the swimmers should swim thirty 50-yard (or meter) efforts, beginning one on each minute. "Repeats" refer to the series of swims swum in an interval training or repetition training workout. All repeats are timed, either by the coach, an assistant or manager, or by the swimmer himself using a large pacing clock. Below are listed some examples of terms and phrases used in the workouts that follow, along with a description of the terms. For a more detailed description of these terms and the principles on which the methods are based refer to Chapter VIII.

Examples

SWIM 15 × 100 I.T. ON 2 MIN.   This should be interpreted to mean 15 efforts of 100 yards (or meters) each, each repeat to be done in an interval training manner, and beginning each repeat every two minutes.

SWIM 5 × 100 R.T. AT LEAST 5 MIN. REST.

> Freestylers—51 seconds or better.
> Backstrokers—58 seconds or better.
> Breaststrokers—65 seconds or better.
> Flyers—56 seconds or better.

This means that the swimmer should swim five efforts of 100 yards (or meters) each in a repetition manner (near maximum effort) and with at least five minutes rest between each 100. Time goals are also given.

KICK 20 LENGTHS, THEN 4 × 100 ON 3 MIN.   The swimmer is directed to kick the first 20 lengths at a moderate pace with no time to be recorded. He then should kick four efforts of 100 yards (or meters) each, starting each repeat on every third minute.

SWIM SIM. 200 (100–5 SEC., 50–5 SEC., 25–5 SEC., 25–START ON 45).   In this case the swimmer should swim a simulator; after the first 100 take five seconds rest, then swim a 50 and take five seconds rest, swim a 25 and take five seconds rest, then swim another 25. He should leave when the sweep hand on the pace clock reaches 45; in this way the five seconds' rest will be cancelled and the total swimming time will be recorded as though the swimmer had started with the hand on zero.

SWIM BROKEN 400, 10 SEC. AFTER EACH 100, START ON 30.   The swimmer should swim four repeats of 100 yards (or meters) each, taking precisely ten seconds of rest after each 100. By starting when the second hand reaches 30, the rest time will be cancelled and the total swimming time can be read directly from the pace clock.

SWIM 8 PROGRESSIVE 400's, ON 8 MIN.   This indicates to the swimmer that each succeeding 400 should be faster than the preceding one. Other types of sets of repeats are: straight sets in which the times of each repeat are held relatively constant; fast-slow set in which one repeat is fast and the next slow, repeating this pattern throughout the set; decreasing distance sets in which, on each succeeding repeat swim, the distance is decreased and the speed increased (such as 400–300–200–100); and simulators in which a form of decreasing distance is also used as the set progresses, with the difference being that only a short rest interval is used between efforts as compared with a long rest in the decreasing distance set. The simulator set is an attempt to simulate the pace and effort the swimmer will have to use in the actual race.

A Year's Training Schedule

The schedule outlined here corresponds to the program charted in Table IX–2. It provides for peak performances in March and April for the indoor season and in July and August for the outdoor season. The workouts in this schedule are typical, and a large variety are given in order that the reader may have a wide selection from which to choose. Different formats of the workouts are also provided so that the reader may select the one best suited to his training conditions. Additional workout routines are supplied throughout the book and in particular in Chapter XIV, *The Training Schedules of Some Champions.*

Coaches frequently set up their training programs so that the routines are similar or, in some cases, identical throughout the year. This can become monotonous even to a person who is new to the sport of swimming, and it can mean *finis* to a swimmer who has been in the sport for many years. For this reason it is well to change routines each year and to use a wide variety of workouts within each season.

It is also a good idea to divide the swimming season into four phases: pre-season training, the preparatory phase, the hard-training phase, and the tapering phase. This arrangement helps vary the routine and gives the swimmers some help in their attitudes toward the whole season. Instead of one long, continuous season which sometimes seems endless to the swimmer, he now has four shorter phases to swim through. As he finishes each phase, he gets a mental lift from this accomplishment.

PRE-SEASON TRAINING. Pre-season work, particularly dry land exercises, has been proven helpful to most swimmers, especially to the swimmer who has been inactive out of season. While it is true that there will be some conditioning carried over from the preceding season, the amount will vary depending on the length of the layoff period and the inactive or active manner in which the person has been living. Such activities as running, dry land exercises, and playing tennis will help maintain a certain level of fitness during this layoff period.

It is important to remember that the effects of training are specific, and that there is only limited carry-over value from one activity to the other, such as from track to swimming. If a person has no water available, he may have to settle for a program of dry land exercises, running, bicycling, or some other activity in order to maintain his fitness.

During the pre-season phase the coach may decide to use dry land exercises (either supervised or unsupervised) with the addition of some mild swimming. The coach may also decide to conduct classroom sessions a few times a week which will be devoted to stroke mechanics. He may show movies and lead discussions on stroke mechanics, training, or any phase of the swimming program. Pre-season training may also include such activities as water-polo and running.

THE PREPARATORY PHASE. This phase of the indoor season for most college, high school, and age-group teams begins in October or November and extends through November or December. Seasons vary somewhat in different parts of this country and among different countries; the following plan is for an indoor season with the swimming phase lasting for six months—October through March.

The lectures and movies begun during the pre-season phase should be continued, and a good deal of time should be devoted to stroke work, starts, and turns. Most coaches find that they do more work on stroke technique in this period and in the tapering period than during the hard-training phase.

Generally, during this preparatory period the swimmers tend to work at a level of effort lower than that of the next phase. The preparatory phase is just what its name implies and is designed for the following purposes: (1) to improve the swimmers' strength and flexibility through dry land exercises, (2) to improve the stroke mechanics, starts, and turns of the swimmers, and (3) to prepare or condition the body for the hard work that is to come in the next phase.

During this period the swimmers should do most of their workout using over-distance training, fartlek training, and interval training. Very little repetition training, sprinting, or simulators should be used.

One Week of Typical Workouts in the Preparatory Phase. Unless otherwise stated all three categories of swimmer will do the workouts as listed.

Monday
1. Discussion of stroke mechanics for 20 minutes.
2. Thirty minutes of organized dry land exercises.
3. Thirty minutes of fartlek swimming.
4. Ten minutes of fartlek kicking.
5. Ten minutes of fartlek pulling.

Tuesday. The last-named exercises for this day may be done before or after the swimming, depending on convenience. If a choice is available, however, the exercises should be done before swimming.
1. Swim continuously for 30 minutes.
2. Kick continuously for 15 minutes.
3. Time 800 yards of pulling.
4. Work a half hour on dry land exercises.

Wednesday. This workout introduces some interval training into the practice.
1. Swim 500 yards moderately hard.
2. Kick 500 yards moderately, then kick 3 × 100 on 2 minutes.
3. Pull 500 yards moderately, then pull 3 × 100 on 2 minutes.
4. Swim a mile, stopping for 5 to 10 seconds of rest after every 50 yards, slow I.T.
5. Half hour of dry land exercises.

Thursday
1. Half hour of stroke technique discussion during which movies are shown and work is done on underwater stroke mechanics.
2. Swim 500.
3. Kick 500.
4. Pull 500.
5. Time 1000 yards, pacing.

Friday
1. Warm up 1000 yards swimming fartlek method.
2. Kick 1000 yards fartlek method.
3. Pull 8 × 100 yards on 2 minutes S.I.T.
4. Dry land exercises for 30 minutes.

Saturday. 3000 yards workout *on the house.* In this workout the swimmers can do anything they want to do as long as they cover the distance prescribed.

Sunday. Day off.

As this phase progresses into the season, repeat swims should gradually be introduced into the workouts, along with repeat kicks and pulls. At first, not much emphasis should be placed on timing the swimmers, but it is a good idea to begin timing them and asking them to keep a mental record of their times, to average them, and to keep a record of this average in their swimming logs or diaries. All swimmers should be encouraged to keep a daily record of their workouts. The swimming team manager should keep a master log which should contain all of the workouts plus each boy's average time for a series of repeats.

By the first part of December (or November, depending on the time they begin swimming in meets) the swimmers should be doing interval training workouts about three days a week. Stroke work should continue, for this is the ideal time in the season to make major stroke corrections, but a beginning emphasis on speeding up repeat times should be felt by the swimmers. For example, if a swimmer did 15 × 100-yard swims with 30 seconds rest in an average of 64 seconds for freestyle last week, he should try to drop this time to 63.5 this week, and try to lower it again next week. There should be no sharp dividing point between the end of the preparatory phase and the beginning of the hard-training phase. The entire preparatory phase consists of a steadily increasing emphasis on adding to the number of days spent on the interval training type of routine and on improving the quality of the work.

Five Days of Sample Workouts during the Latter Part of the Preparatory Phase.

Monday
1. One half hour lecture or movie devoted to stroke mechanics.
2. A half hour of dry land exercises.
3. Swim a half mile continuously, at moderate speed.
4. Kick 400 yards moderately, then time 500 kick time trial.
5. Pull 400 yards moderately, then time 500 pull time trial.
6. 16 × 50 yard swims with 10 seconds rest.

Tuesday
1. A half hour of dry land exercises.
2. A half hour devoted to starts and turns (lecture followed by actual pool work).
3. Kick 880 moderately.
4. Pull 500, then 4 × 100 pull repeats, 30 seconds rest.
5. 8 × 200 swims with 60 seconds rest (sprinters, 20 × 50 with 60 seconds rest).

Wednesday
1. A half hour of dry land exercises.
2. Fifteen minutes of lecture on pace.
3. Warm up 200 yards.
4. Pace 880 swim, moderate effort (sprinters, pace 500).
5. Kick 500.
6. Pull 500.

7. Pace 800, swimming as fast or faster than the first (sprinters, 500).

Thursday
1. A half hour of dry land exercises.
2. Fifteen minutes of work on starts and turns.
3. 10 × 100 swims, 15 seconds rest (distance men, 5 × 200, 15 seconds rest).
4. Kick 500 yards, then time 200 kick.
5. Pull 500 yards, then time 200 pull.
6. 5 × 100 swims, leaving on 3 minutes (sprinters, 5 × 50).

Friday
1. Warm up 500 swim with moderate effort.
2. 8 × 50 swims with moderate effort.
3. Kick 500, moderately.
4. Pull 500, moderately.
5. Time a mile swim (sprinters, time 800).

It is a good practice, when possible, to have organized dry land exercise drills as long into the season as they do not interfere with the amount of time spent in the water. While some swimmers are timing repeats or longer distances, the others can be working with dry land exercises or isometric contractions while waiting their turns to swim.

More Examples of Preparatory Phase Workouts. The following workouts are additional examples of workouts which can be used during this period. A team may use one type of workout one year and another the next. In fact, the coach should change workouts daily, weekly, monthly, and even yearly. Excessive use of too many different workouts and different styles of workout within a single season, however, can be as disastrous as too much rigidity.

No swimmer should attempt to do all of the following workouts in one season. If the coach and swimmer find the workouts they are using to be monotonous and they want a temporary, or even permanent, change, these workouts will serve as a guide. The skull sessions, dry land exercises, movies, and so on may continue to be included in these workouts at the discretion of the coach; they are not listed herein, however.

Sample workouts
   I. Swim locomotor (1 slow, 1 fast, 2 slow, 2 fast, 3 slow, 3 fast, 4 slow, 4 fast, 6 slow, 6 fast, 4 slow, 4 fast, 3 slow, 3 fast, 2 slow, 2 fast, 1 slow, 1 fast) for a total of 52 lengths in a 25-yard pool.
     2. Kick locomotor (as above).
     3. Pull 1000 yards at a steady rate.
  II. 1. Pull 800 yards.
     2. Kick 800 yards.
     3. 3 × 800 progressive set, I.T. swims, 4 minutes rest.

III. 1. Swim 70 × 25 yards, S.I.T., 5 seconds rest each 25.
   2. Kick 36 × 25, 5 seconds rest interval (R.I.).
   3. Pull 36 × 25, 5 seconds R.I.
IV. 1. Swim 40 lengths, every third length fast.
   2. Kick I.T., progressive 4 × 200, R.I. 2 minutes.
   3. Pull I.T., progressive 4 × 200, R.I. 2 minutes.
 V. 1. Swim 800 yards pace.
   2. Kick 400.
   3. Swim 800 pace, faster than the first one.
   4. Pull 400.
   5. Swim 800 pace, faster than second one.
VI. 1. Fartlek swim for 15 minutes.
   2. Fartlek kick for 15 minutes.
   3. Fartlek pull for 15 minutes.
   4. Fartlek swim for 15 minutes.
VII. 1. Swim 10 × 100 S.I.T., 10 seconds R.I.
   2. Kick 8 × 100, 10 seconds R.I.
   3. Pull 500 with moderate effort.
   4. Swim 8 × 100 S.I.T., 10 seconds R.I.
VIII. 1. Swim broken 400, 8 × 50, 5 seconds R.I. start on 50.
   2. Kick 500, moderately.
   3. Pull 500, moderately.
   4. Pull broken 500, 8 × 50, 5 seconds R.I.
   5. Kick broken 400, 8 × 50, 10 seconds R.I., start on 50.
   6. Pace a moderate 400 for time.
IX. 1. Kick 800, every third length fast.
   2. Pull 800, every third length fast.
   3. Swim pace 800, 400, 200, 100.
 X. 1. Swim 30 × 50 S.I.T., one slow, one fast; time fast ones.
   2. Kick 10 × 100, one slow, one fast; time fast ones.
   3. Pull 10 × 100, one slow, one fast; time fast ones.

HARD-TRAINING PHASE. This phase should last eight to twelve weeks: the indoor (winter), December, January, February; the outdoor (summer), June, July, and part of August. It is during this phase that the hardest training takes place, both in total distance and intensity.

Most coaches and swimmers will find it profitable to engage in two workouts a day at this time. The hardest training that most swimmers do usually occurs during the summer season when the swimmers do not have the pressure of schoolwork to consider, and may devote their primary efforts to training for swimming. In the summer our team does two very hard workouts per day of approximately 3000 to 4000 meters each. In the indoor season, when the swimmers are in the hard phase of training, I ask the swimmers to take one hard workout of approximately 4000 to 5000 yards during the afternoon and a second workout of 1000 to 2000 yards, either in the morning or in the evening, depending upon their available time.

During this phase it is well to emphasize the importance of working hard. To express the idea of the importance of training hard, Figure XII–1 illustrates the *hurt, pain, agony* concept of training.

Training Methods. All of the training methods that have been discussed will be used during this phase, with particular emphasis on those involving speed: over distance, fartlek, interval training, repetition training, sprint training, time trials, and actual competition. As this phase progresses the swimmer should increase his speed work—repetition training, sprint training, and so on.

One Week of Typical Workouts in the Hard-training Phase

Monday. First workout
1. Swim 500.
2. Time 500 swim.
3. Kick 400, then 10 × 50 on 1½ minutes.
4. Pull 400, then 10 × 50 on 1 minute.
5. Swim F.I.T.:

Sprinters	Middle Distance	Distance	Rest Interval
300	400	500	6 min.
200	300	400	4 min.
100	200	300	3 min.
50	100	200	

6. Sprint 4 × 25.

Monday. Second workout

Sprinters & Middle Distance	*Distance*
1. Warm up 8 × 50 on min.	1. Warm up 400 swim.
2. Kick 200.	2. Pace 2 × 800,
3. Pull 200.	5 minute rest,
4. 6 × 100 on 2½ minutes.	

Tuesday. First workout
1. Warm up 200 yards.
2. Swim broken 400 (10 seconds after each 50, starting when pace clock second hand reaches 50).
3. Kick 36 lengths (900 yards), sprinting every third length.
4. Pull 18 lengths (450 yards) butterfly, then time 500 yard pull.
5. Swim F.I.T., straight set, 30 × 50 on 60 seconds.

Tuesday. Second workout
   Sprinters
1. Swim F.I.T. 10 × 25, 10 seconds R.I.
2. Pull 10.
3. Kick 10.
4. Swim R.T. 6 × 50 on 3 minutes, each one within 2 seconds of your best time.
   Middle Distance
1. Swim F.I.T. 10 × 25, 10 seconds R.I.
2. Pull 200 time.
3. Kick 200 time.
4. Swim I.T., 4 × 200 on 5 minutes.
   Distance Men
1. Swim F.I.T. 10 × 25, 10 seconds R.I.
2. Pace 1650, within 40 seconds of your best time.

Wednesday. First workout
1. Swim 3 broken 400's (10 seconds R.I. after each 50 and 3 to 6 minutes between each 400).
2. Pull 4 × 200 I.T. on 5 minutes.
3. Kick 6 × 100 I.T. on 3 minutes.
4. Swim I.T. straight set 15 × 100 on 2 minutes.
5. Relay take-offs and one length sprints.

Wednesday. Second workout
All swimmers—1600 yards on the house.

Thursday. First workout
1. Swim 500, then 8 × 50 S.I.T. on 60 seconds.
2. Kick 10.
3. Simulator:

100 for Sprinters (start on 50)	200 for Middle Distance (start on 45)	500 for Distance Men (start on 30)
50, 5 sec. R.I.	100, 5 sec. R.I.	200, 10 sec. R.I.
25, 5 sec. R.I.	50, 5 sec. R.I.	100, 5 sec. R.I.
25	25, 5 sec. R.I.	75, 5 sec. R.I.
	25	50, 5 sec. R.I.
		50, 5 sec. R.I.
		25

4. Kick 500 for time.
5. Pull 36 lengths, every third one fast.
6. Swim progressive set.

Sprinters	*Others*	*Distance Men*
5 × 150	5 × 300	5 × 500

7. Sprint 2 × 25, then 1 × 50.

Thursday. Second workout
1. All swimmers swim 6 × 100 S.I.T. on 1:45.

2. *Sprinters*	*Others*	*Distance Men*
Swim F.I.T.	Swim F.I.T.	Swim F.I.T.
6 × 75	4 × 150	4 × 300

Friday. First workout. Swimmers may be tired by this day and, if they have a tough meet on Saturday, may want to reduce the intensity of the workouts. In the following workout 3500 yards are covered, but in a manner that will not tire the swimmer. All swimmers do the same workout.
1. Swim 30 × 50 I.T. slow-fast set on 60 seconds.
2. Kick 500 yards, then 1 × 100 and 1 × 50.
3. Pull 500 yards, then 1 × 100 and 1 × 50.
4. Pace 2 × 100, 3 minutes R.I., 5 to 8 seconds off of best time.
5. Push off I.T. 8 × 25, 10 seconds, R.I.
6. Sprint 2 × 25 from a dive.
7. Swim 250 yards easy.

Friday. Second workout

1. *Sprinters*	*Middle Distance*	*Distance*
Swim I.T.	Swim I.T.	Swim I.T.
12 × 50 progressive on 60 seconds.	6 × 100 progressive on 2 minutes.	4 × 200 progressive on 4 minutes.

2. Kick 10, then 6 × 25.
3. Pull 10, then 6 × 25.

Saturday. Day of competition with meet in afternoon.
1. Warm up in the morning.
2. After the meet—take a workout of approximately 1000 to 1500 yards. Do a straight set such as 20 × 50 I.T. on 50 seconds, or 10 ×100 I.T. on 2 minutes.

Sunday. Day off.

Additional Examples of Workouts during the Hard-Training Phase. As suggested earlier, during this phase the swimmers should not make a point of trying all of these workouts. They should, however, measure their progress by comparing their times in the various workouts they choose to do. These sets will be different for the different categories of swimmers. For example, they may use the following sets—each set to be done on a different day:

Sprinters and Middle Distance

1. 4 × 400 I.T. on 8 minutes.
2. 8 × 200 I.T. on 6 minutes.
3. 15 × 100 I.T. on 2 minutes.
4. 30 × 50 I.T. on 1 minute.

Distance

1. 8 × 500 I.T. on 8 minutes.
2. 16 × 200 on 4 minutes.
3. 20 × 100 on 2 minutes.
4. 30 × 50 on 1 minute.

The swimmers may also want to use given sets of repetition training to measure their progress. The frequent repetition of certain workouts or parts of workouts (perhaps weekly or bi-weekly) can provide short range goals to motivate the swimmers.

High-pressure Workouts. These workouts are strong goal workouts which, repeated identically several times throughout the weeks of hard-training, provide goals in which the swimmer tries to better the times achieved during the last practice session when he did an identical workout or set of repeats.

I. 1. Swim progressive 2 broken 400's (8 × 50 with 10 seconds R.I., starting on 50). Distance men swim progressive 3 × 400, 10 seconds R.I. after each 100, start on 30.
    2. Kick 300, then 3 × 200, 3 minutes R.I.
    3. Pull 200, then 5 × 100, 1½ minutes R.I.
    4. Swim straight set 15 × 100 I.T. on 2½ minutes R.I. (distance men do 20 × 100 on 2 minutes R.I.).
II. 1. Swim 16 × 50 I.T. on 60 seconds.
    2. Pull 20, then 8 × 50 on 60 seconds.
    3. Kick 20, then 8 × 50 on 1½ minutes.
    4. Swim straight set 8 × 200 I.T. on 6 minutes.
       Distance men warm up with 10 × 50:
            kick 10;
            pull 10;
            16 × 200—first 8 × 200 leaving on 3 minutes (average time for good college swimmers, 2:05), last 8 × 200 on 4 minutes (average time, 2:01).
    5. Swim 3 × 25 sprints, take long rest (1 to 4 minutes) then swim 1 × 50.
III. 1. Warm up 500 swim of moderate effort.
     2. Kick 500.
     3. Swim 30 × 50 F.I.T. on 60 seconds.
     4. Kick 4 × 100 I.T. on 3 minutes.
     5. Pull 400, then 3 × 200 on 6 minutes.
     6. Swim 6 × 25 sprints from dive.
IV. 1. Warm up swim 8 × 50.
    2. Swim for time: sprinters—200; others—300; distance—1000.
    3. Kick 500, then time 400.

    4. Pull 400, then 8 × 50 I.T. on 1½ minutes.

    5. Time repetition training, 5 minutes R.I.: sprinters—4 × 100 (around 51 seconds); others—4 × 150; distance—4 × 300 (under 3 minutes).

V. 1. Swim 500 easy.

    2. Swim 8 × 50 I.T. on 60 seconds.

    3. Kick 10.

    4. Swim simulator over distance:

       sprinters—200 (100, 10 seconds R.I.; 50, 5 seconds R.I.; 25, 5 seconds R.I.; 25);

       middle distance—300 (150, 10 seconds R.I.; 50, 5 seconds R.I.; 50, 5 seconds R.I.; 25, 5 seconds R.I.; 25);

       distance—800 (300, 10 seconds R.I.; 200, 10 seconds R.I.; 100, 10 seconds R.I.; 100, 5 seconds R.I; 50, 5 seconds R.I.; 50).

    5. Pull 20, then 10 × 25, 10 seconds R.I.

    6. Kick 16 × 25, 10 seconds R.I.

    7. Repetition training, long R.I. of 4 to 8 minutes, 95 per cent effort: sprinters—4 × 75; middle distance 4 × 100; distance 4 × 200.

Low-pressure Workouts. These workouts can be alternated with the high-pressure workouts. They should be approached by the swimmer with the idea that he should work hard, but, since the sets of repeats are broken up more than they are in the high-pressure routines, the goals will not be as easily identified, thus they are inherently lower pressure. Excessive use of these routines may prove harmful since they are intended for only occasional use, to condition the swimmer and, simultaneously, remove the pressure to constantly better his previous workout times.

I. 1. Warm up alternate progressive-regressive 20 × 50 I.T. on 60 seconds.

    2. Kick 20 (500 yards).

    3. Pull 20 (500 yards).

    4. Alternate 100 kick and 100 pull on 2½ minutes, repeat until 6 ×100 have been kicked and 6 × 100 have been pulled.

    5. Swim, coming back faster than going out: sprinters—8 × 100 on 3 minutes; others—4 × 200 on 6 minutes; distance—3 × 400 on 8 minutes.

    6. Sprint 4 × 25 from push-off.

II. 1. Swim 8 × 100 I.T. on 1:45 minutes.

    2. Kick 20, then 16 × 25, every other one fast.

    3. Pull 20, then 8 × 50, every other one fast

    4. Swim 1 × 400, 1 × 200, 4 × 100, 8 × 50 (all swimmers do these repeats, going in two waves).

       7 × 25 all-out.

III. 1. Swim 800 yards.

2. Swim 1 broken 400 (4 × 100, 10 seconds R.I., starting on 30).
3. Swim 1 broken 200 (4 × 50, 5 seconds R.I., starting on 45).
4. Kick progressive 8 × 100 I.T. on 3 minutes.
5. Pull progressive 4 × 200 I.T. on 5 minutes.
6. Swim, taking long rest: sprinters—100, 75, 2 × 50, 4 × 25; middle distance—200, 100, 4 × 50, 2 × 25; distance—400, 300, 4 × 100, 2 × 25.

IV. 1. Swim 500 warm up.
  2. Pull 4 × 150 I.T. progressive on 4 minutes.
  3. Swim 10 × 100 I.T. progressive on 2 minutes.
  4. Kick 500, then 16 × 25 on 30 seconds.
  5. Swim 15 minutes fartlek.
  6. Sprint 75, 50, 25.

V. 1. Swim 1 broken 800, 10 seconds R.I. after each 100, starting on 50.
  2. Kick 500.
  3. Time hard swim of 95 per cent effort on your distance.
  4. Kick 4 × 50, 8 × 25, short rest.
  5. Pull 500 butterfly, 500 your own stroke.
  6. Repetition training: sprinters—4 × 50, 2 × 25; middle distance— 2 × 100, 3 × 50, 2 × 25; distance—2 × 200, 2 × 100, 2 × 25.

Examples of the Second Daily Workout. The following workouts are examples of workouts that can be used for the second workout in a day, particularly during the school year. They may be a bit too easy for the second workout during the summer training schedule. They take between 30–45 minutes to complete.

I. 1. Swim 10 × 25 warm up I.T., 10 seconds R.I.
  2. Swim I.T.: sprinters—6 × 100 on 3 minutes; middle distance—4 × 200; distance—3 × 400.
  3. Sprint 4 × 50.

II. 1. Swim broken 800 (16 × 50, 10 seconds R.I.), starting on 30.
  2. Kick 300, then 2 × 100.
  3. Pull 500, fartlek.
  4. Swim pace: sprinters—200; middle distance—300; distance—500.

III. 1. Warm up 500.
  2. Pull 2 × 200, 3 minutes R.I.
  3. Swim I.T.: sprinters—4 × 100 on 3 minutes; middle distance—6 × 100 on 2 minutes; distance—4 × 200 on 3 minutes.

IV. 1. Swim 8 × 50 I.T. on 50 seconds.
  2. Kick 300.
  3. Pull 300.
  4. Sprint 4 × 25, then 3 × 50.

V. 1. Swim 300 warm up.
  2. Kick 200, then 2 × 50 on 1½ minutes.

3. Swim over distance pace: sprinters—400; middle distance—800; distance—1650.

THE TAPERING PHASE.   The success of an entire season of work can depend largely upon this relatively short phase of the season. This period comes toward the end of the season and is in preparation for the final big meets of the year. It lasts from two to four weeks. Swimmers frequently make the mistake of tapering for every meet. A typical high school or age-group swimmer might have a meet every week and sometimes two or three a week. If a swimmer tapers for each meet, he will discover that he is losing half his workout days. A taper of one day—at the most, two days—should be attempted for meets during the hard-training phase. If the meet is a small one, it might be better to continue to work through it.

The tapering period for the indoor season usually begins early in March, since most of the big meets are in the latter part of March or the first part of April, or over the last two to four weeks of the season. The transition from the previous phase to the tapering phase should not be marked at first. At least two to three days a week should consist of moderately hard work. For example, instead of doing 30×50 in a standard high-pressure workout of the previous phase, the number of 50's may be reduced to 12 or 20; instead of doing 15×100 swims, the number may be reduced to 6, 8, or 10.

There are five general purposes of the tapering period:

1. To permit the swimmer to be completely rested for the big meets.
2. To sharpen up on stroke mechanics, starts, and turns.
3. To work on pace and speed.
4. To do enough training so as not to lose any conditioning gained in the previous phase.
5. To prepare the swimmers psychologically for the big competition.

The general plan of changing the training routine is:

1. To reduce the total distance from that swum during the previous phase and to do fewer repeat swims.
2. To decrease the relative amount of kicking and pulling.
3. To increase the interval of rest between the repeat swims and to increase the speed of the repeats.

The Variable Taper.   Laboratory research has shown that some of the physiological changes acquired by a finely trained endurance athlete can regress in as few as four to six days of relative inactivity. In other words, it may take only a few days of decreased workouts to lose some of the conditioning gained in the hard-training phase. For this reason, I advocate a *variable taper*. In this taper three kinds of days may be alternated with one another: (1) hard days, (2) moderate days, and (3) easy days. The concept behind this kind of taper is that the hard days will maintain the conditioning of the swimmer, the easy days will permit him to rest, and the moderate days will supply some of both. This taper also permits some margin of safety in case the coach or swimmer errs in his judgment.

The swimmer does not have to follow a consistent pattern of alternation, but may have two easy or two hard or moderate days in succession. The coach and the swimmer must decide on the combinations.

A typical week during this tapering period is represented below:

Monday (hard day)
1. Warm up 500.
2. 16 × 50 swims on 60 seconds.
3. Kick 500, moderate effort.
4. Pull 500, moderate effort.
5. Swim 200 (sprinters, 100, distance men, 400).
6. Swim 10 × 100, 2 minutes R.I. between each 100 (sprinters, 10 × 50, distance men, 5 × 200).
7. 8 × 25 swims, with a start and turn.

Tuesday (moderate day)
1. Warm up 10 × 50, every other one hard.
2. Time distance to be swum in meet, swimming at moderate speed.
3. Kick 250, then 4 × 50.
4. Pull 250, then 4 × 40.
5. 16 × 50 on 1½ minutes, moderate effort (distance men work on pace, 100's and 200's).

Wednesday (hard day)
1. Warm up 500.
2. 8 × 50 swim, leaving on 60 seconds.
3. Kick 20, then kick 4 × 100 hard.
4. Pull 20, then pull 3 × 100 hard.
5. 2 × 200, 3 minutes R.I.
6. 1 × 400 at moderate effort (sprinters, 1 × 100, distance men, 4 × 400).

Thursday (moderate day)
1. Warm up 500.
2. 8 × 50 swims, every other one hard, on 60 seconds.
3. Kick 20 easy (no pulling).
4. 8 × 100, 2 minutes R.I.
5. Work on pace for event to be swum (sprinters time a moderate 75 and several 50's; 200 men time a moderate 150, then 100, then 2 × 50; distance men pace 300 or 200, then some shorter distance).

FIG. IX–3.   Planning a Season's Program

The following outline will not fit every team's needs, for in different areas the actual competitive seasons may vary by as much as two months. It is designed so that swimmers will reach peak condition in March and early April for the indoor season, and in August for the outdoor season. Any team must adjust the schedule to fit its particular season. This program also outlines an *ideal* training program.

September—The Casual Month

September is to be taken easy by the swimmer, so far as his training is concerned. He may concentrate on dry land exercises and play water polo. He may swim a bit if he wishes, but should stay away from high-pressure or interval training workouts and time trials. Work in the water should be concentrated on stroke work. Lectures and movies on strokes, turns, and starts should begin.

Type of Swimming Training: Endurance work—either over distance training or fartlek training, little or no speed work. Get in the water two or three times a week.

SEPTEMBER

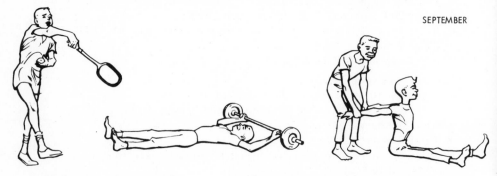

Engage in another activity for respite

Build strength and flexibility with dry land exercises three times a week

When swimming, use fartlek or over distance training; no speed work

Use movies and lectures to explain training techniques and stroke mechanics

OCTOBER

Work harder on dry land exercises three to five times a week, one hour a day

Spend a little more time in the water, but continue with endurance training three to five times a week

Play water polo if you wish

Work on stroke mechanics. Underwater coaching is best

Skull sessions: work on starts, turns, stroke, diet, training principles

October—Early Preparatory Work

The tempo of this month's work on dry land exercises should be picked up, and the swimmer should also start spending more time in the water. Water polo is a good activity and can be substituted for some of the swimming workouts. Work should begin on stroke techniques and starts and turns; later in the season there will not be time to discuss these aspects in detail, so concentrate on them now. This is also a good time to work on strokes other than those which are the specialty of the swimmer.

Type of Swimming Training: Over distance, fartlek, and slow interval training. Still not too much speed work, as in sprint or repetition training.

NOVEMBER

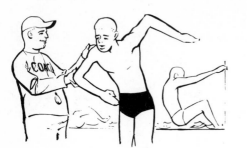

Continue work on stroke, starts, turns, relay take-offs

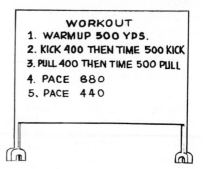

WORKOUT
1. WARMUP 500 YDS.
2. KICK 400 THEN TIME 500 KICK
3. PULL 400 THEN TIME 500 PULL
4. PACE 880
5. PACE 440

Sample of over distance workout

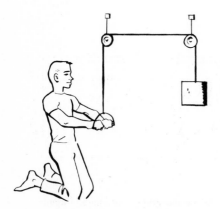

Swimmers may have to reduce time spent on dry land exercises

HONOLULU 1260 MILES

Swim over distance in workouts to lay good foundation, also fartlek training and some slow and moderate interval training four to six times a week

November—Preparatory Phase

Dry land exercises should continue, but the amount of time spent on them should be reduced if they interfere with time spent in the water. The swimmer should not be pushed far into the "hurt, pain, agony" approach. A good foundation should be made in endurance conditioning, but some moderate speed work should also be introduced.

Type of Swimming Training: Emphasis continues to be on endurance training—fartlek, over distance, slow interval training. With the introduction of some speed work, there should be a higher level of effort, with few maximum efforts in practice other than a few short sprints.

December—Hard Training Begins

This month should be devoted to bridging the gap between the preparatory phase and the hard-training phase. The workouts should become more difficult; more interval training and some repetition training should be introduced. It is still too early to go all out for speed work. Exercises should be continued (ten to thirty minutes a day) with the greatest concentration on isometric contractions. The total distance for the workout should exceed two miles and in the case of the eager swimmers two workouts a day may be introduced two or three times a week.

Type of Swimming Training: Integrated workouts should begin, which include all methods of training. The amount of speed work should be increased and some repetition and sprint training introduced.

DECEMBER

Keep record of times

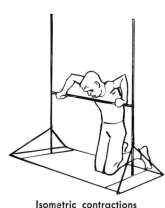

Isometric contractions

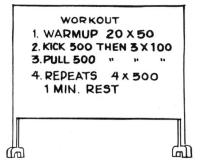

"Eager beavers" can work out twice a day

WORKOUT
1. WARMUP 20 X 50
2. KICK 500 THEN 3 X 100
3. PULL 500   "   "   "
4. REPEATS   4 x 500
   1 MIN. REST

Introduce more interval training—six to nine workouts a week

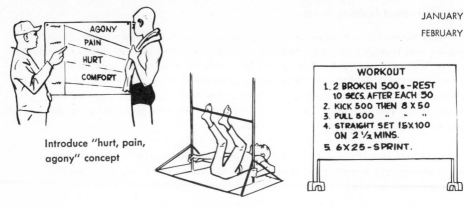

Introduce "hurt, pain, agony" concept

Do some isometric contractions

Hard interval training and repetition work, workouts twice a day when possible

BEST STRAIGHT SETS				
NAME	30X50	15X100	8 X 200	4 X 400
JONES	31.3	65.6	2:19	5:01

Try to improve on best previous workout times

Remember to study!

January and February—Hard Training Phase

The toughest workouts of the indoor season should come during this period. Even though there are usually a great many meets during these months, nevertheless nearly every workout should be of the integrated type. Two workouts a day should be taken, if schoolwork and pool schedules permit. The "hurt, pain, agony" concept should be pushed. High-pressure or strong-goal workouts should be alternated with equally hard but low-pressure routines. Little layoff or tapering should be done for small meets. The swimmer should be watched for fatigue and should be sure to get proper diet, sleep, and rest. Exercises should be continued, but with discretion, so that they do not interfere with swimming workouts.

Type of Swimming Training: Integrated workouts with an increasing amount of speed work should be used. The swimmers should be divided into three groups appropriate to their events and should be worked accordingly.

March—Tapering Phase

Ten days to two weeks before the biggest meet the tapering phase should begin. Exercises may be stopped unless the swimmer feels their cessation will upset his schedule. During this taper, the general plan is to do fewer repeats with longer rest intervals between each repeat. The total amount of kicking and pulling in workouts should also be reduced. Swimmers should concentrate on speed and pace work, resting, and preparing psychologically for the tests ahead.

Type of Swimming Training: Integrated workouts similar to those used in January and February, but with slightly more emphasis on repetition and sprint training. Be careful not to oversprint or to work too often at the 100 per cent level.

MARCH

Alternate rest and work

Get ready psychologically

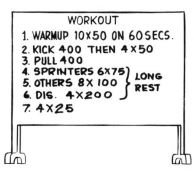

WORKOUT
1. WARMUP 10×50 ON 60 SECS.
2. KICK 400 THEN 4×50
3. PULL 400
4. SPRINTERS 6×75 ⎫
5. OTHERS 8×100 ⎬ LONG REST
6. DIS. 4×200 ⎭
7. 4×25

Begin tapering phase, decreasing total amount of work. Concentrate on pace and other details of race

Work on turns and starts

APRIL

MAY

Dry land exercises

Back to over distance and low pressure workouts

Don't lose the feel for your strokes

Get good grades

WORKOUTS FOR APRIL & MAY

IN APRIL WE WILL DO MOSTLY OVERDISTANCE AND FARTLEK TRAINING WHEN WE TRAIN. IN MAY WE WILL START SOME INTERVAL TRAINING WORK.

Typical workout pattern

April and May—Summer Season Preparatory Phase

If the swimmer plans to train and compete during the summer, he should try to retain some of the conditioning he worked so hard to acquire during the indoor season. He can do this by swimming a moderate workout two to five times a week and by doing dry land exercises. The workouts should be low-pressure, over distance workouts, particularly during the early part of this period. As the period progresses, some interval training should be introduced. A complete layoff during this time is undesirable and leaves the swimmer unfit for the hardest training period of the entire year.

Type of Swimming Training: Over distance, fartlek, or slow interval training.

June and July—Hard-Training Phase

These should be the hardest training months of the year. Two workouts (perhaps even three for distance men) should be taken daily, four-and-a-half to six-and-a-half miles per day. Some dry land exercises should be taken, concentrating heavily on isometric contractions. Nearly all of the workouts should be of the integrated type. One day or at least one-half day a week should be taken off from practice. Strong emphasis should be placed on the "hurt, pain, agony" concept. Since the physical stress of hard training is so great during this period, such things as overfatigue and excessive weight loss should be watched for carefully in the swimmer. Careful attention should also be given to diet, rest, and sleep habits. Stroke work is important. Even though the workouts are hard, if the swimmers are strongly motivated, they will enjoy them. The zest for training should never be lost.

Type of Swimming Training: Integrated workouts—varied to suit the needs of three groups: sprinters, middle distance, and distance swimmers.

JUNE-JULY

Still do some strength-
ening exercises

Stress high quality work, but
keep zest for training

Hard interval training two
or three times a day—total
distance: four to six miles

Watch diet carefully
Get plenty of rest and
sleep

Avoid excessive fatigue
—a sign of failing adap-
tation

AUGUST

Rest and prepare psychologically

WORKOUT
1. WARM UP 200 SWIM 8X50
2. PACE HARD 200
3. 6X100 SWIM - 2 MIN. REST
4. KICK 500 EASY
5. PACE THROUGH YOUR RACE 90% EFFORT
6. SPRINT 4X25 - 1X50

Decrease total amount of work

Sharpen up starts and turns

THAT 200 WAS 1:57 — NOW PICK UP THE PACE ON THE NEXT ONE!

Do speed and pace work

August—Tapering Phase

A taper of ten days to two weeks duration should be adopted in order to prepare the swimmer for his big meets. He should cease all dry land exercises. Two workouts a day should be continued, but the total distance swum should be decreased. In general, the plan should be to decrease the number of repeats swum and to increase the rest interval between them.

Type of Swimming Training: Integrated workouts.

Friday (easy day)
1. Warm up 500.
2. 8 × 50 swim on 1½ minutes, moderate speed.
3. Kick 500 yards.
4. Work on pace for event (distance men, 300 or 200; middle distance, 100 or 150; sprinters, 50 or 75).
5. 4 × 50 hard, long rest of 2 to 3 minutes.
6. 4 × 25 hard, long rest of 2 to 3 minutes.

Saturday (day of meet)

One of the main concerns during the tapering period is to prepare the swimmers psychologically and to give them enough rest. Swimmers who are prepared physically but not psychologically will not perform up to their maximum potential.

As has already been stated, it is important that during the tapering period the work is not reduced to the extent that the swimmers lose their conditioning. If the coach feels that this is occurring, he may have to return to several days of workouts of the type used in the hard-training phase. If there is a lapse of two weeks between big meets, it is also a good practice to return to the hard-training type of workout for a period of three or four consecutive days.

Dry Land Exercises

The physical conditioning required for good swimming performance is made up of three major components: (1) strength, (2) endurance, and (3) flexibility.

1. *Strength* can be defined as the ability of a muscle or a group of muscles to overcome resistance or create tension—push, pull, or lift.

2. *Endurance* is the ability of a muscle or the body as a whole to repeat an activity many times. There are two types of endurance: muscular endurance, which is the ability of muscles to perform a task many times, and circulo-respiratory endurance, which is the ability of the circulatory system to supply blood to active muscle plus the capability of the respiratory system to supply oxygen to the blood and eliminate the carbon dioxide and metabolites created in active muscle.

3. *Flexibility* or mobility is the ability of the joints and the body as a whole to move easily through the normal range of movement.

A dry land exercise program, when properly designed and

followed, can build strength and flexibility faster than these traits can be built by training with swimming alone. This is the only justification for a dry land exercise program.

Exercises can also be designed to aid in the acquisition of muscular endurance, although this is not their primary purpose. Cardio-respiratory endurance and muscular endurance are built primarily in the swimming drills.

A review of the literature on dry land exercises for swimmers reveals a list of over 500 exercises. One book lists almost 200 such exercises. Most of them are of doubtful value; certainly the average coach or swimmer does not have time to wade through this miasma. Almost any form of exercise will contribute to the organic fitness and general strength of an individual, but the Herculean task of running through a long series of daily exercises which may or may not contribute to a person's speed and endurance in the water lacks appeal for the average competitive swimmer. He is interested in getting the most benefit from the time and effort invested, and for this reason should not engage in exercises of dubious merit. With this in mind, the writer has sorted through, borrowed, and, in some cases, originated exercises which appear, on the basis of anatomical and mechanical principles, to be highly efficient in achieving this goal. Electromyographic research has been used for the purpose of evaluating these exercises.

STRENGTHENING EXERCISES

The use of heavy resistive exercises is now accepted practice for competitive swimmers. However, caution must be exercised when using them. While many calisthenics may be of little or no value, they generally are not harmful; in the case of a weight-training routine, it is entirely possible that a person might develop hypertrophy (enlargement) of the muscles to the point that their size becomes a handicap. In the program outlined in this chapter only those exercises have been selected which develop the muscles of prime importance in the propulsive phase of swimming the four competitive strokes. A swimmer planning his dry land exercise program should not enter into a general body building program. The exercises he uses should be designed specifically to strengthen and improve the endurance of the muscles that anatomists call the "prime movers." In swimming, these muscles are those that propel the swimmer through the water. It is also important that these muscles be exercised as much as possible in the same manner as they are used in the swimming strokes.

Indiscriminate Use of Weight Exercises Can Be Detrimental

A physiological principle states that the strength of a muscle is directly proportional to the cross sectional area of the muscle. To illustrate this principle, a muscle having one square inch of cross sectional area can create a force of 70 pounds; after exercising with weights the muscle has doubled its cross sectional area and has also doubled in strength. At the same time it has also doubled in weight. It is in this latter characteristic that the harmful effect of a poorly planned program is found. A swimmer can develop muscles that are not "prime movers" and put on as many as 20 or more pounds. These muscles are not contributing to the forward propulsion of the body and, in some cases, are just along for the ride. They slow the swimmer by creating more inertia and resistance, and by diverting blood flow and oxygen from the prime mover muscles. When only the prime movers and some associated muscles are increased in strength and, consequently, in size, the weight gain is not excessive, relative to the functional strength the swimmer has gained.

In the exercise program outlined here, the emphasis is on developing strength in the muscles that pull the arms through the water. No exercises are included that intentionally develop the muscles that recover the arms. Recovery muscles need not be tremendously strong since they recover the arms through the air (except in the breaststroke) and encounter little resistance. They work primarily against the inertia of the arms and are sufficiently developed by the exercise they get while performing the actual swimming movements.

Prime Mover Muscles

1. ARM DEPRESSORS—latissimus dorsi, pectoralis major, teres major, and triceps. These muscles pull the arm through the water and provide the main source of propulsion for the four competitive strokes.

2. INWARD ROTATORS OF THE ARM—teres major, subscapularis, latissimus dorsi, and pectoralis major. In all four competitive strokes the rotators of the arm are used when the strokes are swum correctly. To illustrate this action, hold the arm horizontally in front of you and bend the elbow 45°, then lift the elbow and lower the hand.

3. WRIST AND FINGER FLEXORS—flexor carpi, ulnaris, and palmaris longus. Many swimmers lack the strength in these muscles to handle all the resistance their hands encounter in the water; for this reason they "let go" during the pull by extending their fingers and wrists.

4. ELBOW EXTENSORS—triceps. As a swimmer finishes his arm pull in the butterfly, crawl, and backstroke, he uses this powerful extensor of his elbow to thrust the water backward.

5. LEG AND ANKLE EXTENSORS—quadriceps extensors, gastrocnemius, and gluteus. All of these muscles are involved in the start and the push-off, and their development is important to the swimmer for that reason. They are also the prime movers in the breaststroke kick.

Some muscles perform what might be called supplementary work in that they assist, but do not cause, the movement. The *trunk muscles,* both the anterior group and the lateral and posterior group, are in this category. They act as links between the power applied in the front by the arms and that applied in the back by the legs. They stabilize the body and provide a streamlined position for the trunk.

Some Principles in Developing Muscular Strength and Endurance

The statement of a few principles may help the reader understand better how to design a dry land exercise program in such a way as to receive maximum benefits from it. The first two of the following principles concerning progressive resistive exercises are known as DeLorme's principles.[1]

1. Strength is built in a muscle by the use of high resistance-low repetition exercises, such as by five to ten repetitions of a supine pullover with a weight of 50 to 75 pounds.

2. Endurance is built in a muscle by the use of low resistance-high repetition exercises, such as by doing 300 or more repetitions of the same exercise as above with a weight of 15 to 25 pounds.

At this point a third principle not mentioned by DeLorme may be added:

3. Exercises that use moderate resistance and moderate numbers of repetitions, such as doing the same exercise as above with 35 repetitions and a weight of 35 pounds, build some strength, although not as much as the first type of exercise, and some muscular endurance, although not as much as the second type.

Once the type of exercise or stress to be placed on the muscle has been decided, to a great extent the quality to be built in the muscle has also been decided. This again is an example of the specificity of training.

---

[1] Thomas L. DeLorme, "Restoration of Muscle Power by Heavy-Resistance Exercises," *The Journal of Bone and Joint Surgery,* XXVII, No. 4 (October 1945), 666.

1. *Strength-building Exercise:*
   High resistance—75 lbs.
   Low repetitions—5

2. *Intermediate Exercise Builds Equal Amounts of Strength and Endurance:*
   Moderate resistance—35 lbs.
   Moderate repetitions—50

3. *Endurance-building Exercise:*
   Low resistance—15 lbs.
   High repetitions—150

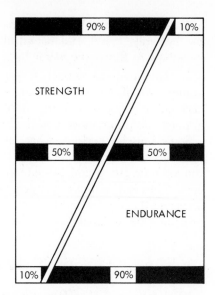

FIG. X–1.   Relative Percentage Contribution of Various Types of Weight Training Exercises to Strength and Endurance

In the first type of exercise the muscle is being *overloaded* by increasing the intensity of the exercise. In the second type the muscle is being overloaded by increasing the duration of the exercise. In the third type there is a combination of the two practices.

OVERLOAD PRINCIPLE.   When speaking of exercise, the *overload principle* is frequently mentioned. Unfortunately, the term *overload* has the connotation of excessive strain or harm to the muscle. A better way to express what is meant might be to say that a greater load or stress is placed on the muscle than it is normally exposed to.

Values of the Different Types of Resistance

As has been described previously, the development of a quality in a muscle is dependent primarily upon two factors: the amount of resistance and the number of repetitions. The type of resistance the muscle works against, whether it be a barbell, stretch cords, the weight of the person himself, the weight of another person, or isometric contractions, is of little consequence. However, in certain forms of exercise the amount of resistance is easily measured, as in weight lifting. For this reason, most of the exercises described in this chapter are those in which some form of weight lifting is involved. The writer also believes in the merit of the other forms of exercise.

Method of Determining the Amount of Weight To Be Used

There is not complete agreement among authorities as to precisely the best procedure for building strength. A general policy that should be followed in a strength building program is to choose the amount of weight for doing a given exercise that will permit the person, with effort, to do 10 to 15 repetitions. As the person improves in strength, the amount of weight used will have to be increased. If the weight is not increased, the muscle will not continue to gain in strength. The term *progressive-resistance exercise* has been applied to this type of program.

If the swimmer also wants to develop a certain amount of muscular endurance, he should reduce the amount of weight used and increase the number of repetitions.

Determining the Number of Repetitions

Normally the number of repetitions to be used with a particular exercise is determined prior to the determination of the amount of weight to be used. The number of repetitions to be used to build maximum strength should ordinarily range between three and ten.

An Integrated Strength Building Program

In training for a given race, a swimmer does not swim all his repeat swims at one distance or at one speed. He swims over distance, under distance, and on distance as well as different intensities of effort. This type of program is referred to as an integrated program of training. In applying this practice to dry land exercise at Indiana University, we do not stick with only one type of program in building strength and endurance. Generally, the following program is used:

1. Exercises with moderately heavy weight and with the number of repetitions held at ten, usually two or three sets of ten repetitions each. This type of exercise is used about 60 per cent of the time, or perhaps on Monday, Wednesday, and Friday of a week.

2. Exercises in which the amount of weight is reduced from that used in exercise 1 above and the repetitions are increased to from 35 to 100, with only one set being done. This form of exercise is done about 30 per cent of the time, or perhaps on Tuesday and Thursday.

3. Occasionally, about once every two weeks, exercises are attempted in which the maximum weight that a person can lift one to three times is used. This type of exercising takes only about 10 per cent of the total exercising time and is used to measure progress and to help in establishing new levels of weight load to be used in exercise 1 above.

THE APPLICATION OF ISOMETRIC CONTRACTIONS TO
TRAINING FOR SWIMMING

Several years have passed since the introduction of isometric contractions to training for sports activities. During this time a great deal has been written on the subject, both pro and con. Unfortunately, most of this material has been written by people who have not worked with isometrics in a practical situation. Brief research projects, in which a small number of subjects have been used and whose researchers display a limited knowledge of the principles involved, have resulted in both detractors and exaggerators of the claims for isometric contractions. At Indiana University we have been working with isometric contractions in both the laboratory and in a controlled, practical situation with our swimming teams. We feel that isometric contractions at the college, high school, and age-group levels have their limitations as well as their values. It is a fact that they have become a permanent, integral part of our physical education and athletic programs.

Research has shown that strength can be built faster through the supplementation of a weight training program with isometric contractions. The theory behind this claim is that the period of stress during an isometric contraction is longer than it is when the person is lifting a weight. As soon as the person overcomes the inertia of the weight, the stress factor upon the muscle decreases.

Although isometric contractions are not the answer to a complete exercise program (and few people have made this claim), they can be used as a means of developing strength. There is one additional and important benefit to be derived from their use which has been overlooked, particularly by their detractors. This is the practice of teaching proper mechanics in sports activities with the implementation of isometric contractions. An illustration of the application of this practice can be made in describing its use in teaching the crawl or butterfly arm pulls. Most coaches know it is very difficult to teach the average swimmer to swim with his elbow up during the first part of his pull. We have tried using films, mirrors, lectures, and work in the water. It is particularly hard to teach this principle to age-group swimmers. My introduction to isometrics was a result of an effort on my part to improve the methods of teaching swimmers to swim with their elbows up. I reasoned, "Why not have the swimmer try to learn to pull correctly by having him push his hands downward on an immovable bar while holding his arms in the desired position with the elbows up?" I felt the swimmer would thus be able to *see* the desired position visually and kinesthetically, and would be likely to develop a feel for the proper arm position.

How to Use Isometric Contractions

Isometric contractions can be performed against an immovable object or against a movable object, such as a barbell. In Figure X–2 the subject is performing an isometric contraction while holding a barbell in back of his head with the elbows bent at 90°. This particular isometric contraction is designed to strengthen the triceps muscle.

The length of time the weight should be held depends upon the weight being used and the physical condition of the exerciser, but it should be somewhere between six and twelve seconds. The person should only do two to four repeti-

FIG. X–2. Isometric Contraction Using a Barbell

tions of this isometric contraction. The isometric contraction should be held halfway through the full range of movement of the exercise, or at the point at which the greatest effort is needed to hold the weight steady.

Intermediary Drills

A muscle that is contracted isometrically in only one position will tend to become strongest in that position. In order to develop strength through the full range of movement of a muscle, it is recommended that a series of isometric contractions be used at various angles throughout the full range of movement. The name applied to a series of this kind of isometric contractions is *intermediary contractions.*

To develop strength through the full range of movement of the muscle, the intermediary contractions should be done at three, four, or five positions spaced at equal distances through the range of movement. Figures X–18, X–19, X–20, and X–21 illustrate the positions spaced in this way. Each position should be held for a period of five seconds, then the weight should be moved to the next position and held for another count of five, and so on. One to two sets of intermediary drills should be used at each exercise session. A rest period of about half a minute should be allowed between the two sets. Although isometric and intermediary contractions build strength quickly, they should not be used exclusively. Isotonic exercises (with movement) are a necessary component of any complete program.

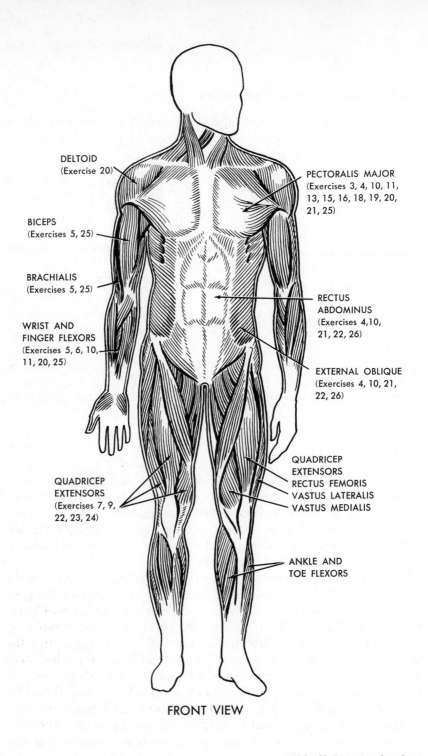

DELTOID
(Exercise 20)

PECTORALIS MAJOR
(Exercises 3, 4, 10, 11,
13, 15, 16, 18, 19, 20,
21, 25)

BICEPS
(Exercises 5, 25)

BRACHIALIS
(Exercises 5, 25)

RECTUS
ABDOMINUS
(Exercises 4,10,
21, 22, 26)

WRIST AND
FINGER FLEXORS
(Exercises 5, 6, 10,
11, 20, 25)

EXTERNAL OBLIQUE
(Exercises 4, 10, 21,
22, 26)

QUADRICEP
EXTENSORS
RECTUS FEMORIS
VASTUS LATERALIS
VASTUS MEDIALIS

QUADRICEP
EXTENSORS
(Exercises 7, 9,
22, 23, 24)

ANKLE AND
TOE FLEXORS

FRONT VIEW

FIG. X–3. Muscle Chart

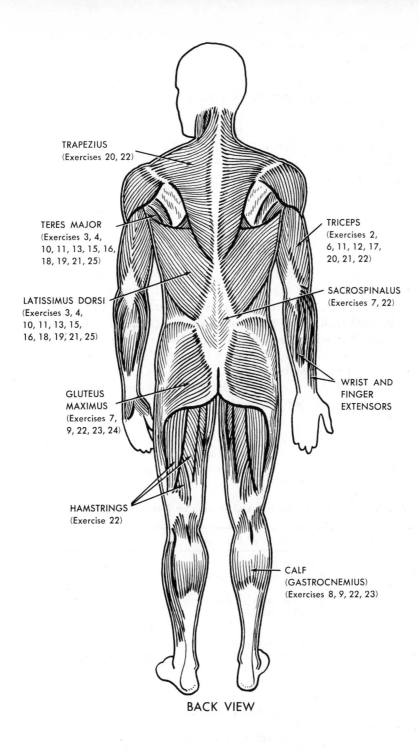

TRAPEZIUS
(Exercises 20, 22)

TERES MAJOR
(Exercises 3, 4,
10, 11, 13, 15, 16,
18, 19, 21, 25)

LATISSIMUS DORSI
(Exercises 3, 4,
10, 11, 13, 15,
16, 18, 19, 21, 25)

GLUTEUS
MAXIMUS
(Exercises 7,
9, 22, 23, 24)

HAMSTRINGS
(Exercise 22)

TRICEPS
(Exercises 2,
6, 11, 12, 17,
20, 21, 22)

SACROSPINALUS
(Exercises 7, 22)

WRIST AND
FINGER
EXTENSORS

CALF
(GASTROCNEMIUS)
(Exercises 8, 9, 22, 23)

BACK VIEW

FIG. X–3. Continued

285

EXERCISE PROGRAMS FOR THE VARIOUS STROKES

There are over 200 muscles in the body. Each has a specific action that is peculiar to itself. There is practically no exercise that a person can do that will contract only one muscle. Every exercise in this chapter involves the use of many muscles; a given exercise, however, will place a greater load on some of these muscles than on others. For example, the performance of the supine pullover exercise will contract many muscles, but will place the greatest overload on the arm depressor muscles. A given exercise consequently can be used to develop a specific muscle or muscle group.

Shown in Figure X–3 are muscle charts depicting many of the large muscles and muscle groups, and the exercises used to develop these muscles. Research and common sense indicate that each stroke requires a different emphasis on the various muscle groups. For this reason it is advisable that, when possible, the exercises be adapted to suit the stroke or strokes for which the swimmer is training. Table X–1 lists the numbers of the exercises best suited for benefiting each particular stroke. It is not suggested that a swimmer do all of the exercises listed each day. The type and number of exercises he will do depend upon the equipment, the time available, and his specific needs. A swimmer should concentrate on eliminating his weaknesses; if he is very strong, but lacks flexibility, he should do more stretching exercises and fewer strength building exercises out of the total number he plans to do.

TABLE X–1.   Dry Land Exercises Classified by Stroke

Stroke	Type of Exercise	Exercise Numbers
Freestyler and Butterfly	Stretching exercises	27, 28, 32, 33, 34, 35, 36, 37
	Strengthening exercises with weights	1, 2, 3, 4, 5, 6, 7, 8, 9, 10, 14
	Exercises with stretch cords or pulley weights	15, 17, 19
Breaststroker	Stretching	22, 23, 29, 30, 31, 37
	Strengthening exercises with weights	1, 2, 3, 4, 7, 8, 9, 13
	Exercises with stretch cords or pulley weights	15, 16, 18, 19
Backstroker	Stretching	27, 28, 32, 33, 34, 35, 36, 37
	Strengthening exercises with weights	1, 2, 3, 4, 5, 8, 9, 11, 12
	Exercises with stretch cords or pulley weights	16, 17, 19

GENERAL INSTRUCTIONS FOR WEIGHT LIFTING EXERCISES

1. The directions for each exercise should be followed carefully.

2. The weight should be lifted at a steady rate and should not be thrown upward. The weight should be lowered at the same rate at which it was lifted because the muscle also gains in strength and endurance as a result of the stress placed upon it during the lowering of the weight.

3. Do not try to lift too heavy a weight. Begin with a weight that can be handled easily, and progress cautiously.

4. In determining the amount of weight and the number of repetitions for a given exercise, follow the instructions presented earlier in this chapter.

5. If the swimmer decides to integrate all three forms of exercise into his program, they should be done in the following sequence: (1) isometric contractions, (2) intermediary contractions, and (3) isotonic exercises (with movement).

6. Warm up before beginning to lift weights. Always do Exercise 1 first, as a warm up.

FIG. X–4. **Warmup Drill**

Exercise 1. Warm up Drill

This exercise should only be done isotonically. It should precede all other exercises. The amount of weight used should be moderate in order that the exercise may be done without undue exertion.

STARTING POSITION: Barbell is on floor, slightly in front of feet. Lean over by bending at knees and hips, grasp barbell with palms downward at shoulder width.

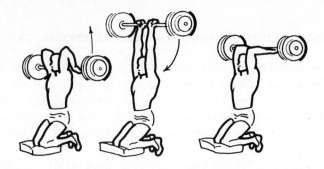

FIG. X–5.   Elbow Extensor

ACTION: Pull the barbell from the floor to overhead position at arms' length in one movement. Repeat ten times. Keep the back straight.

Exercise 2. Elbow Extensor

STARTING POSITION: Kneeling on cushion or pad (this exercise can be done standing erect if the ceiling is high enough), barbell is held straight overhead with the elbows extended, palms forward gripping the bar six to twelve inches apart.

ACTION: The barbell is lowered by flexing the elbows without lowering them. Then return to starting position. Keep back straight.

MUSCLES DEVELOPED: Elbow extensors—the triceps.

Exercise 3. Variation of Elbow Extensor

Follow the instructions for Exercise 2, except lower the barbell only halfway down. Then return to starting position. Also hold isometric contractions at this same position.

FIG. X–6.   Arm Rotator

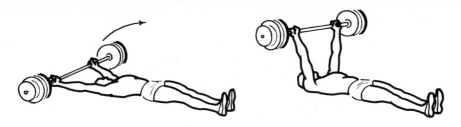

FIG. X–7. Supine Arm Pullover

Exercise 4. Arm Rotator

STARTING POSITION: Lying on back with top of head almost touching bar, grasp barbell with palms up and wide grip, so that the elbows are bent 90° and are on the ground at shoulder level.

ACTION: Raise bar in an arc to vertical position by rotating upper arms. Keep the elbows on floor. Return to starting position. Do not arch back.

MUSCLES DEVELOPED: Medial arm rotators: pectoralis major, subscapularis,[2] latissimus dorsi, teres major.

Exercise 5. Supine Arm Pullover

STARTING POSITION: Lying on the floor on the back, barbell held in wide grip, palms up, arms extended overhead.

ACTION: Without bending the elbows pull the barbell in an arc up to a vertical position. Return to starting position. Do not arch back.

MUSCLES DEVELOPED: Arm depressors: pectoralis major, latissimus dorsi, teres major. If the back is kept flat this is also a good exercise for the abdominal muscles: rectus abdominus and external obliques.

[2] Deep muscle, not shown on muscle chart. It lies under the scapulae (shoulder blade).

FIG. X–8. Double Wrist Curls

FIG. X–9.   Backward Arm Press

Exercise 6. Double Wrist Curls

STARTING POSITION: Sitting on edge of chair or squatting on the heels, grasp barbell with palms upwards. Flex elbows 90° and support forearms on the knees. The bar should not be placed on the palm of the hand, but permitted to rest on the fingers.

ACTION: Raise and lower weight through the fullest possible range of movement by flexing and extending the wrists.

MUSCLES DEVELOPED: Wrist and finger flexors.

Exercise 7. Backward Arm Press

STARTING POSITION: Stand with feet apart, body bent 90 degrees at the hips with the trunk leaning forward. Grasp bar with hands, palms facing backward. Bend knees slightly. Bar is held across back of upper thigh, elbows bent 50° to 80°.

ACTION: Swing bar upward in an arc by extending elbows and elevating upper arm. Return to starting position.

MUSCLES DEVELOPED: Elbow extensors: triceps, wrist and finger flexors.

FIG. X–10.   Half Squats

FIG. X—11. Full Squats

Exercise 8. Half Squats

STARTING POSITION: Standing erect, feet slightly apart, bar resting on the shoulders behind neck, hands grasp the bar in a wide grip with the palms facing upward.

ACTION: Perform a half squat by bending at the knees until they are bent at a right angle. Keep back as erect as possible with head up. Return to starting position.

MUSCLES DEVELOPED: Extensors of the knees and hips: quadriceps extensors and gluteus maximus.

Exercise 9. Full Squats

This exercise is the same as Exercise 8 except that a full squat rather than a half squat is accomplished. Extreme caution should be exercised because a full squat with a heavy weight can be somewhat hazardous. It is recommended that this exercise be done with a moderate weight. It is considered a very good exercise for stretching the Achilles tendon,[3] particularly if the heels are kept on the floor.

[3] Large tendon on the back of the ankle that attaches the calf muscle to the heel.

FIG. X—12. Straddle Lift with Full Squats

Exercise 10. Straddle Lift with Full Squats

STARTING POSITION: With legs spread 18 inches, straddle barbell with one foot in front of the other. Bend at the knees and hips and grasp the barbell with one hand in front and the other behind the legs. The thumbs of the hands face forward. Keep the elbows straight and the head and shoulders erect.

ACTION: Lift the bar by straightening the legs. Return to starting position.

Exercise 11. Straddle Lift with Half Squats

This exercise is the same as Exercise 10 except that the weight is lowered only halfway to the floor. The starting position is the erect position and the weight is lowered and then returned. If there has been a history of knee injury or of chronically weak knees, half squats rather than full squats are recommended.

Exercise 12. Rise on Toes

STARTING POSITION: Stand erect with feet slightly apart and with the barbell resting on the shoulders behind the neck, hands gripping the bar in a wide position with the palms upward.

ACTION: Elevate bar by elevating the heels and rising forcefully up onto the balls of the feet and the toes. Return to starting position.

MUSCLES DEVELOPED: The calf muscles, which are the plantar flexors of the ankle: gastrocnemius and soleus.

FIG. X–13.   Rise on Toes

Exercise 13. Variation of Rise on Toes with Toes Elevated

This exercise is the same as Exercise 12 except that the toes and balls of the feet are elevated upon a board two to three inches high. The heels are lowered to the floor for the starting position. This exercise is preferred to Exercise 12 and should be used if a board is available. It permits a greater amount of contraction and also stretches the Achilles tendon.

Exercise 14. Jumping Quarter Squats

STARTING POSITION: Stand erect with bar resting on shoulders at back of neck. With one foot slightly in front of the other, grasp barbell firmly so that it does not bounce up and down on the shoulders.

ACTION: Bend knees only slightly, raise heels slightly off floor. Jump up and down, emphasizing a vigorous drive of the legs and extension of the ankles, and reverse the feet on each jump. Do this exercise only isotonically; repeat 10 to 30 times.

MUSCLES DEVELOPED: This exercise develops speed and power in the hip and knee extensors and the plantar flexors of the ankles: gluteus maximus, quadriceps extensors, gastrocnemius, and soleus.

FIG. X–14.   **Jumping Quarter Squats**

EXERCISES WITH THE LATISSIMUS APPARATUS

One of the best means of imitating the actual arm motion in swimming the crawl and butterfly strokes, while lifting weights, is through the use of a piece of weight lifting equipment known as a latissimus apparatus.

FIG. X–15. Lat Apparatus

The principles used in determining the amount of weight and number of repetitions for other weight lifting exercises also come into play when using this equipment.

The latissimus apparatus (or *lat machine,* as it is known among coaches and swimmers) is available from companies which sell weight lifting equipment, or it can be improvised with two overhead pulleys, a rope, and some weights made from cans filled with concrete. A special grip handle, such as is being used in Figure X–15, is preferred to the straight bar used by most weight lifters or that comes as standard equipment.

Exercise 15. Forward Arm Depressors

STARTING POSITION: Kneeling on a pad or cushion with the body erect and the arms extended overhead, hands grasping the grip with the palms facing inward.

ACTION: Pull the arms downward, keeping the elbows outside of the hands. As the arms are depressed downward, begin to bend the elbows and, at the same time, keep them up by rotating the upper arms in the same manner as described in Chapter II, *The Crawl Stroke*. Do not drop the elbows as would be done in performing a chinning motion on a horizontal bar. Pull the hand grips down until the elbows are fully extended and the hands touch or almost touch the upper legs. Do not arch the back.

MUSCLES DEVELOPED: Arm depressors, arm rotators, elbow extensors, and wrist and finger flexors. If the back is kept straight, this is also an excellent exercise for the abdominal muscles: rectus abdominus and external obliques.

Backstroke Arm Pull

The two exercises following more closely simulate the arm movement in the backstroke than any other weight training exercise. They must be done on a specially built piece of equipment called a double latissimus apparatus (or double lat machine), as shown in Figure X–16.

FIG. X–16.   Double Lat Apparatus

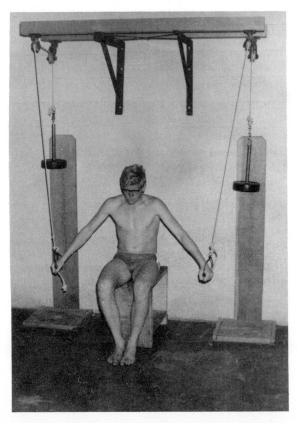

Exercise 16. Sidewards Arm Depressor

STARTING POSITION: Sitting on a stool or chair, the arms are held over-head with the palms facing outward and grasping the pulley handles.

ACTION: As the arms are pulled down laterally (sidewards), the elbows are bent and the upper arms are rotated inwardly as described in Chapter IV, *The Backstroke*. As the arms pass below the horizontal, the elbows start to extend and reach full extension when the hands touch the upper thighs.

MUSCLES DEVELOPED: Arm depressors, arm rotators, elbow extensors, and wrist and finger flexors.

Exercise 17. Elbow Extensor Exercise

STARTING POSITION: Sitting on stool, grasp pulley handles, keeping the hands at the sides.

ACTION: Keep elbows stationary and pull handles down by extending elbows.

MUSCLES DEVELOPED: Elbow extensors and wrist and finger flexors.

Exercise 18. Breaststroke Arm Pull

STARTING POSITION: Sitting on a stool or chair, cross hands and grasp handles on the opposite side from the hands. Start with arms stretched overhead, palms facing outward as when swimming the breaststroke.

ACTION: Depress arms simultaneously and diagonally forward and to the side. Bend the elbows and rotate the upper arms. Imitate the motion of the breaststroke arm pull as described in Chapter V. Return arms up in same manner as they were pulled down. Avoid dropping the elbows; that is, don't pull them into the ribs.

MUSCLES DEVELOPED: Arm depressors, arm rotators, wrist and finger flexors.

Exercise 19. Arm Rotator Exercise

This exercise can be done on either the latissimus or double latissimus apparatus.

STARTING POSITION: Sitting on a bench or kneeling on a pad or cushion, grasp the handle or handles with the elbows held at shoulder height in front of the shoulders, flexed at a 90° angle, the forearms held up in a vertical position. Without depressing (lowering) the elbows, pull the handles down by rotating the upper arms until the arms are fully rotated.

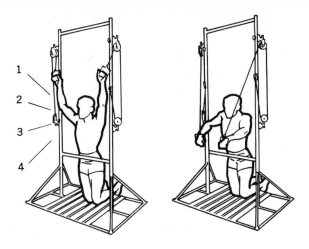

FIG. X–17. Forward Arm Depressor (with Isogym and stretch cords)

EXERCISES WITH STRETCH CORDS OR PULLEY WEIGHTS

If the swimmer does not have barbells or a latissimus apparatus, he can increase his strength by using pulley weights or stretch cords. The stretch cords can be attached to an apparatus such as the Isogym [4] in a pulley arrangement (shown in Exercises 15, 16, 17, 18, and 19), or they can be attached to a fence, a door, or any stable object, and the exercises performed while the person is standing with his body bent at the hips and his torso leaning forward.

If the exercises are performed on the pulley weights, the subject may lie face down on a bench about chest height or stand in the manner already suggested for the use of stretch cords. When using stretch cords, the person has a difficult time determining precisely how much tension is being created when he exerts effort upon the handle. He should, however, try to maintain sufficient tension on the cords to be just capable of completing the desired number of repetitions. This rule also applies to the amount of weight to be used with pulley weights.

The swimmer can increase the resistance created by the stretch cords either by raising the handles higher on the cords (as used on the Isogym) or by stepping backward, away from the point of attachment of the cords, so that the initial tension on the stretch cords is greater.

It is difficult to create as much resistance with pulley weights or stretch cords as it is with the barbells or latissimus apparatus. For this reason, more repetitions of each exercise should be done when this equipment is used, less strength and more endurance being built in this case.

[4] James E. Counsilman, *Isometric Contractions and Isogym,* device manufactured and distributed by the Hamlin Metal Products Corp., Akron, Ohio. Booklet included with device.

The swimmer should do two to three sets of each of the following exercises, with 50 to 150 repetitions in each set. Once again the number of sets and repetitions he does will depend upon the quality he wants to build, the level of his conditioning, and the time available for exercising.

Exercise 20A. Forward Arm Depressor (with Isogym and stretch cords)

Follow the instructions described for Exercise 15.

FIG. X–18.   Forward Arm Depressor (with stretch cords)

Exercise 20B. Forward Arm Depressor (with stretch cords)

This exercise is done with the stretch cords attached at waist height. The swimmer leans over as described previously and pulls the arms through as described in Exercise 15.

Exercise 20C. Forward Arm Depressor (with pulley weights)

Follow directions described for Exercise 20B.

FIG. X–19. Sideward   Arm   Depressor   (with Isogym and stretch cords)

FIG. X–20. Elbow Extensor (with Isogym and stretch cords)

Exercise 21A. Sideward Arm Depressor (with Isogym and stretch cords)

As closely as possible, follow the instructions outlined for Exercise 16.

Exercise 21B. Sideward Arm Depressor (with stretch cords)

Exercise 21C. Sideward Arm Depressor (with pulley weights)

If using a bench with this exercise, the swimmer may lie on his back.

Exercise 22A. Elbow Extensor (with Isogym and stretch cords)

As closely as possible, follow the instructions for Exercise 17.

Exercise 22B. Elbow Extensor (with stretch cords)

Exercise 22C. Elbow Extensor (with pulley weights)

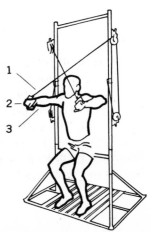

FIG. X–21. Breaststroke Arm Pull

Exercise 23A. Breaststroke Arm Pull (with Isogym and stretch cords)

As closely as possible, follow the instructions for Exercise 18.

Exercise 23B. Breaststroke Arm Pull (with stretch cords)

Exercise 23C. Breaststroke Arm Pull (with pulley weights)

FIG. X–22. Arm Rotators

Exercise 24A. Arm Rotator (with Isogym and stretch cords)

As closely as possible, follow the instructions for Exercise 19.

Exercise 24B. Arm Rotator (with stretch cords)

Exercise 24C. Arm Rotator (with pulley weights)

CALISTHENIC EXERCISES FOR SWIMMERS

It is difficult to design calisthenic exercises for swimmers which exercise the prime mover muscles in the exact manner in which they are used in swimming. In those cases in which there is too little or a complete lack of equipment, however, calisthenics are better than no exercises at all. The writer has used calisthenics and isometric contractions with age-group teams for years, and feels they have been beneficial. They can be done on a pool deck, and the swimmers can use their own weight or the weight of their partners for resistance.

Exercise 25. Push-ups

This exercise is more effective if the swimmer can do the push-ups keeping only his finger tips on the ground.

REPETITIONS: 15 to 60.

MUSCLES DEVELOPED: Elbow extensors, pectoralis, and anterior portion of deltoid.

Exercise 26. Overhead Arm Depressors (a paired exercise)

The subject performing the exercise (Subject A) lies on his back and places his arms overhead. With each hand he grasps the opposite elbow. Subject B places his hands on Subject A's elbows, assumes a front leaning rest, as if doing a push-up, and straddles Subject A's feet with his own feet. Subject A pushes up and forward with his arms against the resistance by Subject B until his arms are in a vertical position. He then slowly lowers his arms to the ground as Subject B keeps a constant pressure on Subject A's elbows. The back should be kept flat on the ground and not arched.

REPETITIONS: 5 to 35.

MUSCLES DEVELOPED: Arm depressors and abdominal muscles.

Exercise 27. Squat Thrusts with Push-ups

Standing erect with the arms at the side, bend the knees and assume a squat position. Then thrust the legs backward in a front leaning rest position. Perform one or two push-ups, then return to the standing position. Do this exercise at a fast rate of speed.

REPETITIONS: 5 to 20.

MUSCLES DEVELOPED: Trunk muscles—both flexors and extensors, triceps, all leg muscles.

Exercise 28. Jumping Squats (either half or full)

During the past few years the value of full jumping squats has been under question because of possible injury to the exerciser's knees. If the subject is in good physical condition, has properly conditioned his legs, and does not do an excessive number of repetitions, full jumping squats can be done with no harmful effect. Full jumping squats are particularly valuable for increasing the strength and flexibility of the legs for breaststrokers. Swimmers of the other strokes gain no particular advantage from doing full jumping squats over half jumping squats.

STARTING POSITION AND ACTION: The swimmer stands erect with his arms at his sides. He bends his knees and drops downward into a full or half squat position and springs upward as high as he can, meanwhile throwing his arms upward as if he were doing a basketball jump. He continues to do this exercise continuously until he has completed 10 to 40 repetitions in a series. Begin with only a few repetitions and progress slowly.

MUSCLES DEVELOPED: Hip and knee extensors and ankle plantar flexors.

Exercise 29. Quarter Squats, Piggy-back (a paired exercise)

The subject performing the exercise permits subject (of approximately the same weight) to straddle his back in a piggy-back manner. He then bends his knees and performs quarter squats.

REPETITIONS: 4 to 20.

CAUTION: In order to avoid excessive strain on the knees, the performing subject should be careful not to bend his knees too much.

MUSCLES DEVELOPED: Hip and knee extensors.

Exercise 30. Chin-ups

If a chinning bar is available, chinning exercises are good for strengthening the arm depressor muscles. They also develop the biceps muscles, which are not prime movers. The arm depressors are used in a slightly different manner in this exercise than they are used in the swimming strokes. For this reason, the chinning exercise is inferior to the latissimus apparatus exercise in developing the arm depressors, but may be used if no latissimus apparatus is available.

MUSCLES DEVELOPED: Arm depressors, elbow flexors, and wrist and finger flexors.

Exercise 31. Sit-ups

Lie on the back, bending the knees slightly, fingers interlaced at back of the neck. Keeping the feet on the ground (if necessary, have someone hold the feet down or anchor them under something), swing the body up and forward until the head almost touches the knees.

REPETITIONS: 10 to 50.

MUSCLES DEVELOPED: Trunk and hip flexors—rectus abdominus, external obliques, psoas magnus. [Note: The trunk flexors (rectus abdominus, external obliques) are important muscles for swimmers. If a good weight training program is used, there is no particular need for the swimmer to do sit-ups as a regular exercise, inasmuch as he will receive enough exercise (isometric) when he performs the supine pullover (or overhead arm depressors, in the case of calisthenics) and when he works with the latissimus device. If the swimmer has weak abdominals and is not involved in a weight program, sit-ups are recommended.]

THE USE OF OTHER STRENGTHENING EXERCISES AND ISOMETRIC CONTRACTIONS

All of the exercises described above are designed specifically to strengthen the muscles associated with swimming. The writer does not mean to imply that these are the only exercises that will strengthen these muscles. There are literally dozens of other exercises which are also beneficial, such as isometric contractions with or without equipment, exercises with medicine ball, exercises with the exergenie, and rope climbing. Time and space prevent a complete inventory. When doing other exercises, the swimmer should use those which use the muscles in a manner similar to the action described in this chapter.

If a child is not engaged in a good school program of physical education or has a very low level of general strength, there may be a need for a general body building program. Such a program would include exercises to condition not only the prime movers for swimming, but also the other muscles and muscle groups.

STRETCHING EXERCISES

Flexibility, or mobility, is a desirable trait for an athlete because it permits maximum exploitation of strength, speed, and coordination. Once again the specific type of flexibility desirable varies with the sport or within a given sport. In swimming, the particular stroke is the determining factor. Research conducted at Indiana University indicates that members of the varsity swimming team are more flexible in the shoulders and ankles than any other group of athletes tested.

As in the case of designing a strength building exercise program, a poorly planned stretching program can result in a tremendous waste of time with minimal, or even detrimental, results.

Flexibility varies considerably from one person to the next. A large-boned, heavily muscled person (mesomorphic body build) is usually less flexible than a small-boned, less heavily muscled person. His lack of flexibility can be attributed largely to the size of the bones and the structure of the joints which restrict movement. The athlete cannot change joint structure; he can improve the flexibility of his joints by increasing the ease and range with which the interfering muscles can be stretched. The fascia or connective tissue which surrounds the muscle fibers and the entire muscle is the particular component of the muscle which limits movement, and must be stretched. The best way to improve the ability of the muscle to be stretched is to engage in the actual activity, or engage in a specifically designed stretching exercise program, or a combination of these two methods. In the sport of swimming, combination of the two methods is commonly used. As an example, the ankles become more flexible because of the stretch placed on the anterior leg muscles (ankle flexors—tibialis anterior, and so on) during the downbeat of the kick, as the crawl flutter kick is employed in swimming drills. Simultaneously, the efficiency of the kick is also improved. The same muscles are also stretched when Exercises 34 and 35 are used.

Areas of Desirable Flexibility

There are two main areas in which good flexibility is critical for all strokes: (1) the ankle joint, and (2) the shoulder joint. Considerable time has been spent by Japanese swimmers in developing good hamstring flexibility (forward bending, such as is done in accomplishing a jackknife dive). I feel that the normal range of movement in this area is sufficient to handle all requirements of the competitive strokes, and that little or no exercise need be devoted to improve this type of flexibility, with the exception of the particular individual who is abnormally low in this flexibility (that is, if he cannot keep his knees straight when he bends over to touch his toes with his hands).

ANKLE FLEXIBILITY. It is desirable for all swimmers who use the flutter kick or fishtail kick (backstrokers, freestylers, and butterflyers) to have good flexibility in plantar flexion of the ankles; that is, to have the ability to point or extend their feet in almost a straight line with their lower legs (as when a ballet dancer performs on her toes). This particular action will permit the swimmer's feet to be in a good position to push the water in a more backward direction during the propulsive phase of his kick, thereby making his kick more effective. To improve this type of flexibility, the anterior muscles of the lower leg (dorsiflexors of the ankles and toes) must be stretched.

Breaststrokers should have flexibility of the ankles in precisely the opposite direction, that is, dorsiflexion of the ankle. This is the ability to flex the ankle toward the shin bone. This type of flexibility permits the breaststroker to place his feet in good position to push the water backwards at a point earlier in his kick than otherwise, and thus have a more effective kick. To achieve this desired type of flexibility, the muscles on the posterior aspect of the lower leg (the gastrocnemius and soleus) must be stretched.

SHOULDER FLEXIBILITY. Flexibility in the shoulder joint, particularly in the backward direction, is desirable, as it facilitates arm recovery in the crawl and butterfly strokes and permits an easier pull in the backstroke.

To achieve the desired flexibility, the anterior muscles of the shoulder joint (the anterior deltoid and the pectoralis muscles) must be stretched.

Method of Stretching

Flexibility can be most effectively improved by paired or forced stretching exercises. These are exercises in which the muscles are stretched at a steady rate either by another person or by resistance of some other type, such as a weight or the weight of the person's body itself.

Free swinging exercises, such as Exercises 39 through 42, also contribute but are not as effective in increasing flexibility as are stretching exercises. Possibly the reason for this is that in free swinging exercise the stretch on the muscle results from the inertia of the swinging limb and, of necessity, must be applied at a fast rate. This fast stretching motion causes stimulation of a protective stretch reflex which works to prevent the muscle from being overstretched. As a result, the muscle that is being stretched contracts and resists being stretched more than when steady forced stretching is applied.

Measuring Flexibility

In research projects, flexibility is measured with special equipment, and careful objective measurements are taken. There are, however, some very simple, if less reliable, methods of measuring flexibility without equipment which can help the swimmer evaluate the flexibility of his ankle and shoulder joints. Girls are generally more flexible than boys, and a person loses some flexibility as he ages, particularly following the onset of puberty. The following measurements are just approximations. In order to achieve a better comparative evaluation of his flexibility, a swimmer can compare his performances on the following general tests with those of his teammates.

ANKLE FLEXIBILITY. Plantar flexion—the subject sits on the deck with his legs held together and his knees fully extended. He plantar flexes his feet as much as possible. If the angle formed between his shin and the top of his feet is almost 180° or a straight line, he has better than average flexibility. The more acute the angle, the poorer his ankle flexibility and, consequently, everything else being equal, the poorer his flutter and fishtail kicks will be.

Dorsiflexion—the subject assumes the same position described above. He now dorsiflexes his feet. If the angle formed between his shin and the top of his feet is 100° or less, he has average or better than average flexibility.

Another method of testing the ankle and leg flexibility needed by breaststrokers is to have the swimmer stand erect with his hands behind his neck and his feet facing directly forward and touching one another at the toes and heels. He should now try to bend down in a full squat position without taking his hands from in back of his neck or separating his knees, and without allowing his heels to leave the ground. If the swimmer lifts his heels or loses his balance and falls backward, he is below average in dorsiflexion and needs to stretch the calf muscles of his legs if he wants to develop a good breaststroke kick.

SHOULDER FLEXIBILITY. Backward flexion—in order to measure shoulder flexibility, instructions should be followed carefully. Subject A sits on the deck with his back straight and vertical. The legs are extended in front of the body, legs together and knees straight. The arms are held in front of the body at exactly shoulder height and with the palms facing one another. Subject B, standing in back of Subject A, leans forward and with his hands pulls Subject A's arms backward in a horizontal plane without permitting Subject A's palms to turn upward or downward or the elbows to bend. He continues to pull, taking particular care not to lower or raise the arms, until the arms are as far backward as they can go without causing undue pain. Subject A should resist the tendency to lean forward and to rotate his palms downward as the arms are moved backward. He should also concentrate on keeping his back straight and not bending his knees. If the swimmer's arms can come within six inches of touching one another without too much effort on the part of Subject B, the swimmer has normal flexibility. If the arms touch or cross over, the swimmer has better than average flexibility.

Exercise 32. Ankle Stretcher (plantar flexor)

Subject A sits on deck with his legs held together and extended in front of him. Subject B assumes kneeling position at the feet of Subject A. He places his hands so the palms cover A's toes and the lower part of his insteps. He pushes downward and forcibly plantar flexes A's ankles. He repeats this action 15 to 30 times. A keeps his knees straight throughout.

Exercise 33. Ankle Stretcher (plantar flexor)

Place a towel or pad on the deck. Assume a kneeling position and plantar flex the feet so the insteps of the ankles are facing downward on the towel, then sit back on the bottoms of the feet. Place the hands on the floor in back of the feet. Rock backward, lifting the knees off the ground and placing the weight of the body over the feet so the ankles are forcibly stretched. Repeat 10 to 20 times.

Exercise 34. Achilles Tendon Stretcher (dorsiflexor)

Subject A can either sit on a bench or on the deck. Subject B kneels down and firmly grasps one of A's feet by placing his left palm in back of A's heel. He places the right hand with his palm over the ball of the foot and forcibly dorsiflexes the ankle. Repeat 10 to 20 times.

Exercise 35. Achilles Tendon Stretcher (dorsiflexor)

The subject takes a standing position approximately three to four feet back from and facing a wall or fence, one leg slightly behind the other. He then leans forward and places his arms against the wall or fence so his body is held at a 45° angle. The subject, keeping the back leg straight and bending the other, exerts his body weight upon this back leg and tries to force the heel of the back foot downward, thereby stretching the calf muscle and the Achilles tendon. Repeat on each leg 20 to 30 times.

Exercise 36. Achilles Tendon Stretcher

The subject stands erect with his hands behind his neck, legs together and feet facing straight forward. Without removing his hands from behind his neck, allowing his knees or feet to separate, or the heels to leave the ground, he does full squats to the point that the buttocks touch the backs of the feet. When all the way down, he bounces up and down (about six inches) several times, then returns to standing position. Repeat eight to ten times.

Exercise 37. Shoulder Stretching Exercise

The method of doing this exercise is identical to that described for testing shoulder flexibility earlier in this chapter (page 306). After the arms are all the way back, they should be moved forward about six inches and then pulled back again in a steady oscillating manner four to five times. The arms should then be returned forward and the entire process repeated five to ten times.

Exercise 38. Shoulder Stretching Exercise

Subject A sits on the deck with his back straight and his hands interlaced behind his neck. Subject B stands in back of A, grasps A's elbows with his palms facing backward, and places one of his knees against A's back. He then forcibly pulls the elbows backward and slightly upward until A feels some pain. When the arms are back, they are bounced forward and backward slightly three to five times. They are then moved forward before being returned to the stretching position again, and the stretching motion is repeated. Repeat five to ten times.

Free Swinging, Shoulder Stretching Exercises

Exercise 39. Forward Windmilling

Standing erect, the arms are swung in a circular motion in the lateral plane, much in the same manner and direction as when doing the butterfly arm stroke. Repeat 15 to 30 times.

Exercise 40. Backward Windmilling

Same as Exercise 39, except that the arms are swung in the opposite direction. Repeat 15 to 30 times.

Exercise 41. Horizontal Swinging

Standing erect, the arms are held forward at shoulder height in front of the chest, palms facing one another. The arms are swung directly backward on the horizontal plane as far as they will go with the elbows straight on the first swing. On the next swing the motion is the same, but the elbows are bent at a 90° angle. The exercise is continued, alternating straight and bent elbows, until the exercise has been repeated 15 to 30 times.

Exercise 42. Overhead Stretching

Standing erect with the arms held at the sides, the arms are swung forward and upward over the head with the elbows straight and the hands grasping one another, palms facing forward. They are then bounced backward twice and returned to the starting position. Repeat 15 to 30 times.

The four preceding exercises are a good set to use to stretch out the muscles before swimming.

WHEN SHOULD THE EXERCISES BE DONE?

Chapter IX, *Planning a Season's Swimming Training Program,* presents a detailed discussion of the placement of exercises in the total program. This will, therefore, be a brief and general statement only.

At any time in the season, the swimmer who is on a heavy strengthening exercise program will probably be somewhat slower in swimming practice than if he were not doing strengthening exercises. His slowness is the result of his muscles being tired from the dry land exercises. The eventual effect of the exercise program, however, is to make the swimmer swim faster. Swimmers just embarking on a dry land, strengthening program often get discouraged when their muscles become stiff and sore, and they fear they may be losing their strokes. They may then drop the program before their muscles have had time to adapt. They must understand what is happening in order to persevere through the period of adjustment.

The strengthening program should be decreased or stopped completely before the big meets at the end of the competitive season, so the muscles may rest. It is unwise, however, for a person who is extremely weak and needs the added strength to go the entire competitive season using no strengthening exercises.

Strengthening exercises may be done before or after swimming workouts, but are more effective if they are done before the swimming practice; that is, before the muscles are tired.

Stretching exercises should be done throughout the swimming training season. The person who is low in flexibility should do the exercises prior to each swimming practice session. Before any swimmer swims in cold water he should use stretching exercises as a means of aiding his warm-up and possibly of preventing injury to the muscles. This is particularly important in the case of breaststrokers who have knee trouble or adductor muscle trouble.

WHO NEEDS DRY LAND EXERCISES?

Some holders of world records have never done dry land exercises. Does this mean that the average swimmer does not need to do them?

The fact can be interpreted in many ways, depending upon the attitude and beliefs of the interpreter. This writer believes these swimmers might have swum even faster if they had had a good exercise program. Such swimmers are also, doubtless, inherently strong and flexible and do not need strengthening and stretching as much as some less flexible and less strong individuals. This writer has trained swimmers, such as Chester Jastremski, Lary Schulhof, and George Breen, who are extremely strong and muscular. They are mesomorphic in body-build, being large-boned and heavily muscled. They needed little strength building and, after three years of routine strengthening exercises, were placed on a mild strengthening exercise program. Each of these was relatively low in flexibility and was always kept on a rigorous stretching exercise program.

The opposite was, and is, true of Fred Schmidt, Ted Stickles, Tom Stock, and Charles Hickcox. These four boys are very flexible but lacking somewhat in strength. They are more ectomorphic (lean, small-boned, less muscular) in body type than the three just described. As their careers advanced, these swimmers were kept on a rigorous strengthening program, and the amount of time spent on stretching exercises was reduced. These illustrations demonstrate that an exercise program should vary somewhat from one individual to the next, particularly as his swimming career advances. As has been stated, a swimmer should concentrate on eliminating his deficiencies.

It is also possible that, when a swimmer reaches maturity and is sufficiently strong, there will be less or no need for a hard strengthening exercise program. However, it seems unlikely that a swimmer should ever completely eliminate the stretching phase of his exercise program.

THE VALUES OF PHYSICAL ACTIVITIES OTHER THAN SWIMMING FOR SWIMMING

Years ago cross-country running was included as a part of a swimmer's training. Obviously, the idea behind this practice was that the swimmer would condition his cardio-respiratory system and develop endurance. There is no doubt that engaging in such other activities as running, bicycling, tennis, and soccer during the off-season is good for the general condition of the swimmer and may be preferred to dissipating or doing nothing.

This is particularly true when a swimmer swims during only one season of the year. Experience has shown, however, that attempts to develop endurance for swimming by running, bicycling, and similar activities is quite ineffective. The swimmer might more profitably spend his time building strength and flexibility through dry land exercises and endurance in the swimming pool. The value of engaging in other physical activities is to provide the swimmer with a change in activity and environment in order that he may not become bored with training for swimming. The athlete needs an occasional break, not only from training for his particular sport, but also from hard training of any sort. For this reason he should try some recreational activities which offer him enjoyment and relaxation, whether it be archery, bowling, baseball, or dancing.

XI

Age-Group Swimming

The international success that American swimming has enjoyed since the 1960 Olympic Games can be traced to a great extent to the age-group swimming program. This program provides an opportunity for children to train for competitive swimming at an early age, and to develop the skills and conditioning that will be needed when they are ready for senior competition. A careful look at the data listed about each swimming champion in Chapter XIV will reveal that the majority of these champions began competitive swimming between the ages of 8 and 12.

Since competitive swimming began, there had been periodic attempts to organize it by age or ability classifications. The most successful attempt in this direction occurred in the early 1950's when the National Amateur Athletic Union formulated national age-group rules and divided competition for swimmers into age-group categories. Age-group rules remain under the jurisdiction of the Amateur Athletic Union, and these rules are printed in the AAU Swimming Guide.[1]

[1] Available from Amateur Athletic Union, 231 West 58th Street, New York, New York, 10019. Cost—$3.00.

Although they change somewhat from year to year, the fundamental rules have remained the same and are listed below:

1. Associations may have age-group competition consisting of four age groups as follows: 10 and under, 11–12 years, 13–14 years, and 15–17 years. Times may be submitted for Age-Group Records and five best times recognition for an age-group swimmer participating in any sanctioned Junior and Senior AAU competition. . . .

3. The eligibility of a participant for a particular age-group will be determined by his date of birth in his respective age-group. Age on the first day of the meet shall govern for the full meet. Participants must swim in their respective age brackets.

7. The five (5) best times nationally in each age group shall be published. . . .

Age-group swimming is subject to its own specific rules plus the general rules that govern AAU swimming. Competition for age-group swimmers and senior swimmers is held within each AAU association. Any person or group interested in obtaining information about these competitions should contact the AAU officers in his district. The names and addresses of the persons to contact may be found in the AAU Swimming Guide or by contacting the National AAU Office.[2] Age-group activities are covered by many local and sectional periodicals and by one national periodical.[3]

DEVELOPING A SOUND PHILOSOPHY OF
AGE-GROUP SWIMMING

Swimming in an age-group program can be a wonderful experience for a child or it can be an upsetting one, depending upon his coach and parents and the manner in which the program is conducted. I have been associated with age-group swimming as a coach since its inception, and have been fortunate enough to have my four children involved in the program as swimmers. I am convinced of the values of a well-conducted age-group swimming program. I, and many other people as well, however, recognize the possibilities for abuse that can develop in such programs as Age-group Swimming and Little League in which, due to the age of the participant, there is a tendency for the parent to become closely associated with the team or club situation. This association is often vital to the existence of the program, for the parents frequently

[2] See footnote 1.
[3] *Swimming World*, edited by Al Schoenfield, 12618 Killion Street, North Hollywood, California.

provide the necessary means of transportation to meets and practice, act as officials at meets, do committee work, and otherwise perform in capacities which make the program successful.

Human nature, however, is such that a person loses most of his ability to remain detached and objective in matters concerning his children. For this reason alone the job of an age-group coach will never be an easy one. The standard joke concerning the most desirable age-group coaching position is that of a coach in an orphans' home. It is a fact that the greatest attrition in the age-group coaching ranks occurs in clubs in which the coach works directly under the control of a parents' group.

Many of the problems that develop could be circumvented if, early in the formation of an age-group program, a sound philosophy were developed and adhered to. Once interest in an age-group program begins developing in a community, it usually grows rapidly, with scant attention to its real purpose on the part of coach, parents, or swimmers. If the program is permitted to develop without a statement of objectives, it too often becomes one in which the coach, parents, and officials have failed to give much consideration to the fact that the only justification for the program is that it exists for the benefit of the children, and not for the glorification of parents, coach, or swimming officials. Most of the abuses prevalent in age-group swimming could be virtually eliminated if all persons concerned would keep this philosophy in mind.

ESTABLISHING OBJECTIVES FOR AN AGE-GROUP PROGRAM

Every age-group team should follow such guidelines for their programs as will reflect a sound philosophy towards training and competition on the part of all concerned. In setting up a constitution and by-laws for the club's charter, this philosophy should be a primary consideration and, after the club is in operation, should not be filed away with the constitution, but should be an integral part of the conduct of each practice session and meet and of the general attitude of the coach, assistant coaches, parents, officials, and children.

When setting up these guidelines for an age-group program, several factors should be considered.

The program should serve the interests of all the children, not just the highly skilled. Over 500,000 children are competing in age-group swimming in the United States today. Only a fraction of 1 per cent of these children will ever be national champions or make an Olympic team. The goals of a program should not be tailored to suit the needs of this select few, but of the whole group.

Not every child can be a great swimmer. No matter how hard their parents or coach push and drive, some children, through no fault of their own, can achieve only mediocre success at best. If the program is well planned and directed, every child can gain from his experience whether or not he ever wins a single race.

Although there may be some upsetting times for the child, as well as some disappointments, the total experience should be an enjoyable one. A program that puts so much emotional pressure on everyone concerned that there are crying scenes, angry words between parents and children, coach and children, and coach and parents is obviously a program with misplaced emphasis.

> Through ten years of age-group swimming I've seen prejudices and hatreds between people all over the country. Swimmers in the older age groups notice and realize these hatreds continually grow. There are hatreds between coach and coach, parent and coach, and swimmer and parent. The swimmer can idolize his or her coach but mommy or daddy hate him because their little Johnny isn't progressing. These hatreds will keep growing because the competition is stiffer and the goals are higher. I and many of my friends were never pushed, because we had parents who cared, and cared the right way . . . the helpful way in a manner that would keep and improve our interest and liking for the sport of swimming.[4]

Some Suggested Objectives of Age-group Swimming

1. To provide opportunities for social and emotional development.
2. To furnish a wholesome and worthwhile physical and recreational outlet.
3. To provide opportunity to learn sportsmanship and make swimmers aware of team cooperation.
4. To provide educational opportunities.
5. To provide opportunities to learn good health habits.
6. To provide training and competition to all swimmers who desire it.
7. To provide a wide base of experienced swimmers in order to contribute to the increased skills and knowledges needed at the high school, college, and Senior AAU level of swimming.

These objectives are accomplished through:

1. Properly supervised and organized practices and meet situations with opportunity for team functions not limited to just swimming.
2. Proper types of practices and meets for the level and skill and scope

---

[4] Art Brandt, University Heights, Ohio, "An Age Group Swimmer Speaks Out," *Swimming World,* VII, No. 1 (January 1966), 11.

of achievement of the several ages and abilities on a team or within an individual's ability.

3. Coaching by competent persons with a preferred background of college or university training and a membership in an accepted coach's association.

4. Directed learning at practices and meets and scholarship opportunities at colleges or universities.

5. Health habits as learned directly from proper coaching techniques and indirectly from dietary directions, exercise schedules, lectures, and demonstrations.

6. Opportunities provided by clubs, schools, recreation departments, and other agencies for training; and competitive opportunities provided through: (1) dual meets, (2) intra-club, (3) closed league, (4) city recreation meets, (5) school, and (6) AAU; so that no person is denied the opportunity to practice and/or compete.

7. Competently organized practices and competitive opportunities, with tensions minimized and developments within the scope and good sequential development of all swimmers. As they progress from lower age levels through high school, college-university, and Senior AAU levels, outstanding experienced swimmers should be produced.[5]

It should be noted that nowhere in this list is the objective of the development of national champions or a winning team mentioned. Mediocrity should be no one's goal; everyone should strive for excellence. However, the real winner in age-group swimming is often not the winner of the race, for he (or she) may be achieving his goal at the cost of failure to attain some of the other goals available in such a program. Trophies, medals, and national age-group records are poor objectives by comparison with those listed above. In many respects age-group swimming is a preparation for life. The hardest worker in the pool does not always win the race, any more than does the student who studies the hardest always make the best grades. Every age-grouper can learn, however, that to get the most from his potential he must apply himself and work hard, intelligently, and consistently. The transfer of this principle to everything he does and will do later depends on the effectiveness of the program in which he is involved in achieving the objectives described above.

Creating Proper Attitudes

The desire to achieve the most from himself should come as much as possible from within the individual. To motivate the person toward

---

[5] Report compiled and submitted by a committee of coaches and officials of the U.S. at the request of Mr. Harold Heller, Chairman of Age-group Swimming of the AAU, 1964.

this end is the real essence of good coaching and good parental guidance. The child is too often goaded into working hard by promises of rewards if he is successful or threats of punishment if he fails. The goals set by coach and parent are often not realistic when considered in the light of the child's potential. If the goals are set too high, a real conflict may be created in the child's mind, and the fact that his interest in continuing to swim may be jeopardized is the least of the psychological implications.

A hypothetical case is often the best way of illustrating a point, and the counterpart of this one may be found in nearly every club or team situation that I know about. Sam was a great swimmer at an early age and went two years undefeated in all his events. He and his father were constant companions and traveled about the country to enter meets that were often hundreds of miles away. At age 13 Sam began losing a race now and then. When he lost Sam's father would "freeze him out"—walk away without talking to him. When he won Sam got a slap on the back, a milk shake, and his father's affection. He began to associate his father's affection and love with his own swimming success. As he lost more and more often, he developed a feeling of insecurity which, during his mid-teens, caused certain psychological problems.

Every child reacts differently to the same situation. Some children would have been affected very little, but the experience could never be beneficial for the child. In such a case the father is to blame, not the age-group swimming program.

The parent described above might be considered the "high-pressure" type. At the opposite extreme is the "low-pressure" parent who boasts that he does not pressure his child into doing anything. If he doesn't want to go to practice, the parent doesn't make him; if he doesn't want to swim in a meet, the parent doesn't make him. This kind of permissiveness might seem to be sound psychology, but it often has a far different result from the one the parent had planned, if it contributes to the child's inability to follow through on any project he undertakes. As long as the child is a member of a team, the coach must have the cooperation of the parents in seeing to it that the child fulfills his obligation to the team. His responsibilities include regular attendance at practice, competing when he is requested to do so, and rallying to his team's support at meets in which he has not been asked to swim. When a parent permits or even encourages the child to shirk these obligations, he is damaging the child's character by conditioning him to be unreliable and inconsiderate. When this situation occurs, the best course for the child and the team is to drop the child from the team roster.

One of the most common criticisms of the age-group swimming program is that it is too competitive. Very young children have little competitive drive; their competitive spirit develops as they mature. Some children develop this drive precociously and to a greater degree than do other children. Aggressive, highly-driven parents are often unhappy if their children do not develop this competitive drive to the extent the parent would like. Parents must realize that slow development of competitive drive at an early age is normal and perhaps more desirable than precocious or forced early development.

One prominent age-group swimming coach expresses his opinion:

> Many people want to know why swimmers quit at such a young age. I believe the reason is that they have been pushed too hard too young. If these swimmers weren't expected to perform as big leaguers at such an early age, and for such a lengthy period of time, they might have a different outlook on swimming, as a sport, both before and after college.[6]

It is important that everyone learn to compete and develop some competitive spirit. It is also important for children to learn to adapt to reasonable levels of emotional stress. The small disappointments they must learn to handle as youngsters prepare them for the larger ones they are certain to experience as adults.

A swimmer conditions his body physiologically for greater physical efforts by progressively increasing the physical stress he places on it; that is, as the body adapts to the stress of short, easy workouts, the swimmer increases the amount of stress by doing longer, harder workouts. He must also condition himself psychologically in a similar manner.

A child encounters small situations in which emotional stresses are placed on him, such as swimming in a local club meet in the 8 and under age-group category, 25-yard freestyle. First place prize is a blue ribbon and the congratulations of his parents. He gets a bit nervous and there is some emotional stress. He is able to adjust to it with no problem.

As his career advances, he is, at the age of 13, winning medals and trophies instead of ribbons. He now gets his picture in the paper and a number of his contemporaries are a bit jealous of him. He is still able to handle the emotional stress, however, and has made all the necessary adjustments. Eventually, at the height of his swimming career at age 19, he finds himself standing on the starting block in the finals of an Olympic event. The emotional stress is tremendous, but, because of his previous experience, he is able to handle it as well as many other emotional stresses associated with success in any area.

Compare this person with the individual who has had none of these

6 Pete Accardy, Burbank Swim Academy, Burbank, California, "A Coach Speaks Out—Is Age Group Getting Out of Hand?" *Swimming World*, VII, No. 1 (January 1966), 11.

or any similar experiences. It seems certain that a person whose character has been properly tempered in this manner is better equipped for adult life than one who has been protected from competition of any sort. Character and personality are the result of two factors: (1) inherent qualities and (2) the stresses placed upon the individual and the adaptations that he makes to these stresses. A properly conducted age-group swimming program can do a great deal to help develop desirable personality traits and prepare the child for adulthood.

THE ROLE OF THE AGE-GROUP COACH

In the crucial transition period of increasing competitive drive, the child needs a compassionate teacher who displays more than his ability to be well-organized and his thorough knowledge of stroke mechanics, important as these factors are in the effective coach. An age-group coach should not be selected merely because he is ambitious and gets good results, but because he knows how to handle and understand children. The paradox is that the latter kind of person is often the one who consistently develops outstanding swimmers.

This writer had the pleasure of seeing one of the greatest of all age-group coaches, the late Jim Clark, formerly of the Indianapolis Athletic Club, at work in his prime. All the children who swam for him admired and respected him. They enjoyed their association with him and he enjoyed coaching them. He worked them hard, but had few harsh words for them. He motivated them without being extremely severe. Many of his swimmers have told me, after they had grown into adulthood, that it had been a very satisfying experience to swim for Jim Clark because they knew he always had their best interests at heart.

A coach working with children during their formative years can do a great deal to develop desirable or undesirable attitudes. The children under his guidance unconsciously adopt the attitudes the coach displays. If the coach disputes decisions, behaves in an unsportsmanlike manner, and has temper tantrums, he will find these traits appearing in some of his athletes.

Most swimmers develop a strong loyalty to their coach and have confidence in his ability. This confidence can be undermined by an over-critical parent who questions the coach's ability and methods, his decisions about meets, entries, and so on. If, after the coach has been given a fair opportunity to prove himself, he is judged incompetent by a majority of the parents, it would be a wiser course of action to find another coach than to attack the present one in the hearing of his swimmers. A coach who must constantly be protecting himself from the criticism of his team's parents is in danger of losing much of his capacity to coach effectively.

A coach's job is to supervise the entire swimming program. He cannot be subservient to the wishes of the parents' group. In matters affecting training and competition he must be in charge; he must make final decisions concerning events and meets that various swimmers should enter. He must not abdicate his right to make the decisions he feels best serve the interests of the team and program. Coaches make errors in judgment, just as we all do; compassion and understanding on the part of the parents is a necessary prerequisite for a successful age-group program.

ORGANIZATION OF PRACTICE FOR AGE-GROUP TEAMS

Age-group swimmers train under all sorts of conditions and at all times of the day. Each team has problems which are peculiar to its situation. However, there are some conditions common to most programs, the primary one being adequate time in the pool. Competitive teams are usually left with the most undesirable hours, those during which the pools are not being used by classes or the public. To obtain optimum use of the pool in the time available, the program must be well organized.

The large number of swimmers and the differences in their level of ability make it necessary for most clubs to divide the team into two or more groups. One age-group team solved its organizational problems by dividing its team into three groups on the basis of ability, with the boys and girls working out together. Instead of using the terms *first team*, *second team*, and *third team*, colors were used to designate the teams— Blue, Red, and Green.

The Blue Team has a membership of 20, with an age-spread from 10 to 17 years. This group comprises the more skilled and experienced swimmers who are capable of taking harder workouts than the other teams. The members of this team are more dedicated and willing to work hard. They average six workouts a week during the winter (from 6:00 to 8:00 P.M. Monday through Saturday) and 12 during the summer (from 6:30 to 8:00 A.M. and from 5:00 to 6:30 P.M. Monday through Saturday). Their average daily distance swum is 2500 to 3800 yards per day in winter and 4000 to 7000 meters per day in summer.

The Red Team comprises 25 members whose ages range from 8 to 15 years. This team is next in terms of skill and experience in competitive swimming. The members of this group work out six times a week in the winter (6:00 to 8:00 P.M. Monday through Saturday), covering from 2500 to 3000 yards per session, and seven times a week in the summer (12:00 Noon to 1:30 P.M.), covering 3000 to 5000 meters per day.

TABLE XI–1.   Organizational Plan for Workouts for an Age-group Team

	Monday	Tuesday
BLUE TEAM	6:00 to 6:30 P.M.—Exercise in weight room, supervised by asst. coach. 6:30 to 7:00 P.M.—Share pool with other two groups, using two lanes each. Warm up 500 kick, 500 pull, 400 swim in circle. 7:00 to 8:00 P.M.—Share pool with Red Team, three lanes each. Do 6 × 200 repeats with 3 min. rest interval. Then kick 4 × 100, pull 4 × 100, sprint 6 × 50.	6:00 to 6:30 P.M.—Have the pool to itself. Warm up with 300 swim, then swim 16 × 50. 6:30 to 7:30 P.M.—Share pool with Red Team, using three lanes for each. Kick and pull 500 each, then 6 × 50 kick, 6 × 50 pull. 7:30 to 8:00 P.M.—Do sprint and relay take-offs along with Red Team.
RED TEAM	6:00 to 6:15 P.M.—View movies and discuss stroke mechanics, discussion led by asst. coach. 6:15 to 6:30 P.M.—Return to pool for isometric contractions. 6:30 to 7:00 P.M.—Share pool with other two teams, using two lanes. Warm up 400, pull 400, kick 400. 7:00 to 8:00 P.M.—Share pool with Blue Team, do 8 × 100 repeats, 3½ min. rest interval, kick 4 × 50, pull 4 × 50, sprint 3 × 50.	6:00 to 6:30 P.M.—Exercise in weight room, supervised by asst. coach. 6:30 to 7:30 P.M.—Share pool with Blue Team, swim 400, kick 400, pull 400, swim 16 × 50. 7:30 to 8:00 P.M.—Do sprints and relay take-offs with Blue Team.
GREEN TEAM	6:00 to 6:30 P.M.—Have pool to itself, handled by head coach for first half hour, taken over by asst. coach for balance of session. Swim 200 to 300 yards, then do series of 6 to 12 × 50 in circles. 6:30 to 7:00 P.M.—Share pool with other two teams, using two lanes each. Kick and swim another 200 yards each, then finish with 25-yard sprints (4 to 8, depending on level). 7:00 to 7:30 P.M.—Exercise in weight room doing mostly calisthenics and isometric contractions. Some time devoted to discussion of rules and stroke mechanics.	No workout on Tuesday.

The Green Team has a membership of about 30 members, ages 5 to 11. This team works out two times a week (from 6:00 to 8:00 P.M.) during the winter, and six times a week (from 12:00 Noon to 1:30 P.M.) during the summer. These children have reached a low level of swimming achievement, but can cover from 800 to 1500 yards per session in winter and from 1000 to 2000 meters per session in summer. Since this team is composed of the beginning group of competitive swimmers, a great deal of their time in the pool is spent in learning the fundamentals of the four competitive strokes and the rules governing their use, and in becoming accustomed to working out. This group is also divided into two sections: the Lions and Tigers. These groups are formed on the basis of ability, the Lions being the beginning group and the Tigers the more advanced.

The organizational plan in Table XI–1 is intended for the use of a team much like the one just described for a typical Monday and Tuesday during the winter season. Nearly all swimming, kicking, and pulling is done in circles. The pool is 42 feet wide and has six lanes. The lane markers are left in during practice.

It can be seen from the table that a single coach cannot handle a large age-group practice alone. He needs the help of assistant coaches or group leaders; team managers are also helpful for keeping records, timing, and generally supervising workouts.

This plan will not suit the needs of all teams, but is a solution for a typical situation confronted by many age-group teams. It may serve as a guide for those interested in establishing a program.

MOST-ASKED QUESTIONS ABOUT AGE-GROUP SWIMMING

Question 1. How hard should an age-group swimmer work?

Answer. People who are not involved with age-group swimming are usually amazed when they see or hear of a ten-year-old swimmer whose workouts involve distances of several miles a day and who may be doing as many as ten or fifteen 100-yard repeat swims. As a result, we get questions like this: "Can the children's growth be stunted by the hard work?" "Can the hard work hurt their hearts?" and so on.

It *is* a good policy to require that each participant pass a medical examination administered by the child's family physician as a prerequisite to membership on an age-group team. This is to assure the club and coach that no child with a pathological condition which might be aggravated by exercise will be harmed by the program. It is generally agreed that, unless there is some predisposing pathological condition, a child's heart cannot be harmed by exercising. It is possible for the child to be overworked and fatigue himself to the point that he becomes more susceptible to other ailments. Most coaches, however, are sensitive to this factor and will reduce the child's work load or lay him off completely when this begins to occur.

I am constantly amazed at the amount of work some young age-groupers can absorb. Below are some workouts of one of the most outstanding age-group swimmers of all time.

Duncan Scott at age 12 set 23 national age-group records. His best times as a twelve year old (long course) were:

Freestyle: 50 meters—:27.7, 100 meters—:60.7, 200 meters—2:12.1
Backstroke: 50 meters—:32.2, 100 meters—:68.9
Butterfly: 50 meters—:29.1, 100 meters—:65.1
Breaststroke: 50 meters—:36.1, 100 meters—1:23.1
Individual Medley: 200 meters—2:30.7, 400 meters—5:31.0

Duncan swam in one meet at age 4, in one meet as a 5 year old, two meets as a 6 year old, and began training regularly as a 7 year old. He works out twice a day in the summer and once or twice a day during the winter season. He does the first half of his workout all freestyle, the second half equally divided among the other strokes. He participates in golf, bowling, and tennis and has won his school championship in the rope climb and number of push-ups accomplished. He likes to play basketball, football, and track, but does not participate in organized programs in these sports.

Duncan does very little kicking in practice because he hurt his knee and feels that kicking aggravates the condition. He does some pulling, but not very much.

His three favorite workouts (25 meter pool) are listed below:

I. Swim 4 × 400 meters freestyle with 1 minute rest interval; average time—5:00.2.
Swim 32 × 50 meters on 60 seconds (8 of each stroke).
II. Swim 2 × 200 meters butterfly with 4 minutes rest interval; average time—2:48.9.
Swim 6 × 200 meters freestyle with 1 minute rest interval; average time—2:24.
Swim 32 × 50 meters with 1 minute rest interval (8 of each stroke).
III. Swim 3200 meters.
Swim 8 × 50, 2 of each stroke.

Some of the swimmers included in Chapter XIV, *The Training Schedules of Some Champions,* are still in the age-group category. Their workouts reveal how hard some of them work. Not all age-group swimmers would want to work this hard even if they were physically capable of doing so.

Ever since the age-group program began, people have speculated as to whether the swimmers who work hard and develop early will *level off* or *burn themselves out,* to use the phrases often heard. Some of the greatest age-group swimmers ever developed in this country have been Chet Jastremski, Don Schollander, John Nelson, Dick Roth, Bill Utley, and many others who have gone on to set world or national records. Other age-group stars have dropped out of swimming at an early age, while still others have continued to swim as seniors and have improved little or not at all. Many swimmers showing little promise as age-group swimmers have gone on to become champions—Mike Troy, Jed Graef, and Steve Jackman, to name a few.

To express it more simply, no one can evaluate and predict accurately the eventual success or failure a swimmer will attain; there are too many variables. One of the biggest factors in the rate of progress of an age-group swimmer is the rate at which the child matures physiologically. Girls mature sooner than boys and reach their peak of performance at an early age. Children who mature early, particularly those who reach puberty at an early age, make premature gains and subsequently level off somewhat earlier than the average child. Some children, on the other hand, are late developers, and often make their greatest gains in the late teens.

It can be seen from the foregoing discussion of a few of the factors which affect an age-group swimmer's career that there are as many possible outcomes as there are individuals. Obviously, not all children who take dancing lessons, learn to figure skate, or play the piano will go on to become prima ballerinas, Olympic Champion figure skaters, or concert pianists. It also seems to be an unreasonable generalization to say that early hard work burns out a promising age-group swimmer.

Question 2. Should an age-group swimmer train on all strokes or concentrate on the one or two at which he is best?

Answer. Specialization at an early age may eliminate any chance the child has to develop the other strokes. Specialization should come later, when the swimmer has had an opportunity to give each of the strokes a fair trial. On the other hand, if he tries to train equally hard on all four strokes, he may not have any success and may become discouraged to the point of quitting. He should, therefore, be allowed to spend the greatest part of his training time (perhaps 75 per cent) on the stroke that seems to offer him the best opportunity for success. The balance of his time should be spent working on the other strokes.

Question 3. Should an age-group swimmer compete in other sports?

Answer. The amount and the extent to which an age-grouper should participate in other sports is an individual proposition and depends on how keen he is to progress in swimming. Many parents and coaches make the mistake of limiting the child's activities to swimming alone, and thereby provide a boring routine against which the child may eventually rebel. On the other hand, it is unlikely that anyone can participate, much less excel, in all sports at a time when there is a trend toward sports' specialization.

During the break between seasons it is a good change for a swimmer to engage in other sports, at least recreationally. A layoff of a year or so has not been very successful among those who have tried it. During the time they have been out, their swimming contemporaries have continued to improve, and upon their return to the sport they become discouraged.

Question 4. How many meets should an age-group team schedule during each season?

Answer. The average age-group child enjoys the meets even though he may get a few butterflies before his events. He also enjoys the traveling and the general experience. Some parents and coaches complain of too few meets, others of too many. One mother told me that her child swam in over 50 meets in one year. My natural reaction was to ask her, "When does he train?" It is certainly possible to find meets to enter during ten months of the year or more. Restriction of the length of seasons and the number of meets for the benefit of the coach and swimmers may be the answer to the problem of too many meets; those who complain of too few, if they are willing and able to travel, can find a schedule of meets in the *Amateur Athlete,* the monthly publication of the National AAU, or in *Swimming World,* the previously mentioned swimming periodical. Other solutions to the problem of too few meets are inter-squad meets, dual meets between local clubs, or membership in a conference of local clubs with a regularly scheduled list of dual meets and a conference championship.

One of the biggest problems in the training program for age-group swimmers is that the swimmers have little opportunity to build a good foundation of stroke work and fundamental conditioning. Most children are required to do too many short repeat swims and sprints in order that they may be kept in good racing shape for most of the year. They need a good foundation of longer swimming, fartlek, over distance, and slow interval training work before they are thrown into a sprint program. Below is the general program used by an actual team and a list of the restrictions governing their competition.

Summer Season

1. No more than a total of *six* away meets.
2. No more than two days of swimming meets per week during the busiest part of the season.

3. No meets during the months of April and May and only two meets during the month of June (the bulk of the meets to come during July, August, and the first part of September).

Winter Season

1. No more than a total of seven away meets.
2. No more than three days of swimming meets per two weeks during the busiest part of the season.
3. No meets during the months of October and November, and no more than two meets during the month of December (the bulk of the meets to come during January, February, and March).

Children should try to follow the general plan of a seasonal program which is somewhat similar to the one shown in Chapter IX. Too much of a good thing can spoil the appetite for it. A year-round program loaded with too many meets can do exactly this to our age-groupers.

Question 5. How do you keep your age-group swimmers doing hard workouts over a long period of time?

Answer. The easiest way for a coach and his team to maintain a schedule of hard work over a long period of time is to *over-motivate* his swimmers. This can be accomplished in a number of ways: (1) by arranging a heavy schedule of meets over a longer-than-usual season, (2) by offering incentives in the form of bigger and better trophies, (3) by providing more publicity through the newspapers, a club newsletter, and magazines, or (4) through the promise of attractive trips and special awards. Over-motivation, however, increases the pressures on the children, and should not be resorted to as the only means by which children can be motivated. Swimmers *should* be given a program that varies as the season progresses (as described in Chapter IX, *Planning a Season's Swimming Training Program*). This variety helps prevent or, at least, forestall boredom. A coach who is a good psychologist can keep his swimmers interested in training and can motivate them without exerting undue pressure or using such doubtful practices as those described above. The main motivating factor the coach has going for him is the interest that he has in each swimmer. This interest keeps him encouraging them, knowing all of their times, setting reasonable goals for each, and being observant of their response to practice.

XII

Organization of Practice

The biggest single problem facing most swimming teams is too little pool space and too few hours of available pool time. Swimming teams usually train during the least desirable hours of the day, when there is little demand on the pool for swimming classes or recreational swimming. To get the maximum use of these facilities for the large number of swimmers in a good competitive swimming program, a successful team must have a highly organized program and well organized practice sessions.

Most swimming teams, particularly large age-group teams, must be divided into two, three, or even four groups. The following team division was used by the City of Commerce, California,[1] which had a good age-group team, a good senior AAU team, and good diving teams in both men's and women's divisions. The water polo team was also outstanding.

[1] The City of Commerce team combined with the Los Angeles Athletic Club in the summer of 1966.

CITY OF COMMERCE TEAM DIVISIONS

A. Novice Team (first step after swim lessons)

Coached by Andy Lewis and comprised of about 60 members of all ages, these beginning competitors ranged in age from 7 to 16.

B. Age-group Team

Coached by Kyle Lawton, this team was composed of about 60 members of ages 7 to 17, who ranged in ability from beginning competitors through top age-groupers. This group was selected on the basis of ability; they moved up from the novice team to this team when they were considered ready.

C. Senior Team

Coached by Don Gambril, there were about 40 members on this team ranging from 12 years on up. They were selected on the basis of ability, and tryouts were held each year during Christmas vacation for the age-groupers. Any swimmer achieving a national standard time automatically qualified.

D. Diving Teams

1. Novice team—coached by Sam Hernandez.
2. Senior team—coached by Bud Lyndon.
About 40 divers made up this team.

E. Water Polo Team

Coached by Neill Kohlhase, this team was composed of from 25 to 30 members.

It becomes apparent upon calculating the number of swimmers, divers, and water polo players that were involved in the City of Commerce program that the facilities were being well used. It is also clear that no one coach could possibly handle all of these activities personally, aside from the safety hazards and lack of individual attention that would result from such understaffing. When the team is divided into groups, it is not necessarily inevitable that they must all work out at different times. Depending upon the facilities and staff available, it was possible that all three swimming team groups mentioned above could be working out at the same time. Chapter XI outlines the organization of one age-group team in which three groups of swimmers are all at practice at the same time. At one point, while one group is swimming, another group is exercising, and the third is attending a session in the classroom on stroke mechanics.

A coach must make the decision to use the allotted time in the pool for one large group or several small ones. Since most successful teams have adopted the latter practice, it must be the more efficient of the two arrangements. It is true that each team will have a reduced total time in the water, but the quality of that time will be higher and the time out of water not wasted if the coaches are ingenious.

This discussion has so far ignored the second important reason for dividing the team into groups, although the discussion of the City of Commerce program suggests it. This is the unsatisfactory situation that would exist if swimmers of different levels of ability were to be worked out together. Apart from the fact that swimmers of less experience and ability cannot take the hard workouts, those of superior ability need stroke work and individual attention to bring about the refinements necessary for outstanding performances.

In the hypothetical case of a team with 80 members and a daily scheduled time in the pool from 4:00 to 6:30 P.M., the team could be divided into two groups: Group A, the most skilled group, composed of 40 swimmers, and Group B, the remaining 40 swimmers. Group B might work out in the pool from 4:00 to 5:00 P.M., and from 5:00 to 5:30 do dry land exercises either in a special area or on the pool deck. Group A might work from 4:30 to 5:00 P.M. on dry land exercises and then work in the water from 5:00 to 6:30 P.M.

PURPOSES OF GOOD ORGANIZATION
IN PRACTICE SESSIONS

Well organized practice sessions are a necessity to the general morale of the entire team. They also serve several other purposes:

1. Permit maximum use of the facilities. One good policy for all clubs pushed for pool time is never to allow pool space to sit idle. Practice should be arranged so the available water is being used at all times.

2. Assure the coach that each swimmer is highly motivated to work hard and is provided with the opportunity to train adequately.

3. Permit a good system for timing practice lengths.

4. Assure that the lazier swimmers will be pulled along to work harder

with the rest of the team. In a well organized practice a loafer will stand out like a sore thumb. Hopefully, self-pride will assert itself and such a swimmer will not want to appear to disadvantage in the opinion of his peers. In a loosely organized program in which swimmers do not work out together, it is possible for a swimmer to "goof-off," with his team-mates and the coach none the wiser.

5. Permit the coach to evaluate the progress of each individual as well as the team as a whole.

Poorly organized practices, with excessive permissiveness and poor dis-cipline the rule, can result in inferior conditioning for all but the highly motivated few.

On the opposite end of the scale, overly organized practices with absolutely rigid control can result in a tense practice session which, although it will result in good conditioning sessions, may eventually cause the swimmer to regard the whole swimming situation resentfully. The ideal practice session is one that is well organized and in which there is a relaxed, yet highly motivated, attitude on the part of the swimmers.

Discipline in practice sessions is necessary. Workouts should begin on time and the swimmers should be punctual. They should not be permitted to drift in late and leave early. If this does occur, particularly on the part of the stars of the team, the coach will find he is losing control of the situation.

Using a Pace Clock

The pace clock has become a very important piece of equipment around which to organize practice. The most important benefit of using one is that it enables the coach to devote more time to actual coaching while each swimmer times himself. He is no longer a slave to the stop-watch, but can devote his time to coaching stroke mechanics, watching turns and push-offs, and generally motivating his swimmers. More im-portantly, the practice of timing oneself has an additional advantage; as the swimmer times himself he becomes more conscious of these times. Self-timing also enhances the swimmer's pace-learning process.

Learning to keep his own times is easy. At first, the swimmer—particu-larly the age-grouper—can only be expected to keep track of his times if he starts when the second hand is on zero or on 30. Then, if he finishes on 33 or on 3, he knows he has swum his 50-yard effort in 33 seconds. After a while he will learn to start when the second hand is at the 15 second and 45 second mark and still keep accurate account of his times. Eventually he will be able to start when the second hand is at any point on the clock, and still be able to keep his time accurately and quickly.

The swimmer should learn to use the pace clock in this manner so that he may be able to do the various types of repeats: long rest repeats, short rest repeats, broken swims, simulators, and so on.

An example might be that of a boy who wants to swim the 1650 free-style (short course) and wants to hit 1:05 for each 100. Every four lengths he glances at the clock as he turns and gets his time. If he sees 1:03, he knows he was too fast. If he sees 1:08, he was too slow. Over a period of time the swimmer will begin to learn the pace. Another way to work on pace is to have a swimmer start swimming at a fairly fast speed, say 1:02 per 100. As soon as he goes over 1:02 he stops, rests, then starts over again. A variation of this technique is another use of the pace clock: set a goal for each swimmer of 1:15 for breaststrokers and 1:07 for back-strokers for each 100. Instead of leaving on 60 and finishing on 15 and 7 respectively, have the swimmers start on 45 and 53 and try to finish on 60. This is an effective method of learning pace as well as a good workout variation. Meanwhile, the coach does not have to keep timing every repeat of every swimmer. He is free to make suggestions and corrections in stroke mechanics.

At this point, it is important to note that in order to assure the success of the pace clock, each swimmer must realize the importance of accurate timing. As improvement is measured by the actual seconds and tenths of seconds a swimmer can cut off his time, he must be sure that each time he gets for himself is as exact as possible. To aid him in making this observation, two checks have been found to be most satisfactory: the coach can make occasional spot checks on each swimmer to be sure he is getting the correct times, and a manager or some other reliable person can start each group together. The swimmer should start his repeat swims so that the clock's second hand hits the desired number before he starts to dive in or before he takes his hand away from the gutter in preparation for the push-off. Most "cheating" against the clock comes from swimmers leaving early, that is, before the second hand hits the desired number.

The Placement of the Pace Clock

The pace clock may be placed in several positions around the pool. This placement is mainly a matter of the coach's preference, the swimmers' preference, and the restrictions of the pool. One position might be the end wall of the pool enclosure from which the clock can be easily read as the swimmers finish, lift their heads, and look at their times. A second position might be the deck on the side of the pool at the end. Here, the swimmer finishes and looks to the side to get his time. In this case he is looking straight at the clock and will get an accurate time. The third, and recommended, location is on the wall, six to ten feet up from the deck, on the side and in a line parallel with the end of the pool. This location gives the swimmer the best chance to get an accurate time. As soon as the swimmer finishes, he looks to the side and gets his time. A pace clock with a face three feet in diameter is big enough so that even the swimmers in the lane farthest from the clock can read their times to within three or four tenths of a second.

Ideally, two pace clocks should be used in each pool, placed in the recommended position at both ends of the pool. This permits the team to work out in wave patterns, using a wave of swimmers at each end.

When the pace clock cannot be located permanently, portable deck models will serve, but special care must be taken to protect against electric shock. Small battery-driven, portable pace clocks are advisable when the swimmer must work under conditions where the danger of electric shock is possible.

WORKOUT DRILL PATTERNS

When swimming, kicking, and pulling lengths in workouts, the most commonly used workout drill patterns are: (1) circle swimming patterns and (2) wave patterns. These two permit maximum use of pool space, while allowing swimmers to train without interference from the other swimmers. Swimmers can also practice continuous, long distance swimming or interval training swimming using either of these patterns, and still time themselves accurately on the pace clock.

Wave Pattern Drills

When doing wave pattern drills, the swimmers are divided into two or more groups, and these groups, depending on conditions, can be placed at the same end or at opposite ends of the pool. When the groups are placed on opposite ends of the pool, it is recommended that there be a pace clock at each end.

When working out in wave pattern, all the members of the first group start together and swim in a line abreast. The next wave, depending on the situation, starts some time later in order that they may swim in back of the other group without the groups interfering with one another.

EXAMPLES OF WAVE PATTERN DRILLS. 1. Two or more waves starting five or more seconds apart. This type of pattern is limited to swimming one length of the pool at a time. The coach might divide the team into four groups. All members of a given group would start simultaneously on a signal or a given time on the pace clock. Shortly thereafter, the succeeding group would start, and so on. As soon as all groups were finished, the whole group would be started again. If the team were training in a 50-meter pool and the four groups were started five seconds apart, and if the slowest swimmer in the last heat swam each 50 meters in 45 seconds or less, the swimmers would be swimming one 50-meter repeat per minute, or 30 × 50 meters in 30 minutes.

In setting up the groups it is important that consideration be given to the fact that a slow swimmer not be placed in the same lane as a faster swimmer in the following heat. If this does occur, it is possible that the faster swimmer will catch up and interfere with the slower swimmer. This problem can be solved by having the faster swimmers swim in the earlier heats or by having swimmers of comparable ability swim in the same lanes.

If the team has to be divided into as many as six or more groups, it might be more efficient for the swimmers who have just completed their repeat swim to get out of the pool and walk back to the starting end of the pool to begin again. This type of routine permits maximum use of the available swimming area when extremely large numbers of swimmers are involved.

2. Two or more groups starting from opposite ends of the pool. When this type of pattern is used, the swimmers can swim repeats of two or more lengths. The group may be divided into two groups, one group placed at each end of a 25-yard pool. The coach assigns each group to do 15 × 100, one every two minutes. The two pace clocks are synchronized. Group 1 leaves when the pace clock's second hand hits zero. The breast-strokers and some of the other, slower swimmers can leave five to ten seconds ahead of the other swimmers in order that they may not get in the way of the succeeding swimmers. When the first wave is on its fourth and last length and is far enough in front of the next group so it cannot be caught, the second group starts its repeat 100. In the example used here, the second group starts one minute after the first group. This time interval between starting the two waves in a 25-yard pool could only be used by good senior and advanced age-group swimmers. Two waves of slower swimmers would probably have to start a 100 on every two and a half or three minutes.

This technique can be used for 50's, 100's, 150's, and 200's. Once the swimmers go 300 yards or more, little is gained by having the groups leave from opposite ends of the pool. If four groups are used, two groups can be placed at each end of the pool. This type of routine permits more swimmers to work out at a given time, but also necessitates a longer rest interval between each repeat swim. This sometimes is desirable, some-times not. When using wave pattern drills, extremely short rest repeats (such as 30 × 50 with ten seconds rest) are not possible unless one wave completes the entire set of repeats, followed by the second wave doing its entire set.

A FEW POINTS TO CONSIDER IN WAVE PATTERN DRILLS.   1. Do not use lane markers—they cut down the effective swimming area.

2. Allow three to four feet pool width per swimmer, with slightly more for butterfly swimmers. In a pool 30 feet wide, a maximum of seven to eight swimmers can work out in one wave; in a pool 42 feet wide, a maximum of eleven to twelve swimmers.

3. This type of workout pattern permits the coach to check the time of each swimmer as he finishes. It is more difficult for the coach to do this when the swimmers are swimming a circle pattern.

4. This type of pattern does not permit as many swimmers to work out as does the circle swimming pattern. It can be used effectively in short course pools 30 feet wide with up to 16 swimmers at a time in a workout, and in a pool 42 feet wide by as many as 24 swimmers. When using circle swimming patterns this number can be almost doubled.

5. The swimmers who have just completed their repeat swims should either get out of the pool as soon as they have finished or position them-selves in the water in such a way as not to interfere with the swimmers in the succeeding wave.

Circle Pattern Drill

This type of pattern permits the largest numbers of swimmers to train at a time (outside of one form of wave pattern mentioned above). This method also lends itself easily to interval training and is better suited to swimming long distances of 800 yards and further than the wave pattern.

When a circle pattern is used, it is wise to use lane markers as guides in directing the swimmers in straight formation. The groups, one to each lane, are lined up in the water ready to start. The first swimmer in each group starts at a given time (perhaps zero on a pace clock) by swim-ming down one side of the lane marker (the right side of the lane as he swims down it), being careful to avoid touching the marker in order that it might not affect his stroking. When the swimmer starts to turn, he cuts across to the middle of the lane and, when he pushes off, cuts across to the other side of the same lane he came down, or in a counter-clockwise pattern. Shortly after the lead swimmer begins, the number two swim-mer starts, that is, when the second hand hits five seconds; the third swimmer then starts when the second hand hits ten, the fourth on fifteen, and so on. Each swimmer times himself and takes into consideration the position of the second hand when he started his repeat swim.

On the short repeat swims (50's, 100's, 150's) the swimmers should start far enough in back of the preceding swimmer so they do not catch him. In setting up the various groups, it is important that swimmers of comparable speed be put together. This may necessitate some swimmers doing their swimming drills with one group, their kicking drills with another, and their pulling drills with still a different group.

In the longer races it may be necessary for a swimmer to pass a preceding one. When this occurs, the swimmer being passed should move close to the outside of the circle against the lane marker, while the swimmer doing the passing swings closer to the middle of the lane. The interval of time between the start of each swimmer's effort depends on how many swimmers are assigned to each lane, what distance the swimmers are swimming, and the desired interval of rest. When swimming 50's in a 25-yard pool, this interval can range from two seconds up to a maximum of ten seconds. In a 50-meter pool, the interval may vary from two seconds to 20 or even, rarely, to 30 seconds.

THE DISADVANTAGES OF CIRCLE PATTERN SWIMMING.   So many swimmers, particularly age-groupers, have swum so many of their lengths in a circular pattern that they swim this way in meets. Backstrokers and freestylers who do all of their swimming in the same circular direction, due to the fact that they tend to turn on one hand all of the time, learn to turn well only on that hand. In order to accomplish a turn that will take them to the other side of the lane, they reach across toward the middle of the lane with the outside hand (in backstroke this is the left hand, in freestyle it is the right). To correct this fault, it is helpful for the swimmers to do some of their circular drills in a clockwise direction and some in a counter-clockwise direction.

A FEW POINTS TO CONSIDER IN CIRCLE PATTERN DRILLS.   1. Lane markers should be kept in the pool; they help the swimmers swim straight.

2. This type of drill permits a greater number of swimmers to train at the same time and permits a greater variety in type of training than does the wave pattern. Its use, however, demands that the swimmers swim straighter and provides more opportunities for the swimmers to interfere with one another.

3. Up to seven swimmers can use a single lane in a 25-yard pool, or up to 42 swimmers can train at one time in a six lane 25-yard pool. In a 50-meter pool this number can be increased up to 15 per lane.

4. The groups should be classified on the basis of their ability in order that the swimmers will not interfere with one another.

The two types of drill just described will take care of the organization of more than 90 per cent of the water work for most swimmers. During the novice stages of training for competitive swimming, the swimmers can profit from such drills as kicking or pulling while hanging onto the edge of the pool. Most beginning competitive swimmers will profit more from swimming widths of the pool than from swimming lengths. Drills in which the swimmer is concentrating on learning turns should be done across the pool's width.

MOTIVATION OF ATHLETES DURING PRACTICE SESSIONS

Training for swimming is not like training for basketball, soccer, and other team sports in which there is a game situation. As the swimmer swims the lengths, his head is buried in the water, his vision is blurred, and his sense of hearing is deadened so he cannot listen to music or hear any sounds clearly. There is no change in environment such as the cross-country runner or bicycler enjoys. The swimmer swims up and down the pool in what, to the casual observer, must be an intolerably boring routine that would try the patience of a Spartan. In spite of this, more people are turning to competitive swimming all the time; in the United States over half a million swimmers, most of them in the age-group program, train in this manner, seem to be highly motivated, and seem to enjoy this training regimen to some extent. Obviously there is some compensation for the hard work; the coaches must be doing something right in their efforts to motivate their swimmers during practice sessions.

Retaining the Zest for Training

The basic problem in motivating athletes during practice seems to be *how best to make a period of physical stress a pleasant and rewarding experience.* An athlete should look forward to practice with anticipation, and should not merely consider it a period of drudgery that is a necessary prerequisite for him to perform well in competition. Practice should be an entertaining and satisfying experience and should challenge the swimmer intellectually as well as physically. The real success of a highly motivated program may be partially manifested by the manner in which the athletes approach practice sessions. If a swimmer drags into the locker room expressionlessly and comes onto the deck apathetically, there is real danger of staleness setting in.

The dream of every coach is to have all his team members approach practice with the aforementioned zest, to come in for their practice sessions with enthusiasm and eagerness. This team attitude during practice does not just accidentally occur; it is the by-product of a carefully planned program. To develop this attitude, at Indiana University we have developed certain specific procedures.

Educating the Athlete

The swimmer and coach have a common goal—of getting the best possible performance out of the swimmer. The coach knows why the swimmer should train hard, that is, what physiological changes occur as a result of a good interval training program. The coach knows why the swimmer must swim his repeat swims in a given time and why the swimmer must develop certain stroke mechanics in order to develop maximum efficiency. Too often, however, he forgets that he will get better cooperation from his charges if he explains not only exactly what they are expected to do, but why.

At Indiana University, in the beginning of each season, lectures are given to the entire team in two general areas: (1) conditioning and (2) stroke mechanics. In the area of conditioning, such points as the difference between the various types of training are discussed. The important concept that conditioning is nothing more than physiological adaptation to the stress of exercise is constantly repeated to the swimmers. To get maximum adaptation the swimmer must, therefore, expose himself at least occasionally to near-maximum stress. In order to put across this idea, the terms hurt-pain-agony are used. For example, a swimmer must begin doing a set of repeat swims, such as 15 × 100, at a fast speed. These will hurt him at first, but after he does a few it will become even harder to keep each 100 at the same speed as he progresses into the *pain* area; finally, at the end of the repeat swims, it will be so hard to swim these repeat swims in the prescribed time that the swimmer will be in the *agony* phase of exertion. These terms are not scientific, but they do convey the idea of putting forth a hard effort, and they provide the mental attitude needed for this approach. We try to build pride in the ability of the swimmers to push themselves hard in this manner when it is requested of them. The other team members have contempt for a laggard or a person who does not *put out* in practice. Social pressure is thus imposed on him to produce in practice or be ostracized.

Stroke mechanics are discussed in detail. Discussion of a semi-technical

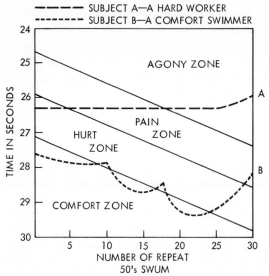

FIG. XII–1. **Hurt-Pain-Agony Chart**

This chart is not meant to be objective or realistic, but it does depict a "state of mind." A coach wants every swimmer to give his very best and to learn to "put out" in practice. Only then can a swimmer achieve top conditioning. While some of the terms here are not scientific, they do convey an unmistakable idea to the swimmer.

In this chart the four areas depicted represent the amount of effort and, consequently, the degree of hurt, pain, or agony which the swimmer feels as he swims each 50-yard repeat.

Subject B is a swimmer who is getting little conditioning from swimming these 30 × 50's. He wants to do everything in the comfort area. He does not want to hurt himself. He miscalculates on two occasions, however, in which he misjudges his effort so that he does hurt himself. On the last few 50's he does push himself a little bit and goes faster. Some swimmers will do this to salvage some self-respect from their poor performance.

Subject A has the mental attributes which characterize great swimmers. He pushes himself from the very beginning. At first, it may take only 80 per cent effort to swim a 50 in 26 seconds and will only hurt a little. As fatigue accumulates he must push himself more to do 26 seconds—perhaps to 90 per cent effort—and will go into the pain area. As he nears the end of the series of 50's, he pushes himself to the extent that he is in the agony phase of exertion—perhaps even to 100 per cent effort.

This hurt-pain-agony concept, together with the emphasis on the part of the coach to "push hard," is a good example of a high-pressure workout, and should not be used exclusively.

nature takes place concerning such topics as fluid mechanics, Newton's laws of motion, strongest angle of pull, and formation of the bow wave. In this manner we feel both the coaches and the swimmers can learn together and also become identified with one another to a higher degree. It is obvious that the athlete who understands the purposes of each phase of his training program and stroke work will give the coach more cooperation and will be more highly motivated in practice sessions than one who is completely uninitiated.

Variety in Practice Sessions

In planning practice sessions it is important for the coach to know with what type of people he is dealing. If all his swimmers are intensely devoted, highly motivated people with good psychological endurance, he can plan a program which complies with all the tenets of scientific training based on physiological principles without so much regard for the psychological aspects—particularly that of boredom.

If, on the other hand, they are not highly motivated, he must devise means of motivating them. If they are of low or average psychological endurance, he must be on his toes constantly, giving his swimmers variety in workouts and finding other means of motivating them. The 1964 Men's Olympic Swimming Team, which was coached by this writer, was given a battery of standardized psychological tests. The team, in general, showed the following traits: (1) high ambition, (2) great independence and individualism, and (3) low psychological endurance in comparison with the average for champion athletes. Evaluation of the tests caused the writer to make the following assumptions:

1. Because of the high ambitions of this group, they could be given very hard workouts.

2. Because of their high level of individuality and independence, two policies should be followed in practice: the purpose of each phase of the workouts should be explained so as to provide the swimmers with an understanding of why they were doing a given thing and get better cooperation from them, and to bring the men into the planning of the workouts.

3. Because of their relative low scores for champion athletes in psychological endurance, it was decided to give them plenty of variety in their workout sessions, and also to devise means of maintaining interest and motivation when their attention might begin to wander. Some of these methods will be discussed later.

The swimmer who does the same workout in practice each day is certainly not presented with a daily challenge, but, on the contrary, with a wearying and boring routine. A daily challenge can be presented by varying his workout. One day, as the principal part of his interval training workout, he may do 30 × 50 yard repeat swims with 30 seconds of rest between each swim. The second day he may do 15 × 100 yard repeat swims with one minute rest. The third day he may go 20 × 75 with 45 seconds rest. The fourth day he might possibly go the following set— a mixed set of repeats:

		Number		Distance	Rest Interval
Mixed Set	1.	5	×	100	1. min.
of	2.	7	×	75	45 sec.
Repeats	3.	10	×	50	30 sec.

The fifth day he may go a fartlek (speedplay) workout, in which he might swim one and a half miles continuously, doing frequent sprints of 25, 50, and 75 yards during the course of the continuous swim, with the rest of the lengths swum at a moderate pace.

It is, however, important that a training program have some general plan, and that the variety of the training not be so great that each day the swimmer has merely a smorgasbord of bits and pieces of mixed sets which provide neither short nor long range goals.

The Use of Straight Sets for Motivation and Evaluation

It is wise to have some straight sets of repeat swims to be used regularly in the training program as guides in evaluating the swimmer's progress. An example of these straight sets which will be used on different days for a person training for a 200-meter event would be 30 × 50, 15 × 100, 8 × 200, 4 × 500. Each one of these workout routines would be used perhaps once each week or two to evaluate and motivate. When these workouts (which we like to call *standard* or *straight* set of repeats) are used, we like to emphasize the hurt-pain-agony idea previously discussed. They are thought of by the swimmers as high-pressure repeats and cannot be used every day. They may be used for two or three days in a row, but generally should be alternated with low-pressure workouts in which the swimmers may do a mixed set such as that described on page 221. In such practice sessions, less emphasis is placed on the quality of work; the attitude of the coach is more casual, but he also uses such sessions to work on stroke mechanics, turns, starts, and so on. Figure IX–3 shows how this occurs.

Kicking and Pulling Add Variety

Some coaches doubt the value of kicking and pulling drills in conditioning the athlete. When a swimmer hangs onto a kick board and uses his legs only, a greater physical stress is imposed on his legs than can be imposed on them when he is just swimming. The same is true of his arms when his legs are tied and he pulls himself through the water. A typical workout might include the following kicking and pulling drills:

1. Kick 400 yards on a board at a moderate speed, then kick 8 × 50 yards with 30 seconds between each 50.

2. Pull 200 yards easily, then time 3 × 200 yards, arms only, with a rest interval of three minutes between each 200.

The next day the amount and distances kicked and pulled might be reversed. In addition to placing a greater overload on the arms and legs than can be achieved while swimming, kicking and pulling drills permit more variety in practice sessions and provide more long and short range goals as incentive. They also help the swimmer discover the weakest factor in his stroke and are thus a motivator to improve stroke mechanics.

Self-planned Workouts and Team-planned Workouts

In 1964 in Tokyo this writer saw a trackman at the Olympic Village call long distance every other day to the United States in order to talk to his track coach at home. This might seem an example of flattering loyalty, indicating that the coach was so outstanding and had the confidence of the boy to such a degree that the boy could not do without him. There is another interpretation, however, perhaps less flattering: the coach had failed to guide the boy towards self-reliance. To develop this quality and to further motivate practice sessions a coach might, on a given day, let the captain or another team member plan the workout, or ask each man to plan his own workout. It is the experience of this writer that such a workout is often harder than that the coach would have given the team. When using this method, let the person know on the previous day that he has the assignment of putting the next day's workout on the board.

Occasionally the team will come in for workouts and find written on the blackboard where that day's workout usually appears: "*ON THE HOUSE WORKOUT*. Do your own workout. Plan your repeat swims, kick and pull, etc. Do enough so that your total distance in practice is not less than two miles and not more than two and a half miles."

Several times a season, at team meetings, the general plan of workouts is discussed and any complaints or suggestions are aired in order that the swimmers be involved in the program intellectually as well as physically. It is also possible that the coach may learn something in these skull sessions. They are, however, a possible source of dissension if the coach is not self-assured or is easily upset. Team meetings should be held regularly, but can be overdone. At Indiana, a team meeting is held every Tuesday, the meetings lasting 20 to 30 minutes. This writer will normally spend one to three hours planning the material he wants to cover. Such things as the workouts and their purpose, the progress of the team, and plans for the next competition might be discussed.

Rewards as Motivators

While excessive use of physical rewards in training may be a doubtful practice, they can be used as a symbol of recognition of a job well done, and can serve as motivators. An example is the reward of a few jelly beans given to the swimmer doing his best set of repeats or achieving some goal set by the coach. Once a season, at Indiana University, we have what we call "jelly bean day." Any swimmer achieving a given time in an over distance time trial (880 yards) receives one pound of jelly beans. The times are 9:10 for 880 freestyle, 10:20 for butterfly, and 11:30 for breaststroke. The writer feels it is an important part of the boys' training schedule to do some over distance, swimming hard. It is easier to motivate them and they swim faster for one pound of jelly beans and the success it symbolizes than they would if the coach were merely to assign an 880-yard swim in practice without the formality of "jelly bean day." College boys, and this coach, at least, are just grown-up children, and are motivated by the same means as are age-group swimmers. Coaches who forget this fact and are nothing but "cold turkey" at practice are missing a lot of enjoyment for themselves and their swimmers.

In the case of the 1964 Olympic Team, this writer took a great many stroke movies, both out of water and under water, in order to increase interest and motivate the boys to work on their strokes, starts, and turns. Another means of having fun at practice was to take funny movies, using trick photography so the boys might appear to be going backwards or at a ridiculously fast speed, or pictures showing all thirty boys and their coaches getting out of one small car.

Children are particularly fond of such gimmicks as used by one coach who owns a beautiful Stetson cowboy hat. Each week he lets the child who has worked the hardest wear the hat for a week. Trophies awarded to the most improved swimmer, the hardest working swimmer, and so on, help by providing motivation to work harder in practice.

Creating the Proper Physical Environment

A pool in which a team trains should look like a competitive pool. Pace clocks for timing, record boards, pictures of individual swimmers and a team picture should be displayed in the pool office or around the pool. The atmosphere of the pool should be conducive to development of a good attitude. A pool can be a barren and depressing area without this paraphernalia. Continued distractions, such as the presence of recreation swimmers during practice, can do a lot to decrease the effectiveness of practice. Ideal conditions for training are few, but they must be aimed for, since the physical environment can affect the mental set of a swimmer. Listed below are a few items that help create the proper environment:

1. Goal Board—a goal board lists the best average times of all the team members for every straight set of repeats. This is kept for the purpose of measuring progress.

2. Record Board—a record board should list pool records and team records for all of the events, as well as the national records for these events. The presence of such a board creates the goal in each swimmer's mind to see his name listed there, without creating intolerable pressure to excel.

3. Swim Programs—swim programs can be as elaborate as time and money will permit.

4. Pictures of the Outstanding Swimmers—such pictures should be framed and hung in the pool office. Pictures of the teams that win championships should be prominently displayed.

5. T-shirts—distinctive t-shirts that identify the swimmer with the team are a real asset and a help to team morale. The same applies to any piece of equipment which is exclusive to team members and helps the association and identification of the swimmers with the team.

6. Newsletters—newsletters and programs should be devoted primarily to promoting the sport and the team members.

7. Special Awards—when they are not overdone, such awards help motivate the swimmers. Suggested awards: most improved swimmer, high point winner, best attitude award, hardest worker award.

8. Special Events—dances, picnics, hikes, pingpong, handball, or tennis tournaments improve team morale and spirit.

9. General Enthusiasm—a swimmer stays out for a team if he enjoys the experience. If the coach, the spectators, the parents, and all of the team members are enthusiastic, this, more than all of the above listed items, will assure the team of a good environment. The tangible forms, however, do aid in promoting enthusiasm. They make it easier for the swimmer to put effort into his workout sessions.

The Coach's Role in Motivating Practice

All of the previously mentioned methods of motivating practice are of secondary importance to the role of the coach. Just as a good mother and wife can make a drab house a cheerful place for her husband and children to return to, so a great coach can make a drab pool, which has none of the aforementioned gimmicks, a pleasant place to spend a couple of hours a day. The coach sets the mood at practice. This mood must be confident and relaxed, not tense and nervous. The coach is the swimmers' guiding light and, as such, he should be inspirational and enthusiastic.

The old belief that a coach should be a stern disciplinarian who drives the athletes through their hard training routines much as a mule driver drives an unquestioning mule team across Death Valley must be replaced with the belief that the coach is an educated director of young people who are striving for a common goal. He must not drive them relentlessly, but should guide them intelligently toward this goal.

The coach wants the athlete to identify himself with the coach and, as has been mentioned, the most effective way is for both to identify with a common goal. This goal is the success of the individual swimmer and the team, not only in the pool, but in all matters affecting the swimmer's life—school work, social adjustment, and so on. The coach whose interest in the athlete lies only in his athletic success will be less effective than the coach who has a sincere interest in the athlete's over-all development. Too often athletes are used by both their coaches and parents as a means of attaining their own goals or achieving vicarious satisfaction. Selfish motivation of this nature will eventually be detected by the athlete and will decrease his motivation to succeed.

It is extremely difficult for an intelligent, mature athlete to form an identification with a coach who sets himself up as a dictator, and whose authoritarian manner must be accepted unquestioningly. Athletes of low intellect, weak or unstable personality, or those who are lacking in maturity, may respond to a martinet, but if, in a free world, we do not look upon such tactics with favor in other aspects of human relationships, certainly we should not in athletics. This is not to say that permissiveness should be allowed to become excessive, to the point that the coach loses control of the team. He should see that intelligently planned rules of training are enforced. Not everyone has all of the attributes necessary to become a good coach. Those who do not have them often do not develop them because of a distorted idea of the role of a coach.

A good swimming coach must have knowledge and ability in three areas: (1) knowledge with which and ability to evaluate stroke mechanics, (2) knowledge with which and ability to interpret proper conditioning procedures—both dry land exercises and water work, and (3) knowledge with which and the ability to handle and work with athletes, that is, to be an effective psychologist. This last trait is the most important of the three, for in order to put to use the first two abilities, he must have the third.

The coach should be at every practice. He cannot be an absentee coach who merely posts the workout and leaves. Neither does it work to have two coaches who alternate workouts to make it easier for both of them. The interest that the coach has in each team member must be evident. He can show this interest by knowing all of the various times the swimmers have swum in their workouts and races. He must know more about the swimmer than just his performances in the pool. In practice, *he should talk to each swimmer each day.* His attitude with every athlete should be cooperative and positive.

In practice sessions the coach must set high goals for the athletes. These goals must be in line with the swimmer's ability, for if they are too high, the swimmer will become discouraged when he finds they are unattainable.

It is the coach's job to build morale during the practice sessions. He should realize that most athletes are unsure of themselves and should not be stripped of their dignity through harsh words and treatment. One of the laws of learning is that a person tends to want to repeat a pleasant experience and not repeat an unpleasant one. The coach should remember this in his handling of athletes during practice. Constant abuse of the athlete by the coach during practice certainly will not build morale.

Personalities vary among coaches as among all humans, and it follows that their coaching styles will also vary. Each coach should adopt a pattern to suit his particular personality. If one coach tries to handle the sessions in a manner similar to that of another coach with a totally different personality, he may not succeed. One of the greatest motivators to keep an athlete working hard in practice is the affection and respect he has for his coach. This affection and respect is not automatically the coach's due; it must be earned. In order to earn it, he must present the athletes with a good training program and with well-planned and organized practice sessions.

THE PROBLEM OF TOO MUCH MOTIVATION DURING PRACTICE SESSIONS. In the past few years, the knowledge of training techniques has improved considerably, and these improvements have been propagated widely. Most coaches and athletes understand the importance of swimming hard in practice. Both short and long range goals, in terms of times swum in practice, are being used and misused. An occurrence that seems more frequent as athletes become aware of the importance of working hard in practice and the coach motivates toward harder work in practice is that of swimming much faster in practice than in meets. A continual over-emphasis in times swum in practice and a continual use of high-pressure workouts can result in this situation. It can usually be avoided by the means mentioned in this chapter and by the coach constantly reminding himself that practice must be intense and highly motivating some of the time, but it should be fun at all times.

THE ASSISTANT COACH.   The assistant swimming coach or coaches often determine the quality of swimmer with which the head coach will eventually be working. Although it is not always possible, it is best to define clearly the lines of authority to be held by the assistant coach. Thus, he may be assigned to work with a certain group of swimmers, such as the novice group or the freshman team. It is important that the head coach do nothing to undermine the authority of the assistant, and vice versa. Each team situation will dictate a somewhat different role for the assistant coach. For this reason, a general statement here of his duties would not apply in most cases.

THE TEAM MANAGER.   One high school coach, when asked by the press who he felt had been the most important man on his team of high school state champions, replied: "My manager."

The manager and his staff can take care of dozens of jobs which, if the coach had to do them, would prevent him from doing a good job of coaching. A résumé of the manager's responsibilities follows:

1. Keeping a master log—this log lists each day's workouts and the times done by all of the swimmers in practice.

2. Keeping the record board and goal board up to date.

3. Seeing that all of the equipment and supplies are available and maintained. This includes kickboards, towels, pulling tubes, office supplies, and vitamins.

4. Answering the phone and taking messages for the coach.

5. Running errands.

6. Helping to arrange for officials and equipment for swimming meets.

7. Arranging for programs and newsletters to be printed and distributed.

8. Keeping clippings and scrapbook.

9. Helping to time swimmers.

10. Helping to complete entry blanks for meets.

11. Helping to take care of the dozens of other details that crop up continually.

XIII

Some Additional Principles of Training

Everyone knows that world records are not set by chance, but not so many know the series of circumstances that are prerequisite to such an achievement. Can such a performance as Don Schollander's four first places in the 1964 Olympic Games, or Martha Randall's great swimming in the summer of 1965, be attributed solely to the ability of the performers? Certainly ability means a great deal, but no one's maximum performance can be achieved unless it is preceded by months, even years, of the observation of certain training principles. For example, Roger Bannister, a medical student when he became the first person to reach the goal of running a sub-four minute mile, attributed much of his success to his study of the physiological principles involved in training and in running the actual race. If it is true, and I believe it is, it follows that a coach must be more than a graduate athlete who is well versed in the mechanics and strategy of his sport. Through the training routine he uses to condition his athletes, he is trying to change and improve many of their physiological processes. The human body has certain capabilities and limitations, and the level of an individual's performance depends largely upon the degree to which he has reached his optimum potentialities. The coach must have at least elementary knowledge of physiology in order to handle the conditioning of these wonderfully adaptable and yet sensitive organisms properly.

In Chapter VIII, conditioning was defined as "the sum total of all the physiological, anatomical, and psychological adaptations made by the organism to the stress of the training program." This statement brings forth the obvious conclusion that the degree of stress to which the swimmer is exposed in his training program determines the degree of his conditioning. This is true only insofar as other factors, such as sleep, rest, and diet, aid or deter in this adaptive process. For example, a swimmer who is in a hard training program, but who is not getting adequate sleep and diet, may fail to make these adaptations to the extent he would have had he observed certain principles of training.

The ultimate conditioning a swimmer will achieve is dependent upon the following factors:

1. Stress factor—the workouts—day by day, week by week training program.
2. The careful control of all of the factors that contribute or detract from the conditioning process.
   A. Contributing factors
      1. Freedom from disease and illness
      2. Proper diet
      3. Proper sleep and rest
      4. Proper mental attitude
      5. Proper training environmental conditions or absence of detracting stress factors in practice, such as proper water and air temperature
   B. Detracting factors
      1. Illnesses
      2. Inadequate diet
      3. Excessive fatigue (inadequate sleep or rest)
      4. Poor mental attitude
      5. Use of tobacco, alcohol, or drugs

When a swimmer fails to make the normal improvements in conditioning in the course of a training program, he and his coach may carefully scrutinize the training program for the causes, when the real cause might be a detracting factor such as improper diet or use of alcohol or tobacco. Another might take the opposite approach and attribute the lack of improvement to a detracting factor, attempting to compensate for it through the use of massive doses of wheat germ oil or whatever fad is prevalent at the time, and ignoring an evaluation of the training program. Both factors are important and should be considered in such a situation.

The training program (or stress factor) determines the original direction of the adaptive processes. The contributing or detracting factors, however, can change the direction so that the organism either achieves optimal adaptation or reaches the level of failing adaptation.

THE STRESS CONCEPT

Gaylord Hauser once said, "We are what we eat." I like to think of it somewhat differently: *we are what we are because of the stresses placed upon us and the adaptations we have made to these stresses, both physical and otherwise. The state of our bodies, our minds, and our personalities is the result of these adaptations.* The Utopian view of an existence without any form of stress, either physical or mental, is not conducive to the development of a person well prepared for existence in a competitive society. Hans Selye, Canadian researcher, who has done more than any other person to develop the concept of stress and adaptation to stress, has made the following statement in his book, *The Stress of Life:* "Stress . . . gives an excellent chance to develop potential talents, no matter where they may be slumbering in the mind or body. In fact, it is only in the heat of stress that individuality can be perfectly molded." [1]

Parents who try to protect their children from stress do as much to cripple the development of their potential as those at the other extreme who expose their children to too much or too many forms of stress, to the point that the child is incapable of adapting. In competitive swimming, a well designed and conducted program theoretically arranges for the proper amount of both physical and psychological stress to be placed on the individual in order that he may become a better person, prepared for future stresses. There are three questions which must be asked constantly by both coach and parent:

1. Can we anticipate what stresses—both emotional and physical—will be placed on the individual in the future?

2. Does this program prepare him for the future, that is, does it inoculate him for future physical and mental stress?

3. Does this inoculation wear off, or does it have a certain residual effect?

If the program is well conducted, it will have tried to anticipate future stresses, and imposed current stresses in such a way that adaptation will occur. As for the answer to the third question: we can only assume that there will be residual effect that will help the individual the rest of his life. Observation and experience would lead us to believe that this assumption is a reasonable one.

[1] Hans Selye, *The Stress of Life* (New York: McGraw-Hill Book Co., 1956), p. 277.

What Is Stress?

Every person is constantly exposed to some form of stress. The swimmer in a race is exposed to both physical and psychological stress. His parents and coach are not exposed to the same physical stress, but they are, to a greater or lesser degree, exposed to the same psychological stress. Even the starter, judges, and timers are exposed to stress. Theoretically, none of them will ever be quite the same as they were before this exposure. All stresses leave us somewhat changed.

Exactly what is stress? Hans Selye, who has been a pioneer in the development and research of the area of the concept of stress, and who has written six books and over 600 articles on the subject, readily admits that the term is an abstraction. In his book, as Selye initially defines it, "stress is essentially the rate of wear and tear on the body." [2] Celeste Ulrich states, "Whenever the homeostatic balance of the body is upset, the human organism attempts to adjust in such a way that the balance is restored. Until the balance is restored, a state of 'stress' exists." [3]

Selye found that no matter what type of stress the organism was exposed to, if this stress was intense and prolonged enough, it would result in a nonspecific general response—along with the specific effects peculiar to that type of stress. This response, as measured in experimental animals, he called the *triad response*. The triad response consists of three types of changes:

1. *An enlargement of the adrenal cortex.* Whenever the organism is exposed to stress, there is a corresponding increase in the activity of this gland, particularly the cortex tissue. The hormones secreted by this gland help mobilize the body's defenses to withstand the stress. These small glands, located directly on top of the kidney, are made up of medullary and cortex tissue. The gland, particularly the cortex tissue, attempts to improve its ability to keep pace with the demands made upon it during stress by enlarging. If intense stress is continued too long, despite the enlargement of the gland, it will eventually lose some of its ability to secrete hormones and the organism will be in a stage of failing adaptation. In training swimmers we have attempted to measure this stage of failing adaptation by measuring the level of keto-steroids in the urine. Their level is a measure of the degree of activity of the adrenal gland since they are a by-product of the metabolism of the adrenal gland.

---

[2] *Ibid.*, p. 3.
[3] Celeste Ulrich, "Stress and Sport," in *Science and Medicine of Exercise and Sports*, ed. Warren R. Johnson (New York: Harper & Row, 1960), p. 251.

2. *A shrinking of the lymphatic tissue,* and a decrease in the lymphocytes in the blood. Selye found an almost complete disappearance of the eosinophil cells (a lymphatic cell). At Indiana, we have noted this disappearance of the eosinophil cells in swimmers who are trained too hard. Unfortunately, use of the eosinophil level to predict the degree of stress has not been validated and results are inconsistent.

3. *Ulcerations in the lining of the stomach and in the first part of the intestine* (the duodenum). These ulcerations, noted by Selye in experimental animals, were minor ruptures in the small blood vessels and resulted in some bleeding.

We have no way of knowing what comparable changes, if any, occur in man after intense levels of prolonged stress. The triad response or syndrome occurred under all types of stress, including heat, cold, injection of chemicals, and muscular exertion. He calls this a syndrome of "just being sick." He now defines stress as any factor that elicited the triad syndrome.

Since this response is general and nonspecific, does it have any practical application for the coach and the athlete? Are they not more concerned with the specific response of the body to the stress of training? They are attempting to bring about specific changes which will enable the swimmer to perform better and are not interested in bringing about the onset of this general response. Before showing how knowledge of the triad response or syndrome can be applied to training methods, further discussion of Selye's theories about stress might be helpful.

Selye found that the organism's response to stress followed three stages, which he referred to as the general adaptation syndrome (GAS):

1. Alarm reaction—this is the initial response of the body to the stress factor. Selye felt it represented a general call to arms of all of the defense forces in the organism. In exercise, this alarm reaction would consist of an increased heart rate, increased secretion of adrenalin from the adrenal gland, the dumping of sugar from the liver into the bloodstream, and so on. The acute (short range) adaptations to exercise occur during this stage.

2. Resistance stage—the changes which occur in this stage are quite different and, in many instances, the exact opposite of those in the first stage. The heart rate will, for example, become more efficient and the resting heart rate will decrease. The adrenal cortex, which discharged its hormones into the bloodstream during the first stage (alarm reaction), may have depleted the stores of the gland. During the second stage the adrenal cortex tissue improves its ability to secrete these hormones by accumulating an abundant reserve of secretory granules. The chronic (long lasting) adaptations to training occur during this stage.

3. Stage of exhaustion—after prolonged exposure to intense levels of stress, the organism may have depleted its ability to adapt to all types of stresses and may start to break down.

Applying Stress Concepts to Training Methods

1. In attempting to apply the GAS to the training program, the athlete is pushed well into the second stage, but not into the third stage. This concept of training is shown in Figure IV–1.

2. The degree of the triad syndrome response is directly proportional to the intensity and duration of the stress factor. It is not desirable to push the swimmer so hard that he manifests all of the symptoms of the triad response to an extreme degree.

There is a possibility that researchers may ultimately find a means of measuring some of the symptoms of the triad syndrome validly, and evaluate the extent to which an athlete can be trained without pushing him too far. At this time, the level of eosinophils in the blood and the level of keto-steroids in the urine have been used with only mild success.

3. By using interval training, that is, short periods of rest between relatively intense periods of stress, the possibility of pushing the swimmers into the later stages of the triad response or the last stage of GAS has been avoided, while the specific adaptations that we are striving for have been acquired.

Long over distance swimming is not intense enough to bring about the desired specific changes. Repeated all-out efforts over the race distance (such as a 100 or more) are severe enough in terms of intensity to bring about these changes, but are of such duration that their continued use would bring about the onset of the third stage of GAS or the later stage of the triad response.

It has been my observation that few swimmers are so strongly motivated as to be capable of pushing themselves into the exhaustion stage as a result of exercise alone. All of us have a natural reluctance to push ourselves this hard. Normally, localized muscular fatigue causes us to diminish our activity before the stage of exhaustion has been reached.

In fact, unless we are strongly motivated, not many of us are willing to push ourselves sufficiently hard to go far enough into the stage of resistance to bring about maximum adaptation. For this reason, I feel it is important to call upon the emotions to reinforce the stimuli to work harder in order to bring about greater physical stress. Only in this manner is the swimmer able to accept the hurt-pain-agony approach to his workout that is described in Figure XII–1. As the swimmer gets near the final phase of preparation before the tapering period begins for the big contest, it is important to use this emotional stress as a stimulating factor.

Stresses Are Cumulative

Selye states that every person has only a certain amount of *adaptation energy* for use against stress factors. If the athlete at a given time uses most of this adaptation energy in trying to adapt to a stress situation other than his swimming training, such as staying up late at night and losing sleep, he will have less adaptation energy to spend on his training program. Consequently, he will not adapt and will either have to remove or reduce the other stress factor, decrease the swimming training, or fall into the stage of failing adaptation.

An athlete cannot be exposed to too many stresses of an intense nature at the same time he is training hard. Most college swimmers I have coached have been able to handle adequately and adapt to the stresses of college course work and training for swimming. The moment other stresses, such as family problems or girl trouble, are superimposed on the first two stresses, the athlete often exhibits signs of failing adaptation.

No matter how involved the discussion of stress may become, it inevitably finishes with the same conclusion: too little stress, physical or otherwise, does not bring about the desired changes, while too much stress is equally harmful in that the organism is incapable of adapting to it. Methods of detecting signs of too little or too much stress will be discussed later in this chapter under the heading *Fatigue and Staleness*.

Specific Adaptations to the Stress of Training

A swimmer presents a different picture physiologically when he is "out of shape." When he conditions himself through his training program, he brings about specific adaptations which are primarily physiological, but which also involve certain psychological and even anatomical changes.

The physiological changes are many, and frequently complex. To discuss each of these in this chapter would be impracticable. Since many of them are of practical importance only to the physiologist, only the gross physiological changes which occur and which are important to the coach and athlete will be discussed.

In this chapter, physiological principles and their application to the training program will also be discussed. In the past three decades a great deal of research has been conducted in this area. Many previous misconceptions have been disproved; some prevail despite proof to the contrary. One such opinion concerns the harmful effect of exercise on the heart, and it will be discussed later.

Most people are familiar with the acute effects which follow the onset of exercise, such as the increase in heart rate and breathing rate, but these effects are temporary, lasting only during the period of exercise and recovery. Chronic effects have been studied, and although there is not always complete unanimity of opinion among researchers, on the basis of a study of this research, the following statements can be made with a high degree of validity.

SKILL AND EFFICIENCY.   Athletes in the various sports place emphasis upon the development of different qualities in their training programs. The distance runner or distance swimmer naturally places his emphasis upon developing endurance, the sprinter upon speed, and the wrestler on strength. All training programs attempt to develop one thing in common, and that is skill. The skills used in some activities, such as the team sports of basketball, football, and soccer, are more complex than the skills used in running and swimming. For this reason the time spent on the acquisition and perfection of these skills takes up most of the training program. However, no matter what the activity, if the proper mechanics and technique are practiced, there will be an increase in the skill and efficiency of performance. By practicing the proper movements in the proper sequence and continually repeating them, as is done in practicing the proper swimming turn, nervous patterns are being established. The greater the number of times that impulses are sent over these nervous pathways, the more firmly established they become, until what has been practiced becomes mechanical or habit. This explains why drill on proper fundamentals is important; it also explains why bad habits, once formed, are hard to break.

It is also true that the more a skill is practiced correctly, the better the athlete learns to use only the muscles involved in performing this particular skill. He thereby reduces the amount of energy necessary to perform a given amount of work. Increases in skill and efficiency frequently may be the first changes which occur as a result of training.

EFFECT UPON THE MUSCLES.   A muscle can develop two qualities: strength and/or endurance. Each quality is dependent upon a different adaptation. It is a well established physiological principle that the strength of a muscle is proportional to its cross-sectional area. To strengthen a muscle, its functional size must be increased. This increase beyond the muscle's normal size is referred to as hypertrophy. In the case of hypertrophy, there is no increase in the number of cells (hyperplasia) as was formerly believed; rather, the individual fibers increase in size. There seems to be a relatively equal increase in the sarcoplasmic material and the connective tissue in the muscle. The muscle not only becomes stronger, but it becomes tougher and has improved tonus. It will suffer less from trauma and, contrary to the opinion of many persons, does not lose any of its ability to perform refined movements.

All types of exercise will not improve muscle strength. The law of use and disuse applies to muscle as it does to other organs of the body. If a muscle is not used, it will atrophy or shrink in size. If it is used, it will develop, and the extent to which it develops will depend upon the demand made upon it. The size of a muscle and, consequently, the strength of a muscle is increased fastest by working with loads which are near-maximum.

What changes have occurred in the distance swimmer's muscles that permit him to have greater endurance? When laboratory animals which were run in wire rotating cages for several hours a day over a period of two months were examined, it was found there was an increase in the number of functional capillaries—up to 40 per cent in active muscles. It would appear that this increased vascularization was brought about by exercise of the moderate-resistance, high-repetition type. The increase in the number of functional capillaries could account to a large extent for the increase in endurance noted in the animals. That a similar vascularization occurs in man under the same conditions is likely. The increased number of functional capillaries could aid in the removal of the waste products of exercise, and would facilitate the transportation of oxygen and blood sugar to the exercising muscle. In exercised animals it was also found that the active muscles contain more glycogen than the muscles of control animals. This factor would also contribute to the local muscular endurance. Possibly one of the great advantages of interval training is its ability to bring about an increase in the number of functional capillaries, plus an increase in muscle glycogen, in a shorter time than can any other method of training.

In a group of runners, including both sprinters and distance men, a negative correlation was found to exist between leg strength and the time for a mile run. The contention that the type of training in which distance men engage does not build strength to the degree that it does in the type in which sprinters engage would seem to be borne out.

Both strength and endurance are desirable qualities to develop in all activities, so it is important that all training programs be designed to build these qualities. In swimming, building strength and endurance in the muscle is handled by running both over- and under-distances in the workout. A swimmer who is training for the 440-yard event will frequently swim over a mile in his workout to improve endurance; he will also swim sprints to improve his speed and strength.

HEART SIZE.   Myocardium, or heart muscle, is similar to skeletal muscle in that it increases in size and strength in relation to the demand made upon it. Consequently, when a person engages in any activity, whether it be football, cross-country racing, or manual labor, which puts a demand upon the circulatory system to supply more blood to the exercising tissues, it is logical to assume that the heart muscle will hypertrophy.

Studies of champion distance runners, cyclists, swimmers, and other endurance athletes have shown a larger than normal heart in many cases. Whether these athletes developed larger hearts as a result of their training program or are champion endurance athletes partially because of their larger hearts is not always clear, due to a lack of control in such studies.

Whether enlargement, if it does occur, is due to hypertrophy or dilatation is another debatable question. If only dilatation occurs, it might imply a detrimental effect. Since heart size is determined in man by means of chest X-rays, it is difficult to prove either view conclusively. Studies of laboratory animals have shown that the increase in heart size due to an exercise program was accompanied by an actual increase in the weight of the hearts of the exercised animals over that of the control animals. This would indicate that, if there were dilatation, there was also hypertrophy. The hearts of exercised rats were also found to return to normal in size and weight within three to four weeks of the cessation of exercise.

The increase in heart size is accompanied by ability to pump greater amounts of blood. The amount of blood the heart pumps in a minute is referred to as *minute volume*. Muscle cells can only function properly when they are provided with oxygen and food materials, when their waste products (lactic acid, carbon dioxide, and so on) are removed promptly, and when their temperature, acidity, and water balance are controlled. The maintenance of the proper internal environment of the cell is the function of the blood and the circulatory system. To sustain prolonged activity the swimmer must, therefore, be able to circulate large quantities of blood. It can safely be stated that the heart of a swimmer who sets a world record in a distance event has developed a large minute volume during exercise.

The term *athlete's heart* is an unfortunate one that is frequently associated with a pathological condition by the layman. An athlete's heart is a normal heart which may be somewhat larger, and have a slower rate and greater stroke volume. It is important to remember that after the end of training the heart will regress to normal size. There is no evidence to prove that this enlargement or regression will in any way affect the function of the heart valves and cause murmurs or leakage.

In a publication of the American Medical Association, the following statements are made:

> The notion that the athlete's heart is an abnormally enlarged heart is a myth. The heart of the trained athlete is now considered normal and its counterpart—the loafer's heart—abnormal. . . . There is no evidence to show that exercise has ever damaged a normal heart in a properly conditioned healthy athlete. Hearts are weakened by disease or congenital defects, not by participation in sports. However, since considerable stress is necessary to "train" a heart and keep it trained, this same stress can be detrimental or debilitating if disease or defect is present. Thus, cooperative medical and athletic supervision is a must for activity programs.
>
> Medical evaluation should precede the onset of a rigorous exercise program by sports enthusiasts of any age.[4]

HEART RATE.   The heart rate, because of the ease with which it can be measured, has been studied extensively. There are many factors which affect the heart rate: age, posture, emotional state, temperature, the ingestion of food, drugs, and exercise, to name a few. The normal range of resting heart rate is from 50 to 100 beats per minute. It tends to be lower among people who are in training, particularly for endurance activities.

The rate goes up with the anticipation of exercise. Emotions affect the heart rate remarkably. I have taken pulse rates of coaches during the time their swimmers were performing and found some of them to have registered rates over 120.

The increase in heart rate is proportional to the intensity of the exercise. This means that, as the swimmer swims slowly, he experiences a slight increase in heart rate, perhaps to 120 beats per minute. As he sprints, a great increase occurs, perhaps to as high as 180 or 200 beats per minute. This particular fact permits the use of heart rate during or immediately after exercise to be a measure of the intensity of the exercise. This principle is used in Chapters VIII and IX in helping identify the various methods of training.

The heart rate after exercise tends to return faster in a well trained (for endurance) individual. This fact is used by Forbes Carlile[5] to

---

[4] *Tips on Athletic Training,* VII, American Medical Association Publication Series (Chicago, Illinois: 1965), 6-7.

[5] Forbes Carlile, *Forbes Carlile on Swimming* (London: Pelham Books, Ltd., 1963), pp. 119-21.

assess training progress and to predict the possible all-out performance of the individual at a particular stage of training. The rise of the heart rate is greater as a result of short sprinting, but the return of the heart rate after short sprints is faster than it is after long sustained swimming.

We take heart rates frequently during practice, in order to evaluate the degree to which the swimmers are exerting themselves, but also as a means of motivating them.

Resting heart rate, heart rate after exercise, and the rate of return of the heart rate to normal after exercise are all greater as the person becomes fatigued and goes into the stages of failing adaptation. Table XIII–1 shows the heart rate for Chet Jastremski on three occasions during his training in the summer of 1964: Column 1 after one and a half weeks of training, when he was feeling relatively well and was not excessively fatigued from his training program, Column 2 after four weeks, when he had been pushed near the point of failing adaptation, and Column 3 during the tapering period nine weeks later and immediately before the Olympic Trials where he set a world record in the 200-meter breaststroke.

The chart lists the three main items that a swimmer can use to evaluate his progress: (1) heart rate, (2) number of strokes per length, and (3) the time in which he swims his repeat swims. As all of these decrease, he can feel assurance in the belief that his conditioning is improving. There are times, however, when he must push himself sufficiently hard to expect all of these factors to regress in order to bring about maximum adaptation. This decrease in efficiency is shown in Column B in the table and in Figure IX–1.

The mechanism involved in the decrease of heart rate as a result of training is not clearly understood. The heart is supplied with two nerves —the vagus nerve and the sympathetic nerve. When the vagus nerve is stimulated there is a decrease in heart rate, and when the sympathetic nerve is stimulated there is an increase. The rate decrease caused by training is believed to be due to an increased vagal tone. A decreased rate permits a greater period of relaxation, during which venous blood can fill the heart to a greater extent. The greater the venous return during this phase, the greater the volume of blood ejected with each heart beat. This volume is referred to as *stroke volume*. As a result of this decreased rate and increased stroke volume, the heart can use less energy to perform a given amount of work.

RESPIRATORY EFFICIENCY. Another big factor in circulo-respiratory endurance is, as the term implies, respiratory efficiency. A common misconception is that respiratory efficiency can be measured by measuring vital lung capacity, which is the greatest volume of air that can be

TABLE XIII–1. Workout: 30 × 50 Leaving on 60 Seconds in a 50-Meter Pool

	Subjective Feeling	Average Time per 50 Meters	Number of Strokes per 50 Meters	Resting Heart Rate, Taken Upon Arising in Morning	Heart Rate After Last 50 Meters *	Heart Rate Return 8 min. After Exercise
A) June 14—After 1½ weeks of hard training	Tired, but not excessively so	:41.6	32.5	64	180	99
B) July 20—After about 4 weeks of training	Very tired, subjective feeling of chronic tiredness	:42.4	34.1	70	188	108
C) August 20—After 8 weeks of hard training and 1 week of tapering	Rested and more energetic	:38.1	31.2	60	176	92

* Taken for only ten seconds, then multiplied by 6.

expelled in a single exhalation after a maximum inhalation. Although vital lung capacity does increase somewhat with training, the main increase in respiratory efficiency is believed to be due to changes in the composition of the blood and in the alveoli—the small air sacs in the lungs where the oxygen and the carbon dioxide are exchanged between the air in the lungs and the blood in the pulmonary capillaries. As a result of training, the alveoli in animals have been reported to develop partitions which increase the amount of surface area exposed to the air in the lungs, thereby increasing the rate of oxygen exchange.[6]

The increase in vital lung capacity, which is apparent, is thought to be the result of increased strength of the respiratory muscles and an increase in the size of some of the alveoli, which during rest or mild exercise are not used. There is a decrease in a trained person's breathing rate and an increase in ventilation depth. During exercise the trained person can handle a greater volume of air and more oxygen can be absorbed through the lungs into the blood stream.

LEVEL OF BLOOD SUGAR.   The resting level of sugar in the blood is not affected appreciably by training. During rest the normal level of blood sugar is 70 to 100 mgs. per milliliters of blood. As the blood sugar decreases during exercise, adrenalin is released by the suprarenal glands, causing the release of sugar from the liver. During exhaustive exercise the level of blood sugar may drop below the resting level. When this level drops too low—a condition referred to as hypoglycemia exists—the person must diminish activity because of blood sugar exhaustion. Marathon runners who have had to drop out of a race due to exhaustion have been found to have had extremely low levels of blood sugar, while the runners who finished high in the race were found to have had at least normal levels of blood sugar. This ability of the athlete to maintain high levels of blood sugar during exhaustive exercise is believed to be related to the ability to store more sugar in the muscles and in the liver.

RED BLOOD CELLS.   The main method of carrying oxygen is in the blood via the hemoglobin in the red blood cells (erythrocytes). The oxygen carrying ability of the blood can be increased by increasing the number of red blood cells and the hemoglobin content of the blood, and this is what probably occurs during certain types of training. The red blood cells are produced in the red bone marrow, and the stimulus to their production is a low level of oxygen (anoxia) in the blood going to that area. This condition of anoxia can be caused by vigorous, prolonged exercise, and it is only as a result of exercise of this type that any increase in red blood cell count would occur. There seems to be a gen-

---

[6] Charles H. McCloy, *An Outline of Physiology of Exercise* (mimeographed pamphlet, State University of Iowa, 1949), p. 9.

eral belief that this is what does occur as a result of endurance type of training, but researchers offer such a wide variety of results that the evidence is not conclusive. During five consecutive summers (1960–1964), under carefully controlled conditions, we noted a statistically significant rise in the number of red blood cells and the hemoglobin content of the blood as a result of six weeks of training in over 50 per cent of the swimmers tested. In only a few cases was there a drop in the number of red blood cells. In the remaining cases there was no significant change. The improvement in times made by the swimmers slightly favored the swimmers who experienced a rise in their red blood cell count and hemoglobin content of the blood.

The capacity for absorbing and carrying large amounts of oxygen during periods of extreme exertion appears to be one of the outstanding characteristics of well trained athletes. A trained athlete can incur greater levels of oxygen debt, thereby permitting him to exercise a longer period of time. This ability is believed to be associated with the alkali reserve.

ALKALI RESERVE AND BLOOD pH. During exercise carbonic acid and lactic acid (the by-product of the breakdown of glucose) enter the blood stream and tend to lower the alkalinity of the blood. The normal range of pH (acidity or alkalinity) for the blood is 7.4 to 7.8 (slightly alkaline). The addition of these acids to the blood would quickly upset the pH if it were not for the neutralizing effects of the buffers in the blood. Acids in the blood—other than carbonic acid, which is buffered by hemoglobin—are buffered in the main by bicarbonate in the blood which is referred to as the alkali reserve. A trained person is able to maintain a higher pH level (more alkaline) during exercise, and this condition may be related to an increased alkali reserve. Some studies report increases in the level of alkali reserve during training while others report no change. Since a trained person is capable of creating higher levels of blood lactate (buffered lactic acid), it follows that he can continue to exercise longer than can a person who is able to tolerate only lower levels. This ability to tolerate high levels of blood lactate is not fully understood. The ingestion of food substances which have a high alkaline content in an effort to increase the alkaline reserve in the blood has not proven beneficial.

Factors Which Contribute to or Detract from Adaptation

SLEEP AND REST. A size eight shoe will not fit everyone's foot. Similarly, a certain number of hours of sleep cannot be prescribed for everyone with the expectation of a perfect fit. Some individuals obviously require more sleep than others.

Bill Utley, National NCAA and AAU individual medley champion, sleeps ten hours a night when he is not in training, and 12 hours a night when he is in training. Chet Jastremski sleeps six hours a night when not in training, and seven hours a night when training hard.

There is a great deal of difference in the manner in which people sleep. Sleeping habits not only vary between individuals, but also in the individual's daily experience. Most healthy persons change one gross bodily position to another 20 to 45 times in one night of eight hours. Athletes, prior to a contest, change body positions several times more often than they do under normal conditions. This type of sleep is called *restless sleep* and, as the term implies, is not as beneficial as the normal type of sleep. Massage, seeing a movie or watching television, a slight or moderate workout, or a warm glass of milk have been shown to improve the athlete's ability to maintain normal sleep habits prior to the contest.

Individuals who are excessively fatigued frequently sleep *like a log;* that is, they move very rarely. This type of sleep is also not as restful as normal sleep. General massage and a light meal have been reported by various coaches to aid in preventing this type of sleep, which often follows the game or contest.

The ingestion of caffeine and cocaine several hours before going to bed may cause irritation of the urinary bladder, thereby inducing sleeplessness. Thus, an athlete should avoid having coffee, tea, and soda pop before going to bed.

When a swimmer is training extremely hard, two or three times a day, he may find a nap of 15 minutes to one hour during the day and, preferably, between practice sessions to be a helpful addition to his regular night's sleep. In training the Olympic Team in 1964, I observed that nearly all of the swimmers enjoyed their afternoon naps. When they had to forego them for some reason, they performed poorly in the afternoon practice.

Rest, as distinct from sleep, implies a period of relative inactivity when the body can relax and make at least partial recovery from the fatigue of the previous workout. We have found that swimmers who try to train hard twice a day and continue to do hard physical work six to eight hours a day cannot sustain the routine over a long period of time. They need rest between the two workouts. The stress of working superimposed upon the stress of training hard is simply too much to permit adaptation.

Some coaches work on the principle that, if the swimmer works extremely hard for a period of several days, he should be given a day's rest or, perhaps, a couple of days of diminished work. One day off a week if the swimmer has trained hard on the other six days will give the swimmer both the physical and psychological rest which he may need.

FATIGUE AND STALENESS.   In every sport we have the phenomenon which we call *staleness*. Exactly what is it? Is it psychological or physiological? Can it be measured? Can it be avoided? These are questions with which every coach should be concerned. I will try to answer these questions on the basis of psychological and physiological principles as established by experts in these areas.

What is staleness? Generally, it is thought of as that condition under which the performance of the athlete is affected detrimentally for a more or less long period of time. This decreased efficiency is believed to be due to overtraining or overwork. The decreased level of performance can be due to either physiological or psychological causes, or to both.

Perhaps the two types of staleness cannot be separated, for as one progresses, so does the other. However, for the purpose of discussion convenience the two will be separated.

Physiological staleness.   This type of staleness, as the name implies, results from some change in the physiology of the athlete which affects his performance harmfully. When this type of staleness occurs, the athlete usually has a drawn look and loses weight. If strength tests were taken previous to and during the slump, they would show a decided decrease in strength. Several studies have been made which show these statements to be true. A simple test item like the grip strength test will indicate a decrease. The person may complain of feeling continually fatigued and he may loaf through the practice sessions. This tired feeling has been termed *chronic fatigue*. When it occurs, the heart rate, especially after exertion, will be higher than it was when the athlete was in top shape. Dark circles will appear under the eyes as the fat pads disappear. The skin on the fingers may appear to be tight and drawn. The skin—particularly of the face—may be sallow as the person loses his color. These changes occur so gradually that they may go unnoticed by both the coach and the athlete. However, by careful observation, the coach can generally determine the cause of this type of staleness. Violation of some of the principles of training is usually the cause.

The athlete may be working so hard that he uses more energy than he can replace by food or rest. He is constantly drawing on his reserve (or, as Selye called it, adaptation energy), but he is not replenishing this reserve between workouts. If he is unable to do so, he is operating *in the red*. Outside activities may account for the overwork; in some cases, it may be inadequate sleep or improper diet which is contributing or is even a major factor. Illnesses so minor as to go unnoticed but which weaken the athlete may precipitate a condition of chronic fatigue, which in turn could well be the cause of physiological staleness. Physiological staleness is a predisposing factor to illness.

Psychological staleness. This type of staleness is marked by a loss of interest in training and even in competition. The athlete may not even admit to himself that he has lost the *drive* or *zest* for his particular activity. There is a decrease in the level of his performance accompanied by a definite slump in the morale of the athlete and, frequently, in that of the whole team. The athlete may experience an anticlimactic feeling, a sort of letdown, which leaves him bored with his task. Interest must be maintained in order to avoid this type of staleness.

As the age-group swimmer who had been pushed all season long to win all of his races and set national age-group records said after finally losing, "I was all wrung out." There must even have been some feeling of relief when the winning streak was broken. His performances got progressively worse and people said that he was stale.

Psychological staleness can also be the result of certian physiological changes. Every coach is familiar with the way emotions affect the athlete's sleep, his diet, his workout routine, and so on. Individuals respond individually to this type of staleness, but generally they show an appreciable loss of interest. Others may feel it coming on and fight it by a demonstrative show of enthusiasm which, if analyzed, appears to be somewhat forced. Some may appear to be bored, while still others seem to be nervous and jumpy. When a coach hears an athlete say repeatedly, "I'll be glad when the season is over," he had better see to it that some changes are made in his team's workouts, for he has just noticed one of the first symptoms of staleness.

Continual emotional peaking for each meet is the surest way of bringing on psychological staleness, because emotional stimulation cannot be imposed repeatedly without cost to the individual. The price he must pay is psychological fatigue. At the other extreme is boredom, a factor which can result in staleness if some thought is not given to avoiding it. This is one of the reasons that a chapter on planning a season's program is included in this book (Chapter IX).

Staleness is similar to a contagious disease in that it is easier to prevent than it is to cure. The coach must plan his training program from the very beginning with its prevention in mind. He should never tell an athlete or a team that they are stale, for they will use this excuse as a hook on which to hang their poor performances. The athletes may become conditioned to the term *staleness* and accept it as inevitable. The coach should never—or seldom—use the term, but he should certainly combat it and watch for signs of it.

BREAKING TRAINING. In a questionnaire completed by 97 swimmers attending the East-West Swimming Meet held annually at Fort Lauderdale, Florida, all but one of the swimmers thought that smoking would harm their performance. If an athlete believes smoking will hurt his

performance, the chances are that it will, even if there were no physiological basis for his belief. This clearly points up the harm in the "one
glass of beer" or "one cigarette" attitude. There may be no way of
measuring any detrimental physiological effect from such a small in-
fraction of the training rules, but the psychological effect may manifest
itself in the offender's performance on the field. Combined with the effect
on the morale of the team when it discovers that one or more of its
members has been breaking training, it is easy to see the advantages of
adhering to strict training rules.

Continued breaking of training will not only have psychological implications, but will also result in a deterioration of the offender's physiological condition. His functional performance will diminish and, particularly, the endurance phase of his conditioning will be affected.

Smoking.   We often see swimmers who want to have their tobacco
and their swimming too. They rationalize their smoking by saying, "It
won't hurt me." Along with risking the chance of lung cancer, they are
affecting their swimming careers. Nowhere is there any medical evidence
—notwithstanding the attractive advertisements to the contrary—to show
that smoking improves health or physical performance. On the contrary,
a growing mass of evidence indicates that smoking decreases the smoker's
life expectancy and is detrimental to physical performance. Tobacco contains toxic substances which have a harmful effect on the heart and fix
onto the red blood cells, decreasing their ability to transport oxygen.
Smoking causes a decrease in the permeability of the walls of the alveoli,
thereby decreasing the ability of the lungs to absorb oxygen. The following statement was made in a bulletin published by the American
Medical Association:

> Tobacco smoke is irritating to the mucous membranes of the nose, throat,
> and other respiratory passages. Smoking is known to constrict the small blood
> vessels and to increase the heart rate. There is little doubt that smoking
> can influence athletic performance, particularly in stress situations. Some
> persons appear to be more resistant to the effects of tobacco than others.
> Even assuming the effects on a particular athlete to be slight, the difference
> between winning and losing may often be just as slight.[7]

In a study which compared 14 smokers with 14 non-smokers, it was
found that there was damage to the lung tissue of the smokers which
affected the function of the lungs.[8]

---

[7] *Tips on Athletic Training*, VII, American Medical Association Publication Series
(Chicago, Illinois: 1965), pp. 6-7.
[8] Oliver E. Byrd, *Health* (Philadelphia: W. B. Saunders Co., 4th ed., 1961),
p. 203.

Dr. T. K. Cureton, of the University of Illinois, tested 271 male swimmers and found that the non-smokers, on the average, were able to hold their breath 21 per cent longer and swim the 100 yards distance 18 per cent faster than the smokers.[9]

Smoking also seems to affect coordination. At the University of Wisconsin students were asked to hold a small metal stylus in a small hole, trying not to touch the sides. Electrical connections registered the number of times it touched. Regular smokers were 60 per cent more unsteady than non-smokers.[10]

The evidence continues to pile up against the obnoxious weed, which by law must be labelled as toxic.

Alcohol. The swimmer who is likely to say, "One cigarette doesn't hurt" is also the one likely to say, "One beer won't hurt you."

In 1960 and 1964, at the Olympic Games, it was pointed out to me by various people that some of the European athletes drank wine and beer with their meals. I observed that these countries were not the countries that were winning the medals, particularly not in the sport of swimming.

An important aspect of training is the physiological effect that alcohol has upon the body. Many people have the erroneous idea that alcohol increases their ability to do work. Actually, the reverse is true. It has been shown that even small amounts of alcohol, such as would be present in a pint of beer, decrease the ability of the person to do work by 8 to 10 per cent. In order to determine the effect of alcohol on muscular efficiency, Professor Durig, a mountain climber, experimented by climbing Mount Belkencrat in the Alps after having taken two and a third glasses of beer, and again after taking none. On the day he took alcohol it took 21.7 per cent longer to reach the top of the mountain than on the days he took no alcohol.[11]

In a 62 mile marathon race in Germany, drinkers were compared with non-drinkers. The first four men to cross the line were abstainers. Over half of the drinkers did not finish, while only a small percentage of the abstainers did not complete the race.[12]

Alcohol is a depressant, that is, it reduces the activity of the brain and results in a reduction of attention, a lessening of discretion and control. It causes a loss in muscular coordination, as evidenced by the staggering drunkard. All of these effects are acute, that is, temporary. Consistent use of alcohol, however, has long-lasting or chronic physio-

---

[9] *Ibid.*, pp. 202-203.

[10] Roger W. Riis, "How Harmful Are Cigarettes?" *Readers Digest,* LVI, No. 333 (January 1950), 5.

[11] Jesse F. Williams, *Healthful Living* (New York: The Macmillan Company, 1956), pp. 68-70.

[12] *Ibid.*, p. 70.

logical effects. These effects are ultimately debilitating to the average person and disastrous for the athlete. Many *near-great* swimmers have lost a championship in the bar. No one can expect to engage in smoking and drinking with impunity.

THE USE OF ERGOGENIC AIDS. Ergogenic aids are intended to increase the ability of the body to do more physical or mental work. The American Medical Association says:

> The mystique of the readiness of the athlete for competition intrigues the sports enthusiast. Unique training table menus, timely whiffs of oxygen, special dietary supplements, and particular exercise rituals have their regular turns in testimonials which supposedly explain sudden or sustained prowess of some athletes. Also, the alleged use of hypnotism or anti-fatigue drugs is occasionally credited with being of advantage to the athlete who indulges in them.
>
> The facts are:
> · Not one of the practices above is essential to athletic achievement.
> · Some of them are hazardous practices, particularly when carried to extremes.
> · For safe and effective performance, there still is no alternative to the fullest utilization of one's natural resources through good personal health practices, optimum conditioning, and confidence in one's ability based upon careful coaching and medical supervision.[13]

Ten years ago the barrier to the sub-four minute mile was broken. Now running the mile in the 3:50's is commonplace, although it used to be considered impossible. This and other supposedly impossible standards have been surpassed in recent years simply by spartan self-discipline and effort, focused on peak condition and extreme refinement of skill.

This surge of new records has tended to produce pressures for continued record breaking. The result is a greater temptation for the impatient coach or athlete to resort to shortcuts and artificial aids which fall into the category of fads, fallacies, and quackery.

DIET AND NUTRITION

It is not uncommon for me to be asked, "Coach, what should I eat to develop strength and endurance?" My reply is that no one ever ate his way to good physical condition. Strength, endurance, and the other desirable qualities are improved through training, not eating.

It appears to be in the nature of most swimmers, perhaps most athletes,

[13] *Tips on Athletic Training,* pp. 8-9.

to be on the lookout for a gimmick or aid which will give them that extra bit of improvement that will set them above the rest. Even world record holders of intelligence and education are not exempt from this urge: one such person took 12 forms of dietary supplements ranging from kelp tablets to wheat germ oil.

It is not my intention to minimize the importance of a good, well balanced diet, but rather to discourage the adoption of dietary fads which might be used in lieu of a well balanced diet.

A great deal of experimentation has been conducted in the area of diet and athletics, most of which is contradictory. At this time, there is little conclusive evidence that there is any dietary supplement which will appreciably improve the level of performance of an athlete, provided he is already getting a balanced, mixed diet. During a rigorous training schedule the swimmer may need to augment his diet quantitatively in order to balance the increased caloric expenditure of his training program. A normal 150-pound male has a basal (resting) caloric need of 1200 calories per day. With normal activity, this need increases to 3000 to 4000 calories per day. Under rigorous training for swimming, four and a half to six miles of hard swimming per day, his caloric need will rise to 7000 calories or more. If the swimmer uses a well balanced diet to meet the additional caloric demand, there is no danger of dietary deficiency. If his diet does lack essential nutrients, he will perform better if these deficiencies are corrected.

A Well Balanced Diet

Not all athletes know what a well balanced diet consists of. Athletes often eat what they like and try to compensate for their poor eating habits by taking dietary supplements, such as vitamins or protein supplements.

One such swimmer whom I coached and who set world records in the backstroke, Tom Stock, had so many food likes and dislikes that his diet was limited almost exclusively to doughnuts, sweet rolls, dry breakfast cereals, and hamburgers. He disliked vegetables, salads, and fruits, and he tried to compensate for their lack by taking vitamins and other dietary supplements. This practice always turns out to be inferior to a well balanced diet, as well as more expensive.

Bogert lists five factors which predispose against a person changing his nutritional habits:

1. Ignorance and prejudice.
2. Racial habits.
3. Fads and false advertising.

4. Complacency.

5. Poverty.[14]

In swimming, items 1, 3, and 4 seem to cause most of the problems we encounter. In working with some of the Mexican swimmers in the summers of 1964 and 1965, however, I became aware that poverty may have contributed to some individual swimming difficulties. This should not be the case in the United States, where the swimmers are living and eating at home. Some swimmers, living away from home and trying to live on a shoestring budget, may sacrifice good eating habits and suffer dietary deficiencies in an effort to save a dollar.

A mixed diet of essential nutrients is composed of six categories: carbohydrates, fats, proteins, minerals, vitamins, and water. Carbohydrates, fats, and proteins, the organic foodstuffs in our diets, can be used interchangeably by the body to supply energy. They, along with water, form the most abundant nutrients in our diets. The minerals and vitamins are needed in only small amounts and act primarily as body regulators by promoting oxidative processes and normal functioning of all tissues. Water also has a regulatory function and makes up approximately 70 per cent of the total body weight.

Protein is composed of amino acids. The body needs approximately 25 different amino acids, eight of which cannot be synthesized and must be obtained from specific foods. Most of these amino acids can be obtained from animal protein, but they can also be obtained from such other sources as grains. Most of the protein received by the average swimmer comes from meat, fish, eggs, and milk. Protein cannot be stored and must be included in the daily diet.

The body uses protein for growth and to rebuild tissues, particularly muscle tissue. The ingestion of a high protein meal such as a big steak dinner two to three hours before competition has become a tradition among athletes. Such a dinner may be satisfactory so far as taste is concerned, but it has no practical value as a quick source of energy. A high carbohydrate meal before strenuous and prolonged work has been shown to be more advantageous. The protein requirements of the body vary with the rate of growth and the total energy output. A reasonable protein allowance is 10 to 12 per cent of the total diet for people not in training, and 12 to 17 per cent for those in a strenuous training program. This means that one average portion of meat together with eggs, milk, and other protein foods is adequate even for an athlete. The practice of adding protein to the diet through protein supplements is useless in spite of advertisements to the contrary. The Russians claim: "For people not active in sports the daily quantity of protein in their food must be

[14] Jean Bogert, *Nutrition and Physical Fitness,* 7th ed. (Philadelphia & London: W. B. Saunders, 1960), p. 9.

1.5 grams per kilogram of body weight. . . . For sportsmen, due to the high intensity of the interchange of matter during the fulfillment of physical exercise, the need for protein is significantly higher, from 2 to 2.5 grams per kilogram of weight." [15] These two statements do not conflict, since the athlete consumes a greater total volume of food when training.

Carbohydrates include sugars and starches and supply quick energy to the body. Carbohydrate derivatives may be converted to fats. Glycogen, a form of carbohydrate, is used in the body as the fuel of muscular contraction. Most carbohydrates ingested by the average swimmer come from bread, potatoes, the yellow vegetables, sugars, and grains in their various forms.

Fats are concentrated sources of energy and are relatively hard to digest. They can be converted into carbohydrates in the body. Most of the fats ingested by the average swimmer come from oils or shortening used to prepare fried foods, butter or margarine, animal fats in meats, and salad oil. Their excessive use before competition should be avoided.

Minerals. At this time we know of between ten and fifteen different minerals which must be supplied in varying amounts:

Calcium—used in building bones and teeth and needed for the normal clotting of blood. Calcium helps to regulate muscle and nerve activity. Rich sources of calcium are found only in dairy products, such as milk, cheese, butter, and ice cream. Green leafy vegetables like broccoli and the legumes contain calcium, as does dried fruit. It is easy for a person who does not eat enough of the aforementioned foods to be deficient in this important mineral. Without the liberal use of milk and its products, it is very difficult to meet the minimum daily requirement of .8 gram of calcium for a normal adult. Children's requirements are relatively larger.

Phosphorus—found abundantly in all animal protein foods, such as meat, fish, poultry, eggs, and cheese, as well as in whole grain breads, cereals, legumes, and nuts. Phosphorus is a factor in the oxidation of all three forms of energy foodstuffs, and forms the rigid structure of bones and teeth. In our modern society, few people suffer from a deficiency of phosphorus.

Potassium—found in milk, dried fruits, bran flakes, wheat germ, cane molasses, catsup, red kidney beans, and so on, it plays a role in muscle contraction and in nerve impulse transmission. It is found in cells in which it regulates acid-base balance and water content. The total potassium content of the body increases when the total muscle bulk is in-

---

[15] N. Jakovlev, "The Nutrition of the Athlete," *Little Library of the Athlete Series,* (Moscow: Physiculture and Sport, 1961), p. 10.

creased. For this reason many persons interested in increasing muscle size have tried eating foods high in potassium. So far, this has not been shown to be of benefit. Very little has been written about potassium deficiency in the diet, and its deficiency may not be a consideration.

Sodium—although sodium is a very common metallic element, it is never found in a pure metallic state, but always in combination with some other substances, as it is in common salt (sodium chloride). In the body it is needed for muscle contraction and helps to regulate water balance and acid-base balance. Its deficiency is easily regulated by satisfying the taste for more salt.

Iron—found in lean meat (particularly liver), leafy vegetables, legumes, whole grains, and dried fruits. Milk is relatively low in iron. Iron is used by the red bone marrow in the manufacture of red blood cells. It is a component of the hemoglobin of the red blood cells. Hemoglobin carries oxygen to the muscles' cells and carbon dioxide away from them. Iron deficiencies are rare among athletes and need not exist at all if the athlete eats enough of the foods mentioned above.

At Indiana University, under carefully controlled experimental conditions, we have used iron dietary supplements of various forms in an effort to raise the red blood cell count and hemoglobin level of the swimmers when they are in heavy training. So far we have had no results except in cases in which the swimmer was suffering from some form of anemia.

Other mineral elements:

Copper—studies of copper in the diet show that even a mediocre American diet provides enough of this mineral to meet the daily requirement.

Cobalt—only very small amounts are needed and there is no danger of a deficiency in the American diet.

Iodine—with the widespread use of iodized salt there is practically no danger of iodine deficiency even in areas formerly known as goitrous regions.

Other mineral elements found in trace amounts in the human body are manganese, magnesium, zinc, fluorine, molybdenum, and silicon.

Vitamins are organic compounds found in the body in only small amounts, but are nevertheless essential to normal growth and maintenance of health. Their action is similar to that of the trace minerals in that their absence or presence determines whether the body functions properly. There are about 15 vitamins that are known to be needed by humans.

Humans can obtain vitamins in their normal diets by eating plants in which they are formed by the action of sunlight, or by eating meat from animals which have eaten these plants. Green leafy vegetables have a high content of most vitamins; legumes, nuts, and whole grains also contain high levels of some vitamins. Fruit and vegetables, with a few exceptions, contain smaller amounts of these vitamins. Such other factors as the stage of ripeness and the method of preparation also affect the vitamin content in any of these foods. Milk, eggs, fish, and lean meat also provide certain vitamins.

1. Vitamin A is found in butter, whole milk, egg yolk, and fish oils. Carotene, which can be changed into vitamin A in the body, is found in carrots, squash, sweet potatoes, corn, and leafy green vegetables. Vitamin A is needed for normal growth of the bones and teeth, for healthy skin, and mucous membrane lining of the respiratory system and the digestive tract. It also helps the eyes adjust to changes in light intensity.

2. Vitamin B_1 or thiamine has its best source in whole grains, organ meats (heart, kidney, liver), pork, and legumes. It is also found in moderate amounts in bread, cereals, meats, fish, poultry, eggs, and dairy products.

3. Vitamin B_2 or riboflavin has its sources in liver, cheese, eggs, leafy vegetables, lean meats, legumes, and milk. It helps produce energy through metabolism of fats, carbohydrates, and proteins. It is needed for health of the skin, nerves, and eyes.

4. B Complex Vitamin (niacin). The following listed foods contain either niacin or tryptophan (niacin can be synthesized in the body if the tryptophan is present in the food taken in): milk, eggs, cheese, meats (particularly organ meats like liver and heart), fish, and peanuts. Niacin is needed for normal functioning of the digestive tract and efficient use of food, and also for healthy skin. Deficiency results in pellagra.

5. Vitamin B_6 or pyridoxine has its best sources in liver, the muscle meats, certain vegetables, and whole grain cereals. It plays a role in converting tryptophan to niacin and also helps the body to utilize amino acids. It may also function in fatty acid metabolism.

6. Vitamin B_{12} or cobalamin has its best sources in liver, kidney, and fresh muscle meats. Synthesis by intestinal bacteria may be sufficient to meet the needs of most adults. This vitamin has been called the antipernicious anemia factor because of its role in the development of red blood cells.

7. Vitamin C or ascorbic acid has its best sources in uncooked fruits and vegetables, particularly citrus fruits, strawberries, cantaloupe, green leafy vegetables, peppers, broccoli, and cauliflower. Cooking and canning destroys much of the Vitamin C in these foods. Its presence promotes healthy teeth and gums, bones and joints, connective tissue, and muscle.

It aids in resistance to illness, particularly respiratory infections, and is intimately related to function of the adrenal gland. The daily requirement for an adult is around 75 mg, for girls over 12 it is 80 mg, and for boys it is 100 mg. This requirement can be provided by a six ounce glass of fresh orange juice. This vitamin is probably one of the most important for the athlete in a rigorous training program. It is considered to be a *stress vitamin* by the Russians; they used large doses of vitamin C as a part of their training regime with both the 1960 and 1964 Olympic Teams. While in heavy training during both indoor and outdoor season, we supplement normal vitamin C intake of the swimmers' diet with additional daily doses of 200 to 300 mg. The Russians recommend that the daily minimum level of vitamin C intake for athletes training for endurance events be 100 mg, that during periods of active rest (when not training hard) it be 100 mg, when training hard, 250 mg, and when near the competition, 300 mg.[16] Van Huss [17] reports favorable results in the recovery rate of laboratory animals which had been administered vitamin C supplements before exercising over those who took none. All research seems to indicate an increasing need for vitamin C during the stress of a training program. Vitamin C cannot be stored in the body; any excess amounts are harmless and will be eliminated in the urine.

8. Vitamin D has its best source in sunshine, cod liver oil, enriched milk, fish, eggs, and butter. Vitamin D is necessary for absorption of calcium from the intestines and is thus essential for formation of bones and teeth. Caution should be exercised to avoid the ingestion of massive dosages of vitamin D, since serious toxic effects can result. A lack of vitamin D causes rickets. There is little danger of a deficiency of vitamin D due to exposure to the sun that most people receive and the enrichment of our food, particularly milk, with vitamin D supplement.

9. Vitamin E (the tocopherols: alpha, beta, gamma, and delta) has its best source in wheat germ oil, corn and other vegetable oils, whole grains, leafy vegetables, liver, meat fats, butter, and milk. It protects vitamin A and carotene from oxidation and it also may exert a specific influence on oxidations in body tissues. Wheat germ oil, which is high in vitamin E content, has been used for the past ten years or more by many swimmers to improve endurance. Little conclusive evidence has been presented to show that its supplementary feeding does improve endurance or favorably affect any phase of the performance of athletes.

---

[16] Jakovlev, "Nutrition of the Athlete," p. 18, Table 14.
[17] Wayne D. Van Huss, "What Made the Russians Run?," *Nutrition Today*, I, No. 1 (March 1966), 20-23.

10. Vitamin K has its best source in green leafy vegetables, egg yolk, and liver. This vitamin helps to form prothrombin, which is necessary for the clotting of blood. Its deficiency hardly ever exists.

Selecting a Daily Diet

It is not to be expected that all swimmers will regulate everything they eat carefully, evaluating the amount of this or that particular vitamin or mineral they have just ingested. The foregoing discussion of the various nutrients can, however, serve as a general guide in helping the swimmer select his food in such a way that he will receive a well balanced diet.

A general policy for the swimmer in a hard training program to follow in selecting his diet would be to select some of the following foods each day:

1. Milk—a minimum of one pint per day; one quart a day would be even better.
2. Protein—one generous portion of meat or fish, two eggs, some cereal or whole grain.
3. Fats—sufficient butter fat will be present in the milk and animal fat in the meat.
4. Carbohydrates—bread (whole grain bread is superior), cereal, potatoes, sugar (as on cereal or in tea).
5. Leafy green vegetables—he should have either a fresh salad or some other form of leafy green vegetable, such as spinach, kale, or turnip greens.
6. Vegetable or fruit juice, or fresh fruit.
7. Vegetables—cooked carefully to preserve vitamin content, such vegetables as peas, beans, and carrots.

Pre-meet Meal

A swimmer should not change his eating habits drastically on the day of competition. He should, however, avoid certain foods which tend to upset his stomach and make him perform poorly, and he should try to eat foods that will be easily digested and converted into energy. It is a good policy to finish eating a moderate-sized meal at least two and a half to three hours before competing.

So many of the practices concerning eating before competition are based on fads, fallacies, or false claims made by advertisers. More frequently, however, the bad eating habits prior to competition are based on the almost complete indifference and lack of knowledge of the swimmer. For example, take a high school student-swimmer: every day before he goes to practice he stops by the high school hangout and buys a hamburger and french fries. An hour later he is working out with no stomach discomfort. The day of the state high school meet he follows the same procedure, but, on this day, his stomach does not react in the way it has done all year and now causes him a good deal of discomfort. The result is that he performs poorly.

When a swimmer gets nervous or keyed up for a meet, his digestive process is affected. Food goes from the stomach into the upper part of the intestines through an opening controlled by the pyloric sphincter muscle surrounding this opening. The sphincter permits food to enter the intestine only under certain conditions. Food is not acceptable when it is in large pieces or when its fat has not been emulsified with the contents of the stomach. Heavily-spiced foods, when they first enter the stomach, are also not permitted to leave. These foods must be churned about and changed until they are of the consistency and nature that will be accepted by the intestine. No actual diffusion of food occurs in the walls of the stomach; the active internal digestion of the food begins only in the intestine. Foods that are hard for the stomach to process tend to stay longer and delay the opening of the pyloric sphincter. This partially explains the reason why athletes should avoid greasy and highly seasoned foods in the meal prior to competition.

The pyloric sphincter is supplied with sympathetic nerves which also cause it to constrict when a person becomes excited. When this occurs, it becomes difficult to get all but the most easily digested food out of the stomach and into the intestine. The combination of excitement and the ingestion of hard to process foods are the cause of distress to the high school student-athlete.

The following is a list of some foods to avoid in the meal just prior to competition:

1. All greasy foods such as french fried potatoes, fried chicken, greasy hamburgers, gravies, and pies.

2. Highly seasoned foods such as chili, pizza, and barbecued meats.

3. Hard-to-digest vegetables such as radishes, onions, cucumbers, and raw vegetables.

4. Large servings of such protein as steak and fish.

5. If milk, milk shakes, or other forms of daily products are hard for the individual to handle when he is nervous, he should avoid them.

The following is a list of foods easily handled before competition:

1. High carbohydrate foods such as bread, rolls, cake, sugar in some form, and mashed or baked potatoes.

2. Moderate portions of lean meat, broiled fish, or eggs prepared in little or no fat (preferably poached).

3. Fruit, vegetable juices, or tea with sugar.

4. Cooked vegetables, canned fruit, or gelatin desserts.

Typical meals before competition:

1. Glass of orange juice
   Two to four slices of bread (toasted, if preferred) with jelly and a small
     amount of butter
   Two to four poached eggs
   Glass of skimmed milk
2. Bowl of canned soup (these contain only small amounts of fat)
   Roast beef sandwich (no gravy)
   Mashed potatoes
   Tea (hot or cold) with sugar
   Cooked vegetable
   Flavored gelatin
3. Glass of fruit juice
   Lean, broiled steak (six to eight ounces)
   Baked potato
   Cooked vegetable
   Rolls or bread
   Two scoops of sherbet
   Tea
4. Fruit salad
   Broiled fish
   Cooked rice
   Cooked vegetable
   Rolls or bread
   Cake
   Tea or skimmed milk

The Value of Ingesting Various Forms of Sugar

The use of honey, dextrose, or some other simple form of sugar prior to competition has been practiced by athletes for many years in an effort to receive an extra source of energy. Most researchers agree that in a short race, such as most swimmers engage in, this practice has no value. Only when exercise is strenuous and prolonged, as in a marathon run or a distance swim of possibly two miles or more, will the level of blood sugar fall below the normal resting level.

The body must deplete its stores of sugar from the muscles, the blood, and then the liver before supplementary feeding of sugar will be of significant help. This depletion of sugar will not occur in swims of 200-, 400-, or possibly even 1500-meters.

It is possible that towards the end of a hard workout of two and a half to three miles, a swimmer may run levels of blood sugar lower than the resting level. To investigate this possibility, Dr. Anthony Pizzo tested the Indiana University swimmers every half hour during a two hour morning practice session under three conditions: (1) with no breakfast or nutrition for a 12 hour period, (2) with a regular breakfast, and (3) with a fluid diet supplement which was high in simple sugars. The results showed that, in all cases, there was no significant drop in the level of blood sugar at any point during the workout regardless of the breakfasted or unbreakfasted condition of the group of swimmers. Toward the end of the experiment, however, it was discovered that, in some cases, when the swimmer worked out without having eaten for 12 hours, the nitrogen level in his urine was significantly higher than if he had taken some nutrition. This would indicate a higher metabolism of protein and that possibly the muscles were using protein for fuel. These findings are contrary to those of other research projects, and are mentioned here as a possible area for future research.

W. W. Tuttle learned that a person performed better on maximum work output tasks and had better choice reaction time if he had had a breakfast than if he had had only a cup of coffee.[18]

I believe that a swimmer should eat something before taking a hard workout in the morning. At Indiana University, before we had our own 50-meter pool, we worked out from 6:00 to 8:00 A.M. in the local municipal pool. If the boys wanted to eat a large or even moderate-sized breakfast before workout and not practice on a full stomach, they had to get up at 4:30 A.M. Rather than do this, they got up at 5:30 A.M. and drank a can of commercially prepared liquid diet supplement which contained 400 calories. This did not cause any gastric upset and provided the boys with something to "swim on." After working out they ate a moderate normal breakfast. Eating only twice a day is not a good practice for athletes, and some research indicates that eating as often as four to five moderate meals a day may be superior for athletes to eating the normal three large meals.

---

[18] W. W. Tuttle, M. Wilson, and K. Daum, "Effect of Altered Breakfast Habits on Physiologic Response," *Journal of Applied Physiology*, I (1949), 545.

XIV

The Training Schedules of Some Champions

This chapter is not an attempt to analyze minutely the year-round training schedules of the swimmers it includes. It is, rather, a brief summary of some of their training techniques, the purpose of which is to show the reader anything that is distinctive about these swimmers' training or tapering methods, dry land exercise programs, or any other phase of their schedules. The material for the chapter has been gathered by personal interviews with or questionnaires directed to the swimmers or their coaches, articles published by the swimmers or their coaches, and actual observation of their workouts. When such information as height and weight of the swimmer, average times for various sets of repeats, times for kicking and pulling, and so on, was available, it has been included. This information can be used by swimmers and coaches for comparison with the same items in their own programs.

In many cases the workouts listed are for a short course pool, while in others they are for long course. Where times for both short course (expressed in yards) and long course (expressed in meters) were available, they are given. Whenever a swimmer has held a world record, I have listed him as such regardless of whether he still holds it. Most of the swimmers discussed in this chapter train twice a day during the hard-training phase of their programs. Where their favorite workouts are listed, the swimmers were asked to give the harder workout of the two they would take in a single day. Sometimes a whole day's routine is outlined.

In some cases the rest interval (R.I.) is indicated, as "on 1 minute," "on 3 minutes," and so on; in other cases it is the actual length of the rest interval, expressed as "10 sec.," "1 min.," and so on. The former indicates that the swimmer begins another repetition swim on the period of elapsed time since the beginning of the previous effort.

Swimming champions enjoy the same prerogatives as all of us to change their ideas and concepts or to change their workout routines. The fact that the training methods listed in this chapter were used by these champions in the past (at the time of the interview) is no assurance that they or their teams are presently doing similar workouts. Such other factors as height, weight, and best times in meets and in practice are also, obviously, subject to change.

In cases in which the swimmers were not sure of their average time in repeat swims or their best times on kicking or pulling drills, these had to be left out. I have found from experience that most swimmers choose a number of sets of repeats that they use to judge their progress. They are aware of their times in these sets, but are not always aware of what they do in other sets.

In those cases in which the swimmer has swum for me, I have included more information about him, because of the availability of this information from our daily practice log.

The swimmers have been categorized by stroke and by the events they train for: (1) Freestyle sprinters, (2) Freestyle middle distance and distance swimmers, (3) Butterfliers, (4) Backstrokers, (5) Breaststrokers, and (6) Individual medleyists. A separate category has been included for team workouts of the 1964 U.S. Olympic Team.

How to Use this Chapter

A coach or swimmer can use this chapter not only as a general guide in setting up his program, but also as a guide in determining such specific details of programs as the number of repeats for a given distance, the amount of rest to use, and the average time to be achieved in the various repeat swims.

A note of caution must be inserted concerning the average repeat times achieved by a swimmer. The fact that a swimmer can achieve the same time averages that another swimmer, Steve Clark, for example, did for a series of 30×50 yard repeats with 30 seconds rest does not mean that the swimmer will be able to swim the 100-yard freestyle in the same time that Steve did (:45.6). I have had two swimmers who have done as fast or faster than Steve did for similar sets of 50's, yet they could only go :47.8 and :48.2 respectively for the 100-yard distance.

Some swimmers can do much better repeat swims in practice than others, and this is particularly true when distance swimmers are compared with sprinters. A swimmer should not try to do his best series of repeats each day. The times listed as the best repeat swims are precisely that, and not what the swimmer would expect to do each day.

A comparison of the swimmer's kicking and pulling times with those of the champions for the various distances can also give him a rough idea of that part of his stroke which is less efficient than it should be and needs the most work. It must be noted that some swimmers when pulling merely drag their feet (this generally permits the best times), others support them with a board, while still others may put a rubber band or a small tube around their legs. Any of these methods will result in different times and it is hard to compare the times achieved using one method with those using another. Most swimmers, however, kick in a similar manner, that is, while holding a kick board, so comparison of kicking times is more valid.

The reader will also find some valuable information on tapering and warm up and may want, at different times, to try various methods used by the champions. Only through experimentation can the swimmer find the particular method best suited to him.

FREESTYLE SPRINTERS

Dawn Fraser

Australian Olympic Champion—100 meters (1956, 1960, 1964). World Record—100 meters Freestyle, :58.9, and 200 meters, 2:11.6. Dawn won her 1964 title at the age of 27. Height—5'9", weight—159 pounds.

Coached by Harry Gallagher of Melbourne, Australia.

Dawn only trains one season a year, as do most Australians. Both in and out of season Gallagher has his swimmers do dry land exercises to build and retain strength. During the season 10 minutes of isometric contractions are done prior to swimming. Lacking these exercises, Gallagher feels his swimmers would lose some strength. Gallagher tries to train his swimmers below the stress-sign level; if they become cranky and have long faces around the pool, he reduces their work load.

Dawn has been accused of doing very little training in preparation for competition. The table below indicates that her training is considerably harder than the public had been led to believe by the press. The number of miles that Dawn swam each half month is indicated, along with her best time for 100 meters swum during that period. The level of hemoglobin in Dawn's blood is also shown in percentage, with 100 per cent being normal.

	Miles in Training	Hemoglobin Level	Best Time Trial
First half of Aug., 1962	33	88%	
Second half of Aug., 1962	33	90%	:62.4
First half of Sept., 1962	32	88%	
Second half of Sept., 1962	34	86%	:62.2
First half of Oct., 1962	36	88%	
Second half of Oct., 1962	36	92%	:62.0
First half of Nov., 1962	14 (fewer because of taper)	98%	:59.9

The above tabulation reveals that, during the period, Dawn averaged over 2 miles training per day. Only about 15 per cent of this work was done on leg kicking, more emphasis being placed on pulling than on kicking. Most of Dawn's work was carried out at a fast pace; it was not unusual for a session of 2 miles to be executed at higher than 90 per cent effort, primarily of interval training type.

I asked Gallagher for a typical workout, one of the hardest that he would give Dawn during the period of preparation for a big competition, such as the Australian National Championships or the Olympic Games. He uses a 2-week taper to rest Dawn for her big meets, so the workout outlined below would occur between 2 and 8 weeks before a big meet.

MORNING WORKOUT

1. Long, slow warm up of from 440 to 880 yards.
2. Two to 4 broken 440's (10 sec. between each 55, 3 to 4 min. rest between each 440). Her times will average between 5:00 to 5:10 for each broken 440.
3. 440 continuous kick on a small board (her time usually is over 8 min.—Dawn is a poor kicker).
4. 440 pull (with legs in a rubber band); her times are usually around 6:30. Her pull is much better than her kick. Movies which we have studied of her underwater pull show that Dawn pulls more like the good men swimmers than perhaps any other girl swimmer. Terri Stickles' pull is similar to Dawn's.

5. Two to 4 broken 220's (4 × 50 meters with 10 sec. rest, 3 to 5 min. rest between each 220). Her times are usually under 2:25.

Total distance: 1½ to 2½ miles; total time: 1 hour and 15 min. to 2 hours.

AFTERNOON WORKOUT

1. Ten min. of isometric contractions.

2. Two broken 440's (8 × 55 yards with 10 sec. rest, 5 min. rest between 440's) at 85 per cent effort, both under 5 min. Occasionally she breaks 4:50; her best is 4:34.4.

3. 220 kick on a board, 85 per cent effort, under 4 min. occasionally.

4. 220 swim—either individual medley or butterfly, 75 per cent effort.

5. 16 × 50 pull with legs tied by a rubber band. Dawn determines her own rest, but must complete the whole series in 30 min. Her times average around 37 sec. per 50.

6. 16 × 50 swims, each of which must be under 30 sec. Once again she determines her rest period, but the 50's must be completed in 30 min. Therefore, she is swimming one 50 approximately every 2 min. Some days she may go 8 × 110 yard swims instead of 16 × 50. She also must complete the 8 × 100 in 30 min. and try to break 68 sec. on all of them.

7. If any time remains, they work on starts and turns.

Total distance: 2 miles; total time: 2 hours.

Total distance for the day: 3½ to 4½ miles.

On a given day Gallagher may vary the amount of rest between 50's and 100's, depending on whether he is working for endurance or speed. For example, Dawn has done 8 × 110 swims, leaving every 2 min. Her best average time for a series of these is :68.2.

Dawn does occasionally swim longer repeats, such as continuous 220's and 440's, but Gallagher apparently believes more in the value of repeating shorter distances. He has also made the statement, "decrease rather than increase the annual mileage as the years progress [I assume here that he means as the swimmer grows older], but balance this decrease with faster and specialized work."

The above workout for one day totals from 3½ to 4½ miles, and yet it has been said that Dawn averaged a little over 2 miles per day. This apparent discrepancy can be explained in terms of days off from workout for rest or for competition, when little mileage would be recorded. If Dawn began to feel excessively tired, she might take a half day or a whole day off. Gallagher has used the level of blood hemoglobin, pulse rate, and other physiological measures to help him be aware when Dawn was getting too fatigued.

A gradual taper of 2 weeks with a very mild last few days, consisting of only a mile or less of swimming, usually got Dawn ready for her top performances.

Pokey Watson

World Record holder, 200 meters—2:10.5. Best Times: (long course) 50 meters—:28.9, 100 meters—:59.9, 400 meters—4:42.0; (short course) 50 yards—:24.4, 100 yards—:53.4, 200 yards—1:54.1, 400 yards—4:09.0. Age—17, height—5'9", weight—145 pounds. Began swimming competitively at age 9.

Coached by George Haines, Santa Clara, California.

Pokey does a little weight lifting and some isometric contractions. She pulls with a rubber band, holding a kick board between her ankles. She generally works out twice a day, sometimes increasing to 3 times during the swimming season.

FAVORITE WORKOUTS

The following 4 workouts are taken from Pokey's log book; they were done on 4 different days.

SHORT COURSE

  I. 1. Swim 400 to 600 yards warm up.
      2. Swim 4 broken 200's (4 × 50 with 10 sec. R.I. between each 50); times—2:10, 2:03, 2:02, 1:53.
      3. Pull 3 × 300 (about 2 to 3 min. rest); times—3:36, 3:26, 3:21.
      4. Kick 800 yards, alternating 1 hard length with 1 easy.
 II. 1. Swim 600 yards warm up.
      2. Swim 8 × 200 (about 2 to 3 min. R.I.); times—2:06, 2:07, 2:09, 2:14, 2:10, 2:11, 2:11, 2:11.
      3. Pull 5 × 100.
      4. Kick 5 × 100.
      5. Swim 10 × 25 sprint, holding breath.

LONG COURSE

III. 1. Swim 800 meters warm up.
      2. Swim 4 × 400 progressive series (about 4 to 6 min. R.I.); times—5:01, 4:55, 4:52, 4:48.
      3. Kick 5 × 100.
      4. Swim 20 × 50 (2 sets of 10 each with R.I. of 30 sec.).
      5. Pull 2 × 300; times—3:45 and 3:50.
IV. 1. Swim 800 meters warm up.
      2. Swim 20 × 100 (4 sets of 5 each in which each set is faster than the

previous one); average times of sets—1:15, 1:12, 1:09, 1:06.

3. Kick 10 × 50.
4. Pull 4 × 200.
5. Swim 10 × 50.

TAPER (QUOTED DIRECTLY)

"We usually start tapering about a week before we get to the Nationals and we get to the Nationals the Monday before they begin. We stress about twice as much speed work."

1. Swim 800 warm up.
2. Swim 4 × 100 from a dive with about 5 to 6 min. R.I.; times—1:03+, 1:02+, 1:04+, 1:03+.
3. Kick 10 × 50.
4. Pull 2 × 300.

WARM UP BEFORE COMPETITION

1. Swim 600 warm up.
2. Kick 400.
3. Pull 200.
4. Swim some sprints, 25's or 50's.
5. Swim another 100 or 200 easy.

BEST REPEATS

| Short Course (yards) | | | | Long Course (meters) | | | |
| | | Average | | | | Average | |
Dist.	No.	Time	R.I.	Dist.	No.	Time	R.I.
50	10	:26.0	on 60 sec.	50	10	:29+	on 60 sec.
100	5	:55.5	on 5 min.	100	5	1:03.0	on 5 min.
200	6	2:07.0	on 5 min.	200	6	2:20	on 5 min.
400	2	4:22.0	on 8 min.	400	4	4:53	on 10 min.
				800	2	9:58	on 15 min.

BEST KICKING AND PULLING TIMES

(Short Course) Pulling: 50 yds.—:28, 100 yds.—:59.0, 200 yds.—2:03.5, 400 yds.—4:20.0; (Long Course) Pulling: 50 meters—:30.0, 100 meters—1:06.0, 200 meters—:2:19.0, 400 meters—4:48.

Steve Clark

Winner of three Gold Medals in the 1964 Olympic Games—400- and 800-meter Freestyle Relays and 400-meter Medley Relay. World Record —100-meter Freestyle :52.9. Best Times: (short course—50 yards) :20.9, 100 yards—:45.6, 200 yards—1:43.1. Age—21, height—6', weight—162 pounds. Began swimming competitively at age 9.

Coached by George Haines of the Santa Clara Swim Club and Phil Moriarity of Yale University.

Steve does dry land exercises using barbells, no isometric contractions.

FAVORITE WORKOUTS (LONG COURSE)

I. 1. Warm up, swim 400.
    2. Swim 10 × 25 sprints.
    3. Swim 10 × 100 on 5 min., R.I. averaging around 60 sec.
    4. Kick 3 × 200 semi-hard.
    5. Pull 3 × 200 (half of kick board with rubber band between legs).
    6. Swim 4 × 50 hard, 2 min. R.I.
    7. Loosen up swim of 200 meters.

II. 1. Swim ¼ to ½ mile to loosen up.
    2. Sprint a few 25's.
    3. Swim 2 × 400 meters, 5 min. R.I., average 4:50.
    4. Swim 2 × 200, 3 min. R.I., average time 2:15.
    5. Swim 2 × 100, 3 min. R.I., average time :60.
    6. Kick 4 × 100.
    7. Pull 4 × 100.
    8. Swim 8 × 25 hard.
    9. Swim easy 200 to loosen up.

III. "When workouts get monotonous, I do the following":
    1. Warm up with ½ mile swim.
    2. Pull 8 × 100, 1½ min., R.I., average 1:10 to 1:12.
    3. Kick 8 × 100, ½ min. R.I., average 1:35 or better.
    4. Swim easy 200.
    5. Swim 30 × 25, 20 sec. R.I., for speed.
    6. Rest 10 min., then swim 4 × 50 hard or 2 × 100 hard.
    7. Swim 8 × 25 hard.
    8. Swim easy 200 to loosen up.

TAPER

Two weeks of short speed workouts (1 hour) without getting extremely tired. Long warm up and short swims for pace. Twice a day.

1. Warm up ½ to 1 mile (may do some 25 sprints, some pull and some kick).
2. Swim 2 × 100, pace for 200 (or 2 × 50 sprint pace for 100).
3. Swim 2 × 50, pace for 200 (or 4 × 25 sprint pace for 100).
4. Loosen up with an easy swim.

WARM UP FOR MEETS (DIRECT QUOTATION)

"For trials, I need ½ mile to 1 mile to get decently loose the first time I get in the water. Swim easy 400 meters, kick and pull 100 to 200 meters. Swim 200 easy, sprint 4 or 8 push-off 25's or pace a 50 on the way for a 200. Sprint 1 or 2 × 50, if I feel like it.

"For finals, already warmed up if trials are on the same day. Swim ⅛ to ¾ miles depending on how I feel. Sprint (push-off usually) a few 25's or 15 yards."

BEST REPEATS

Short Course (yards)		Average		Long Course (meters)		Average	
Dist.	No.	Time	R.I.	Dist.	No.	Time	R.I.
50	30	:26+	30 sec.	50	40	:30+	30 sec.
100	10	:52.0	4 min.	100	10	:65	1 min.
200	8	1:59+	2½ min.	200	6	2:16	2½ min.
500	5	5:20	6 min.	400	4	4:44	5 min.
				800	2	10:08	12 min.

BEST KICKING AND PULLING TIMES

Kicking: 50—:32, 100—1:10
Pulling: 50—:24.5, 100—56,
       200—2:00

Kicking: 50—:37.5, 100—1.24,
       200—3:20, 400—7:00
Pulling: 50—28, 100—2:18,
       400—5:00

Gary Ilman

Winner of two Gold Medals, 1964 Olympic Games—400-meter Freestyle Relay and 800-meter Freestyle Relay. Best Times: 100 meters—:53.9, 200 meters—1:59.1. Age—21, height—6'2", weight—195 pounds. Began swimming competitively at age 14.

Coached by George Haines of Santa Clara Swim Club and Nort Thornton of Foothills Junior College.

FAVORITE WORKOUT

1. Swim 1 × 400.
2. Swim 2 × 200, 3 to 5 min. R.I.
3. Swim 4 × 100, 1½ to 2 min. R.I.
4. Swim 8 × 50, 30 sec. to 1 min. R.I.
5. Pull 3 × 300, 3 min. R.I. (drag feet).
6. Kick 4 × 100, 1½ min. R.I.
7. Swim 8 × 50, 30 to 60 sec. R.I.

TAPER

About ten days before the big meet, he does more speed work.

1. Warm up well.
2. Swim 8 × 25, 30 sec. R.I.
3. Kick 4 × 50, 30 to 60 sec. R.I.

4. Pull 4 × 50, 30 to 60 sec. R.I.
5. Swim 2 × 100 with long rest.
6. Swim 10 × 50 from dive, 60 sec. R.I.
7. A few 25 sprints.

WARM UP BEFORE COMPETITION

1. Swim 400 to 600 yards.
2. Kick 400.
3. Pull 300.

BEST REPEATS

	Short Course (yards)	Average			Long Course (meters)	Average	
Dist.	No.	Time	R.I.	Dist.	No.	Time	R.I.
50	16	:24.8	on 1 min.	50	10	:28+	on 1 min.
100	20	:55+	on 2 min.	100	15	:65.5	on 2½ min.
200	8	1:55+	on 5 min.	100	8	:62+	on 2½ min.
400	4	4:09	on 10 min.	200	4	2:12	on 4 min.
				400	4	4:47	on 10 min.

FREESTYLE MIDDLE DISTANCE AND DISTANCE SWIMMERS

Terri Stickles

Bronze Medal winner—1964 Olympics, 400 meters-Freestyle, 4:41.7. Best Times: (short course) 50 yards—:24.9, 100 yards—:54.7, 200 yards—1:59.2, 400 yards—4:15.1, 500 yards—5:19.2; (long course) 100 meters —61:9, 200 meters—2:12.9, 400 meters—4:41.2. Age—19, height—5'10", weight—150 pounds. Began competitive swimming at age 11.

Coached by George Haines of Santa Clara Swim Club.

Terri does no weight lifting, but does isometric contractions and exercises with stretch cords.

FAVORITE WORKOUTS (SHORT COURSE)

I. 1. Warm up total of 500 yards (some kick, some pull, some swim).
   2. Swim 12 × 25 (begins doing these in 15+ sec. working down to 14.0 sec.
   3. Swim easy 200.
   4. Swim 8 × 200 on 5 min., average 2:14+.
   5. Swim easy 200.
   6. Kick 8 × 50 on 1 min., average 42 sec.
   7. Pull 8 × 50 on 1 min., average 31 sec. (drags feet).
   8. Swim 16 × 25 all-out effort on 30 sec., average 14 sec.

Total distance: 4000 yards.

II. 1. Warm up 500 yards (kick, pull, swim).
 2. Kick 4 × 50, no prescribed R.I.
 3. Pull 4 × 50, no prescribed R.I.
 4. Swim 200 easy.
 5. Swim 8 × 100 on 2 min., average 1:04 and 1:05.
 6. Rest 5 min., then swim 8 × 100 on 2 min., average 1:01 and 1:02.
 7. Swim easy 200.
 8. Kick 400 for time (around 6 minutes).
 9. Swim locomotive (1 hard, 1 easy, 2 hard, 1 easy, 3 hard, 1 easy, 3 hard, 1 easy, 2 hard, 1 easy, 1 hard, 1 easy).
 10. Swim 10 × 25 all-out on 30 sec., average 14 sec.

Total distance: 4000 yards.

III. 1. Warm up 500.
 2. Kick 200 hard.
 3. Pull 200 hard.
 4. Swim 4 × 400 on 10 min. (starting at 4:55, work down to 4:45).
 5. Swim 200 easy.
 6. Kick 3 × 300 hard.
 7. Pull 6 × 150 hard.
 8. Swim 200 easy.

Total distance: 4700 yards.

TAPER

2 to 3 weeks during which more speed work, less mileage, and more rest between repeats are emphasized. More quality swimming with legal starts and turns.

 1. Warm up 800 yards (200 kick, 200 pull, 200 swim).
 2. Swim 8 × 25, build-up.
 3. Swim 2 × 200 with long rest, average 2:05.
 4. Swim 4 × 100 from dive, long rest, average :58.0.
 5. Swim 8 × 50 with long rest, average :27.0.
 6. Kick 4 × 50.
 7. Pull 4 × 50.
 8. Swim 8 × 25 from dive, average 12 to 13 sec.

WARM UP BEFORE COMPETITION

 1. Swim 400.
 2. Kick 200.
 3. Pull 200.
 4. Mild stretching exercises.
 5. Swim 4 × 25 hard, but not all-out.

6. Swim 4 × 50 for pace.
7. Swim 2 to 4 × 25 sprints.
8. Swim easy 200.

BEST REPEATS

| Short Course (yards) | | | | Long Course (meters) | | | |
| | | Average | | | | Average | |
Dist.	No.	Time	R.I.	Dist.	No.	Time	R.I.
50	30	:29.0	on min.	50	30	:33.0	on min.
100	10	1:01.0	on 2 min.	100	10	1:10.0	on 2 min.
200	8	2:12.0	on 5 min.	200	10	2:25.0	on 5 min.
400	4	4:30	on 10 min.	400	4	4:58+	on 10 min.
				800	3	10:20	on 20 min.

BEST KICKING AND PULLING TIMES

Kicking: 50—:38, 100—1:17, 200—
2:48, 400—5:50
Pulling: 50—:27.3, 100—:58,
200—2:12, 400—4:35

Kicking: 50—:42, 100—1:31, 200—
3:15, 400—6:45
Pulling: 50—:31, 100—1:09, 200—
2:28, 400—4:58

Martha Randall

World Record holder in the 400-meter Freestyle event (4:38.0). Best
Times: (short course) 50 yards—:24.9, 100 yards—:53.6, 200 yards—1:56.9;
(long course) 100 meters—1:01, 200 meters—2:11.4, 1500 meters—19:06.0.
Age—18, height—5′5″, weight—127 pounds. Began competitive swimming
at age 10.
Coached by Mary Kelly, Vesper Boat Club, Philadelphia, Pennsyl-
vania.

FAVORITE WORKOUTS: LONG COURSE (METERS)

I. 1. Swim 400 warm up.
    2. Swim 8 × 400 on 6½ min., average 5:10.
    3. Kick 12 × 100 on 2 min., average 1:34.
    4. Pull 12 × 100 on 2 min., average 1:21 (drags feet).
    5. Swim 12 × 100 on 2 min., average 1:12.
II. 1. Swim 400 warm up.
    2. Swim 5 × 400 on 6½ min., average 5:10.
    3. Swim 10 × 200 on 3½ min., average 2:34.
    4. Swim 10 × 100 on 2 min., average 1:12.
    5. Pull 400, no time.
    6. Kick 400, no time.
III. 1. Swim 400 warm up.
    2. Swim 4 × 800 on 15 min., average 10:30.

3. Kick 8 × 50 on 1 min., average :43.
4. Pull 8 × 50 on 1 min., average :35.
5. Swim 8 × 50 on 1 min., average :32.

TAPER

About two weeks, do more speed work.

1. Warm up—kick 200, swim 200, pull 200.
2. Swim 4 × 200 moderate.
3. Pull 4 × 100.
4. Kick 4 × 100.
5. Swim some 50's.
6. Swim some 25's.

WARM UP BEFORE COMPETITION

1. Warm up 400—swim 1 length, kick 1 length, pull 1 length, and so on.
2. Swim 4 to 6 × 50 "or maybe a couple of 100's, if I am to swim a 200 or 400. If I am to swim a 100, I go 4 to 6 × 25."

BEST REPEATS

Short Course (yards)		Average		Long Course (meters)		Average	
Dist.	No.	Time	R.I.	Dist.	No.	Time	R.I.
50	16	:30+	on 1 min.	50	16	:32.0	on 1 min.
100	20	1:04	on 2 min.	100	20	1:11.0	on 2 min.
200	16	2:14+	on 3½ min.	200	16	2:34	on 3½ min.
400	8	4:44	on 6½ min.	400	8	5:10	on 6½ min.
				800	4	10:30	on 15 min.

BEST KICKING AND PULLING TIMES

Kicking: 50—:39, 100—1:18, 200—
         2:46
Pulling: 50—:31, 100—1:05, 200—
         2:17, 400—4:42

Kicking: 50—:41, 100—1:28, 200—
         3:02
Pulling: 50—:35, 100—1:16, 200—
         2:38, 400—5:20

Ginnie Duenkel

Winner of Gold Medal in 1964 Olympic Games—400-meter Freestyle (4:43.3).

Coached by Frank Elm, Rutgers University and Summit Y Girls Team.

Ginnie's summer training schedule began May 13 in a 25-yard pool. She did no dry land exercises during this summer season. For 3 weeks she worked out only once a day, covering 2¾ to 3 miles. At any given time during the season she alternated 3 workouts; the following is an example of one of them.

WORKOUT IN MAY

1. Warm up easy swim of about 440 yards.
2. 4 × 500 repeat swims, 6 min. R.I.
3. 4 × 200 kick, 1½ min. R.I.
4. 4 × 200 pull, 1½ min. R.I.
5. 4 × 200 repeat swims, 2 min. R.I.

WORKOUT IN JUNE

Three different workout routines were used at this point.

1. Warm up.
2. 5 × 400 meter repeat swims, 4 min. R.I.
3. 32 × 50, one per min.
4. 10 × 100 kick, 1 min. R.I.
5. 10 × 100 pull, 1 min. R.I.
6. 2 × 200 individual medley.

EXAMPLE OF A WORKOUT IN JULY

By this time Ginnie was working out twice a day; her total daily distance averaged from 5 to 7 miles a day.

Morning Workout

1. Warm up.
2. 4 × 800 repeat swims, 4 to 5 min. R.I.
3. 32 × 50, one per min.
4. 5 × 200 pull, 1½ min. R.I.
5. 5 × 200 kick, 1½ min. R.I.
6. 2 × 200 medium swim.

Afternoon Workout

1. Warm up.
2. 32 × 100, 1 to 2 min. R.I.

Ginnie swam approximately 25 to 28 1500-meter swims in the summer of 1963, in preparation for the National Swimming Championships.[1]

Pam Kruse

National AAU Champion, 500-yard Freestyle. Best Times: (long course) 100 meters—1:01.3, 200 meters—2:09.7, 400 meters—4:33.7; (short course) 100 yards—:54.0, 200 yards—1:54.0, 500 yards—5:06.9. Age—16, height—5'5", weight—125 pounds. Began competitive swimming at age 11.

---

[1] Frank Elm, "How I Trained Ginnie Duenkel and the Summit Girls Team for the National AAU Championships," *Swimming World*, V, No. 3 (March 1964), 4, 11.

Coached by Bob Ousley, Pompano Beach, Florida.
Pam does some weight lifting and a few isometric contractions.

FAVORITE WORKOUTS

Pam does not have specific favorite workouts, but, during the week, she likes to do the following straight sets of repeats.

1. Swim 10 × 200 on 3 or 3½ min., or
2. Swim 6 × 500 on 8 min., or
3. Swim 3 × 1000 on 15 min.
4. Swim 2 × 1650 on 30 min.
5. Swim 20 × 100 on 1½ min.

Prior to doing one of the above straight sets of repeats, Pam warms up with a combination of 1500 yards of kicking, pulling, and swimming. She swims a total of 3500 to 5000 yards per workout for a duration of 1½ to 2 hours. She works out twice a day, averaging 7000 to 8000 yards per day.

TAPER

Pam tapers beginning 7 to 10 days before big meet; she cuts down from 7000 yards daily until the last 3 days, during which she goes only about 1800 yards. She also increases her speed and pace work during the taper.

WARM UP BEFORE COMPETITION (1650 YARD RACE)

1. Easy 300 to 500 swim warm up.
2. Kick 300 yards.
3. Swim other strokes—400 yards.
4. Swim 50- or 100-yards pace, total of 700 to 800 yards.

For the shorter races Pam does more short work and a few hard sprints.

BEST REPEATS

Short Course (yards)		Average		Long Course (meters)		Average	
Dist.	No.	Time	R.I.	Dist.	No.	Time	R.I.
50	20	:29	on 1 min.	200	8	2:25	on 4 min.
100	20	:62.7	on 1½ min.	400	8	5:02	on 8 min.
200	10	2:11.7	on 3½ min.				
500	6	5:36	on 8 min.				

Roy Saari

Winner of the Silver Medal, 1964 Olympic Games—400-meter Individual Medley, and Gold Medal—800-meter Freestyle Relay. Best times: (short course) 100 yards—47.9, 200 yards—1:42.9, 500 yards—4:42.0, 1650 yards—16:39.9; (long course) 1500 meters—16:58.7, 400 meters—4:13.6, 200 meters—1:59.2. Age—19, height—6'2", weight—190 pounds. Began swimming competitively at age 5½.

Coached by Uurho Saari of El Segundo High School and Peter Daland of Southern California University.

Roy does no dry land exercises, but plays water polo, which he feels helps to condition him.

FAVORITE WORKOUTS (LONG COURSE)

I. 1. Swim 3 × 800, 5 min. R.I.
    2. Kick 4 × 100.
    3. Pull 4 × 100 (drags feet).
    4. Swim sprint 4 × 50 on 3 min.
II. 1. Swim to loosen up.
    2. Swim with 2 min. R.I. 16 × 100:
       4 × 100 Butterfly.
       4 × 100 Breaststroke.
       4 × 100 Backstroke.
       4 × 100 Butterfly.
    3. Kick 3 × 200.
    4. Swim sprint 50.
III. 1. Swim 10 × 200, 1½ min. R.I.
    2. Kick 4 × 100.
    3. Pull 4 × 100.
    4. Swim 4 × 100, 5 min. R.I., one of each stroke.

TAPER

Eighteen days before the beginning of the 1964 Olympic Games, Roy wrote the following description of his taper. "I feel that I can afford to start tapering now. For the next eight days I would like to do more speed work, but not so much that I feel exhausted 24 hours a day. For the last ten days all I want to do is light loosening-up workouts and a few easy pace swims. I feel the important thing from here on in is not to panic and overwork. The best thing I can do now is rest!"

WARM UP BEFORE COMPETITION

"I just do easy loosening-up laps until I feel about right. No time trials!"

BEST REPEATS

| | Short Course (yards) | | | | Long Course (meters) | | |
| | | Average | | | | Average | |
Dist.	No.	Time	R.I.	Dist.	No.	Time	R.I.
50	10	:24.2	on 60 sec.	50	16	:29+	on 60 sec.
100	10	:56+	on 2 min.	100	12	1:04	on 2 min.
200	5	1:58	on 5 min.	200	5	2:10	on 6 min.
400	4	4:07	on 10 min.	400	4	4:35	5 min.
				800	3	9:26	3 min.
				3000	1	36:48	——

Don Schollander

Winner of four Gold Medals in 1964 Olympic Games: 100 meters, 400 meters, 400-meter Freestyle Relay, and 800-meter Freestyle Relay. Best Times: (long course) 100 meters—53.3, 200 meters—1:55.7, 400 meters—4:11.6; (short course) 100 yards—46.8, 200 yards—1:41.2, 500 yards—4:44.5. Age—20, height—5'10", weight—172 pounds. Began swimming competitively at age 9.

Coached by George Haines of Santa Clara Swim Club and Phil Moriarty of Yale University.

Don trains nearly year round and has done a lot of work with dry land exercises and isometric contractions. He has worked with the latissimus machine, barbells, and exercise stretch cords.

FAVORITE WORKOUT (SUMMER, 1964)

I. 1. Swim 400 meters as easy warm up.
   2. Kick 200 meters easy.
   3. Pull 200 meters easy (drags feet).
   4. Swim 10 × 100 meters, 1 min. R.I., average 64 to 66 sec.
   5. Pull 4 × 300 meters with 1½ to 2 min. R.I.
   6. Kick 3 × 400 meters with 3 to 5 min. R.I.
   7. Swim 4 × 50 sprint pace with long rest (3 min.).
II. Don describes this workout as the hardest one he does.
   1. Swim 400 as warm up.
   2. Kick 200.
   3. Pull 200.
   4. Swim 4 × 400, 5 to 7 min. R.I.
   5. Swim 2 × 100, 1 to 2 min. R.I.
   6. Kick 2 × 100, 1 to 2 min. R.I.
   7. Pull 2 × 100, 1 to 2 min. R.I.
   8. Swim 4 × 50 very hard, 2 min. R.I.

III. 1. Swim 400 warm up.
   2. Kick 200.
   3. Pull 200.
   4. Swim 4 × 200, 2 to 3 min. R.I.
   5. Swim 10 × 200, 1 to 1½ min. R.I.
   6. Swim 8 × 50, 30 to 45 sec. R.I.

TAPER

Two weeks long—more speed and pace work, with a lot of rest.

1. Swim 400 warm up.
2. Kick 200.
3. Pull 200.
4. Swim 4 × 50 warm up.
5. Swim 4 × 25 warm up hard.
6. Swim 4 × 100, average 60 sec.
7. Swim 2 × 50, hard and from dive.
8. Swim 4 × 25 sprints.

WARM UP BEFORE COMPETITION

1. Swim easy 400.
2. Swim 100 freestyle, picking up speed.
3. Kick 200 warm up.
4. Kick 100 fast time.
5. Pull 150 warm up.
6. Pull 50 fast.
7. Swim 100 pace.
8. Swim 50 pace.
9. Swim 2 × 25 pace.
10. Swim 3 × 50 sprint.
11. Swim 2 × 25 sprint.

Comment: Don's warm ups are long and might well tire the average swimmer. The day he won the Olympic 100-meters event in the freestyle, he kicked 800 meters to loosen up his legs, which felt tight.

BEST REPEATS

Don likes to do his repeats in a progressive manner, that is, to get faster as the set of repeats goes along. In training for the Olympic Games Trials on August 14, 1964, he went the following 400-meter repeats long course with a 5 minute rest interval——4:32.8, 4:33.9, 4:32.9, and 4:23.8. On the same day, in his second workout in a short course pool (25 yards), he swam 20 × 100 with only 15 seconds rest interval and averaged 58 seconds per 100 yards, swimming the last two 100's in :53.8 and :53.2. The day before this, Don had swum two 1500 meter (long course) swims with a 10 minute rest interval in the times of 18:09 and 18:18. On September 22, 1964, he swam 6 × 200 meters with 5 minutes rest in 2:11, 2:10.4, 2:09.4, 2:07.9, 2:06.7, and 2:05.6.

| | Short Course (yards) | | | | Long Course (meters) | | |
| | | Average | | | | Average | |
Dist.	No.	Time	R.I.	Dist.	No.	Time	R.I.
50	12	:24+	on 1 min.	50	40	:30.2	on 1 min.
100	10	:54+	on 2 min.	50	10	:27.7	on 1 min.
100	20	:58+	15 sec.	100	15	1:04.0	on 2½ min.
200	5	1:52+	on 4 min.	100	8	1:02	on 2 min.
400	4	under	2 to 4	200	6	2:00	
		4 min.	min. R.I.	400	4	4:29	5 min.
				800	2	9:16	10 min.

BEST KICKING AND PULLING TIMES

Kicking: 100–1:05
Pulling: 50–:25, 100–:53

Kicking: 50–:35.5, 100–1:15,
 200–2:45, 400–6:02
Pulling: 100–:63, 400–4:38

Michael Burton

World Record holder, 1500-meters Freestyle–16:34.1. Mike Burton is probably one of the hardest working swimmers of all time. He trains about 10½ months of the year. His coach feels that Mike's greatest attribute so far as his swimming success is concerned is his tremendous desire to succeed. He describes Mike as very ambitious and very humble. He falls into the category of athletes known as "agonists," that is, he seems to enjoy hurting himself in both practice and competition. He has come as close to swimming the 1500-meter race at a near maximum pace as anyone has ever done. Best Times: (long course) 100 meters–:56.4, 200 meters–1:59.1 (relay start), 400 meters–4:12.3, 800 meters–8:45.5, 1500 meters–16:34.1; (short course) 200 yards–1:47.8, 500 yards–4:37.0, 1650 yards–16:08.0.

Mike's split times for his World Record 1500-meter swim are as follows:

100– :59.8	600– 6:30.9	1100–12:08.9
200–2:05.0	700– 7:38.6	1200–13:16.3
300–3:10.9	800– 8:46.3	1300–14:23.5
400–4:17.4	900– 9:53.9	1400–15:30.1
500–5:24.2	1000–11:01.4	1500–16:34.1

Age–20, height–5'7½", weight–160 pounds. Began swimming competitively at age 11, but swam only during the summer season until he reached the age of 15, when he began training for both the indoor and outdoor seasons.

Coached by Sherman Chavoor, Arden Hills Club, California.

Mike does both weight training and isometric contractions. He watches his diet carefully and, during the competitive season, goes to bed between 8:30 and 9:00 P.M.

For about 4½ months of the year Mike works out once a day. During the indoor competitive season (January, February, March) Mike works out twice a day; during the outdoor season (June, July, August) he works out 3 times a day, averaging about 11,000 to 12,000 meters daily.

TYPICAL WORKOUTS

Early season—either in the fall (September and October) or spring (April or May).

Burton's coach likes to have all of his swimmers do many lengths of swimming the various strokes. The workout would be considered low-pressure in that everything is done without being timed.

1. Swim 4 to 5 × 200 butterfly (R.I. not rigidly controlled).
2. Swim 2 or 3 × 500 breaststroke.
3. Swim 2 or 3 × 500 backstroke.
4. Swim 8 × 50 butterfly, 8 × 50 backstroke, 8 × 50 breaststroke, and 8 × 50 freestyle.

Another early season (January) short course workout is timed.

1. Swim 500 warm up.
2. Time 1650—time 17:20 to 17:30, R.I.—5 min.
3. Time 1650—time 17:55 to 18:10.
4. Pull 1650, no time.
5. Swim 4 or 5 × 200—time 1:56 to 2:00, with 1 min. R:I.

SUMMER WORKOUT—THREE TIMES A DAY

I. Morning workout—long course—total distance—6000 meters, time—2½ hours.
  1. Swim 500 meters warm up.
  2. Swim 4 × 800 meters, R.I.—3 to 5 min., average time—9:35 to 9:45, best time for one of these in the summer of 1966—9:10.
  3. Swim 3 × 400, R.I.—2 min., average time—4:35 to 4:39.
  4. Swim 3 or 4 × 200, R.I.—1 min., average time—2:09 to 2:11.
  5. Swim 3 or 4 × 100, R.I.—1 min., average time—1:06 to 1:08.
II. Noon workout—short course—approximate distance of 5000 yards, time—1½ to 2 hours.
  1. Swim a few hundred yards to loosen up.
  2. Kick or pull 2 × 800 moderately hard, but not for time.
  3. Swim 30 × 50 on 1 min., using all strokes.
  4. Swim 1650 continuously, but not for time.
  5. Swim some hard repeats, either 50's or 100's, the number depending on how tired the swimmer is.
III. Third workout—if the two previous workouts, which were very hard, were

used, the third workout might be relatively light. The following workout is a hard third workout which would be used if Mike were feeling relatively good. Long course

1. Swim a few hundred meters warm up.
2. Swim 2 × 800 meters, R.I.—5 min., average time—9:35 to 9:40.
3. Swim 15 to 20 × 100 meters, R.I.—1 min., average time—1:05 to 1:06.

Twice a week during the season Mike times a 3000 meter trying to go under 40 minutes. Three times a week he does 15 × 100 meters with a rest interval of 10 seconds (or 100 yards, short course), trying to hit 1:06.5 for each 100 meters.

TAPER

Chavoor says, "It really takes a lot of guts to taper," so he is very cautious and reduces Mike's total distance from 12,000 meters a day to about 6000. The taper starts 10 days before the big meet. There is more speed work with a longer rest interval between repeats. The amount of pulling is decreased. The day before the meet Mike swims about 1 to 1½ hours.

WARM UP BEFORE COMPETITION

1. Swim about 1000 meters to warm up.
2. Swim a series of 8 to 10 × 50 meters, getting down to :27.
3. Swim 5 or 6 × 100 with approximately 1 minute R.I., concentrating on pace for the race (before setting the world record for 1500 meters, Mike swam these in :65.5 average).
4. Kick a few lengths.

BEST REPEATS

Short Course (yards)				Long Course (meters)			
		Average				Average	
Dist.	No.	Time	R.I.	Dist.	No.	Time	R.I.
50	20	:25.5	30 sec.	100	15	1:04	1 min.
100	15	:59	10 sec.	100	15	1:06.5	10 sec.
200	10	1:58	1 min.	200	10	2:08	2 min.
500	6	5:10	2 min.	400	8	4:29	4 to 5 min.
				800	4	9:20	5 min.

Murray Rose

Gold Medal winner in two events in the Olympics of 1956—400 and 1500 meters, and in the 400-meter event in 1960. World Record holder—1500 meters—17:01, and 400 meters—4:13.4.

Coached by Sam Hereford of Sydney, Australia, and Peter Daland of Southern California University.

During the 1964 season, when Murray Rose set the world record, he began training in May 2 or 3 times a week. Early in June he began training twice a day hard. For the first 2 weeks of hard training the emphasis was on distance swimming with a short rest, a total of 5 to 6 miles per day. Repeats consisted primarily of 800's, 400's, and 200's; 400's were usually done in a series of 10 with a rest interval of 2 minutes. Once or twice a week Murray timed a 3000-meter swim.

He continued this training routine with little change until 2 weeks before the national meet where he set the world record at 17:01. During the last 2 weeks Murray concentrated more on speed in the afternoons, doing more 50's, 100's, and 200's. In the morning he concentrated on more quality and cut the number of 400's to 6, but kept the rest interval at 1 to 2 minutes. Two weeks before the meet he averaged 3 miles a day, and the week before the meet averaged only 1 mile a day, primarily high quality and pace work. The 50's and 100's during this time were done from a dive with 3 to 5 minutes rest interval.

Murray likes to warm up 1000 yards to 1 mile. He swims easily for about a half of the mile and then tries to do push-off 100's on the watch or a few push-off 50's working on pace. His warm up ends with a few easy lengths swim.[2]

John Nelson

Silver Medal winner in 1964 Olympic Games in 1500 meters (17:03). Best Times: 400 meters—4:11.8, 200 meters—1:57.6. Age—19, height—5'6", weight—143.

Coached by Robert Ousley, Pompano Beach High School, Florida.

John does not do dry land exercises; he works out twice a day when training hard.

FAVORITE WORKOUTS

I. 1. Warm up 400 meters.
    2. Swim 8 × 400, on 8 min., average under 4:40.
    3. Swim 2 broken 400's, 10 sec. R.I. after each 100.
    4. Kick 500.
    5. Pull 500.
II. 1. Kick 500.
    2. Pull 500.
    3. Swim 10 × 200 on 5 min., average under 2:16.
    4. Swim 10 × 100 on 2 min., average :65+.

[2] Eric Hanauer, "Murray Rose on Training," *Swimming World*, VI, No. 2 (February 1965), 4-5.

TAPER

Two to three weeks in duration, John does pace work and a lot of broken 400's, particularly the week before the big meet. A typical workout during this time in the morning would be: kick and pull 1500 each, alternating 500 kick, 500 pull, and so on. In the afternoon swim 8 × 400.

WARM UP BEFORE COMPETITION

1. Swim lazy 300, some of each stroke.
2. Kick 200, 150 flutter and 50 frog.
3. Pull 200 free.
4. Swim 4 × 50 for pace.

Robert Windle

Olympic Champion—1500-meter Freestyle (17:01.7). Best Times: (long course) 100 meters—:54.9, 200 meters—2:00.1, 440 yards—4:15.0, 800 meters—8:59.6; (short course) 100 yards—47.9, 200 yards—1:43.9, 500 yards—4:48.2, 1650 yards—16:50.2. Age—20 years, height—6', weight—173 pounds. Began swimming competitively at age 13.

Coached by Don Talbot of Sydney, Australia, and James Counsilman, Indiana University.

Bob does pulley weight exercises, but has also done some weight lifting and isometric contractions.

FAVORITE WORKOUTS

I. 1. Warm up with 400 meter swim.
   2. Swim 20 × 200 meters on 3 min.
   3. Sprint 6 × 25.
   4. Swim 400 easy.
II. 1. Warm up with 400-meter swim.
   2. Kick 400, no time.
   3. Swim 20 × 100 on 1:45.
   4. Pull 400, no time (small tube around ankles).
   5. Swim 8 × 50 from dive.
   6. Swim 400 easy.
III. 1. Warm up with 400 swim.
   2. Swim 4 × 800, 1 min. R.I.
   3. Swim 6 × 25 sprint.
   4. Swim 400 easy.

WARM UP BEFORE COMPETITION

1. Swim 4 to 8 × 50 on 60 sec.
2. Swim easy 400.

3. A few hard 50's.
4. Swim 4 to 6 × 25.
5. Loosen up 200 meters.

BEST REPEATS

Short Course (yards) Average				Long Course (meters) Average			
Dist.	No.	Time	R.I.	Dist.	No.	Time	R.I.
50	30	:27	on 50 sec.	50	32	:31.0	10 sec.
100	15	:56	on 1:45 min.	100	15	1:05+	on 1:45 min.
100	20	:58+	on 1:15 min.	200	20	2:17	on 3 min.
200	8	1:53	on 6 min.	400	8	4:41	on 6 min.
200	16	2:00	on 3 min.	400	5	4:33	on 8 min.
400	4	4:03+	on 10 min.				
400	8	4:12	on 6 min.				
500	4	5:06	on 10 min.				
880	3	9:16	on 17 min.				

BEST KICKING AND PULLING TIMES

Short course

Kicking: 50–:37, 100–1:19, 200–2:47, 440–6:36

Pulling: 50–:25, 100–:56, 200–2:00, 400–4:12, 440–4:38

Long course

Kicking: 50–:47, 100–1:44, 200–3:41, 400–7:59

Pulling: 50–:30, 100–1:04, 200–2:19, 400–4:52

Steve Krause

Former World Record holder in the 1500-meters Freestyle, 16:51.0; Best Times: (short course) 100 yards–:50.3, 200 yards–1:47.6; (long course) 100 meters–:57.0, 200 meters–2:03.2, 400 meters–4:15.6, 1500 meters–16:51.6. Age–16, height–6'2", weight–162 pounds. Began competitive swimming at age 8.

Coached by John Tallman of Cascades Swim Club, Seattle, Washington.

Steve does weight lifting exercises plus some isometric contractions.

Steve does most of his workouts in a short course pool. In the summer of 1966, when he swam the 1500-meter long course in the time of 16:51.6, he was training a total of over 6 miles a day in 3 workouts.

FAVORITE WORKOUTS

I. (long course)
Swim 32 × 100 at 1500-meter pace, leave every 2 min.
II. (short course)
1. Swim 200-yard individual medley warm up.

  2. Swim 200-yard freestyle.
  3. Swim 8 × 440, descending in time from 5 min. to 4:18, leaving every
     7 min.
III. (in a 20-yard pool)
  1. Swim 12 × 40 yards, using all four strokes warm up.
  2. Swim 2 × 440 with 5 min. rest, average 4:35.
  3. Pull 1 × 440.
  4. Swim 2 × 440 with 5 min. rest, time 4:30.
  5. Swim 8 × 40, 2 of each stroke.

TAPER

Tapering begins 3 to 4 weeks before the national meet. Workouts are
decreased in number from 3 to 2 and in distance from 2 miles or over
per workout to 1 mile. Repeat swims are fewer in number and less distance is covered in each repeat. Speed work is increased; for example,
swim 600 warm up, swim hard 200, swim 8 × 100 high quality, swim
8 × 50—2 of each stroke.

WARM UP BEFORE COMPETITION

  1. Loosen up with 600 to 800 swim, progressively picking up speed.
  2. Pace work—swim 3 or 4 × 100 at pace from push-off.
  3. Swim 1 or 2 × 100 from a dive at the speed I want to go out on the first
100 of the race.
  4. Loosen up a little more with some kicking, pulling, and swimming of the
other strokes.
  5. Speed work—sometimes I finish with a couple of hard 50's.

BEST REPEATS

Steve never does any 50-yard repeats short course and seldom does
any 50-meter repeats long course.

20-yard Course				Long Course (meters)			
		Average				Average	
Dist.	No.	Time	R.I.	Dist.	No.	Time	R.I.
100	8	:56	4 min.	100	32	1:09	on 2 min.
440	4	4:33	5 min.	200	8	2:20	2½-3 min.
				400	4	4:37	5 min.
				800	4	11:00	4 min.

Greg Charlton

Holder of World Record for 400 meters—4:08.2, and 440 yards—4:12.2.
Best Times: (long course) 200 meters—1:58.1, 1500 meters—17:03.7; (short
course) 50 yards—:22.3, 100 yards—:48.0, 200 yards—1:45.8, 500 yards—

4:37.8. Age—19, height—6'3", weight—180 pounds. Began competitive swimming at age 9.

Coached by Don Gambril; works out twice a day during the height of the season.

Greg does both weight lifting and isometric contractions. He pulls with a rubber band around his ankles.

FAVORITE WORKOUTS

(Both of these would be done on the same day in a 25-yard pool)

I. 1. Kick 10 × 100 on 1 min. 50 sec., average time—1:28.
   2. Pull 10 × 100 on 1 min. 50 sec., average time—:59.
   3. Swim 6 × 200 on 4 min., average time—2 min. or under.
   4. Swim 15 × 100 freestyle on 1 min. 20 sec., average time—:55+.
   5. Swim 20 × 25 sprints on 30 sec.
II. 1. Kick 10 × 50 on 1 min.
   2. Pull 10 × 50 on 1 min.
   3. Swim 10 × 50 on 1 min.
   4. Swim 5 × 500 on 8 min., average time—5:08.
   5. Swim 10 × 100 any stroke on 2 min.

TAPER

Begins about 2 weeks before the big meet. The type of work depends on how Greg is swimming; in general, there is more speed work.

1. Kick 10 × 50 on 1 min.
2. Pull 10 × 50 on 1 min.
3. Swim 10 × 50 on 1 min.
4. Swim 10 × 100 on 1 min.
5. Swim 10 × 50 hard.

WARM UP BEFORE COMPETITION

1. Swim 500.
2. Kick 200.
3. Pull 200.
4. Swim several 50 sprints.
5. Loosen down 500 easy swim.

BEST REPEATS

	Short Course (yards)				Long Course (meters)		
		Average				Average	
Dist.	No.	Time	R.I.	Dist.	No.	Time	R.I.
50	30	:27+	20 sec.	100	30	:63	1 min.
100	15	:55+	20 sec.	200	16	2:15	2 min.
200	10	1:56	2 min.	400	10	4:45	3 min.
500	6	5:08	3 min.	800	3	9:28	4 min.

BEST KICKING AND PULLING TIMES

Short course
Kicking: 50 yds—:35, 100 yds—1:18, 400 yds—5:58
Pulling: 50 yds—:26, 100 yds—:53, 200 yds—1:57, 400 yds—4:12

Long course
Pulling: 50 meters—:28, 100 meters—1:03, 200 meters—2:18, 400 meters—4:45

BUTTERFLYERS

Sharon Stouder

Winner of three Gold Medals in the 1964 Olympic Games—100-meter Butterfly (:64.7); member of winning 400-meter Medley Relay and 400-meter Freestyle Relay; second place in the 100-meter Freestyle (:59.9). Best Times: (short course) 50 yard Freestyle—:25.0, 100—:54.2, 200—1:59.1, 400—4:20; 50 yard Butterfly—:26, 100 yard—:58.0, 200 yard—2:10.0; (long course) Freestyle—50 meter—:27.5, 100 meter—:59.9, 200 meter—2:14.3, 400 meter—4:48.9; Butterfly—50 meter—:28.5, 200 meter—2:26.3. Age—17, height—5'8", weight—142 pounds. Began competitive swimming at age 8.

Coached by Don Gambril of the City of Commerce, California.

Sharon does most of her workouts using the freestyle; she swims very little of it in the butterfly except when she is getting ready for the big meets. Even at this time she does only part of her workout in butterfly. She considers herself to be primarily a freestyler who swims butterfly as a sideline.

FAVORITE WORKOUTS (LONG COURSE)

I. 1. Swim 400 warm up.
    2. Swim 10 × 50 on 1 min., average :35 sec.
    3. Swim 4 × 200 on 5 min., average 2:30.
    4. Kick 4 × 100, average 1:25.
    5. Pull 4 × 200, average 2:40.
    6. Swim 8 × 50, average :30.0.
    7. Swim 30 × 20-yard sprints on 30 sec.
    8. Kick 500.
    9. Pull 500 (rubber band around ankles).
   10. Swim 500.
II. 1. Kick 10 × 50 on 1 min.
    2. Pull 10 × 50 on 1 min.
    3. Swim 10 × 50 on 1 min.
    4. Kick 2 × 200 on 5 min., average 3 min.
    5. Pull 4 × 100 on 2 min., average 1:14.
    6. Swim 8 × 150 on 5 min., average 1:50.

7. Swim 8 × 50 on 4 min. (4 × 50 fly—:32 and 4 × 50 freestyle—:32).
8. Swim 30 × 20 yard sprints.

III. 1. Swim 400 warm up.
2. Swim a pyramid build-up—50, 100, 150, 200, 300, 400, 300, 200, 150, 100, 50 (pyramid build-up allows 1 min. per length for starting time of the next repeat swim, i.e., if Sharon swam a 100—2 lengths, she begins the next repeat 2 min. after she started the 100).
3. Kick 2 × 400 on 10 min., average 6:15.
4. Pull 2 × 400 on 8 min., average 5:20.
5. Swim 5 × 75 on 2 min., average :52.0.

TAPER

Two and a half weeks before a big meet begin doing more speed work with shorter distances.

1. Swim 20 × 50 on 1 min.
2. Kick 4 × 50 on 4 min.
3. Pull 4 × 50 on 4 min.
4. Swim 4 × 50 on 4 min.
4. Kick 2 × 25.
6. Pull 2 × 25.
7. Swim 4 × 25.

WARM UP BEFORE COMPETITION

1. Swim 800 easy.
2. Kick 400.
3. Pull 200.
4. Swim 4 × 50 on 1 min.
5. Swim 2 or 3 × 25 with long rest.

BEST REPEATS (ALL FREESTYLE)

Short Course (yards)				Long Course (meters)			
Dist.	No.	Average Time	R.I.	Dist.	No.	Average Time	R.I.
50	10	:27+	on 2 min.	50	10	:29+	on 2 min.
100	5	:57+	on 3 min.	100	5	1:05	on 3 min.
200	4	2:07	on 5 min.	200	4	2:28	on 5 min.
500	5	5:48	on 8 min.	400	5	4:56.5	on 8 min.
				800	3	10:14	on 15 min.

BEST KICKING AND PULLING TIMES

Kicking (Crawl): 50—:31, 100—1:10, 200—2:32

Kicking (Fishtail): 50—:32, 100—1:16

Pulling (Crawl): 50—:27.5, 100—:59.2, 200—2:11.3

Kicking (Crawl): 50—:34, 100—1:21, 200—2:50, 400—5:53

Kicking (Fishtail): 50—:35, 100—1:26

Pulling (Crawl): 50—:29.4, 100—1:08, 200—2:27.8, 400—5:10

Pulling (Butterfly): 50–:31.8, 100–   Pulling (Butterfly): 50–:31.8, 100–
    1:05, 200–2:30   1:15

Ada Kok

Netherlands' World Record holder at the 100-meter Butterfly–1:04.5, and 200-meter Butterfly–2:21.0. Age–19, height–6', weight–191 pounds.

INTERVIEW WITH AUTHOR, DECEMBER 29, 1965

Ada rides bicycle daily (1 to 2 hours) in going to and from practice. In the winter she works out once a day most of the time, doing 1000 to 1500 meters in a pool filled with recreational swimmers. She does very little kicking; more pulling than kicking. She tries to do one hard set of repeats each day, such as 5 × 200 meters. She does these in an average time of about 2:45 (short course) with 2 to 4 minute rest interval. The total time of workout is approximately 1 hour. Another set which she does on alternate days is 8 to 10 × 100, average 1:18 to 1:20. She likes to swim freestyle in many of her workouts.

In the summer Ada works approximately an hour in the morning in an indoor 25-meter pool and about an hour in the afternoon in a 50-meter pool. During the summer of 1964, in training for the Olympic Games, she worked as many as 4 hours a day, and she felt this much hard work hurt her preparation for the Games. She tapers 3 days and reduces her workouts to about 500 meters. She warms up very little, generally doing only 300 to 400 meters with no sprints in her warm up.

Susan Pitt

National AAU Champion in the 100- and 200-meter Butterfly. Best Times: (long course) 100 meters–:65.5, 200 meters–2:26.6; (short course) 50 yards–:28.0, 100 yards–:59.2, 200 yards–2:09.6. Age–17, height–5'8", weight–132 pounds. Began swimming competitively at age 10.

Coached by Frank Elm, Rutgers University.

Sue has done no weight lifting or isometric contractions. She does her pulling drills with a kick board held between the legs. Sue works out twice a day during the season and has, on occasion, worked out 3 times a day.

FAVORITE WORKOUTS (LONG COURSE)

Sue might possibly do 2 of the following workouts in 1 day.

I. 1. Warm up 400 easy freestyle swim.
   2. Swim 4 to 8 broken 200 (R.I.–10 sec. after each 50 and a few min-

utes between each broken 200). Three to four of these will be butterfly, the rest will be the other strokes or individual medley.

    3. Kick 8 × 100, 30 sec. R.I.

    4. Pull 8 × 100, 30 sec. R.I.

    5. Swim some hard 25 sprints.

II. 1. Warm up 400 swim easy freestyle.

    2. Swim 2 × 400 individual medley, in 6 min. each.

    3. Swim 2 × broken 400 individual medley, stopping 15 sec. after each 100.

    4. Kick 800 meters using all strokes.

    5. Pull 800 meters using all strokes.

    6. Swim 8 to 10 × 50, half or more of them butterfly.

III. 1. Warm up 400 easy swim freestyle.

    2. (a) Swim 4 to 6 broken 200's, 15 sec. rest after each 50. Best time for broken 200-meters long course—2:16+. Sue's average time is about 2.20 to 2:24; a long rest of 3 to 5 min. is used between each broken 200.

    (b) Swim 8 to 10 broken 100 meters, 10 sec. rest after the first 50. Sue's best time for a broken 100 is :63, average time is between 66 and 69 sec. A long rest of 2 to 4 min. is used between each broken 100.

    3. Swim some sprint 25's with a long rest.

TAPER

Sue starts tapering 5 or 6 days before the Nationals. She does not taper for small meets. During tapering, she concentrates on speed and takes a longer rest between repeats.

    1. Warm up 400 easy swim freestyle.

    2. Swim 2 × broken 200 butterfly.

    3. Kick 200 to 400 easy.

    4. Pull 200 to 400 easy.

    5. Swim 2 to 8 × 50 butterfly (hard).

    6. Swim 4 × 25 all-out sprints butterfly.

WARM UP BEFORE COMPETITION

Before preliminaries:

    1. Swim about 400 easy freestyle.

    2. Kick 200 to 400 easy fishtail and freestyle.

    3. Pull 200 to 400 easy freestyle (primarily).

    4. Swim 200 (or until loosened up) any stroke, mostly freestyle.

    5. Swim 4 or 5 × 50, beginning with medium effort freestyle and ending with 90 per cent effort butterfly.

    6. Swim 1 or 2 hard 25's butterfly.

    7. Loosen down 100 very easy.

Before finals:

1. Swim until loosened up.
2. Kick 100 or 200 easy.
3. Pull 100 or 200 easy, mostly freestyle.
4. Swim a little easy (100 or 200) to loosen up.
5. Swim 2, 3, or 4 × 50, building up to a fairly hard 50 butterfly on the last 50.
6. Swim 1 or 2 × 25 all-out.
7. Swim an easy *loosen-down* [3] 100.

Before the finals of the 100, Sue emphasizes more speed work in her warm up than she does for the 200.

BEST REPEATS

Sue does most of her repeat swims by doing broken swims (see Chapter VIII, pp. 199-233); a broken 200 might consist of 4 × 50 with a 10 second rest between each 50.

Short Course (yards)				Long Course (meters)			
Dist.	No.	Average Time	R.I.	Dist.	No.	Average Time	R.I.
50	4	:30-:33	10-20 sec.	50	4	:32-:35	10-20 sec.

(Sue will do 3 to 6 broken 200's in one workout with several min. rest between each set)

(Several min. rest taken between each set)

100	2	1:06-1:11	15-20 sec.	100	2	1:06-1:11	15-20 sec.

The following 200's are not done as a broken set

200	4 to 8	2:25-2:32	3 min.

Kevin Berry

1964 Olympic Champion in the 200-meter Butterfly in the World Record time of 2:06.6. Best Times: (long course) 100 meters—58.5; (short course) 100 yards—:51.7, 200 yards—1:53.7. Age—20, height—5'10", weight —193 pounds. Began swimming competitively at age 11.

Coached by Don Talbot of Sydney, Australia, and James Counsilman, Indiana University.

Kevin does dry land exercises with weights and also does isometric contractions. He does most of his workouts swimming the butterfly stroke.

---

[3] The term "loosen-down" is used by many swimmers to refer to the period of easy swimming in the warm up that often follows some hard sprinting.

FAVORITE WORKOUTS (LONG COURSE)

I. 1. Swim 400 crawl easy (warm up).
    2. Kick 400 (fishtail).
    3. Swim 4 × 400 butterfly, 6 min. R.I., average 5:06 to 5:12.
    4. Swim 6 × 25 sprints.
    5. Swim 400 crawl easy.
II. 1. Swim 400 crawl (warm up).
    2. Swim 2 × broken 400 (8 × 50, 10 sec. R.I.) first 400 under 5 min., second under 4:40.
    3. Kick 200 easy.
    4. Kick 4 × 100 (fishtail) on 3 min., average 1:30.
    5. Pull 200 easy crawl.
    6. Pull 8 × 50 butterfly on 60 sec., average 36 to 38 sec.
    7. Swim 15 × 100 on 2 min., average 1:08 to 1:10.
III. "I have swum the following workout only a couple of times, but I think it is very good."
    1. Warm up 200 easy crawl.
    2. Do the following swimming repeats, trying to do as many fly as possible; fairly long rest. 800, 400, 200, 100, 50, 50, 100, 200, 400, 800.

TAPER

Six to eight days before the big race. "When I start my taper, I like to reduce my load drastically, as it gives me a good feeling—particularly mentally. I like to do more speed work and sharpen up with 50's and 25's.

WARM UP BEFORE COMPETITION

1. Swim 400 or further easy crawl.
2. Swim 6 × 25 sprints.
3. Pace a 50 from a dive at the speed I want to hit on the way to the 200.

BEST REPEATS

Short Course (yards)				Long Course (meters)			
Dist.	No.	Average Time	R.I.	Dist.	No.	Average Time	R.I.
50	30	:28.0	on 1 min.	50	30	:30.8	on 1 min.
100	15	:59+	on 2 min.	50	32	:35	on 10 sec.
200	8	2:03+	on 5 min.	100	15	1:08+	on 2⅔ min.
440	4	4:51	on 12 min.	100	20	1:09+	on 2 min.
				200	8	2:21+	on 6 min.
				200	16	2:28	30 to 45 sec.

BEST KICKING AND PULLING TIMES

Kicking: 50—:34, 100—1:15, 200—
              2:37, 440—6:12
Pulling: 50—:28, 100—:65, 200—
              2:21, 440—5:52

Kicking: 50—:39, 100—1:27, 200—
              3:15, 400—6:51
Pulling: 50—:35, 100—1:16, 200—
              2:50

Fred Schmidt

1964 Olympic Games Gold Medal winner as member of the 400-meter Medley Relay, his time for the Butterfly leg of the relay was :56.9; Bronze Medal winner in the 200-meter Butterfly event (2:08.0), his best long course time; short course 100 fly—:50.9 and 200 fly—1:51.4. Age—21, height—6'1½", weight—182 pounds. Began swimming competitively at age 8.

Coached by James Counsilman, Indiana University.

Fred likes to do dry land exercises, primarily barbell work and with the latissimus machine, both out of season and during the competitive season, up to within 2 weeks of the big meet.

FAVORITE WORKOUTS

I. 1. Swim 400 yards.
    2. Swim 16 × 50 on 60 sec., half free—half fly, average short course—:31, long course—:36.
    3. Kick 400, then 8 × 50 on 60 sec., average short course—:31, long course—:36.
    4. Pull 400, then 8 × 50 on 60 sec. (using small tube around ankles), average short course—:32, long course—:37.
    5. Swim 30 × 50 on 60 sec., average short course—:28.5, long course—:32.
II. 1. and 2. Same as above.
    3. Kick 400, then 4 × 100 on 3 min., average short course—1:08, long course—1:16.
    4. Pull 400, then 4 × 100 on 3 min., average short course—1:08, long course—1:19.
    5. Swim 8 × 150 on 5 min., average short course—1:33, long course—1:48.
III. 1. through 4. Same as number II workout above.
    5. Swim 15 × 100 on 2½ min., average short course—:59.0, long course—1:09.

TAPER

The last 2 weeks before big meet, do more speed and pace work.

1. Swim 400.
2. Swim 8 × 50 on 60 sec.
3. Kick 400, then 4 × 50.
4. Pull 400.

5. Swim 6 × 100 on 3 min.
6. Swim 6 × 100 on 1½ min.

WARM UP BEFORE COMPETITION

1. Swim 400.
2. Kick 400.
3. Pull 400.
4. Swim 8 × 50 progressive, 1 min. R.I.

BEST REPEATS

	Short Course (yards)				Long Course (meters)		
Dist.	No.	Average Time	R.I.	Dist.	No.	Average Time	R.I.
50	36	:27.7	on 1 min.	50	30	:30	on 1 min.
100	15	:60+	on 3 min.	100	15	1:09+	on 3 min.
200	6	2:07	on 5 min.	200	6	2:27	on 6 min.
400	3	4:45	on 12 min.	400	3	5:17	on 12 min.

BEST KICKING AND PULLING TIMES

Kicking: 50–:27+, 100–:60+, 200–
2:15, 400–4:47, 440–5:14

Pulling: 50–:29, 100–1:05, 200–
2:19, 400–5:00, 440–5:28

Kicking: 50–:33, 100–1:13, 200–
2:37, 400–5:32

Pulling: 50–:34, 100–1:15, 200–
2:42, 400–5:49

Carl Robie

Silver Medal winner in the 200 Butterfly event, 1964 Olympic Games
(2:07.5). Best Times: (short course) 100 yards–52.1, 200 yards–1:52.1;
(long course) 100 meters–:58.1. Age–21, height–5'10", weight–160
pounds. Began swimming competitively at age 10.

Coached by Gus Stager of the University of Michigan.

Carl does most of his practice sessions using the crawl stroke. He does
no dry land exercises. Carl has a great ability to perform in repeat swims.
He works out twice a day when training hard.

FAVORITE WORKOUTS (LONG COURSE)

I. 1. Swim 400 freestyle (warm up).
   2. Kick 400.
   3. Pull 400 (drags feet).
   4. Swim 4 × 400 freestyle, 5 min. R.I., average 4:32.
   5. Kick 800.
   6. Pull 800.
   7. 12 × 50 (butterfly or freestyle), 30 sec. R.I.
II. 1. Swim 400 (warm up).
    2. Swim 6 × 200 butterfly, 2½ min. R.I., average 2:17.

3. Kick 2 × 200 butterfly.
4. Pull 2 × 200 freestyle.
5. Swim 16 × 50, 30 sec. R.I.

TAPER

Five to seven days; more speed work. Works out the same as the 2 above, but the repeat swims are cut in half and are done at a faster rate.

WARM UP BEFORE COMPETITION

1. Swim 400 to 800 warm up, freestyle.
2. Kick 200.
3. Swim 4 × 50.

BEST REPEATS

Short Course (yards)		Average		Long Course (meters)		Average	
Dist.	No.	Time	R.I.	Dist.	No.	Time	R.I.
50	20	:29+	30 sec.	50	16	:31+	30 sec.
100	10	:60	1 min.	100	12	1:07+	1 min.
200	4	2:05	2½ min.	200	4	2:17	2½ min.

BEST KICKING AND PULLING TIMES

Kicking: 50—:31, 100—1:07, 200—
2:30

Kicking: 50—:34, 100—1:14, 200—
2:42, 400—5:31.5

Pulling: 50—:28.0, 100—:58.0, 200—
2:02

Pulling: 50—:30, 100—:64, 200—2:21

BACKSTROKERS

Cathy Ferguson

Olympic Champion (1964) in 100-meter Backstroke and World Record holder in that event (1:07.7). Best Times: (long course) 200 meters —2:27.4; (short course) 50 yards—:28.8, 100 yards—:60.9, 200 yards— 2:12.7. Age—18, height—5'8", weight—135 pounds. Began swimming competitively at age 10.

Coached by Peter Daland of Los Angeles Athletic Club.

Cathy does only one form of dry land exercises—pulley weights.

FAVORITE WORKOUTS

I. 1. Warm up, 8 × 50, 20 sec. R.I.
   2. Swim 8 × 400 yards freestyle, 1 min. 20 sec. R.I. (average short course 400 yards—4:45, long course 400 meters—5:05).

II. 1. Swim warm up, 8 × 50, 20 sec. R.I.
2. Swim 4 × 200 backstroke (average short course 200 yards—2:22.0, long course 200 meters—2:38.0).
3. Kick 400, don't time.
4. Pull 400, don't time.
5. Swim 8 × 50 freestyle (average short course 50 yards—:29.0, long course 50 meters—:31.0).

III. 1. Swim warm up 8 × 50.
2. Swim 5 × 800 freestyle (long course average—10:32).
3. Kick 400, don't time.
4. Pull 400, don't time.

TAPER

Ten to fourteen days; more speed work with more rest.

1. Swim 8 × 50.
2. Swim 4 × 100 backstroke, 3 to 5 min. R.I.
3. Kick 200.
4. Pull 200.
5. Swim 3 × 50, 3 to 5 min. R.I.

WARM UP BEFORE COMPETITION

1. Swim 4 × 50 freestyle.
2. Swim 400 freestyle, don't time.
3. Kick 200 freestyle.
4. Kick 200 backstroke.
5. Sprint 3 or 4 × 50 with long rest interval.

BEST REPEATS

Short Course (yards)				Long Course (meters)			
Dist.	No.	Average Time	R.I.	Dist.	No.	Average Time	R.I.
50	4	:33	10 sec.	50	4	:35.0	10 sec.
100	4	1:06	25 sec.	100	4	1:15.0	25 sec.
200	4	2:22	1 min.	200	4	2:38.0	1 min.

BEST KICKING AND PULLING TIMES

Kicking: 50—:41, 100—1:28, 200—3:02

Pulling: 50—:37, 100—1:17, 200—2:42

Kicking: 50—:50, 100—1:42, 200—3:23

Pulling: 50—:40, 100—1:30, 200—3:00

Judy Humbarger

National AAU Backstroke Champion. Best Times: (long course) 50 meters Backstroke—:32.4, 100 meters—1:09.0, 200 meters—2:28.0; (short course) 50 yards—:28.8, 100 yards—1:01.5, 200 yards—2:11.8. Age—17, height—5'7", weight—143 pounds. Began swimming competitively at age 7.

Coached by Stefano Hunyadfi, Club Olympia, Fort Wayne, Indiana, Judy does some weight lifting and some isometric contractions. She trains for the backstroke, freestyle, and individual medley. In the smaller meets she will compete in all events except the breaststroke, but in the big meets limits her competition to the backstroke and individual medleys. She trains about 10 months out of the year; during the height of the indoor season she trains twice a day, and during the height of the outdoor season, 2 or 3 times a day.

FAVORITE WORKOUTS

Short course (yards):

1. Swim 400 freestyle.
2. Kick 5 × 100 on 2½ min., time—1:25.
3. Swim 4 × 400 freestyle on 6 min., average time 4:50.
4. Pull 10 × 50 on 1 min., swim 2 × 50 of each stroke and 4 × 50 of freestyle.
5. Swim 10 × 100 backstroke on 1½ min., average time 1:08—1:10.

Long course (meters):

Morning:

1. Swim 400 individual medley.
2. Kick 3 × 200 on 5 min., 2 of them freestyle, 1 of them backstroke.
3. Swim 5 × broken 400 freestyle on 8 min., average time 5:15.
4. Swim 10 × 50 on 1 min., 5 of them fly, time :39, 5 of them backstroke, time :36.

Afternoon:

1. Pull 200 warm up.
2. Kick 200 warm up.
3. Swim 4 × 800 freestyle on 15 min., average time 11:15.
4. Swim 8 × 50 on 1½ min., 2 of each stroke.

TAPER (DIRECT QUOTATION)

"Start 10 days before the national meet. Start easing down on workouts. I do more speed work with more rest and a lot of long, easy swimming."

Short course (yards):

1. Warm up 800, a little of each—swim, kick, pull.
2. Swim 1 × 200 backstroke—out easy, back hard, about 2:21.
3. Swim 2 × 100 backstroke, first one at 1:07, second at 1:03.
4. Swim 4 × 50 freestyle with long rest, times—:25+ to :27+.
5. Swim 10 × 25 sprints with long rest, 2 of each stroke, 4 of them freestyle.
6. Swim 1 × 100 easy.

WARM UP BEFORE COMPETITION

1. Swim 400.
2. Kick 400.
3. Pull 200.
4. Swim 200 to 400 yards.
5. Swim 1 × 100 at pace of the stroke being swum that day.
6. Swim 2 × 50 hard.
7. Swim 4 or 5 × 25, all strokes.
8. Swim easy 200.

BEST REPEATS (ALL BACKSTROKE)

Short Course (yards)				Long Course (meters)			
Dist.	No.	Average Time	R.I.	Dist.	No.	Average Time	R.I.
50	10	:30+	1 Min.	50	10	:34+	1:15
100	10	1:10	1½ min.	100	10	1:16	2 min.
200	8	2:22	3½ min.	200	4	2:40	4 min.

BEST KICKING AND PULLING TIMES

Short course

Kicking: 50 yards—:37, 100 yards—1:23, 200 yards—2:55
Pulling (rubber band around the ankles): 50 yards—:31, 100 yards—1:10, 200 yards—2:35

Long course

Kicking: 50 meters—:41, 100 meters—1:38, 200 meters—3:30
Pulling: 50 meters—:35, 100 meters—1:19

Charles Hickcox

National Champion and World Record Holder, 100- and 200-meter Backstroke. Best Times: (long course) 100-meter Backstroke—:59.1, 200-meter Backstroke—2:09.4, 100-meter Freestyle—:53.6 (relay start), 200-meter Freestyle—2:00.1 (relay start), 400-meter Freestyle—4:20.1, 1500-meter Freestyle—17:43.1, 100-meter Butterfly—:57.8, 200-meter Butterfly—2:13.2, 100-meter Breaststroke—1:19.1, 200 meters—2:56.2, 200-meter Individual Medley—2:15.0, 400 meters—4:53.1; (short course) 100-yard Backstroke—:52.6, 200-yard Backstroke—1:55.3, 100-yard Freestyle—:47.6, 200-yard Freestyle—1:46.1, 50-yard Butterfly—:23.0, 100-yard Butterfly—:51.1, 200-yard Butterfly—1:56.1, 100-yard Breaststroke—1:07.1, 200-yard Breaststroke—2:25.2, 200-yard Individual Medley—1:57.9, 400-yard Individual Medley—4:16.3. Age—20, height—6'1", weight—173 pounds. Began swimming competitively at age 13.

Coached by James Counsilman, Indiana University.

Charley does both weight lifting and isometric contractions. His workouts are listed with the backstrokers, although he might as appropriately be listed with the individual medley swimmers. He is also one of the finest butterfly swimmers in the world. He trains twice a day during the indoor season and either 2 or 3 times a day during the summer season. He has a unique combination of tremendous breakaway speed plus above-average endurance. Charles pulls with a tube wrapped around his ankles.

FAVORITE WORKOUTS (LONG COURSE)

A typical summer day with three workouts.

Morning workout:

1. Swim 15 × 100 progressive set (picking up speed on each 100) on 1:45. Freestyle times begin at 1:20 and end at 1:01, backstroke times begin at 1:25 and end at 1:06.
2. Swim pace 400 meters—freestyle in 4:40 or backstroke in 5:00.
3. Kick 400 easy, 100 of each stroke.
4. Kick 4 × 100, 1 of each stroke, on 2:30.
5. Pull 400 easy, 100 of each stroke.
6. Pull 4 × 100, 1 of each stroke, on 2:30.
7. Swim 20 × 50 on 60 sec., average time for freestyle :30, for backstroke :33, for butterfly :31.

Noon workout:

1. Swim 400 individual medley—no time.
2. Swim 3 × 400 with 5 min. rest. Times: 400 free—4:38, 400 individual medley—5:07, 400 back—under 5 min.

Afternoon workout:

1. Swim 16 × 50 on 60 sec., 4 of each stroke.
2. Pace either a 400 or an 800 freestyle or backstroke.
3. Kick 300.
4. Pull 8 × 50, 2 of each stroke.
5. Swim 5 × 100 with 4 to 5 min. rest (swim at least 2 or 3 strokes). Typical good set: 100 freestyle—1:02, 100 free—1:01, 100 backstroke—1:06.1, 100 back—1:03.8, 100 fly—:59.3.

TAPER

Charles likes to taper no more than 1 week. He reduces his workouts to 2 a day with a total distance per day of less than 4000 meters.

1. Swim 8 × 100 progressive set on 2 mins.
2. Kick 400.
3. Kick 2 × 100.
4. Pull 400.
5. Pace 400, backstroke under 4:55 or freestyle under 4:35.
6. Swim 3 × 100 hard.
7. Swim 3 × 50 sprints.

WARM UP BEFORE COMPETITION (LONG COURSE)

Before preliminaries of backstroke race:

1. Swim about 600 to 1000, all strokes.
2. Swim 8 × 50, all strokes, ending with the last 2 × 50 backstroke—:30 or better.
3. Kick 300 to 500 easy.
4. Swim 3 or 4 × 25, at least 2 backstroke at about :13.6.
5. Swim 200 to loosen down.

Before finals:

1. Swim 400 to 600, mostly freestyle, the last 100 or 200 backstroke.
2. Swim 3 × 50 progressive backstroke.
3. Swim 2 × 25 sprint time—:13.6 to :13.9.
4. Loosen down with a 100 swim.

In warming up before swimming the individual medley, equal emphasis is placed on all strokes.

BEST REPEATS (ALL LISTED TIMES ARE FOR BACKSTROKE)

Short Course (yards)				Long Course (meters)			
Dist.	No.	Average Time	R.I.	Dist.	No.	Average Time	R.I.
50	30	:29.0	on 1 min.	50	30	:32.6	on 1 min.
100	15	:60.5	on 2½ min.	100	15	1:08.3	on 2½ min.
200	8	2:04.4	on 5 min.	200	6	2:22.9	on 6 min.
440	4	4:51.2	on 10 min.	400	2	4:51.6	on 12 min.
880	1	9:34.2		800	1	9:59.2	

BEST KICKING AND PULLING TIMES

Short course	Long course
Kicking: 50 yards—:35.2, 100 yards—1:12.2, 440 yards—6:01	Kicking: 50 meters—:38.7, 100 meters—1:29
Pulling: 50 yards—:31.2, 100 yards—1:08.4, 440 yards—5:32.7	Pulling: 50 meters—:34.9, 100 meters—1:19.2

Gary Dilley

Silver Medal winner in 1964 Olympic Games 200-meter Backstroke (2:10.5). Best Times: (short course) 100 yards—:52.5, 200 yards—1:56.2. Age—20, height—6'1", weight—170 pounds. Began competitive swimming at age 12.

Coached by Glenn Hummer of the Huntington, Indiana YMCA and Charles MacCaffree of Michigan State University.

Gary likes to swim a lot of his practice lengths freestyle and has swum the 100-yard Freestyle in a little over 47 seconds.

FAVORITE WORKOUTS

I. 1. Swim 8 × 400 on 8 min.
   2. Swim 32 × 50 on 1 min.
   3. Pull 14 × 100 on 2 min. (drags feet).
   4. Kick 8 × 100 on 2½ min.
   5. Swim 400 easy.
II. 1. Swim 10 × 300 on 7 min.
   2. Swim 32 × 50 on 1 min.
   3. Pull 7 × 200 on 4 min.
   4. Kick 4 × 200 on 6 min.
   5. Swim 800 easy.

TAPER

For 2½ to 3 weeks, concentrating on short sprint work.

Sample workout:
1. Pull 400.
2. Kick 400.
3. Swim 10 to 15 × 50 on 1½ to 2 min.
4. Swim 400 easy.

WARM UP BEFORE COMPETITION

1. After loosening up a little, time a moderate 200-meter swim at around 2:30.
2. Swim 1 × 50 all-out.
3. Swim 3 × 25 progressive sprints.
4. Swim a little to loosen up.

| Short Course (yards) | | | | Long Course (meters) | | | |
Dist.	No.	Average Time	R.I.	Dist.	No.	Average Time	R.I.
100	25	1:03	on 3 min.	50	25	:33.3	on 1 min.
200	15	2:10.3	on 5 min.	100	15	1:10.0	on 3 min.
				200	6	2:27	on 5 min.
				400	4	5:22	on 15 min.

BEST KICKING AND PULLING TIMES

Kicking: 50—:33, 100—1:15

Pulling: 100—1:08, 200—2:20

Kicking: 50—:37, 100—1:27, 200—3:21, 400—6:51

Pulling: 50—:34, 100—1:19, 200—2:40

Jed Graef and Thompson Mann

These two swimmers trained together in the summers under the coaching of Robert Alexander, North New Jersey Swim Club. Their workouts were similar so they are listed together here. Jed Graef won the 1964 Olympic Games 200-meter Backstroke event in the World Record time of 2:10.3. Jed, age–23, height–6'6", weight–200 pounds, began swimming competitively at age 10. Thompson Mann was a member of the winning 400-meter Medley Relay in the 1964 Olympic Games. His time for the 100-meter Backstroke leg of the relay set a World Record for 100 meters of :59.6. Thompson, age–21, height–6'1", weight–170 pounds, began swimming competitively at age 9. The following workout was used daily in the summer of 1964 for a period of 2 weeks in the month of August, prior to their making the Olympic Team. The total distance per day was between 2000 and 3000 meters a day, with approximately 5 minutes rest interval between each item.

1. Pull 50, kick 50, and swim 50.
2. Kick 100 moderately hard.
3. Swim 100 meters double overarm backstroke.
4. Swim 150 meters time trial (know your time).
5. Kick 100 easy.
6. Swim 200 meters hard, accentuating the feeling of a strong, hard catch.
7. Pull 50, kick 50, swim 50.
8. Pull 2 × 50 sprints (drag feet).
9. Kick 2 × 50 sprints.
10. Swim 100 meters for time.
11. Swim 200 hard, but not all-out.

Only Items 4 and 10 are timed.

Once the boys had made the Olympic Team they did workouts identical with those done by the rest of the Olympic Team. Jed was placed in the middle distance category and Thompson in the sprinter category; their total daily distance was increased to between 4 and 5 miles per day.

TAPER

Starts 3 weeks before big meet. They do more speed work and less distance. Daily distance starting 3 weeks prior to a big meet is about 1200 meters. Two weeks before the meet this distance is decreased to about 1000 meters.

WARM UP BEFORE COMPETITION

Approximate total distance—1000 to 1500 meters.

1. Swim 200 easy.
2. Kick 100, pull 100, swim 100.
3. Swim easy 200.
4. Kick 2 × 100 easy.

5. Pull 2 × 100 easy.
6. Swim 4 × 50 timed, 1 to 2 min. R.I.
7. Swim 100 easy.

BEST REPEAT TIMES

JED GRAEF

Short Course (yards)				Long Course (meters)			
Dist.	No.	Average Time	R.I.	Dist.	No.	Average Time	R.I.
50	10	:27.0	on 1 min.	50	20	:33.6	on 1 min.
100	6	:58.0	on 5 min.	100	15	1:11.2	on 2½ min.
200	6	2:05	on 7 min.	200	8	2:23	on 5 min.

BEST KICKING AND PULLING TIMES (LONG COURSE)

Kicking: 100—1:38, 200—3:31, 400—7:33
Pulling: 100—1:19, 200—2:58, 400—6:20

THOMPSON MANN

Short Course (yards)				Long Course (meters)			
Dist.	No.	Average Time	R.I.	Dist.	No.	Average Time	R.I.
50	16	:29.5	30 sec.	50	40	:34.0	on 1 min.
100	12	:59.0	on 4 min.	100	10	1:08.9	on 5 min.
				200	6	2:21.1	on 6 min.
				400	4	5:02.4	on 12 min.

BEST KICKING AND PULLING TIMES (LONG COURSE)

Kicking: 100—1:39, 200—3:40.1, 400—7:53
Pulling: 200—2:56, 400—6:44

Robert Bennett

Bronze Medal winner in 1960 Olympic Games 100-meter Backstroke and again in 1964 Olympic Games in the 200-meter Backstroke (2:13.1). Age—21, height—6'1", weight—185 pounds. Began swimming competitively at age 10.

Coached by Kris Kristensen of the Kris Kristensen Swim School and by Peter Daland of Southern California University.

FAVORITE WORKOUT

1. Warm up, swim 400.
2. Kick 400 (Bob does his kicking and pulling using freestyle most of the time).
3. Pull 400.
4. Swim 4 × 200 meters backstroke on 5 min., average 2:29.
5. Swim easy 200 meters, rest 5 min.
6. Swim 5 × 100 on 2½ min., average :66.0.
7. Swim easy 100 meters freestyle, 5 min. R.I.
8. Swim 8 × 50 on 1 min.

TAPER

Two weeks before the meet, Bob decreases to 1500 meters a day. One week before the race he cuts down to 800 meters a day.

1. Swim 400 easy, rest 5 min.
2. Swim 3 × 100 backstroke, 30 sec. R.I., average 1:10.
3. Swim 2 × 50, 10 min. R.I., average :29.5.

WARM UP BEFORE COMPETITION

1. Swim 400.
2. Kick 200.
3. Practice turns for about 10 min.
4. Swim 2 × 50 at about :33.0.
5. Swim 1 × 50 at :29.5.
6. Swim 300 easy.

BEST REPEATS

Short Course (yards)				Long Course (meters)			
Dist.	No.	Average Time	R.I.	Dist.	No.	Average Time	R.I.
50	20	:30.0	on 1 min.	50	20	:34	on 1 min.
100	10	1:02	on 2½ min.	100	10	1:10	on 2½ min.
200	8	2:15	on 3 min.	200	8	2:40	on 3 min.
				400	4	5:20	on 10 min.

Thomas Stock

Former World Record holder in 100-meter Backstroke (1:00.9) and 200-meter Backstroke (2:10.9). Best Times: (short course) 100 yards— :53.6, 200 yards—1:55.9. Age—20, height—5′6″, weight—134 pounds, began swimming competitively at age 11.

Coached by James Counsilman. Tom had tremendous endurance and swam the greatest repeat swims and distance backstroke times in practice of any swimmer I have heard about. He swam 9:25.2 for an 880-yard Backstroke and 18:07.7 for 1650 yards (short course). In long course he consistently broke 10 minutes for 800 meters and his best 400-meter Backstroke was 4:36.7. He worked hard on dry land exercise, using weights, isometric contractions, and the double latissimus machine.

FAVORITE WORKOUTS (LONG COURSE)

I. 1. Warm up, 400-meter swim.
    2. Kick 400 easy.
    3. Time 400 kicking, around 6:30.
    4. Pull 400 easy.
    5. Time 400 pulling, around 5:40 (tube around ankles).
    6. Swim 4 × 400, 6 min. R.I., average under 5 min.
II. 1. Warm up, 400 meter swim.
    2. Swim 16 × 50 on 1 min., average :33+.
    3. Kick 400 easy.
    4. Kick 4 × 100 on 3 min., average 1:30+.
    5. Pull 400 easy.
    6. Pull 4 × 100 on 3 min., average 1:19.
    7. Swim 8 × 200 on 6 min., average 2:24.
III. Favorite afternoon (second) workout
    1. Warm up, 500 easy.
    2. Kick 500 easy.
    3. Pull 500 easy.
    4. Swim 8 × 100, 3 min. R.I., average :65+.
    5. Swim 4 × 50 on 3 min. R.I., average :31+.

TAPER

Ten days—shorten total distance and speed up repeat swims.

1. Warm up, 400 swim.
2. Swim 12 to 16 × 50, moderate at first, getting progressively faster.
3. Kick 500 easy, 2 to 4 × 50 kick hard.
4. Pull 400 easy, 2 to 4 × 50 pull hard.
5. Either 3 or 4 × 200 or 6 to 8 × 100, long rest.
6. Sprint 2 × 50 all-out.

WARM UP BEFORE COMPETITION

1. Swim 500 to 800.
2. Kick 200.
3. Swim 8 × 50, every other one hard.
4. Pace 1 × 100, "if I still don't feel loose."

BEST REPEATS

Short Course (yards)				Long Course (meters)			
		Average				Average	
Dist.	No.	Time	R.I.	Dist.	No.	Time	R.I.
50	30	:29+	on 1 min.	50	30	:31+	on 1 min.
100	15	:60.2	on 2½ min.	100	15	:67+	on 2½ min.
200	8	2:02+	on 5 min.	200	8	2:21.6	on 6 min.
440	4	4:46	on 10 min.	400	4	4:48.6	on 12 min.
880	1	9:25.2		800	2	9:56.4	on 24 min.
1650	1	18:07.7					

BEST KICKING AND PULLING TIMES

Kicking: 50–:33, 100–1:11, 200–
2:32, 440–5:52

Pulling: 50–:29, 100–1:04, 200–
2:18, 440–5:26

Kicking: 50–:37, 100–1:19, 200–
2:52, 400–6:02

Pulling: 50–:33, 100–1:12, 200–
2:36, 400–5:39

BREASTSTROKERS

Catie Ball

National AAU Champion, 100- and 200-meter Breaststroke. Best Times:
(short course) 100 yards–1:06.6, 200 yards–2:25.0; (long course) 100
meters–1:14.6, 200 meters–2:39.5. Age–16, height–5'4", weight–125
pounds. Began swimming competitively at age 8.

Coached by George Campbell, Jacksonville, Florida. Catie usually
works out twice a day during the height of the indoor and outdoor seasons. Each workout takes about 1½ hours. She does most of her work
in a short course pool (25 yards).

Catie does some weight lifting, but no isometric contractions. She
kicks by holding onto a board and does her pulling with a pull-buoy (a
plastic leg support).

FAVORITE WORKOUTS (SHORT COURSE)

I. 1. Warm up 800 freestyle swim.
    2. Swim 2 × 400, 1 freestyle and 1 individual medley.
    3. Swim 4 × 200, 2 breaststroke and 2 individual medley.
    4. Swim 8 × 100, 2 breaststroke, 2 individual medley, 2 freestyle, 2 of one
       of the other strokes.
    5. Several sprint 50's.
    Total distance of about 3600 yards.

II. 1. Warm up 400 freestyle swim.
    2. Warm up 400 kick individual medley.
    3. Kick 2 × 200.
    4. Pull 2 × 200.
    5. Kick 4 × 100.
    6. Pull 4 × 100.
    7. Kick 4 × 50.
    8. Pull 4 × 50.
    9. Swim 12 × 50 hard, three of each stroke.
    Total distance—3400 yards.
III. 1. Warm up 400-kick individual medley.
    2. Swim 10 × 200, alternating individual medleys and breaststroke.
    3. Kick 2 × 100 breaststroke.
    4. Pull 2 × 100 breaststroke.
    5. Swim 2 × 100 breaststroke.
    6. Swim 2 × 100 freestyle.
    7. Swim 2 × 100 individual medley.
    8. Swim 12 × 50, 3 of each stroke.
    Total distance—3900 to 4000 yards.

TAPER

Begins 2 weeks before indoor nationals and 3 weeks before outdoor nationals. Catie does more speed work during taper.

1. Warm up 4 × 100 kick, R.I. 1 min.
2. Warm up 4 × 100 pull, R.I. 1 min.
3. Swim 5 or 6 × 200, usually individual medleys or freestyle. Rest interval is long (or until Catie says she is ready).
4. Swim 8 or 10 × 100, usually individual medleys or freestyle. Rest interval as in item 3 above.

WARM UP BEFORE COMPETITION

1. Swim 200 individual medley.
2. Kick 200 individual medley.
3. Pull 200 individual medley.
4. Kick 200 to 300 breaststroke.
5. Pull 100 to 200 breaststroke.
6. Swim 1 or 2 × 50 of each stroke.
7. Swim 2 or 3 × 50 breaststroke.
8. Swim 5 or 6 × 25 breaststroke.

BEST REPEATS

Catie does not always time all of her repeats and does most of her series of repeats with only part of the series being breaststroke. The times listed below are for the breaststroke part of the series.

| | | Short Course (yards) | |
| | | Average | |
Dist.	No.	Time	R.I.
50	5	:33.5	on 1½ min.
100	4	1:09.6	on 4 min.
200	2	2:32.0	on 8 min.

BEST KICKING AND PULLING TIMES

Kicking (short course): 100 yards—1:19, 200 yards—2:50
Kicking (long course): 100 meters—1:30, 200 meters—3:05

Claudia Kolb

Silver Medal winner, 1964 Olympic Games in 200-meter Breaststroke (2:47.6). Best Times: (short course) 50 yards—:32.2, 100 yards—1:09.1, 200 yards—2:27.4; (long course) 50 meters—:36.2, 100 meters—1:17.1. Age—16, height—5′6″, weight—137 pounds. Started competitive swimming at age 7.

Coached by George Haines, Santa Clara Swim Club. Claudia also trains for the individual medley.

Claudia does no weight lifting, but does exercise with stretch cords and uses some isometric contractions.

While Claudia is listed here as a breaststroker, she also specializes in the individual medley, where she has held the World Record for the 200 and 400 meters individual medley.

FAVORITE WORKOUTS

I. (short course pool)
   1. Warm up 400.
   2. Swim 8 × 25 moderate.
   3. Swim 2 × 800 freestyle, 7 min. R.I. Times—9:10 and 8:55.
   4. Kick 4 × 200 breaststroke, on every 4 min. Times—2.51, 2:47, 2:45, and 2:42.
   5. Pull 1000, time 11:23 (uses small board to float legs).
   6. Swim 8 × 25 all strokes, leave every 30 sec.
   Total—4200 yards.
II. (long course pool)
   1. Warm up with 400 meters.
   2. Swim 4 × 50 on 1 min.
   3. Swim 8 × 100 freestyle on 2 min., average 1:08 to 1:10.
   4. Pull 4 × 300 on every 5½ min. (2 × 100 butterfly, 1 × 100 breaststroke, and 1 + 100 freestyle).
   5. Kick 8 × 100 breast, on 2 min., average 1:32 to 1:35.
   6. Swim 12 × 50 (6 × 50 butterfly in 34 to 35 sec., 6 × 50 breaststroke in 40 to 41 sec.).
   Total—3600 meters.

III. (long course pool)
   1. Swim 400 meters warm up.
   2. Swim 8 × 200 on 4 min. (4 × 200, time 2:25 to 2:30; 4 × 200, time 2:58 to 3:02).
   3. Kick 2 × 400 breaststroke on 8 min., average 6:30.
   4. Pull 3 × 300 freestyle on 6 min.
   5. Swim 8 × 50 on 1 min., all strokes.
   Total—4300 meters.

TAPER

Two weeks—more speed work and more kicking.

   1. Warm up 400.
   2. 200 total—kick, swim, or pull.
   3. Swim 8 × 25 sprint.
   4. Kick 4 × 200 breaststroke.
   5. Swim 4 × 100 pace, long rest.
   6. Pull 8 × 50.
   7. Swim 8 × 50 from dive.
   8. Swim 10 × 25.
   9. Swim 200 loosen down.

WARM UP BEFORE COMPETITION

   1. Swim 500.
   2. Pull 400.
   3. Kick 400.
   4. Kick sprint some 25's.
   5. "If I'm competing in a race over 100, I do 4 × 50 and 8 × 25 from a dive. If I'm competing in a 100 or less, I do mostly 25's."
   6. Swim easy 200.

BEST REPEATS

| | Short Course (yards) | | | | Long Course (meters) | | |
| | | Average | | | | Average | |
Dist.	No.	Time	R.I.	Dist.	No.	Time	R.I.
50	10	:34.0	on 1½ min.	50	10	:38+	on 1½ min.
100	8	1:12+	on 2½ min.	100	8	1:22+	on 2½ min.
200	8	2:35	on 5 min.	200	4	2:53+	on 5 min.

BEST KICKING AND PULLING TIMES

Kicking: 50—:36, 100—1:16, 200—2:39, 400—5:35, 800—11:50
Swimming: 400—5:18, 800—11:10

Kicking: 50—:42, 100—1:25, 200—2:58, 400—6:15, 800—13:04
Swimming: 400—6:04, 800—12:52

Claudia does most of her pulling freestyle and for this reason has no times for the breaststroke pulling in her practice sessions.

Chester Jastremski

Former World Record holder and National AAU Champion, Bronze Medal winner in 1964 Olympics 200-meter Breaststroke (see also Table XIII–1). Best Times: (long course) 100 meters—1:07.5, 200 meters—2:28.2; (short course) 100 yards—:58.5, 200 yards—2:09.0. Age—22, height—5'9", weight—160. Began swimming competitively at age 8.

Coached by James Counsilman, Indiana University. Chet did weight lifting and isometric contractions until the last 2 years of competitive swimming, at which time it was felt that he was sufficiently strong. From this point on his dry land exercises were confined to stretching exercises. Chet had a very strong arm pull and a relatively poor kick. He swam good overdistance breaststroke times: long course 400 meters—5:21.2, short course 400 yards—4:50, 440 yards—5:19.8, 880 yards—11:01.2. Chet worked out 2 times a day during the season and occasionally 3 times a day. Approximately 80 to 90 per cent of his training was done using the breaststroke. He pulled with a tube wrapped around his ankles.

FAVORITE WORKOUTS

(Short course in yards, the following 2 workouts would be done in the same day).

Morning before Class—7:30 to 8:30 A.M.:

1. Warm up 400 easy swim.
2. Kick 400.
3. Pull 400.
4. Time 440 breaststroke 5:45 to 5:30.
5. Swim broken 400 breaststroke (4 × 100 with 15 sec. rest, average time 1:12).
6. 4 to 6 × 25 sprints.

Afternoon workout:

1. Warm up 400 easy crawl and breaststroke.
2. Swim 16 × 50 on 1 min., progressively increasing speed with last 50 in :31+.
3. Swim hard 440 breaststroke, average time 5:38; best time 5:19.8.
4. Kick 400 easy crawl or breaststroke.
5. Kick 4 × 100 on 3 min., progressing in speed from 1:30 to 1:23 or better.
6. Pull 400 easy crawl or breaststroke.
7. Pull 4 × 100 on 3 min. breaststroke, progressing in speed from 1:23 to 1:15 or better.
8. Swim 15 × 100 on 2½ min. breaststroke, average time 1:11 or better when in good shape. Chet also liked to swim 8 × 200.
9. Swim 3 to 5 × 25 sprints from a dive—trying to be in the low 13 sec. and occasionally breaking 13 sec.

(Long course in meters, the following 2 workouts would be done in the same day).

Morning workout:

1. Warm up 200 easy, swimming crawl or breaststroke.
2. Swim 8 × 50 breaststroke warm up on 1 min. (sometimes these would be done as a broken 400 with 10 sec. R.I. between each 50).
3. Time a fairly hard 800 meters (around 12 min. and occasionally under 12 min.).
4. Kick 400 easy.
5. Kick 8 × 50 breaststroke on 1½ min., beginning at about 55 sec. and dropping the times until the last 50 was about 45 sec.
6. Pull 400 easy.
7. Pull 8 × 50 breaststroke on 1½ min., beginning at about 45 sec. and dropping the times until the last 50 was about 39 sec.
8. Swim 1 × 400 breaststroke at about 6 min.
9. Swim 8 × 100 on 3 min., average time 1:18.
10. Swim 400 breaststroke under 6 min.
11. Swim 2 or 3 all out 50's, each about 33.5 to 35 sec.

Afternoon workout:

1. Warm up 500 swim.
2. Warm up 500 kick.
3. Warm up 500 pull.
4. Swim a few 50's to get the stroke together.
5. Swim 3 hard 200 meters breaststroke with about 5 min. R.I. between each, average time 2:47, 2:43, trying to break 2:40 on the last.
6. Swim 8 × 50 breaststroke with long rest.

Chet started tapering about 2 weeks before the big meet, reducing total amount of work in practice and working a great deal on pace, particularly the first 50 and 100 of the race. Continued twice-a-day workouts.

Morning workout (long course):

1. Swim 12 × 50 warm up, using all strokes.
2. Kick 400 easy.
3. Kick 2 × 100 for speed.
4. Pull 200 to 400 easy.
5. Swim easy-pace 400 breaststroke, around 5:50.
6. Swim 2 or 3 × 200, one individual medley—the other or others breaststroke.
7. Swim some sprints, such as 2 or 3 × 50 or 1 × 50 and 1 × 100.

Afternoon workout (long course):

1. Swim 8 to 12 × 50 breaststroke warm up.
2. Kick 200 to 400 easy.
3. Swim 3 to 4 × 100 breaststroke, progressively increasing speed from 1:21 to 1:12.
4. Swim an easy 400 (untimed).
5. A few sprints, either 25's or 50's.

The last 3 days before the meet, Chet reduced his work to about 1800 to 2400 meters depending on how he felt. He liked to do speed work right up to the day of the big competition (such as 2 or 3 × 100 or 5 to 6 × 50).

WARM UP BEFORE COMPETITION (LONG COURSE)

1. Ten to 15 minutes of stretching exercises before preliminaries.
2. Swim 400 easy warm up, either crawl or breaststroke.
3. Swim 8 × 50 on 1½ min., progressively increasing speed from 50 sec. to about 36 sec.
4. Kick 200 to 400 easy to loosen up legs.
5. Swim 1 × 100 pace, about 1:18 to 1:20.
6. Swim some hard sprints from a push-off (such as 2 × 50 or 3 × 25).

Before finals:

1. Warm up 200 to 400 swimming breaststroke and crawl.
2. Swim 4 to 6 × 50 progressively.
3. Swim an easy 100 or 200 to loosen up.
4. Swim some hard sprints, 1 or 2 × 50 or 2 or 3 × 25.

BEST REPEATS

Short Course (yards)				Long Course (meters)			
Dist.	No.	Average Time	R.I.	Dist.	No.	Average Time	R.I.
50	30	:31.8	on 60 sec.	50	30	:38.1	on 60 sec.
50	8	:30.2	on 3 min.	50	4	:33.4	on 5 min.
100	15	1:09.1	on 2½ min.	100	15	1:18.3	on 2½ min.
100	4	1:03.2	on 5 min.	100	4	1:14.4	on 6 min.
200	8	2:23	on 5 min.	200	8	2:48	on 6 min.
200	4	2:18	on 8 min.	200	3	2:41	on 10 min.
400	4	5:00	on 12 min.	400	4	5:52	on 12 min.
440	4	5:30	on 12 min.	800	2	12:02	on 24 min.
880	3	12:04	on 24 min.				

BEST KICKING AND PULLING TIMES

Short course (yards)
Kicking: 50–:37, 100–1:19, 200–2:51, 400–6:03, 440–6:39, 880–13:52

Long course (meters)
Kicking: 50–:39.7, 100–1:29, 200–3:17, 400–6:47, 800–14:09

Pulling: 50—:32.8, 100—1:11, 200—   Pulling: 50—:36.8, 100—1:19, 200—
2:37, 400—5:28, 440—6:01,   2:51.6, 400—6:08
880—12:27

Tom Trethewey

Member of the 1964 United States Olympic Team and National AAU Outdoor 100-meter Breaststroke champion—1:08.3. Best Times: (long course) 200 meters breaststroke—2:30.3; (short course) 50 yards—:27.2, 100 yards—:60.0, 200 yards—2:10.4 (NCAA Record). Age—21, height—6'1", weight—164 pounds. Began swimming competitively at age 13.

Coached by James Counsilman, Indiana University.

Tom does weight lifting, isometric contractions, and stretching exercises. He pulls with partially inflated tube wrapped around his ankles. Tom swims 80 to 90 per cent of workouts using breaststroke.

FAVORITE WORKOUTS (SHORT COURSE)

I. 1. Swim 400 warm up, some of it crawl.
    2. Swim 16 × 50 on 60 sec.
    3. Pull 400 easy.
    4. Pull 4 × 100 on 2 or 2½ min., average time 1:18.
    5. Kick 400.
    6. Kick 2 × 200 on 6 min., average time 2:50.
    7. Swim 15 × 100 on 2 or 2½ min., average time 1:09 to 1:13.
II. 1. Swim 400 warm up.
    2. Swim 20 × 50 on 60 sec., alternating one hard 50 with one easy 50.
    3. Pull 400 easy.
    4. Pull 2 × 200 for time, 3 min. R.I.
    5. Kick 400 easy.
    6. Time 440 kick (around 6:16—best time was 6:01).
    7. Swim 5 × 150 hard, long rest of 3 to 5 min., average time 1:45.

TAPER

Begins 10 days before big meet, doing more speed work.

1. Swim 400 warm up.
2. Swim 16 × 50 on 60 sec., alternating one hard, one easy.
3. Kick 200 easy.
4. Kick 4 × 50 hard, average time :37+.
5. Pull 200 easy.
6. Pull 4 × 50 hard, average time :38+.
7. Swim 4 to 6 × 100 with long rest of about 3 min., average time 1:05 or better.
8. Swim some 25 sprints from a dive in the low 13 sec.

WARM UP BEFORE COMPETITION

1. Swim 400 to 800 easy freestyle and breaststroke.
2. Kick 400 easy.
3. Pull 400 easy.
4. Swim 8 × 50, altenating hard and easy 50's.
5. Swim 4 × 25 hard.

BEST REPEATS

Short Course (yards)				Long Course (meters)			
Dist.	No.	Average Time	R.I.	Dist.	No.	Average Time	R.I.
50	30	:32.0	on 1 min.	50	30	:38+	on 1 min.
100	15	1:09+	on 2½ min.	50	20	:37.2	on 1 min. 10 sec.
200	8	2:24+	on 6 min.	100	15	1:21.2	on 2½ min.
440	4	5:38.0	on 12 min.	200	8	2:50.0	on 6 min.
880	1	11:16.0		400	4	5:56.2	on 12 min.

BEST KICKING AND PULLING TIMES

Short course	Long course
Kicking: 50 yards–:32.8, 100 yards–1:11.6, 200 yards–2:35, 400 yards–5:25	Kicking: 50 meters–:38, 100 meters –1:21, 200 meters–2:56, 400 meters–6:07
Pulling: 50 yards–:35.0, 100 yards–1:15.0, 200 yards–2:38, 400 yards–5:29	Pulling: 50 meters–:41, 100 meters –1:28, 200 meters–3:07, 400 meters–6:26

INDIVIDUAL MEDLEYISTS

Edward "Ted" Stickles

Former World Record holder of the 400-meter and 440-yard Individual Medley (4:51.0) and 200-meter Individual Medley (2:15.9). Best Times: (Individual Medley short course) 100 yards–55.9, 200 yards–1:59.5, 400 yards–4:16.2. Age–21, height–5'11", weight–160 pounds. Began swimming competitively at age 14. Ted did dry land exercises in the form of weight training, isometric contractions, and stretching exercises.

Coached by James Counsilman of Indiana University.

Ted was one of the first swimmers to train for the Individual Medley. In the summer of 1961 he became the first swimmer to break 5 minutes for the 400-meter Individual Medley, long course. He also was the first swimmer to break 2 minutes for the 200-yard Individual Medley, short course.

Ted did not train with Individual Medley workouts every day. He did have a general pattern of workouts which varied somewhat from week to week. Below is a pattern of workouts he used for one week during the indoor season of 1964 (February).

Monday morning. Work on stroke he would be swimming in a meet on Saturday. In this case, the stroke was butterfly and he did 10 × 100 fly on 2 min., average :63+.

Monday afternoon. Work on all strokes.
1. Swim 500.
2. Kick 500, then 8 × 50 (2 of each stroke).
3. Pull 20, then pull 400 I.M., average 5:30.
4. Swim 30 × 50 on 60 sec.–7 × 50 fly, average 1:30; 8 × 50 back, average :30+; 8 × 50 breast, average :34+; 7 × 50 free, average :28+.

Tuesday morning. Work on weakest stroke, in this case freestyle—swim 5 × 200, average 2:01.

Tuesday afternoon.
1. Swim 500 warm up.
2. Swim 8 × 50–2 × 50 of each stroke.
3. Kick 18, then 4 × 100 (1 of each stroke).
4. Pull 18, then 4 × 100 (1 of each stroke).
5. Swim 4 × 440 (back–5:06, breast–5:37, free–4:46, individual medley, last 140 yards of which were freestyle, 4:58).

Wednesday morning. Work on backstroke and breaststroke, swimming 20 × 50 and alternating strokes.

Wednesday afternoon.
1. Swim 300 warm up.
2. Sprint 8 × 25.
3. Kick 18, then 4 × 50, 8 × 25—all strokes.
4. Pull 18, then 4 × 50, 8 × 25—all strokes.
5. Swim 15 × 100–2 of each stroke, last 7 individual medley.

Thursday morning. Time 880 freestyle under 9:40.

Thursday afternoon.
1. Swim 500 warm up.
2. Swim broken 400 individual medley, 10 sec. R.I. after each 50, time under 4:30.
3. Kick 200, then 200 of each stroke.
4. Pull 800 individual medley, alternately swimming 1 length slow, 1 length fast.
5. Swim 8 × 200 on 6 min. (first 4—one of each stroke; fifth one—100 butterfly and 100 backstroke, time 2:10; sixth one—100 backstroke and 100 breaststroke, time 2:24; seventh one—100 breast and 100 freestyle, time 2:15;

eighth one—a complete individual medley, time 2:11. Finish workout with one all-out 50 in each stroke—times: 50 fly—:25+, 50 back—:27+, 50 breast —:31+, and 50 free—:24+.

Friday morning. Swim easy 880 freestyle, breaking 10 min. Swim 16 × 25, 4 of each stroke.

Friday afternoon.
1. Swim 500 warm up.
2. Swim 16 × 50, every other one fast, all strokes.
3. Kick 20, then 4 × 100, 1 each stroke.
4. Pull 10, then 4 × 100, 1 each stroke.
5. Swim 8 × 100 on 3 min. (2 × 100 fly, 1 × 100 back, 1 × 100 breast, 1 × 100 free, 1 × 100 (50 fly—50 back), 1 × 100 (50 back—50 breast), 1 × 100 (50 breast—50 free), 1 × 100 individual medley.

Saturday. Dual meet without too much competition (previous day's work would have been reduced otherwise).

WARM UP BEFORE COMPETITION (SHORT COURSE)

1. Swim 36 lengths (9 free, 9 back, 9 breast, 9 fly).
2. Swim 8 × 25 freestyle progressive.
3. Kick 16—4 of each stroke.
4. Swim 8 × 50—2 of each stroke, 1 easy and 1 hard.
5. 4 × 25, hard—1 of each stroke.
6. Swim easy 200.

BEST REPEATS (INDIVIDUAL MEDLEYS)

Short Course (yards)				Long Course (meters)			
Dist.	No.	Average Time	R.I.	Dist.	No.	Average Time	R.I.
200	6	2:11+	on 5 min.	200	4	2:26+	on 5 min.
400	4	4:26+	on 10 min.	400	3	5:07+	on 10 min.
800	1	9:06+					

Richard Roth

Gold Medal winner, 1964 Olympic Games, 400-meter Individual Medley—4:45.4. Best Times: (long course) 200-meter Individual Medley—2:14.9, 100-meter Freestyle—:53.6 (relay start), 200-meter Freestyle—1:58.3 (relay start), 400-meter Freestyle—4:18.8, 100-meter Backstroke—1:04.1, 200-meter Backstroke—2:20.4, 100-meter Butterfly—:60+, 200-meter Butterfly—2:15.4, 100-meter Breaststroke—1:14.4, 200-meter Breaststroke—2:41.1; (short course) 200-yard Individual Medley—1:56.0, 400-yard Individual Medley—4:09.5, 100-yard Freestyle—:48.1, 200-yard Free-

style—1:46.0+, 400-yard Freestyle—3:49+, 100-yard Backstroke—:54.9, 200-yard Backstroke—1:57.9+, 100-yard Butterfly—:54+, 200-yard Butterfly—2:01+. 100-yard Breaststroke—1:03+, 200-yard Breaststroke—2:18+. Age—20, height—6'1", weight—195 pounds.

Coached by George Haines, Santa Clara, California.

Dick does no weight lifting or isometric contractions. He pulls with a half of a kick board held between his legs by a rubber band. Dick is extremely strong and yet relatively flexible. He trains primarily for the Individual Medley event. He normally works out twice a day during the season, occasionally 3 times a day.

In response to the 3 questions listed below, Dick gave the following answers.

Question: How do you split up your workout so far as strokes are concerned?

Answer: I used to break up everything as evenly as I could, i.e., if we were going 8 × 200, I would go 2 of each. Now I feel that I get more work out of a series if I try to go it all one stroke and work my time down. Sometimes on a series of 200's I'll go half divided up and half I.M.; 400's I generally go the first couple free and last 1 or 2 I.M. I think my swimming shows that the main stress in my workout is on free and breast. Many times I will separate and work with the distance freestylers or work with the breaststrokers. This year also showed that I didn't work enough back. I saw that in the fly and spent a good deal of time on it, and now I intend to do the same in back. I always kick breast or fly, mainly breast.

Question: What do you feel is the most important thing for an individual medley man to stress in his training?

Answer: I believe that the swimmer needs a good last 200 to win an I.M. In order to have this, I pull all free and kick nearly all breast. I do this on the theory that the breaststroke is where the legs are used most of any stroke. Here I like my legs to take over, because my arms have done most of the work the first 200. My arms rest more or less and are ready for the free. So I believe an I.M. swimmer must have a strong breaststroke, but more important a strong breast-kick (I believe that is why Chet could go I.M. and a guy like Saari dies). Of course a freestyle is most essential, Ralph and Ted suffer here. My personal advice to any aspiring I.M.'er would be to make sure his last 2 strokes are very strong.

In the 200 I believe I suffer most in the fly. I just don't have enough speed. It worked all right until this year when I swam a guy with a real strong free and good breast. I'm sure the same would have happened against Saari had I ever met him. I'd say the most important in the 200 are the fly and free, but you won't do much without the breast.

Question: List any suggestions you think might help an aspiring young individual medley swimmer.

Answer: My advice, in a general fashion, would be to stay away from the age-group program under at least 10 and, preferably, 12 years old. I think the pressure and year round training from 7–12 would kill swimmers off: case in point is _____. When one does get into the age-group program, I believe he should enter every event and set an eventual goal to win every one of them. This was my goal and it was eventually fulfilled.

I guess everyone has an idol he should strive to beat. If he doesn't, I think he should, and he should definitely be in the stroke he is swimming. Mine was Ted Stickles, and I can't tell you how much it speeded my rise to the top by always shooting at him. More than that, I tried to copy him in everything he did and nearly thought he was God.

FAVORITE WORKOUTS

(Can be used for short or long course)

I. 1. Swim 600 warm up.
   2. Kick 200.
   3. Pull 200.
   4. Swim 8 × 50 on 1 min.
   5. Swim 2 × 800, 10 min. R.I.
   6. Pull 3 × 300, 4 min. R.I.
   7. Swim 8 × 50 on 1 min.
II. 1. Swim 600 warm up.
   2. Kick 200 warm up.
   3. Pull 200 warm up.
   4. Swim 8 × 50 on 1 min.
   5. Swim 4 sets of 10 × 50 on 1 min. (2 min. between each set).
   6. Kick 4 × 200 on 5 min.
   7. Swim 8 × 50 on 1 min.
III. 1. Swim 600 warm up.
   2. Kick 200 warm up.
   3. Pull 200 warm up.
   4. Swim 2 sets of 10 × 100 on 2 min. (2 min. R.I. between sets).
   5. Kick 10 × 50 on 1½ min.
   6. Swim 2 sets of 10 × 50 on 1 min. (2 min. R.I. between sets).

TAPER (DIRECT QUOTATION)

"We taper a week to a week and a half before the nationals and about a day before the rest of the team. I do more speed work thinking of the 200 I.M. Then, if the 400 is the first event, I will forget about speed and think of the 400. After the 400 I swim mostly 50's and 25's. Workouts during the taper are similar to those above, but with a long warm up and less total work.

"At the site of the meet, a few days before the meet:

1. Swim 1000 to 1500 warm up on my own, doing all strokes, swim, kick, and pull.
2. I then do some 50 or 100 swims for time, with the team (8 or 10).
3. Swim some high quality 100's, 200's, or 400's, generally freestyle.
4. End up with some swim sprints—50's—4 or 5."

WARM UP BEFORE COMPETITION

"1. Swim 400 to 600 freestyle if cold, then 200 or 300 of the other strokes.
2. Kick 200—400.
3. Sometimes I pull a little, but not often.
4. Swim 3 or 4 pickup 50's on my own, then I do the following:
5. A. Before the 400:   B. Before the 200:
    1. Swim 2 to 3 × 50 fly.   1. Swim 1 or 2 × 50 fly.
    2. Swim 1 × 25 fly.   2. Swim 4 or 5 × 25 all strokes.
    3. Swim 1 × 25 free.

"My entire warm up may take longer, if I don't feel loosened up properly."

BEST REPEATS

	Short Course (yards)				Long Course (meters)		
Dist.	No.	Average Time	R.I.	Dist.	No.	Average Time	R.I.
I.M.				I.M.			
200	4	2:07	on 5 min.	200	3	2:24	on 5 min.
400	2	4:22	on 10 min.	400	4	5:03	on 10 min.
Butterfly				Butterfly			
100	4	:58	on 2 min.	100	4	1:07	on 2 min.
Backstroke				Backstroke			
100	4	1:01	on 2 min.	100	4	1:10	on 2 min.
Breaststroke				Breaststroke			
100	4	1:10	on 2 min.	100	4	1:19	on 2 min.
Freestyle				Freestyle			
100	8	:54	on 2 min.	50	8	:27.0	on 3 min.
400	3	4:04	on 10 min.	100	4	:57.0	on 10 min.
				200	4	2:12	on 5 min.
				400	4	4:40	on 10 min.
				800	3	9:30	on 20 min.

OLYMPIC TEAM WORKOUTS

The following workouts are those used for 1 week of training by the 1964 Men's Olympic Team during September, 1964, in preparation for the Olympic Games which were held a month later in Tokyo, Japan.

The dates of the Olympic swimming events were October 11 through October 18.

The team worked out twice a day, 6 days a week, with Sundays off. The entire team worked out at the same time, but was divided into 3 groups for many of the workouts: (1) Distance Men—those training for the 400- and 1500-meter Freestyle, (2) Middle Distance Men—those training for the 200-meter distance (this would include some swimmers of all the various strokes), and (3) Sprinters—those training for the 100 Freestyle and the Medley Relay.

Those swimmers, such as Schollander (who was training for the 100 and 400 Freestyle), who were swimming events in 2 of the above categories, would work out part of the time with the distance swimmers and part with the middle distance swimmers. This was also the case with Dick Roth, who was training for the 400 Individual Medley.

In many of the workouts the performances of some swimmers are noted. No attempt is made to give a complete summary of every repeat effort swum, kicked, or pulled by the entire team. The reader will observe from noting the summaries of the workouts that most swimmers vary somewhat in their performances from day to day. There is, however, a tendency for some swimmers to be good "repeaters," that is, to accomplish good times consistently in practice. Carl Robie and Don Schollander would fall into this category.

The swimmers swam the strokes under which they are listed unless it is otherwise noted.

September 14 (morning workout)

A. DISTANCE SWIMMERS

1. Swim 400 warm up.
2. Kick 400 warm up.
3. Swim 4 × 50 warm up.
4. Swim 3000 meters hard pace.

Times: Saari—36:48.4, Farley—36:51.6, Nelson—38:07.5.

B. MIDDLE DISTANCE SWIMMERS

1. Swim 400 warm up.
2. Kick 400 warm up.
3. Swim 4 × 50 warm up.
4. Swim 15 × 100 on 2½ min.
5. Pull broken 800, 10 sec. rest after each 100.
6. Pull broken 800, 10 sec. rest after each 100.
7. Swim 8 × 50 hard from a dive.

Average times for the 15 × 100 repeats:

Breaststrokers: Jastremski—1:21, Trethewey—1:21, Anderson—1:22.

Backstrokers: Graef—1:13, Dilley—1:13, Bennett (swam only 8 Backstroke, average time—1:11, the rest was swum Freestyle).

Butterflyers: Robie—1:06, Riker—1:09, Schmidt (swam only 8 Butterfly, average time—1:04.5, the rest was swum Freestyle).

Freestylers: Schollander—:63.5, Ilman—1:04, Wall—1:04, Townsend—:68+.

C. SPRINTERS

1. Swim 400 warm up.
2. Kick 400 warm up.
3. Swim 4 × 50 warm up.
4. Swim 8 × 100 on 5 min.
5. Kick broken 400 (10 sec. rest after each 50).
6. Pull broken 400 (10 sec. rest after each 50).
7. Swim 4 × 50 hard from a dive.

Average times for 8 × 100 repeats:

Backstrokers: Mann—1:11, McGeagh—1:15.

Butterflyers: Schulhof—1:10, Richardson—1:13+.

Breaststrokers: Craig—1:28, Lukens—1:23.

Freestylers: Clark—1:04.5, Townsend—1:08, Austin—1:09.

D. INDIVIDUAL MEDLEY SWIMMERS

Dick Roth did the same workout as the Middle Distance swimmers, but swam 16 instead of 15 × 100. He swam 4 × 100 of each stroke. His average times were: Butterfly—1:10, Backstroke—1:12, Breaststroke—1:23, and Freestyle—1:04.5.

September 14 (afternoon workout)

In this workout all 3 groups did the same workout.

1. Swim 400 easy warm up.
2. Swim 15 × 50 progressive-regressive set on 50 sec.
3. Swim 400 for time (pace the swim so that the second 200 is the same time as the first).
4. Kick 400 easy.
5. Swim 200 pace.
6. Swim 4 × 100 with 30 sec. rest.
7. Swim 5 × 100 from a dive on 4 min.
8. Swim 8 × 50 from a dive on 2 min.

REPEAT TIMES FOR ITEMS 3, 5, AND 7 OF SEPTEMBER 14 WORKOUT

	(3) Pace 400		(5) Pace 200		(7) Average for 5 × 100
Breaststrokers					
Jastremski	5:50		2:48.5		1:21
Anderson	6:05		2:50.7		1:22
Trethewey	5:58		2:49.2		1:22.6
Luken	6:35		3:02		1:32
Backstrokers					
Dilley	5:17		2:32		1:12
Graef	4:59		2:21		1:10
Mann	5:08		2:22		1:09
Bennett	5:01.5		2:25		1:11
Butterflyers					
Robie	4:31.7	Free	2:16.8	Fly	1:05 Fly
Schmidt	5:06	Fly	2:25	Fly	1:06 Fly
Riker	5:03	Free	2:37	Fly	1:09 Fly
Richardson	5:18	Free	2:38	Fly	1:13 Fly
Schulhof	5:06	Free	2:22	Fly	1:08 Fly
Freestylers					
Schollander	4:34.8		2:10.0		1:04.0
Saari	4:35.6		2:18.4		1:06.6
Nelson	4:35.6		2:11.3		1:05.2
Farley	4:39.5		2:18.1		1:06.0
Clark	4:47.7		2:13.0		1:06.1
Ilman	4:40.1		2:16.2		1:07.0
Lyons	5:16.0		2:33.0		1:08.0
Mettler	4:40.0		2:24.3		1:05+
Townsend	5:01.7		2:10.6		1:04+
Wall	4:36.8		2:12.5		1:05.0
Austin	5:24.2		2:40.1		1:11.0
Roth (swam all of this workout Freestyle)	4:37.8		2:12.6		1:04.5

September 15 (morning workout)

All swimmers did the same workout.

1. Swim 400 warm up.
2. Swim 3 × broken 400 (each broken 400 consists of 8 × 50 with 10 sec. R.I. after each 50). Each successive broken 400 should be faster than the previous one, 6 min. R.I. between each broken 400.

3. Kick 400 easy.
4. Kick 400 for time.
5. Pull 400 easy.
6. Pull 400 for time.
7. Swim 4 × 400 with 6 to 7 min. R.I.

TABLE XIV–1.   Repeat Times for Items 2, 4, 6, and 7 of September 15 Workout

	3 Broken 400's			Kick 400	Pull 400	4 × 400 swims			
Breaststrokers									
Jastremski	5:48	5:32	5:18	6:59	6:37	6:00.1	5:51.2	5:48	5:46.9
Anderson (Fr)	5:55	5:35	5:31	6:10	7:48	6:14	5:55.2	5:53	5:50.2
Trethewey	5:50	5:42	5:36	6:39	7:31	6:01	6:01.7	5:55.2	5:50.4
Backstrokers									
Graef	5:04	5:00	5:02	7:25	6:20	5:07.8	5:14.1	5:08	5:03.7
Dilley	5:20	5:00	5:30	7:33	5:46.2	5:19	5:19	5:12.8	5:05.4
Mann	5:05	5:05	5:00	7:53	6:44.2	5:09.2	5:01.4	5:06	4:54
Butterflyers								Free	Free
Schmidt	4:52	4:42	4:42	5:35.6	5:47.6	5:07	5:02.3	4:50	4:46
Freestylers									
Schollander	4:28	4:22	4:11	6:02	4:46.6	4:35.2	4:45.4	4:42.5	4:38
Clark	4:38	4:31	4:26	6:40.5	5:10.2	4:49.4	4:45	4:42.5	4:43.5
Nelson	4:30	4:25	4:12	7:33	5:08	4:36.5	4:45	4:47	4:38
Robie	4:22	4:17	4:16	5:32	4:40	4:30.3	4:39	4:34.9	4:30

September 15 (afternoon workout)

1. Swim 400 warm up.
2. Kick 400 easy.
3. Swim 400 pace.
4. Swim 40 × 50 on 60 sec. in 4 sets of 10 each, each set faster than the previous set and with 3 min. R.I. between each set.
5. Pull, kick, or swim an easy 400.

TABLE XIV–2.   Repeat Times for Four Sets of 10 × 50

	First Set 10 × 50	Second Set 10 × 50	Third Set 10 × 50	Fourth Set 10 × 50
Breaststrokers				
Jastremski	:41.0	:39.2	:38.8	:37.0
Anderson	:43.5	:41.5	:39.5	:39.1
Trethewey	:40.0	:39.3	:38.4	:37.1

Backstrokers

Graef	:35.5	:34.5	:33.8	:33.0
Dilley	:36.0	:34.2	:34.1	:33.6
Mann	:36.0	:35.2	:34.1	:33.5

Butterflyers

Robie	:33.0	:32.6	:32.0	:31.8
Schmidt	:34.0	:33.0	:31.0	:30.5
Riker	:34.0	:34.0	:34.0	:33.0

Freestylers

Schollander	:32.0	:31.0	:30.0	:28.8
Clark	:33.0	:31.5	:30.3	:29.4
Nelson	:33.0	:32.1	:31.0	:29.9
Saari	:33.0	:32.0	:30.5	:29.5

September 16 (morning workout)

All swimmers.

1. Warm up 400.
2. Kick 1 × 400.
3. Pull 1 × 400.
4. Swim 8 × 50 on 60 sec.
5. A. Distance swimmers
     6 × 400 on 8 min.
   B. Middle distance
      Swim 1 × 400 with 5 min. R.I.
      Swim 2 × 200 with 3 min. R.I.
      Swim 4 × 100 with 2 min. R.I.
      Swim 8 × 50 with 1 min. R.I.
      Sprinters
   C. Swim 1 × 400 with 5 min. R.I.
      Swim 1 × 200 with 5 min. R.I.
      Swim 2 × 100 with 3 min. R.I.
      Swim 8 × 50 with 1 min. R.I.

REPEAT TIMES FOR DISTANCE SWIMMERS' 6 × 400

	First	Second	Third	Fourth	Fifth	Sixth
Schollander	4:41.1,	4:42.2,	4:40.0,	4:34.4,	4:30.5,	4:25.2
Saari	4:42.0,	4:43.5,	4:39.0,	4:35.0,	4:34.0,	4:31.4
Nelson	4:42.5,	4:40.0,	4:37.0,	4:33.8,	4:41.5,	4:27.5
Farley	4:42.0,	4:43.0,	4:40.8,	4:35.0,	4:33.0,	4:29.8

REPEAT TIMES FOR MIDDLE DISTANCE SWIMMERS

	Swim 400	Swim 200	Swim 200	Average Time 4 × 100	Average Time 8 × 50
Breaststrokers					
Jastremski	6:01	2:54	2:51	1:22.5	:39.0
Anderson	5:30 Free	2:53	2:45	1:20.6	:40.0
Trethewey	5:53	2:51	2:53	1:22+	:38.8
Backstrokers					
Graef	5:11	2:29.0	2:23.2	1:09+	:34+
Dilley	5:23	2:32.1	2:29.4	1:07.7	:33.6
Bennett	5:18	2:33.2	2:30.0	1:07.2	:33.8
Butterflyers					
Robie	4:36 Free	2:14	2:17.0	1:05.7	:31.8
Schmidt	4:52 Free	2:27	2:23	1:06.2	:31.1
Riker	5:01 Free	2:37	2:21 Free	1:09.2	:31.7

REPEAT TIMES FOR SPRINTERS

	Swim 400	Swim 200	Average Time 2 × 100	Time Average 8 × 50
Breaststrokers				
Luken	5:30 Free	3:10	1:24	:41
Craig	6:02 Free	2:45 Free	1:18	:39
Backstrokers				
McGeagh	5:16	2:32	1:05	:33.4
Mann	5:00	2:22	1:05	:31.8
Butterflyers				
Schulhof	4:54 Free	2:21	1:04.4	:31.1
Freestylers				
Clark	4:38.2	2:14.5	:59.5	:29.8
Ilman	4:39.0	2:12.8	:60.1	:30.2
Lyons	5:00.1	2:24.4	:65.2	:32.0
Mettler	4:59.0	2:14.0	:61.2	:30.5
Townsend	5:02.1	2:15.6	:59.2	:29.9

September 16 (afternoon workout)

1. Swim 400 warm up.
2. Swim 8 × 100, moderate speed, with 10 sec. R.I.
3. Kick 6 × 100 with 1½ min. R.I.
4. Pull 3 × 300 with 3 min. R.I.
5. Swim: A. Distance Men—1 × 800.
       B. Middle Distance Men—3 × 200.
       C. Sprinters—3 × 100.
6. Swim 4 × 50 sprint;
       4 × 25 sprint.

September 17 (morning workout)

All swimmers did the same workout.

1. Swim 400 warm up.
2. Swim 5 × 200 with 3 min. R.I.
3. Kick 400.
4. Pull 4 × 100 on 2 min.
5. Swim 1 broken 400, 10 sec. R.I. after each 100.
6. Swim 1 broken 200, 10 sec. R.I. after each 50.

September 17 (afternoon workout)

1. Swim 400 warm up.
2. Swim 16 × 50 on 50 sec.
3. Kick 400.
4. A. Distance Men
   Swim 1 × 400 (under 4:30), 1 × 200 (under 2:10), 2 × 100 (under :60).

REPEAT TIMES FOR DISTANCE SWIMMERS

	400	200	100	100
Schollander	4:23.5	2:08.5	:58.5	:57.4
Saari	4:27.4	2:07.7	:58.5	:58.1
Nelson	4:24.1	2:08.2	:59.5	:58.8

   B. Middle Distance Men and Sprinters
   Swim 1 × 200, 1 × 150, and 2 × 100.

REPEAT TIMES FOR MIDDLE DISTANCE MEN AND SPRINTERS

	200	150	100	100
Breaststrokers				
Jastremski	2:36.1	1:56.0	1:13.4	1:12.9
Anderson	2:37.9	1:57.0	1:17.1	1:16.0
Trethewey	2:43.1	1:59.2	1:15.5	1:15.1
Backstrokers				
Graef	2:17.0	1:44.2	1:06.4	1:05.4
Dilley	2:18.2	1:44.8	1:07.2	1:06.9
Mann	2:15.4	1:48.0	1:06.0	1:06.2
Butterflyers				
Robie	2:09.0	1:37.0	1:02.5	1:02.0
Schmidt	2:16.3	1:38.0	1:01.4	1:01.0
Richardson	2:24.2	1:50.4	1:14.1	1:10.2
Freestylers				
Clark	2:06.9	1:31.3	:57.2	:56.4
Ilman	2:03.5	1:31.1	:58.5	:58.1

September 18 (morning workout)

This day was a Friday with time trials scheduled for the next day. All swimmers did identical workouts.

1. Swim 400 warm up.
2. Swim 20 × 50 on 60 sec.
3. Pull 400 (no time).
4. Swim 20 × 50 on 60 sec.

REPEAT TIMES FOR 2 SETS OF 20 × 50

	Swam 20 × 50	Swam 20 × 50
Breaststrokers		
Jastremski	:40.0	:38.2
Anderson	:39.4	:38.6
Trethewey	:39.0	:38.3
Luken	:41.0	:40.0
Craig	:42.0	:39.5
Backstrokers		
Graef	:37.0	:32.0
Dilley	:33+	:32.2
Bennett	:37.0	:33.4
Mann	:37.0	:33.0
McGeagh	:34.4	:33.2
Butterflyers		
Robie	:31.1	:28.8 Free
Schmidt	:32.0	:31.0
Richardson	:35.0	:34.0
Schulhof	:33.3	:32.1
Freestylers		
Schollander	:31.0	:29.0
Ilman	:31.0	:29.2
Saari	:31.0	:29.1
Clark	:32.0	:30.0
Nelson	:33.1	:29.2
Austin	:33.0	:34.0
Farley	:34.0	:30.0
Mettler	:30.4	:30.2
Wall	:33.0	:29.4

September 18 (afternoon workout)

All swimmers again did identical workouts.

1. Warm up 400.
2. Swim 8 × 100 progressively.

3. Kick 200 easy.
4. Swim 4 × 100 pace from a dive.
5. Pull 200.

September 19 (Saturday)

MORNING

"On the house" workout. (Each swimmer was directed to do any workout he desired, the only stipulation being that he must cover a total distance of 2 miles or more; each swimmer submitted a card to the coach which outlined his chosen workout.)

AFTERNOON

1. Each swimmer was directed to warm up in the way he might before the finals of the Olympic Games.

2. Swim 10 × "Goal 100's" (hard) in a continuous relay—5 or 6 men to a relay. (This gave the swimmers approximately 5 to 6 minutes rest between each repeat 100. Each swimmer was given a time to better as a goal. If he went over this time more than once, he did not get credit for that particular 100.)

TABLE XIV–3. Times for 1964 Olympic Team Members for 10 × 100 Meter Swims

	Goal	1	2	3	4	5	6	7	8	9	10	11
Breaststrokers												
Jastremski	1:17.5	1:18.2	1:18.3	1:16.9	1:17.1	1:16.7	1:17.2	1:16.1	1:16.3	1:17.4	1:15.2	1:10.3*
Trethewey	1:17.5	1:16.4	1:15.4	1:15.7	1:14.4	1:16.9	1:17.1	1:16.8	1:15.1	1:17.0	1:13.7	
Anderson	1:17.5	1:17.0	1:15.0	1:16.1	1:15.3	1:15.7	1:16.2	1:17.4	1:15.5	1:16.7	1:15.2	
Craig	1:19.0	1:15.5	1:18.3	1:16.0	1:15.5	1:17.4	1:17.1	1:18.2	1:18.2	1:17.3	1:16.1	
Backstrokers												
Graef	1:08	1:06.5	1:06.7	1:06.0	1:08.5	1:07.8	1:06.2	1:07.6	1:07.1	1:08.5	1:06.1	
Dilley	1:08	1:07.0	1:07.7	1:06.4	1:07.7	1:06.7	1:07.1	1:06.4	1:06.5	1:06.7	1:05.7	
Mann	1:08	1:04.1	1:06.0	1:04.4	1:06.5	1:05.9	1:06.7	1:06.9	1:06.8	1:06.4	1:03.7	
Butterflyers												
Robie	1:03	1:02.5	1:02.1	1:01.5	1:02.0	1:01.8	1:01.9	1:02.4	1:02.4	1:02.3	1:01.8	
Schmidt	1:03	1:01.0	1:02.9	1:02.8	1:01.8	1:02.0	1:02.4	1:02.3	1:02.7	1:01.7	1:00.4	
Richardson	1:06	1:02.5	1:03.5	1:04.3	1:04.1	1:05.2	1:04.9	1:05.3	1:05.7	1:06.2	1:03.7	
Freestylers												
Schollander	:58.5	1:02.5	:58.1	:57.3	:57.4	:57.5	:56.7	:57.7	:58.1	:57.8	:56.1	
Clark	:59	1:00.5	:58.8	:58.5	:57.9	:58.0	:58.8	:58.2	:57.9	:57.7	:56.1	
Saari	:59	1:00.1	:58.9	:58.6	:58.8	:57.6	:58.7	:58.8	:58.2	:57.1	:56.6	
Nelson	1:00	:58.0	:59.1	:59.8	:60.0	:58.8	:59.6	:59.1	:59.4	:58.9	:59.0	
Roth	1:00	:58.7	:58.4	:59.4	:59.5	:60.1	:59.3	:58.8	:58.4	:58.9	:58.4	

* Jastremski's second and third 100 meter swims were slower than the goal time; therefore, he had to swim an additional one.

Index